REGULARITY IN SEMANTIC CHANGE

ELIZABETH CLOSS TRAUGOTT
RICHARD B. DASHER

CAMBRIDGE
UNIVERSITY PRESS

CAMBRIDGE UNIVERSITY PRESS
Cambridge, New York, Melbourne, Madrid, Cape Town, Singapore, São Paulo

Cambridge University Press
The Edinburgh Building, Cambridge CB2 8RU, UK

Published in the United States of America by Cambridge University Press, New York

www.cambridge.org
Information on this title: www.cambridge.org/9780521583787

First published 2001
Reprinted 2002, 2003 (twice)
First paperback edition 2005

A catalogue record for this publication is available from the British Library

Library of Congress Cataloguing in Publication data

Traugott, Elizabeth Closs.
Regularity in semantic change / by Elizabeth Closs Traugott and Richard B. Dasher.
   p.   cm. – (Cambridge studies in linguistics)
Includes bibliographical references and index.
ISBN 0 521 58378 0
1. Semantics, Historical.   2. Grammar, Comparative and general.
I. Dasher, Richard B., 1955–   II. Title.   III. Series.
P325.5.H57 T73   2001
401′.43 – dc21   2001025490   CIP

ISBN 978-0-521-58378-7 hardback
ISBN 978-0-521-61791-8 paperback

Transferred to digital printing 2007

This new and important study of semantic change examines how new meanings arise through language use, especially the various ways in which speakers and writers experiment with uses of words and constructions in the flow of strategic interaction with addressees.

In the last few decades there has been growing interest in exploring systematicities in semantic change from a number of perspectives including theories of metaphor, pragmatic inferencing, and grammaticalization. As in earlier studies, these have for the most part been based on data taken out of context. This book is the first detailed examination of semantic change from the perspective of historical pragmatics and discourse analysis. Drawing on extensive corpus data from over a thousand years of English and Japanese textual history, Traugott and Dasher show that most changes in meaning originate in and are motivated by the associative flow of speech.

ELIZABETH CLOSS TRAUGOTT is Professor of Linguistics and English at Stanford University. Her previous books include *A History of English Syntax* (1972), *Linguistics for Students of Literature* (with Mary L. Pratt, 1980) and *Grammaticalization* (with Paul J. Hopper, 1993).

RICHARD B. DASHER is Director of the US–Japan Technology Management Center and Consulting Associate Professor at the School of Engineering, Stanford University. Previous publications include historical work on Japanese honorifics in *Papers in Linguistics* and other research in various scholarly journals.

In this series

Earlier issues not listed are also available

CONTENTS

Contents

Contents

FIGURES

ix

PREFACE AND
ACKNOWLEDGMENTS

The focus of this work is recent developments in cross-linguistic research on historical semantics and pragmatics, with special reference to the histories of English and Japanese. The framework can be characterized as "integrative functionalist" (Croft 1995) in that we consider linguistic phenomena to be systematic and partly arbitrary, but so closely tied to cognitive and social factors as not to be self-contained; they are therefore in part nonarbitrary. One of the linguist's tasks is to determine what is arbitrary, what is not, and how to account for the differences.

We see semantic change (change in code) as arising out of the pragmatic uses to which speakers or writers and addressees or readers put language, and most especially out of the preferred strategies that speakers/writers use in communicating with addressees. The changes discussed in this book are tendencies that are remarkably widely attested, but that can be violated under particular, often social, circumstances ranging from shifts in ideological values to the development of various technologies. "Regularity" is to be understood as typical change, or frequent replication across time and across languages, not as analogous to the Neogrammarian idea of unexceptionless change in phonology.

Richard Dasher takes prime responsibility for the Japanese data, Elizabeth Traugott for the remainder, but both have discussed all the material presented here in countless meetings over nearly fifteen years. The ideas presented here have been explored in several venues. It would be impossible to thank and acknowledge the contribution of all those who have helped make this a better book than it would have been otherwise, but Joan Bybee, Maria Cuenca, Bernd Heine, Paul Kiparsky, Roger Lass, Nina Lin, Alain Peyraube, Eve Sweetser, Chaofen Sun, Shiao-Wei Tham, and Yo Matsumoto deserve special mention, and especially Brady Clark, Andrew Garrett, and Nigel Vincent who gave extensive advice on pre-final drafts. Elizabeth Traugott owes a particular debt to her coauthors on various other occasions: Paul Hopper, Ekkehard König, Rachel Nordlinger, Whitney Tabor, and above all to Scott Schwenter without whose inspiration, intellectual congening, and friendly challenges this book would not have come to fruition. Juno Nakamura gave invaluable help with preparing the manuscript and the indices. Citi Potts saved us from many errors at the copy-editing stage, and Andrew Winnard of Cambridge University Press supervised the production. To all our deepest appreciation.

CONVENTIONS

Here we outline conventions of transcription and periodization for the three languages most fully discussed in this book: Chinese, English, and Japanese.

All languages including Japanese, Chinese, and Greek are transcribed in the Roman alphabet. Macrons indicating reconstructed vowel length are omitted.

All dates of the language stages should be considered to be approximate. Some texts from early in a language stage may show relatively more characteristics of the previous language stage. Some may be deliberately archaizing.

(i) Conventions for Chinese

The transcription employed for Chinese examples is the *pinyin* system of romanization, used in the People's Republic of China. The tone marks of the romanization are omitted.

Approximate stages in the history of Chinese are as in (1):

(1)	Language Stage		Beginning	Ending
	PAC	Pre-Archaic Chinese	1400 BC	1100 BC
	EAC	Early Archaic Chinese	1100 BC	500 BC
	LAC	Late Archaic Chinese	500 BC	200 BC
	EMC	Early Middle Chinese	200 BC	600 AC
	LMC	Late Middle Chinese	600	1250
	EMand	Early Mandarin	1250	1800
	MdMand	Modern Mandarin	1800	present

(ii) Conventions for English

Old English is transcribed without macrons or abbreviations other than ampersand.

Approximate stages in the history of English are given in (2):

(2)	Language Stage		Beginning	Ending
	OE	Old English	450	1150
	EOE	Early Old English	450	800
	LOE	Late Old English	1000	1150

ME	Middle English	1150	1500
EME	Early Middle English	1150	1300
LME	Late Middle English	1370	1500
EMdE	Early Modern English	1500	1770
MdE	Modern English	1770	1970
PDE	Present Day English	1970	present

Dating Old English texts is notoriously controversial. Dates of composition differ extensively from dates of manuscripts. In the case of the epic poem *Beowulf*, the manuscript dates from about 1000, but the date of composition is presumably significantly earlier. Scholars disagree on whether it was composed in the eighth or ninth century (see Bjork and Obermeier 1997); we accept the eighth century date. The dating suggested in this book provides specific dates of composition where reasonably well established; otherwise, we use the dating conventions adopted for the Helsinki Corpus of English Texts (see Rissanen, Kytö, and Palander-Collin 1993) or by the editions from which texts are cited.

(iii) Conventions for Japanese

For Japanese linguistic items, phonemic transcription is used. Thus, for example, the syllables [fu] and [tsu] in Modern Japanese are written as *hu* and *tu*, respectively. Transcriptions of linguistic items from previous stages of Japanese for the most part follow the orthographic conventions of the language at the time, but these may be modified for clarity, e.g. when discussing the history of a single item across several language stages. In particular, the phonological system change of /F/ (bilabial fricative; in preliterary times most likely a stop) to /h/ (which spread at different times depending on the following vowel) is captured by using *F* for Old Japanese transcriptions, *h* for later premodern periods of the language, and the current phonemic shape for the form in the present day language, e.g. *tamaFu* "give" (Old Japanese) > *tamahu* (Late Old Japanese–Early Modern Japanese) > *tamau* (Modern Japanese). Transcriptions of Old Japanese in the present work do not distinguish between the *koo* (A) and *otu* (B) series of vowels.

For Japanese author and book names, including those of primary texts, the modified Hepburn romanization system (see Masuda 1974) is used in order to clarify references to proper nouns that are best known in this transcription. Double vowels, however, are used instead of macrons.

Approximate stages in the history of Japanese (Jp.) are given in (3):

(3)	Language Stage	Beginning	Ending	Corresponding Historical Period	
OJ	Old Jp.	710	800	Nara Period	710–794
LOJ	Late Old Jp.	800	1100	Heian Period	794–1192
EMJ	Early Middle Jp.	1100	1330	Kamakura Period	1192–1333
LMJ	Late Middle Jp.	1330	1610	Muromachi Period	1333–1603

EMdJ	Early Modern Jp.	1610	1870	Edo Period	1603–1868
MdJ	Modern Jp.	1870	1970	from Meiji Period	1868–present
PDJ	Present Day Jp.	1970	present		

The extent to which periodization is arbitrary for any particular text is well illustrated by the *Kyogen* plays. They are considered to be representative of the colloquial language of the Late Middle Japanese period, despite the fact that the written texts of the plays stem from the early seventeenth century. In fact, the language of the plays reflects some layering of Early Modern Japanese elements over a basic language model from the Late Middle Japanese period, plus some set "stage language" phrases (Koyama 1960: 27).

ABBREVIATIONS

Linguistic terms, languages, dictionaries (for full dictionary entries, see Secondary references)

ABL	ablative
AD/R	addressee/reader
AD/R+	addressee/reader and associated social group
ADV	adverbial
AffADHON	affixal adressee honorific
ASSOC	associative (includes genitive uses)
C	conceptual category
CAUS	causative
CDE	conceptualized described event
Ch.	Chinese
COMPAR	comparative
CONDIT	conditional
COP	copula
C-Ref	conceptualized referent (in figures)
C-Ref P	conceptualized referent person (in figures)
CSE	conceptualized speech event
DAT	dative
DEM	demonstrative
DESID	desiderative
DO	direct object
DOE	Dictionary of Old English
Du.	Dutch
EA	epistemic adverbial
EAC	Early Archaic Chinese
EMand	Early Mandarin
EMC	Early Middle Chinese
EMdE	Early Modern English
EMdJ	Early Modern Japanese

Abbreviations

EME	Early Middle English
EMJ	Early Middle Japanese
EMPH	emphatic (particle)
Eng.	English
EOE	Early Old English
EXCL	exclusive (focus particle)
FOC	focus (particle)
Fr.	French
FTA	face threatening act
FUT	future
GER	gerund (verb form)
GIIN	generalized invited inference
Gk.	Greek
Gm.	German
HONP	honorific prefix
HUMIL	humiliative subject
IE	Indo-European
IIN	invited inference
IITSC	Invited Inferencing Theory of Semantic Change
IMP	imperative
INCL	inclusive (focus particle)
INDEF	indefinite
INTENT	intentional
Jp.	Japanese
L	lexeme
LAC	Late Archaic Chinese
Lat.	Latin
LexADHON	lexical addressee honorific
LME	Late Middle English
LMC	Late Middle Chinese
LMJ	Late Middle Japanese
LOC	locative
LOE	Late Old English
LOJ	Late Old Japanese
M	coded abstract meaningful element
MA	manner adverb(ial)
MdE	Modern English
MdJ	Modern Japanese
MdMand	Modern Mandarin
ME	Middle English

MED	Middle English Dictionary
M-heuristic	Manner-heuristic
MJ	Middle Japanese
nec	necessity (in figures)
NEG	negative
NKD	Nihon Kokugo Daiziten
NP	noun phrase
OBJ	object
OE	Old English
OED	Oxford English Dictionary
OJ	Old Japanese
P	phonological element
PAC	Pre-Archaic Chinese
PASS	passive morpheme
PDE	Present-Day English
PDJ	Present-Day Japanese
PERF	perfect (tense/aspect)
PFV	perfective
POL	polite
POSS	possibility (in figures)
POTEN	potential (affix)
PP	prepositional phrase
PROB	probability (verb suffix)
PTC	particle
Q	question (particle)
Q-heuristic	Quantity-heuristic
QUOT	quotative (particle)
RA	respect adverbial (adverbial of "respect in which")
Ref action	conceptualized referred-to action (in figures)
RESP	respectful (suffix, formulaic expression, etc.)
R-heuristic	Relevance-heuristic
S	(morpho)syntactic component
SAV	speech act verb (nonperformative)
SD	social deictic
s-o	scope over (in figures)
SP/W	speaker/writer
SP/W+	speaker/writer and associated social group
SUBJ Ref	conceptualized subject referent (in figures)
SUBJUNCT	subjunctive
s-w	scope within (in figures)

TOP   topic (particle)
T-V   "familiar vs. formal" forms of the second person singular
VPOL   very polite
VRESP very respectful

Symbols

↕   is linked to
→   is realized as
>   changes to
+>   invites the inference
-        morpheme boundary in original language
:   morpheme boundary in English gloss
/   poetic lines breaks in Japanese texts
X/Y   both X and Y (in Figures)
——— = attested as semanticized, and continues to period specified
        (in figures)
- - - = sporadic use; probably not fully semanticized (in figures)
->-= increase in strength of change (in figures)

I
The framework

1.1 Aims of this book

In this book we show that there are predictable paths for semantic change across different conceptual structures and domains of language function.[1] Most especially we will show that, despite century-old taxonomies that suggest that meaning changes are bidirectional, e.g. generalization and narrowing, metaphor and metonymy, when we trace the histories of lexemes cross-linguistically we in fact repeatedly find evidence for unidirectional changes. These changes are of a different sort from those cited in the taxonomies. The taxonomies focus on mechanisms, the kinds of cognitive and communicative processes speakers and hearers bring to the task of learning and using a language. The regularities are, however, shifts from one linguistically coded meaning to another, for example, from obligation to do something to conclusion that something is the case. Such regularities are prototypical types of changes that are replicated across times and languages. They are possible, indeed probable, tendencies, not changes that are replicated across every possible meaningful item at a specific point in time in a specific language, such as the Neogrammarians postulated for sound change. That they recur so often and across totally unrelated languages is, we argue, intrinsically bound up with the cognitive and communicative processes by which pragmatic meanings come to be conventionalized and reanalyzed as semantic polysemies. In particular, they are bound up with the mechanisms that we call "invited inferencing" and "subjectification." This book, therefore, is a contribution to historical pragmatics as well as semantics. We pay special attention to conceptual structures that can broadly be construed as either modal or deictic, or both.

As an example of issues regarding regularity of change affecting semantic code in the sense to be discussed in this book, consider the well-known fact that in Modern English *must* can in some uses be ambiguous. A much-used example is:

(1) They *must* be married.

---

[1] Parts of this chapter, especially 1.3.2, build on Traugott (1995a, 1996/97, 1999a, 1999b).

In this form (1) is ambiguous – out of context, therefore devoid of possible contextual clues; and written, therefore devoid of possible intonational clues. There is an obligation sense as in:

> (2)   They *must* be/get married, I demand it.

and a conclusion/high certainty sense, as in:

> (3)   They *must* be married, I am sure of it.

Must in (2) is known as the "deontic" modal, in (3) as the "epistemic" modal. Similarly, throughout the recorded history of the Japanese language, we find that the verb suffix *-beki* (*-besi*) expresses obligation in some contexts and probability in others. It has often been pointed out that when an item has the meanings of both obligation and epistemic possibility, the obligation sense precedes the epistemic one in the history of the language in question (for English see e.g. Shepherd 1981, Traugott 1989; for Chinese, Sun 1996, Peyraube 1999). What can we make of such similarities among language histories? Are they the result of mere happenstance, or can they be construed as outcomes of similar cognitive and communicative processes?

As is the case with *must*, many forms that express obligation and epistemic possibility are not full lexical verbs, but grammatical forms restricted both syntactically and morphologically in terms of position, cooccurrence, and form. On first pass one might ask whether perhaps the meaning change from obligation to conclusion has something to do with the grammatical status of the forms in question. However, evidence from full-fledged lexical verbs suggests that any link between susceptibility to semantic change and grammatical status of the form is only coincidental. For example:

> (4)   I *promise* to do my best.

a directive imposing obligation on oneself as speaker, historically antedates:

> (5)   She *promises* to be an outstanding teacher.

a statement expressing the speaker's high degree of certainty. Similarly in Japanese the verb *tikau* appears in the earliest stages of the language with the meaning "swear an oath (of allegiance or obligation)" and only much later comes to be used in the meaning "swear (that something is true)." Somewhat akin is the shift from "command" (imposing obligation on the addressee) > "say" (stating that something is true) as exemplified by Japanese *ossyaru* "(respected subject referent) say(s)."

This originates in *ooseraru*, a formulaic derivation of *o(h)osu* "command."[2] The similarities in the semantic changes, and the fact that they occur in different and unrelated languages, English, Chinese, and Japanese, suggest that there must be some overarching principles of language use that account for the replication of meaning changes across languages and categories.

It has long been recognized that phonological change is regular in the sense that certain changes can probabilistically be expected to recur across languages, depending on the phonetic properties in question, e.g. "In chain shifts, peripheral vowels become more open and nonperipheral vowels become less open" (Labov 1994: 601). Work on grammaticalization over the last two decades has shown that morphosyntactic change is regular in a somewhat similar sense, e.g. adpositions may give rise to case morphology, but usually not vice versa (see e.g. Lehmann 1995 [1982]). In the semantic domain, evidence has also been accumulating that there are predictable patterns of change undergone by individual lexemes cross-linguistically. At every level, language use is constrained by the structural properties of the form in question, and the cognitive and communicative purposes for which language is used.

The greatest degree of semantic regularity has so far been found in conceptual structures the lexemes of which are typically associated with grammaticalization, e.g. spatial deixis (*come, go*), temporal deixis (*now, then*), aspect (*have, finish*), modality (*want, will*), and case relations (*belly, head*). However, on closer inspection, members of a far larger range of conceptual domains, especially lexemes that are verbal and (in relevant languages) adjectival or adverbial, also exhibit regular patterns of semantic change. Our purpose is to show that semantic change recurs over a wide range of conceptual structures, whatever the grammatical status of the lexeme in question.

In all cases of linguistic change, the regularities are not absolute.[3] Changes fail to occur, and exceptions can be found. This is particularly true in the semantic domain, given the nature of the lexicon, which is far from immune to reference and therefore to changing life-styles and ideologies. It turns out, however, that irregular meaning changes seem to occur primarily in the nominal domain, which

---

[2] The formula is passive-causative, lit. "(can) be allowed to command." This construction was relatively productive in Middle Japanese as a formula that marked respectful honorification on non-honorific verbs; in this function, the formula did not necessarily express passive-causative meaning.

[3] "Formal" generative theories of language structure have tended to find little of interest in tendencies rather than universally defined, deterministic rules (e.g. Newmeyer 1998). However, functionally oriented theories have always recognized that constraints are violable. The enormous success of Optimality Theory in recent years stems in part from the difficulty in constructing exceptionless universals (Archangeli 1997).

3

is particularly susceptible to extralinguistic factors such as change in the nature or the social construction of the referent. For example, the referents of towns, armor, rockets, vehicles, pens, communication devices, etc., have changed considerably over time, as have concepts of disease, hence the meanings attached to the words referring to them have changed in ways not subject to linguistic generalization. Likewise the meaning of a word can change due to institutional fiat, such as the redefinition in the USA of *harassment* "annoyance" by the Civil Rights Act of 1964. Or it may change due to the decision by certain communities to reclaim for positive purposes of group identification or pride a word that has been used in pejorative ways against them. For example, *Yankee* (possibly derived from Dutch *Jane*, a nickname for "John") was a term used derisively by the British for New England settlers; after the Battle of Lexington (1775), however, New Englanders claimed the name for themselves;[4] similarly, the term *queer* was claimed roughly two centuries later, for example in contexts such as *Queer Theory*. A word being reclaimed at the time of writing by some African Americans is *nappy* (of hair); this term, referring to naturally kinky hair, has become derogatory and highly politicized, but there is a movement to give it a positive, or at least neutral meaning.

At the micro-level each instance of semantic change has its own peculiar characteristics. These may derive from the specific properties of the lexeme undergoing change. Or they may derive from the broader synchronic lexical and grammatical system in the language for expressing the conceptual structure in question (e.g. obligation). Or yet again, these peculiar characteristics may derive from the circumstances surrounding the actuation of the change in a speech community at a particular time. In other words, each lexeme considered on its own, has its own individual history. At the macro-level, however, the direction of semantic change is often highly predictable, not only within a language but also cross-linguistically. This book attempts to account for individual micro-changes within the framework of macro-processes.

Several major studies of semantic change since the end of the nineteenth century, such as Bréal (1964 [1900], 1991 [1882]), Stern (1968 [1931]), and Ullmann (1957, 1964), have proposed taxonomies of semantic changes in terms of opposing pairs of mechanisms like amelioration–pejoration, broadening–narrowing, metaphor–metonymy. These provided ways of classifying changes, but, because each pair was conceived as an opposition, no framework was offered in which to consider overarching types of semantic change, or to imagine unidirectionality of change. Hence no systemic relationship between pairs was or could be posited. Such taxonomies are often still considered to be the current state of knowledge in the field of semantic change. However, interest in the possibility of discovering replicated

---

[4] *The American Heritage Dictionary* (1992: *Yankee*, Word History).

4

unidirectionality in semantic change goes back at least to Stern (1968 [1931]), who showed that terms for "rapidly" came to mean "immediately" in Middle English (ME). His was a study of a particular phenomenon in a particular language at a particular time, and therefore did not catch much attention. Cross-linguistic studies of replicable sequences of change in lexemes came into being with work on color terms (e.g. Berlin and Kay 1969), and on "synaesthetic" adjectives of sensation and perception (e.g. Williams 1976). These were studies of changes within lexical domains, with emphasis on physiological motivations for the changes. More recently the emphasis has been on unidirectionality from one lexical or conceptual structure to another and its motivation in metaphor (an iconic strategy) and implicatures (a metonymic, associative, and indexical strategy), and on evidence for subjectification (e.g. Traugott 1982, 1989, 1995a, Brinton 1988, 1996, Sweetser 1990, Heine, Claudi, and Hünnemeyer 1991). A history of work on semantic change is sketched in chapter 2.

We will argue for an Invited Inferencing Theory of Semantic Change (IITSC) (Traugott 1999a). Being concerned with both cognitive and functional issues, we draw on several strands of research, including: (i) cognitive studies of the structuring of semantic domains (e.g. Talmy 1985, 1988, Langacker 1987/91, Sweetser 1990, Geeraerts 1997), (ii) pragmatics, especially the pragmatics of the conventionalizing of implicatures (we will call them "invited inferences") that arise in language use (e.g. Geis and Zwicky 1971, Grice 1989 [1975], Brown and Levinson 1987 [1978], Faltz 1989, Horn 1984, Levinson 1995, 2000, Clark 1996), and (iii) discourse analysis conceived as the interaction of grammar and use (Hopper and Thompson 1980), but adapted to the study of written texts because these are the prime data for studies of change with a long time-depth (see e.g. Fleischman 1982, 1992). The term "invited inference" is borrowed from Geis and Zwicky (1971). However, as will emerge below, we have a broader interpretation of invited inferences than they, and do not restrict the term to generalized implicatures. In the present context it is meant to elide the complexities of communication in which the speaker/writer (SP/W) evokes implicatures and invites the addressee/reader (AD/R) to infer them. We prefer this term over, e.g. "context-induced inferences" (Heine, Claudi, and Hünnemeyer 1991), since the latter term suggests a focus on AD/Rs as interpreters and appears to downplay the active role of SP/Ws in rhetorical strategizing, indeed indexing and choreographing the communicative act.[5] To the extent possible, semantic change will be contextualized within larger discourse structures, typically across sentence boundaries. The book therefore engages with historical discourse analysis and historical pragmatics (see Fleischman 1992, Jucker 1995).

---

[5] Note, however, that, despite the term, Heine, Claudi, and Hünnemeyer view SP/W as central forces in innovation.

With data taken from various semantic domains and various languages, we find several unifying threads in recurring patterns of semantic change. One is the overarching tendency for meanings to undergo subjectification (they come to express grounding in the SP/W's perspective explicitly), and ultimately intersubjectification (they come to express grounding in the relationship between speaker/writer and addressee/reader explicitly). A further commonality is that meanings expressing proposition-internal concepts may come to have scope over the whole proposition, as in the case of epistemic modals; or over the whole utterance, as in the case of discourse markers that show connectivity between what precedes and what follows; or they may come to have scope over whole chunks of discourse, as in the case of episode markers. Items with such scope serve to anchor the proposition explicitly in one or more of the conditions that hold in a particular speech event, such as the relative spatial, temporal, or social arrangement of the interlocutors, the speaker's attitude toward or assessment of the likelihood of the described event[6] as conceptualized at the time of speaking, or the function of the given utterance in the ongoing construction of the discourse. For example, until recently the Japanese verb *ageru* "give" was a humiliative honorific that indexed the subject (the giver) as lower in social status than the indirect object (the recipient). In present day usage, however, *ageru* in many instances marks the speaker's politeness toward the addressee without indexing the social status of its subject and indirect object. In this addressee honorific use, *ageru* may be used with animals or other social inferiors as its indirect object. As an "addressee honorific," the word anchors the expression of the entire proposition in the speaker–addressee social relationship.

1.2 The theory of grammar and of language use

Since our topic is change and most especially the discourse processes involved in change, we need not only a theory of grammar but also a theory of language use and of the mutual relationship between use and grammar. No one model of grammar is espoused here, but our approach is in principle consistent with the variety of theories associated more or less directly with Construction Grammar and Cognitive Linguistics (see e.g. Fillmore 1982, 1985, Lakoff 1987, Langacker 1987–91, Fillmore, Kay, and O'Connor 1988, Talmy 1988, Sweetser 1990, Jackendoff 1997, Kay 1997, and Goldberg 1995). Our assumption is that structural and communicative aspects of language shape the form of grammar (see e.g. Vallduví 1992, Lambrecht 1994).

If we assume that "grammar" is "linguistic system" and "code" (mostly language-specific, with very little provided by a putative Universal Grammar), the link between

---

[6] We use the term "described event" as a cover term to refer to the actions, states of affairs, and the participants in them that are at the core of clause structure.

"grammar" and "use" is the SP/W – AD/R dyad,[7] who negotiate meaning in interactive ways, both responding to context and creating context (see e.g. Silverstein 1976a, Schiffrin 1987, and various papers in Duranti and Goodwin 1992). Although this dyad may appear symmetric (and indeed has been memorialized as such by models like Saussure's "talking heads"), in fact it is not: SP/Ws have mental states and produce meanings that may or may not be understood by AD/Rs in the way intended. Although both members of the dyad are "ground" in the sense of participants assumed in the context of a particular speech or reading event (for the interactive nature of reading events, see 1.2.3 below), SP/W, when exercising his or her turn, has the central role in the context. As we will discuss below, SP/W's central role calls for a production-oriented view of language change, and accounts for why the major type of semantic change is subjectification. Here it must suffice to say that SP/W is the prime negotiator (with AD/R) of reference and of meaning in general, using indexicals and deictic shifters that permit the assigning of variables for speaker, hearer, time, place, communicative relevance, and social status.

1.2.1 Meaning and grammar

We regard the basic function of language to be to convey meaning. We also take as fundamental the notion that meaning is both cognitive and communicative. Our focus is on the lexicon and the usage patterns of lexical items in constructions. In our view lexemes (Ls) are particular language-specific representations of macro-level conceptual structures (Cs). Cs are highly abstract structures such as MOTION, LOCATION, CONDITION, DEGREE, HUMAN BEING, EPISTEMIC ATTITUDE, and may include non-linguistic meanings, such as those construed by vision. They are more or less stable and consistent across the human species, though they are inevitably somewhat influenced by culture (Györi 1996: 180–181). They are linked to more particular, and more culturally dependent, but still highly abstract linguistic meanings (Ms), subject to constraints on how Ms are combined. For example, the macro-level C of LOCATION is linked to Ms such as IN, OUT, AROUND; the C of HUMAN BEING is linked to MALE, FEMALE, PARENT OF; and the C of EPISTEMIC ATTITUDE is linked to HIGH PROBABILITY, POSSIBILITY, LOW PROBABILITY, etc.[8]

Ms are abstract linguistic representations of, among other things, situation types (processes, activities, and states), the participants in them (functioning in roles

---

[7] The dyad is of course a simplification. In many situations it is expanded to include multiple addressees, and "other participants," e.g. bystanders and eavesdroppers (see Clark 1996: 14, Verschueren 1999: 85).

[8] Cs and Ms are represented in capitals, by convention, to distinguish them from individual lexemes of the same form.

such as agent, experiencer, instrument, location), belief types (modalities), and communicative situations (speech acts). The types are not rigid categories but prototypes – family resemblance structures, members of which are more or less representative of the category (Rosch 1975, Coleman and Kay 1981, Wierzbicka 1985a, Taylor, 1997 [1989]). Being prototype in character in that they are relatively discrete but not categorically so, distinctions between Ms are gradient rather than fully determined. This means that what is at the core of a prototype can also change over time and differ across languages (see Blank 1997, Geeraerts 1997). Such possible differences in frame structure or prototype must be considered in any analysis of diachronic or cross-linguistic data in regard to semantics or semantic change.

Linguistic elements of conceptual structure (Ms and rules of combination) are, by hypothesis, universally available, and are linked to morphosyntactic and phonological structure in ways approximately as modeled in Jackendoff (1997). However, Cs may not be used in all cultures or communities within the same culture with equal saliency: at a detailed level the frame structures and the links between conceptual structure, morphosyntactic structure, and phonological structure may differ across languages and across time. For example, Pederson et al. (1998) show that cross-linguistically there may be different frames of spatial reference: not exclusively the relative space based on projections from the human body that are common in English (*front–back*, *left–right*), but also absolute reference based on fixed bearings such as north and south.

An individual lexeme L is a language-specific combination of elements from each component: a meaningful element M, a morphosyntactic one (S), and a phonological one (P):

$$(6) \quad L \rightarrow \begin{bmatrix} M \\ S \\ P \end{bmatrix}$$

The M and S elements are thought of not as collections of individual properties (such as a feature analysis might suggest), but rather as members of frames (see e.g. Fillmore 1985, Levin 1993, Levin and Rappaport Hovav 1995, and papers in Lehrer and Kittay 1992). For example, *run* conceptually involves (pre-theoretically) an Agent (the mover) and a Path (the trajectory along which the mover moves). Such conceptual frames can have significant syntactic consequences. In the instance of *run*, the syntactic consequences include intransitivity and the possibility of overt expressions of temporal and locational relations (*ran yesterday to the store*). They also have more fine-grained consequences in terms of local constructions. On an abstract level, *run* and *jog* are equivalent, but at a more fine-grained one, they are different; thus running can be competitive whereas jogging is usually not: *Mary ran against Jane*, but *?Mary jogged against Jane*, or *Mary ran a race*, but **Mary jogged a race* (Taylor 1996). As a working hypothesis we assume that differences in syntactic frame reflect differences in constructional meaning.

Differences in conceptual frame are of course also found between corresponding words in different languages, and there may be differences in the frame structure of a C or M as realized by corresponding families of lexemes in two languages. For example, *run* and its Japanese (Jp.) counterpart *hasiru* are essentially intransitive, but they can appear with direct objects that express the traversal of a path. While this pattern in English (Eng.) appears restricted to the completion of a finite path or distance, e.g. *run a race*, *run a mile*, in Jp. it may be used for partial as well as complete traversal: *miti o hasiru* "run (down/along) the street." Such use is characteristic of other motion verbs in Jp. as well, e.g. *tobu* "fly" (*sora o tobu*, literally "fly (through/in) the sky").[9] This class of "quasi-transitive" motion verbs (see Martin 1975: 186–188) provides evidence that the C of MOTION is realized with a somewhat different frame structure in Eng. and in Jp. (see also Fong 1997 on differences between Eng. and Finnish). As another working hypothesis, we assume that differences in syntax reflect differences in conceptual frame.

Despite evident similarities to research in frameworks consistent with Construction Grammar and Cognitive Linguistics, our approach is considerably different in focus. Some differences are directly related to the fact that our topic is language change from a discourse perspective. Specifically, our data are necessarily written texts, not constructed data (except occasionally to highlight a point). Therefore our data are instances of language in use, not of linguistic competence abstracted from context. As we have indicated, our theory thus pertains not only to cognition (mental representations) but also to SP/W and AD/R as dynamic participants. Central to our view of the dynamic nature of language change are the processes SP/Ws and AD/Rs bring "on-line" to the act of language use. Though speakers and hearers draw from paradigmatically organized sets of constructions, lexical items, and other resources, on-line production and processing make use of essentially syntagmatic relations and associations. Therefore, invited inferences and metonymic relationships predominate. We will argue that metaphorical, analogical relationships often provide the background contexts for and often appear as the resulting products of change, but that they are less important in the process of change than are associative, metonymic ones. Furthermore, image-schemata such as are central to Cognitive Linguistic thinking are shown to be only one (relatively small) component of the conceptual structures on which language-users draw.

---

[9] This class of "quasi-transitive" motion verbs differs from other transitive verbs in Jp. For example, unlike true transitives, these motion verbs in their transitive uses do not appear in the passive (**sora ga tobareru* "the sky is flown" is not possible).

Although we do not espouse many of the particular theoretical claims and assumptions of Relevance Theory, most particularly not the emphasis on monosemy and on decoding by addressees, we nevertheless share several of their assumptions. One is that conceptual meanings (Ms in our sense) have to do with entities, activities, attitudes, etc. and, when combined into propositions, may be subject to truth-conditional interpretation; they are, however, not to be identified with truth-conditional meaning (Wilson and Sperber 1993, Sperber and Wilson 1995 [1986]). For example, in (7):

> (7) On the record, I'm happily married; off the record, I'm about to divorce.
>
> (Wilson and Sperber 1993: 19)

on the record and *off the record*, as "illocutionary" or "stance" adverbials, do not contribute to the truth-conditions of the sentence, but they do contribute conceptual meaning. Otherwise, as Wilson and Sperber point out, the sentence would be contradictory.

Like Relevance Theorists, we also assume that there is a division of labor among Ms: some are primarily contentful, others primarily procedural (Blakemore 1987).[10] Meanings expressed by nouns, verbs, adjectives, prepositions, and adverbs in some of their uses are usually of the contentful type. By contrast, procedural meanings are primarily indexical of SP/W's attitudes to the discourse and the participants in it; they index metatextual relations between propositions or between propositions and the non-linguistic context. They include discourse markers (*well, in fact, so* in some of their meanings), various connectives (*and, but*), and express SP/W's view of the way these propositions should be understood to be connected. For example, *so* in:

> (8) a. *So*, what's for lunch?
>
>   b. *So*, our speaker tonight is Bella Johnson.

cannot be analyzed in terms of its contribution to the propositions *X is for lunch, Our speaker tonight is Bella Johnson*, but rather encodes the SP/W's evocation of some connectivity (in the first case to prior expectations that the interlocutor will have planned a menu, in the second to prior expectations that the speaker will be introduced). Further, some forms have both contentful and procedural meaning (Nicolle 1998). They are what Silverstein called "duplex signs" that are

---

[10] Blakemore and, following her, other Relevance Theorists use the term "conceptual" rather than "contentful"; however, we use the latter term (see Sweetser 1990) because both procedural and non-procedural language-specific meanings are representations of more abstract Conceptual Structures (Cs).

"referential–indexical" (Silverstein 1976a: 24–25), and include most notably deictics such as *here, I, come*. They also include epistemic modals. Thus *may* in:

(9)   Bella *may* speak tonight. (= It is possible that Bella will speak tonight.)

contributes to the contentful structure of the utterance (possibility on a scale between high probability (*must*) and low probability (*might*)), but it also indexes subjective attitude (*I think it is possible that Bella will speak tonight*). While modals and connectives have long been accepted as elements of grammar, some procedurals like discourse markers have only recently been included, partly because they have been perceived to have primarily pragmatic meaning connecting discourses rather than sentences, and partly because, in some languages like English, they are syntactically highly variable in position. However, they can link clauses and even phrases, and clearly not only have syntactic status but are also constrained in terms of sequence. They are therefore elements of "grammar" in the sense of "linguistic system" (Fraser 1988: 32). In terms of language use they are at the interface between syntax and discourse.

Although the line between "semantic representation" and "encyclopedic knowledge of the world" is a very fine one, as a general principle we focus our attention on meaning changes that are primarily linguistic and that have implications for constraints on lexical insertion or grammatical function. Without some independent evidence such as changes in morphosyntactic distribution, we have no principled way to demonstrate that a linguistic change has taken place. Changes that are primarily extensional, e.g. depend on material changes in the referent (e.g. Latin *carrus* "four-wheeled wagon" > *car*), will for the most part be ignored.

1.2.2   *Polysemy, homonymy, monosemy*

Our theory of meaning embraces the hypothesis that families of related meanings, or polysemies, can, and indeed must, be identified (see Fillmore 1997 [1971], Brugman 1988, Pustejovsky 1995, to mention only a few). Semantic change cannot be studied without drawing on a theory of polysemy because of the nature of change. Every change, at any level in a grammar, involves not "A > B," i.e. the simple replacement of one item by another, but rather "A > A ~ B" and then sometimes ">B" alone. Older meanings may become restricted in register, and therefore recessive, and may disappear completely, as did *ought* in the sense of "have/owe." In ME *ought* (*to*) was the past tense form of both "have/owe" and of the obligation modal. Both the "have/owe" and the modal senses were derived (by sound and meaning change) from Late Old English (LOE) *ahte* "have," but the original meaning of possession was lost. However, despite what is often thought, the loss of an earlier meaning is relatively rare. What is typical is the accretion of more and more meanings over time, hence the parenthetical status of the lone survivor B in the schema:

$$(10) \quad A > \left\{ \begin{array}{c} A \\ . \\ B \end{array} \right\} \ (> B)$$

The coexistence of variants has been termed "layering" by Hopper (1991); it is a psychological reality for individual SP/Ws, who acquire variants, whether phonological, morphological, syntactic, or semantic, and for communities as change spreads. Older meanings coexist with newer meanings of the same item, as for example, older and newer meanings of *since* (the temporal is older, the causal more recent) and they may influence each other. As we will see, some polysemies continue to coexist over several hundreds of years, although their relationship to each other in terms of saliency may change.

Positing polysemy is often considered problematic. On the one hand there is the synchronic type of analysis that privileges the notion that one-form:one-meaning would be ideal. One-form:one-meaning would appear to give optimal results in an information-based theory of meaning, particularly one in which the work that AD/R brings to the communicative act is concerned, since it would minimize ambiguity. However, there is no evidence that SP/Ws actually strive for this ideal in their everyday use of language (except in the context of various discourses associated with standardization, such as pedagogy, editorial practices, or the claims of pundits about language). While the demands of an increasingly technological society favor the development of rigidly specified lexical distinctions, for example, among diseases, legal rulings, or linguistic terminologies, very few, if any, words in ordinary language have only one interpretation. Even in academic disciplines there are often systemic ambiguities. Thus "semantics," "syntax," "phonology," "grammaticalization," "semantic change" refer both to the phenomenon itself as it pertains to a particular language, and to the putative theory of the phenomenon in the abstract. Although the adage "Languages avoid unnecessary variation" is often repeated, some variation seems to be very necessary, most particularly that associated with multiple meanings.

One approach to coexistent meanings associated with the same form has been to postulate homonymy. On this view, L is a combination of a single semantic reading with a single underlying syntactic function and a single phonological shape. Such an approach was proposed by Katz and Fodor (1963) when they suggested that *bachelor* could be treated as at least four homonyms that are conceptually unrelated despite sameness of form. While most people would agree that the meanings "a man who has never married," "a person holding the lowest academic degree," "young knight serving under the standard of another knight," "a young fur seal without a mate during breeding time," are synchronically distinct in meaning, they might have more difficulty agreeing with McCawley (1968: 126) that *sad* is likewise homonymous in its readings "experiencing sadness, said of a living being," and "evoking sadness, said of an aesthetic object." For one there is a regular relationship between experiencing and evoking that is also found in the various meanings of *happy*, *glad*, and other adjectives of mental state.

Recently Fraser (1996) has taken the position that the manner adverb and sentence adverb meanings of lexemes such as *candidly* should be treated as homonyms (cf. *You should reply candidly* (manner adverb) vs. *Candidly, you should reply* (sentence adverb with the illocutionary function *to speak candidly*)). However, an assumption of homonymy obscures patterned meaning relationships that pertain to sets of adverbs, such as *frankly*, *truthfully*, which, among other things, express a way in which something is done and an assessment of the proposition that follows. Likewise *in fact*, *actually* express both unexpectedness/adversativity and also elaboration/specification/additivity. Furthermore, similar patterns of meaning relationships between adversativity and some kind of elaboration are found cross-linguistically, e.g. *shi* "in fact" (lit. *qi* "its" + *shi* "fruit/fact") in Chinese (Ch.), *zitu wa* "in fact, as for the fact(s)" in Japanese (Jp.); see also the discussion of *en fait/de fait* "in fact" in French (Fr) (Roulet 1987), *infatti/difatto* in Italian (Rossari 1994), and especially *si* in Spanish (Sp.) (Schwenter 1999).

Where there is a synchronic sense relationship there is usually a historical relationship. Typically it is a relationship of an older meaning and a newer one that developed out of it in specific contexts, as in the case of the examples in the preceding paragraph, and of epistemic meanings arising out of obligation meanings. However, synchronic convergence of what appear to be historically unrelated meanings can not be ruled out. For example, dictionaries treat *lap* in the sense of "to place or lay something so as to overlap another" and *lap* "take in a liquid with the tongue" as homonyms. The first is from OE *lapa* "part of outer garment that hangs down" (OED *lap* v^2), the second from OE *lapian* "take in a liquid with the tongue" (OED *lap* v^1). Nevertheless, some speakers might well construe them as related. This is because in the nineteenth century *lap* "take in a liquid with the tongue" was extended to mean "wash against with a slapping sound":

(11) Flinty steps, against which the tide *lapped* fitfully with small successive waves.

(1823 Scott xxxvi [OED *lap* v^1. 4])

Since lapping waves not only involve water and slapping sounds, but also visual overlap (of wave over wave, or of water over steps in the case of (11)), an area of related meaning has developed, and for some SP/Ws *lap* can be considered polysemous in English. It is, however, unlikely that such a convergence of homonyms

13

would occur cross-linguistically; unlike the development of polysemies discussed here, such convergence of homonyms is highly idiosyncratic and irregular. Another, even more idiosyncratic, reason for apparent synchronic convergence of historically unrelated meanings is "folk etymology": the association of a form the meaning of which has become obscure with an extant one. For example, *hangnail* originates in OE *angnægl* "painful corn (on foot)." When *ang* as an independent form was lost (it was reborrowed, however, as an inseparable one in words like *anguish*), the form was reinterpreted as *hang-* and the meaning associated with a pain typically in a different part of the body (hand rather than foot), one associated with a piece of detached skin "hanging" from its normal place.

If plausible meaning-relationships can be shown to hold, most especially if they pattern across members of similar lexical representations, then they can also be considered to operate across syntactic classes (Brugman 1984). For example, the root-epistemic polysemy of *insist* persists *across* the verb *insist* (*that X do/that X is*) and the noun *insistence*. Furthermore, it can operate across phonological splits; an example is provided by OE *an* "one" which split into *a(n)* in its function as article and *one* in its function as numeral and pronoun, as in *Would you like an apple? No, I don't want one*. On this view, a lexeme L may have two or more polysemies (M_1, M_2, ... M_n), and, beyond the outputs of regular lexical processes, two or more idiosyncratic morphosyntactic properties (S_1, S_2) and (more rarely) phonological forms (P_1, P_2):

$$(12) \quad L \rightarrow \begin{bmatrix} M_1, M_2 \\ S_1, (S_2) \\ P_1, (P_2) \end{bmatrix}$$

It is important for our view of meaning change and of polysemy in particular, that a meaning M is understood as schematic, and partially underdetermined. It is a stabilized, institutionalized, and prototypical "magnetic center" that can be contextually interpreted in constrained ways (see Victorri 1997), not a fully determined discrete entity. Our view of polysemy is therefore consistent with the "weak polymorphic model" proposed by Pustejovsky (1995) for the lexicon, in which polysemy is part lexically, part pragmatically determined. We do not, however, embrace his strongly synchronic formalism here.

In our view homonymy should be postulated only when there is no clear semantic relation between the meanings of a phonological string, that is, only when there is what Pustejovsky (1995), following Weinreich (1964), calls "contrastive ambiguity." A methodological problem for the historical linguist is to assess when two polysemous meanings have lost their relationship so as to be associated with two homonymous lexemes. This change presumably occurs at different times for different individuals, but equally presumably it eventually spreads like other changes to a whole community of speakers. For example *well* meaning "in a good/proper manner" and *well* functioning as a discourse marker indicating hesitation, or an attempt to take a turn, are probably regarded as homonyms by most speakers in contemporary Eng., although they were once historically connected.

In the case of phonology, we know that erstwhile allophones have split when they no longer become predictable in terms of environments, e.g./f/ and /v/ came to contrast word-initially in ME, though they were predictable variants in OE ([v] occurred in voiced environments). However, there are few things comparable in lexicology and the surest way to assess homonymy with reasonable accuracy is by tapping speaker intuitions. For example, *still* "without motion, quietly" is no longer associated with *still* in its temporal sense of "without interruption," or in its concessive sense of "however"; and *apprehension* "understanding, dread" is no longer associated with *apprehension* in its meaning of seizure (as in *border apprehensions*). Absent speakers of a dead stage of a language, there is no sure way to tap such intuitions. Nevertheless, evidence is not totally unavailable. Sometimes comments can be found in dictionaries and grammars. There is also negative evidence when a meaning ceases to be used after some period of time, and (less reliably) restriction of at least one (often the older) meaning to a very particular register. For example, *humor* "that which excites amusement" is no longer associated with *humor* "body fluid." Although the two meanings are still used, they appear in totally different registers, the second (and older) in a discussion of ancient views of physiology.[11]

While some contemporary linguists opt for homonymy rather than polysemy even where regular patterns of meaning relationships exist, others opt for monosemy or unitary meaning. For example, Kratzer (1977) seeks the "invariable" or "common kernel" of meaning behind *must* and *can*, since the number of meanings of these Ls is too large to capture (perhaps nonfinite). Likewise Groefsema (1995) argues that a theory of polysemy is too coarse-grained to account for all the synchronic uses of modals like *may, can, must*, and *should* in Present Day English (PDE). Assuming that polysemy requires discreteness, she also argues that it does not provide a principled way to account synchronically for indeterminacy, merger etc. Her view of the semantic change from obligation to conclusion is partly that they have undergone "a development from more specific meanings through implication to more general meanings" (Groefsema 1995: 59). However, absent a principled account of relationships between "specific" and "general" meanings that can constrain the paths of change in actual use, a monosemous approach of this type underdifferentiates the recurring patterns that a polysemous approach can highlight.

[11] A term that has been suggested for historically related forms that are not or are not necessarily construed as related by speakers synchronically is "heterosemy" (Lichtenberk 1991). For the historical linguist this usefully distinguishes between historically related meanings such as those of *still*, and homonyms that have never been related, e.g. *pear* and *pair*.

On the widely accepted assumption that a theory accounting for both synchrony and diachrony is optimal (see e.g. Kiparsky 1982 [1968]), if polysemy is needed for diachrony then it should be for synchrony as well. There is no way to account for change except by appealing to structures and processes that exist synchronically. Our view is that polysemy is therefore central to a theory of semantics and semantic change. It arises out of processes of invited inferencing. How pragmatic inferences are employed in any situation is a matter of language use, which is discussed in the next section.

1.2.3   *Meaning and use*

In thinking about meaning change, and especially about invited inferences arising out of and being exploited in the flow of speech, it is useful to build on Levinson (1995)[12] and distinguish three levels of meaning relevant to a lexeme:[13]

(i) CODED MEANINGS (SEMANTICS). This is a convention of a language at a given time. For example, in PDE, in its function as a conjunction introducing finite clauses, *after* is used to mean "at a time later than," but *since* has both the meanings "from the time that" and "because"; in other words *since* is semantically polysemous, whereas *after* is not. Eng. *as long as* has polysemies "of same length as," "during the time that," "provided that"; by contrast, Fr. *tandis que* < Lat. *tam diu quam* "as long (temporally) as" has polysemies "during the time that," "although" (see 1.3.2 below); in Late Middle Japanese (LMJ) *hodo ni* had the meanings "to the (temporal or quantitative) extent that" and also "because."

(ii) UTTERANCE-TYPE MEANINGS. These are generalized invited inferences (GIINs). GIINs are preferred meanings, and conventions of use in language-specific communities, but may be canceled.[14] They are crystallized invited inferences associated with certain lexemes or constructions that are specific to a linguistic community, and can be exploited to imply/insinuate certain meanings, e.g. in their function as prepositions *after* and *since* can give rise to and be used to implicate causality. Thus *After the trip to Minnesota she felt very tired* +> "because of the trip she felt very tired," *Before TV two world wars; after TV zero.*[15] However, causality is not a coded meaning of *after* or *since* as prepositions, and is easily canceled: *After the trip to*

---

[12] The proposals in Levinson (1995) are developed in far greater detail in Levinson (2000). We are grateful to Stephen Levinson for sharing parts of earlier drafts of Levinson (2000) with us; unfortunately the book came out too late to be discussed here.

[13] In doing so, we recognize that the distinction between the three types of meaning outlined below is not always crystal clear (see e.g. Carston 1995).

[14] GIINs are akin to generalized conversational implicatures or GCIs in Levinson's (1995) terminology.

[15] Billboard seen near San Francisco, August 1998, clearly exploiting the causal implicature, but staying safely within bounds of commonsense (and legalities of truth in advertising).

Minnesota she felt very tired. It turned out she had been sick for quite some time. Such utterance-type meanings may be pragmatically ambiguous (see Horn 1985, Sweetser 1990), but are not semantically ambiguous.

(iii) UTTERANCE-TOKEN MEANINGS. These are invited inferences (IINs) that have not been crystallized into commonly used implicatures.[16] They arise in context "on the fly." They may be based in encyclopedic knowledge, or (in a nonce-situation) on the situation at hand, in which case they are knowledge- or situation-specific. But they may also be based in linguistic knowledge, possibly on a universal basis (subject to particular cultural experiences). Thus it is possible that "at a time later than" may always invite inferences of causality in any language as an IIN, without taking on saliency or being generally exploitable as a GIIN. Note this does not mean that all languages necessarily encode "at a time later than" (though it is probable that they do so), only that if they do so, then causality may arise as an IIN. This allows us to recognize that not all linguistic systems may involve the same conceptual structures, but still to maintain the assumption that if the structures are the same, then the same invited inferences can arise. Each conceptual frame may presumably be used to invite inferences of specific kinds, but this frame will not always be invoked. We have little solid evidence that IINs differ in different communities, although it is often surmised that literacy may affect ways of interpreting utterances (and in different ways in different communities) (see e.g. Olson 1994). Evidence for differences would come from cross-linguistic study of contemporary languages, from metalinguistic comments by authors from different periods, or from a substantial number of replicated changes that no currently known pragmatic principles could account for.

Language users internalize a system or grammar. Drawing on various strategies of production and perception they engage in language use – "activities in which people do things with language" (Clark 1996: 3). Such activities are in most particular instances personal and individual, but they are produced and reproduced within the larger social settings of norms, e.g. of trading transactions, breakfast conversations, religious or institutional activities such as sermons or court orders, trials, proclamations, and through letters, dramas, or novels.

Essential in these activities are (at least) a speaker/writer (SP/W) and an addressee/reader (AD/R) (see 1.2.1). In line with recent work on discourse analysis (e.g. Duranti and Goodwin 1992, Chafe 1994) we conceptualize the reader as an active participant who not only reads passively but also actively makes inferences and may begin to exploit these inferences in a way similar to those of the writer. Recipients of the written word may interact in overt ways, perhaps by responding verbally to a version of a sermon read aloud (or perhaps emotionally to a romance). They always interact covertly, by engaging in processing and interpretation. In any

---

[16] IINs are akin to ad hoc conversational implicatures or CIs in Levinson's (1995) terminology.

event, their main task in response to SP/W is to determine what is meant, in other words, to find the relevance of what has been said to the situation, including the task at hand, and perhaps some larger task such as improvement of knowledge structure. AD/R also exerts influence on the formulation of the linguistic communication by SP/W: SP/W can be assumed to take into consideration expectations about AD/R's knowledge and linguistic competence, other conventions, and also factors such as AD/R's probable degree of attentiveness to the discourse at hand in selecting particular linguistic forms that will likely achieve the desired communicative effect.

In other words, although writing is sometimes thought to be context-free, non-interactive, and monologic (see Ong 1982 for discussion of such views), this underestimates the communicative task of writing. Writers write for audiences. This is particularly true of times prior to printing, when few people were literate and many texts were written down to be read out loud, whether homilies, romances, dramas, or biblical translations. It is clear that Murasaki Shikibu expected the readers of her *Tale of Genji* (*c.* 1001–10 AC) to be intimately familiar with Heian Japan court life and its many conventions. It is true, however, that, except in the case of some private letters, court records, commissioned plays, etc., at least some, if not most, AD/Rs of a written text are often, even typically, unknown and not co-present with SP/W. Other participants include audiences of the type for whom the text was not intended. Although the scribes who wrote down the trials of Throckmorton, More, and others in the sixteenth century recorded spoken language, like present-day court scribes they presumably edited what was said, and not only for the judges but for posterity.

We assume that the interactive choreography of writing, like that of speech, is governed by what Levinson calls a set of principles, heuristics, or "a *generative theory of idiomaticity* ... guiding the choice of the right expression to suggest a specific interpretation, and as a corollary, a theory for accounting for preferred interpretations" (Levinson 1995: 94; italics original). These principles, modified here for the context of writing, are related to Grice's "maxims" (Grice 1989 [1975]), and Horn's "principles" (Horn 1984):[17]

(i) THE Q(UANTITY)-HEURISTIC: "Make your contribution as informative as required, and imply no more thereby," "Say/write as much as is needed for the occasion." This is approximately Grice's Quantity1 Maxim, and pairs with "What is not said/written is not the case." This strategy is highly relative. What is needed on one occasion (such as on first meeting someone, an introductory class, a text book) may be totally unnecessary or even inappropriate on another (such as with long-time friends, an advanced graduate course, a monograph, a letter from an insurance company regarding a claim).

---

[17] For various approaches to these principles, see Atlas and Levinson (1981), Levinson (1983, 1995), Horn (1984), Blakemore (1987, 1990), Traugott (1989), Traugott and König (1991).

(ii) THE R(ELEVANCE)-HEURISTIC: "Say/write no more than you must, and mean more thereby." This is inspired by Grice's Quantity2 Maxim, combined with his maxim of Relevance. It has also been called the Principle of Informativeness (Levinson 1983: 146). It leads to rich interpretations. All writing as well as speech is subject to the R-heuristic. Meaning cannot be constructed without it. For example, readers have to enrich the relationship between the two sentences preceding this one to infer the relevance of writing and speech to meaning, and of being subject to Y to constructing Z. This is not to deny that at certain periods (or in certain communities) exploitation of the R-heuristic may be more highly valued than at others, nor that writers of certain kinds of scientific texts may aim at minimizing the effect of the R-heuristic, while others, such as poets, may seek to maximize it. The point is that it is ubiquitous and unavoidable.

(iii) THE M(ANNER)-HEURISTIC: "Avoid prolixity," or, specially marked, complex expressions warn "marked situation." This approximates Grice's Manner Maxim. In Levinson's and Horn's view, the M-heuristic is relevant only when there are pairs of lexical items, e.g. *house:residence, unnatural:non-natural*. Here we extend the heuristic to pairs that are marked in any kind of special way, whether by register (as in the case of *residence, non-natural*), status as a recognizable borrowed term (*boutique, Weltanschauung, sashimi*), or constructional periphrasis (e.g. *eat up, cross over*). In the case of *eat up* and *cross over* these complex predicates are unmarked with respect to *devour, traverse* where register is concerned, since the single lexical items are the more formal (and borrowed), but with respect to *eat* and *cross, eat up* and *cross over* are aspectually marked. Factors such as this point to the need to interpret "marked expressions" along a variety of dimensions. What will turn out to be a marked expression will be very specific to a language or a community, but we assume that the effect of markedness, however it is expressed, will be consistent across these languages and communities.

As will be discussed in more detail in 2.3.5, the Q-heuristic retards change since it inhibits inferences beyond what is said (it is, however, relevant to change, if mainly in a negative way, since it is associated with standardization, which tends to privilege literal meaning, lack of ambiguity, and conservative linguistic practices). By contrast, the R-heuristic leads to change because it evokes utterance meanings beyond what is said; in other words, it involves "pragmatic strengthening." New uses of old form–meaning pairs often exploit the M-heuristic because they are redundant in the context, and so signal "marked situation."

1.2.4 *Subjectivity, intersubjectivity, objectivity*

Among types of utterance meanings that have come to be of major importance in recent years are those associated with subjectivity. Subjectivity was already mentioned in Bréal's work (1964 [1900]: chapter 25). Elaborated on in

Bühler (1990 [1934]), it was understood to underlie deixis. Subjectivity played a prominent part in the *gengo katei-setu* "theory of language as process" of Tokieda (1941) and subsequent work within the *kokugogaku* (roughly "traditional Japanese linguistics") approach in Japan (see Maynard 1993: chapter 1 for a discussion in English). However, subjectivity did not become a significant topic of research within the international community of linguists until Benveniste raised the question whether "language could still function and be called language" unless it was deeply "marked... by the expression of subjectivity" (1971 [1958]a: 225). Like Bühler and Jakobson, Benveniste saw the SP/W–AD/R dyad as the condition or ground for linguistic communication, and characterized this relationship as one of "intersubjectivity" – in communication each participant is a speaking subject who is aware of the other participant as speaking subject. Discourse "is language in so far as it is taken over by the man who is speaking and within the condition of intersubjectivity, which alone makes linguistic communication possible" (Benveniste 1971 [1958]a: 230). SP/Ws constitute themselves as "subject" in saying "I" and in contrasting themselves with "you." Linguistic codes allow SP/W to appropriate form–meaning pairs, not only in the domain of personal pronouns, but throughout the linguistic system; most particularly this appropriation accounts for the difference between the "syntactic subject"/"sujet d'énoncé" and the "speaking subject"/"sujet d'énonciation" (see also Lyons 1982, 1994,[18] Langacker 1985, 1990).

In language use subjectivity "involves the expression of self and the representation of a speaker's... perspective or point of view in discourse – what has been called a speaker's imprint" (Finegan 1995: 1). As Stubbs (1986: 1) has said:

> whenever speakers (or writers) say anything, they encode their point of view towards it: whether they think it is a reasonable thing to say, or might be found to be obvious, irrelevant, impolite, or whatever. The expression of such attitudes is pervasive in all uses of language. All sentences encode such a point of view ... and the description of such markers of point of view and their meanings should therefore be a central topic for linguistics.

Synchronically, SP/W selects not only the content, but also the expression of that content – which entity is chosen as syntactic subject, whether topicalization is used, present or past tense, etc. In the dynamic production of speech or writing, linguistic material may be used in novel ways to express that subjectivity. Selection from the grammatical repertoire may be conscious or unconscious. Creative writers and rhetoricians tend to be highly conscious of their selections, others less so. Choices are correlated with register (e.g. scientific writing in this century has been expected until recently to be maximally "objective"), and with degree of attention to an

---

[18] Thanks to Susan Fitzmaurice for drawing our attention to Lyons (1994).

audience, whether individual or multiple AD/Rs (here the issue is one of "intersubjectivity"). In all cases choices are particularly highly correlated with strategic intent and explicit coding of that intent.

If the speaker's point of view is pervasive, can there be speaker-neutral or objective language? "Objective" language has often been associated with active, declarative assertions in which the speaker's viewpoint is not explicitly coded. Stereotypically in rhetorical traditions it has been associated with the passive (where the agent of scientific experiment or authorship is demoted into a *by*-phrase or even effaced, i.e. is zero). Scientific writing has come since the seventeenth century to be associated with nominalizations, passives, and other syntactic devices that "objectivize" the task of running experiments and interpreting them. An eighteenth century idea was that "classic" prose is clear, exact, truth-oriented, with an "invisible writer" (Thomas and Turner 1994). In the logical, philosophical, and computational traditions that have not only influenced rhetoric but also underlie much of linguistic work on semantics, objectivity has been linked to truth and information structure. Choices along the objective–subjective continuum are also often correlatable with social role, e.g. positions of authority (Macaulay 1995). In Euro-American traditions, those who wish to exert or draw attention to their authority tend to do so by use of "objective" language, whereas those who either are not empowered or who do not wish to draw attention to their power, tend to use more "subjective" language. But this is not true in all societies. Rather, representation of the nature and status of the source of one's information (hearsay, personal experience, traditional lore), or epistemological stance may be expected of all speakers. This is especially true when a language has grammaticalized "evidentials," or markers of information source, as in the case of Quechua and many other languages (see e.g. Chafe and Nichols 1986, Mushin 1998).

In his important work on subjectivity, Langacker (e.g. 1985, 1995) has adhered closely to Benveniste's original distinction between overt subject of sentence and covert subject of utterance. Langacker has identified subjectivity largely with zero subject or at least "off-stage," implicit expression of the Speaker–Hearer dyad or their point of view, and objectivity with explicit, "on-stage" expression of this dyad (typically as arguments). In this he in part follows not only Benveniste but also the tradition associated with scientific writing and classic prose. We will discuss Langacker's position in some detail in 2.3.4. In this book we take a different approach to subjectivity and objectivity (see Traugott 1989, 1995a, 1999a), although we agree with Langacker that subjectivity and objectivity are matters of linguistic perspective, on the assumption that experience is largely determined by language (though visual, aural, and other perceptions play a role too (see e.g. Jackendoff 1997)).

Since our concern in this book is with ways in which language use leads to new coding of meaning, our prime concern is with subjectivity that explicitly encodes

SP/W's point of view, for example in deixis, modality, and marking of discourse strategies. Likewise, for us, intersubjectivity is most usefully thought of in parallel with subjectivity: as the explicit, coded expression of SP/W's attention to the image or "self" of AD/R in a social or an epistemic sense, for example, in honorification. This focus on encoding makes it possible to pose research questions such as the following (paraphrasing Lyons 1994: 16): do natural languages differ typologically and over time in their encoding of locutionary subjectivity and intersubjectivity, and in the kinds of subjectivity and intersubjectivity encoded?

In thinking about subjectivity and intersubjectivity it is important to distinguish the roles of SP/W and AD/R in the world of the speech event from possible roles that the same individuals may (and often do) play as referents in the world that is talked about. Intersubjectivity crucially involves SP/W's attention to AD/R as a participant in the speech event, not in the world talked about. Consequently, at least in English, intersubjectivity is not necessarily a characteristic of all expressions that make reference to the second person. For example, *I will take you to school* reveals little if any attention on the part of SP/W toward the image or other needs of AD/R in that person's role as an interlocutor in the speech event. Nevertheless, the meanings of the first and second person pronouns *I* and *you* are crucially grounded in the point of view of the speaker, and so they exhibit subjectivity, as do all deictics (see Jakobson 1957, Silverstein 1976a, Fillmore 1997 [1971]). Moreover, in languages with contrasting formal and intimate second person pronouns, e.g. Fr. *tu* and *vous*, the image needs of AD/R must be explicitly addressed in the expression of such propositions, and therefore explicit attention is paid to intersubjectivity. As is discussed in 4.3.3, in the expression *Actually, I will take you to school* the word *actually* likewise addresses SP/W's attitude toward AD/R and has an intersubjective meaning. Subjectivity is a prerequisite to intersubjectivity, inasmuch as SP/W's attitude toward AD/R is a function of the perspective of SP/W.

We consider those expressions most objective that require the fewest inferences depending on SP/W–AD/R. This means that other things being equal (which they are often not), the most objective expressions have the following characteristics:[19]

(i)   they are declarative, i.e. minimally marked with regard to modality,

(ii) all participants in an event structure are expressed in surface structure,

(iii) lexical items are minimally concerned with the interlocutors' perspective (i.e. minimally deictic),

<hr />

[19] As Brady Clark has pointed out, the exact conditions under which these characteristics apply may vary according to register. Recipes in English tend to be imperative, in French they tend to be expressed by infinitives; in both cases the agentive subject is unexpressed, even though, being indefinite, it is not referentially inferable (it is of course contextually inferable).

(iv) the Q-heuristic predominates, i.e. contexts for meanings are provided so that interpretation is strongly determined, and what is not said is implied not to be the case.

On the other hand, the most subjective expressions will have the following characteristics:

(i) overt spatial, and temporal deixis,
(ii) explicit markers of SP/W attitude to what is said, including epistemic attitude to the proposition,
(iii) explicit markers of SP/W attitude to the relationship between what precedes and what follows, i.e. to the discourse structure; many aspects of discourse deixis are included here,
(iv) The R-heuristic predominates.

Intersubjective meanings, by contrast, are "interpersonal" (Halliday and Hasan 1976) and arise directly from the interaction of SP/W with AD/R. In our view intersubjective meanings crucially involve social deixis (attitude toward status that speakers impose on first person – second person deixis).[20] They impact directly on the self-image or "face" needs of SP/W or AD/R (see Brown and Levinson 1987 [1978], Matsumoto 1988, Ervin-Tripp, Nakamura, and Guo 1995). Therefore the most intersubjective expressions have the following characteristics:

(i) overt social deixis,
(ii) explicit markers of SP/W attention to AD/R, e.g. hedges, politeness markers, and honorific titles,
(iii) the R-heuristic predominates, i.e. what is said implies more is meant.

On this view, certain types of expressions may be explicitly subjective, most especially explicit illocutionary expressions such as *I promise to X*, etc. Others may mask subjectivity by drawing on lexemes associated with "objective" truth, e.g. sentence adverbs like *in fact*, though how tenuous this apparent objectivity is will be discussed in chapter 4. As Halliday (1994 [1985]: 362–363) points out, there is a fundamental paradox in the expression of certainty: "we only say we are certain when we are not"; in the "'games people play' in the daily round of interpersonal

---

[20] Other uses of the term "intersubjective" usually assume audience interpretation and understanding. For example, Schiffrin argues that subjectivity and intersubjectivity "emerge from an interaction between what an actor does – including actions intended to be perceived and designed as such and actions not so intended – and an audience's interpretation of all available information" (1990a: 142). Nuyts (1998) uses "intersubjectivity" in referring to evidence known to or accessible to a larger group of people who share the same conclusion as the speaker.

Minimally coded attention to SP/W–AD/R dyad	Maximally coded attention to SP/W–AD/R dyad
Objectivity	(Inter)subjectivity
Q-heuristic	R- and M-heuristics

Figure 1.1. Correlations between degree of subjectivity and heuristics.

skirmishing," subjective opinions which in fact are best expressed by e.g. *I think*, are concealed behind objective-seeming expressions like *surely*.[21]

From the perspective of an information-based, truth-conditional approach to semantics, or an approach assuming one-form:one-meaning, one might ask how it is possible for one lexeme with multiple polysemies to be explicit. The puzzle diminishes, however, when attention is paid to the fact that explicitness is a matter of context, for an individual polysemy does not occur in a vacuum. Polysemies often have different distributional properties, and an explicit use will take advantage of them. One of the striking phenomena that we will come back to again and again in this book is the extent to which language use is redundant. Explicitness is achieved through the choice of Ls in specific syntactic strings, and in specific linguistic (and nonlinguistic) contexts.

In sum, in our view, (relative) objectivity vs. (inter)subjectivity is not only a matter of cognitive stance but a property of language that arises directly out of the SP/W–AD/R dyad and the rhetorical uses to which they put language in communication. SP/W rhetorical purposes motivate uses of the heuristics discussed in 1.2.3. Objectivity is associated with the Q-heuristic, (inter)subjectivity with the R- and M-heuristics. This can be modeled as in figure 1.1. Like the heuristics, objectivity and (inter)subjectivity are both context-dependent and context-creating.

This is a synchronic model. We will see that, from a historical perspective, subjectification precedes intersubjectification.

1.3 Semantic change

In the following chapters we will develop the widely recognized hypothesis that the chief driving force in processes of regular semantic change is pragmatic: the context-dependency of abstract structural meaning allows for change in the situations of use, most particularly the speaker's role in strategizing this dynamic use. As pointed out by Bartsch: "semantic change is possible because the specific linguistic norms, including semantic norms, are hypothetical norms, subordinated to the highest norms of communication (the pragmatic aspect of change)"

---

[21] Halliday terms this "metaphorical representation" of modality.

(1984: 393). We consider the implicatures/inferences in question to be both cognitive (information-related) and communicative/rhetorical (arising out of purposeful negotiation between speaker and addressee). Although we do not use the cybernetic feedback model developed by Lewandowska-Tomaszczyk (1985), we agree wholeheartedly with her claim that meanings have "a starting point in the conventional *given*, but in the course of ongoing interaction meaning is negotiated, i.e. jointly and collaboratively constructed ... This is the setting of semantic variability and change" (Lewandowska-Tomaszczyk 1985: 300).

Semantic change is typically thought of in terms of three research questions (see Geeraerts 1997):

(i) Given the form–meaning pair L (lexeme) what changes did meaning M of L undergo?
(ii) Given a conceptual structure C, or meaning M, what lexemes can it be expressed by?
(iii) Given C, what paths of semantic change can be found to or from other Cs?

Work on Question (i) is known as semasiology. In the semasiological approach, form (morphosyntactic and morphophonological properties) is typically kept constant (though it can be subject to phonological changes). The focus is on the development of polysemies (or, where relevant, splits into homonymies), e.g. *as long as* "equal in length" > "equal in time" > "provided that"; *even* "evenly" > "unexpected member of set of alternatives" (the focus particle use as in *Even Samantha has left*); or *sanction* "approve, authorize" > "impose penalty"). This can be schematically represented as in (13), where "Form" is a cover term for syntax and phonology:

$$(13) \quad L \rightarrow \begin{bmatrix} \text{Form} \\ M_1 \end{bmatrix} > L \rightarrow \begin{bmatrix} \text{Form} \\ M_1 + M_2 \end{bmatrix}$$

Semasiology is the approach that will be the prime focus of the present book, but always within the context of the other two questions.

Work on Question (ii) is known as onomasiology. The focus is on the development or restructuring of coded representations of a particular domain such as COLOR, INTELLECT, or CONDITIONAL. For example, in OE CONDITIONAL was expressed by Ls such as *gif* "if"; *butan* "unless," *nymþe* "unless." In PDE it is represented by *if, when, as long as, suppose, provided that, unless*, etc. Changes in representation of C between time 1 (t_1) and time 2 (t_2) can be schematically represented as:

$$(14) \quad C \qquad\qquad C$$
$$\updownarrow \qquad\qquad \updownarrow$$
$$(L_1, L_2)\, t_1 \;>\; (L_1, L_2, L_3)\, t_2$$

The schema in (14) highlights recruitment of new lexemes to represent C; there are therefore more Ls at t_2 than at t_1. Of course, L_1 or L_2 may eventually be lost, in which case there may be fewer or the same number of Ls at t_n. A major example of the onomasiological approach to semantic change is provided by Buck's (1949) dictionary of Indo-European synonyms, which organizes the material according to such conceptual categories as "mankind: sex, age, family relationship, parts of the body, food and drink, clothing, motion, possession, quantity and number, time, sense perception, emotion, mind, thought, religion."

Answers to Questions (i) and (ii) inform work on Question (iii), which concerns detectable regularities of change across abstract conceptual structures, as evidenced by particular semasiological changes. Here the focus is on the growing evidence for unidirectional relationships in semantic structure such as TEMPORAL > CONDITIONAL (but not vice versa), TEMPORAL > CONCESSIVE (but not vice versa), DEONTIC > EPISTEMIC (but not vice versa), and at a more global level from content meanings based in event-structure to procedural meanings based in discourse. The resulting synchronic implicational relationship is of the type "if a term is concessive it may have derived from a temporal" (e.g. *while, however* [note the *ever* here]), or, in a stronger version, "if L has temporal and concessive polysemies, then the concessive is with strong probability derived from the temporal" (see 2.2.3). This can be represented as in (15):[22]

$$(15) \quad C_2 \supset C_1$$

A word of caution is always necessary when speaking of change in language, or a component of language such as semantics. Despite terms like "language change" or locutions like TEMPORAL > CONDITIONAL, or *must* "be obligated to" > "I conclude that," it is important to recall that natural language does not exist without language-users. The abstract systems that language-users draw on when they do things with language largely[23] differ from speaker to speaker because of the discontinuity of persons and of acquisition. One abstract subsystem may be expanded by links to others, and may eventually be replaced – here as always, the phenomenon of coexistent variation schematized in (10) in 1.2.2 is at work: new

---

[22] Note the implicational $\supset$ is meant to be understood only in the non-deterministic, violable sense "if B then probably A."

[23] "Largely" because there are presumably some aspects of language structure that are universal, such as the existence of Ns and Vs and of hierarchic syntactic structure. We regard most aspects of language structure as language-specific, however.

structures coexist with older ones, and old ones need not disappear. Most especially, one set of links between form and meaning may be expanded by additional links, with old links only occasionally disappearing. Aggregates of differences among systems give us the impression over time of continuous change, but this continuity is only apparent. Therefore, strictly speaking, we should not say that root modals "become" epistemic, or that the individual lexeme *must* "becomes" epistemic *must*; rather we should say that over time speakers come to use *must* to express epistemic as well as root modal concepts. We will, however, use the usual shorthand expressions of "become" and "change" as a convenience.

1.3.1 Mechanisms of semantic change: metaphorization, metonymization

Two major mechanisms of change are usually recognized in mor-phosyntactic and phonological change: reanalysis and analogy.[24] A third mech-anism, borrowing, will not be discussed. For most of this century, reanalysis has been considered the major factor in morphosyntactic change (Meillet 1958 [1912], Langacker 1977, Lightfoot 1979, 1991, Harris and Campbell 1995; but see Tabor 1994a, Haspelmath 1998). Meillet regarded it as the only locus of innova-tive grammatical change ("grammaticalization"); Lightfoot (1979) conceptualized it as the only locus of "catastrophic" syntactic change, i.e. change that can have potentially radical consequences for a linguistic system (his paradigm example is the development of syntactic auxiliaries in English). Nevertheless, understand-ing of the extremely local nature of reanalysis has grown, and analogy/extension have been recognized as holding promise for interesting generalizations. Accord-ingly, there has been increasing interest in the role of analogy (e.g. Kiparsky 1992, Vincent 1994) and in the question of whether a fundamental distinction can actually be made between analogy and reanalysis (e.g. Tabor 1994a).

Likewise in semantic change, two mechanisms are usually recognized, metaphor and metonymy. For example, Nerlich and Clarke have argued that "[t]he trick of being innovative and at the same time understandable is to use words in a novel way the meaning of which is self-evident" (a semasiological claim) and that in essence "there are only two main ways of going about that: using words for the near neighbours of the things you mean (metonymy) or using words for the look-alikes (resemblars) of what you mean (metaphor)" (Nerlich and Clarke 1992: 137). To avoid confusion between the synchronic, static view of these two terms and the view of their processual function as mechanisms, we will refer to them in their dynamic dimension as metaphorization and metonymization. As in the case of

---

[24] Analogy is reconceptualized and redefined as "extension" by Harris and Campbell (1995). Theirs is a study of syntactic change, and the differences in focus will not concern us here.

analogy and reanalysis, the relative importance of these mechanisms has been differently construed over time. For most of the twentieth century metaphor(ization) was considered the major factor in semantic change. Metaphorization is primarily an analogical principle, and involves conceptualizing one element of a conceptual structure C_a in terms of an element of another conceptual structure C_b. Since it operates "*between* domains" (Sweetser 1990: 19; italics original), processes said to be motivated by metaphorization are conceptualized primarily in terms of comparison and of "sources" and "targets" in different (and discontinuous) conceptual domains, though constrained by paradigmatic relationships of sames and differences. Thus it is possible to conceptualize the development of temporal *while* "during the time that" > concessive *while* "although," or *grasp* "seize" > "understand" in terms of a projection or leap across domains. One question, however, is what is meant by "domain" (for an insightful critique, see Croft 1993, Barcelona 2000a, Kövecses 2000). The term is used in a variety of senses. For example, in Sweetser's book, as in this one, semantics, syntax, phonology are considered large-scale domains of linguistic organization and of study; so are large-scale categories like modality, performativity; likewise so are the domains that "model our understanding of the social and physical world," of the "world of reasoning," and of the act of describing the world ("speech acting") (Sweetser 1990: 21). But the term is also often used for irreducible "primitive representational field[s]" (Langacker 1987/91: chapter 4) like space, time, deontic modality, epistemic modality, concession. If irreducible primitives of this type are called "domains," as they often are in work on metaphor, e.g. Lakoff (1987), Heine, Claudi, and Hünnemeyer (1991), then the question of how large a leap has to be to count as a metaphor becomes a major issue. We will be using the term "conceptual structures" for such large-scale domains in an attempt not to prejudge what is in "different domains" (allowing for metaphorization) or the "same domain" (allowing for metonymy).

By contrast, metonym(ization) has until recently usually been considered the poor relation of metaphor(ization). Traditional examples tend to be limited to phenomena such as contiguity or association of an overtly accessible sort, e.g. part–whole, cause–effect (Gibbs 1993), often in physical space, e.g. *cheek* "jaw bone" > "fleshy part above jaw-bone"; part for whole, e.g. *keel* for *ship* (part–whole synecdoche); and ellipsis, e.g. *a Hockney*, for *a painting by Hockney*, Fr. *Place de Grève* "square where strikers met" > *grève* "strike." On the basis of such examples, Ullmann said that metonymy is "less interesting than metaphor since it does not discover new relations but arises between words already related to each other" (Ullmann 1964: 218). Nevertheless, he recognized metonymy as "an important factor in semantic change" (loc. cit.).

But metonym(ization) should also be understood as a conceptual phenomenon (see e.g. Hopper and Traugott 1993: 80–81). Given this perspective, the fundamental importance of metonymy has recently come to be appreciated (see e.g. Barcelona 2000a), and hypothesized to be "probably even more basic to language and cognition" than metaphor (Barcelona 2000b: 4). Stern had already seen this in the early part of the twentieth century when he wrote of "permutation" and "adequation" (both kinds of metonymy; see 2.2.2) as involving "the subjective apprehension of the referent" (Stern 1968 [1931]: 350). For example, he wrote of the association of mental state with its object or cause, e.g. *concern* (n.) "interest (in some matter)" > "(the) matter that concerns" (ibid. p. 376). And focusing on the "syntactical" nature of linguistic metonymization, Kurylowicz regarded it as "the fundamental and overall phenomenon" (1975: 92). Construed as a conceptual mechanism by which invited inferences in the associative, continuous stream of speech/writing come to be semanticized over time, metonymization provides as rich an explanation as metaphorization for semantic change, and in many cases a richer one (Traugott 1988, Traugott and König 1991). Consider the relationship of part to whole. In semantic change, it has often been noted that a term for a part will become a term for a whole, but not vice versa, e.g. FINGERNAIL > FINGER > HAND in Australian aboriginal languages. This can be seen as enabled by the unidirectionality of entailments in part–whole relationships: "'part', by definition, entails some idea of 'whole', but a 'whole' entails no notion of 'part'" (Wilkins 1996: 275–282). Not only strong entailments, but also weaker, defeasible implicatures can enable change. The motivation is the R-heuristic "Say no more than you must, and mean more thereby." Or consider concessive *while*; this can be seen to arise out of association of surprise (special, marked effect) at the explicit marking of two events as taking place at the same time (the motivation is not only the R-Heuristic but also the M-heuristic: "complex expression warns 'marked' situation").

Neither conceptual metaphorization nor conceptual metonymization in principle excludes the other: easily comprehended metaphors are consistent with typical associations; both exploit pragmatic meaning; both enrich meaning. Indeed, we agree with the claim that the target and/or the source of a potential metaphor "must be *understood* or *perspectivized* metonymically for the metaphor to be possible" (Barcelona 2000b: 31; italics original). Since the prime focus of this book in regard to processes of change is on IITSC and invited inferences, it is also on the mechanism of conceptual and discursive metonymization and its role in semantic change. Invited inferencing arises out of implicatures that are regularly associated with linguistic material in syntagmatic space, together with the operation of the R- and M-heuristics on underspecified linguistic material that give saliency to specific aspects of reasoning and rhetorical strategizing in particular contexts. Metaphorization is regarded as not only a constraint on but also often the outcome of metonymic change.

We take the position that the notion of conceptual metonymy needs to be expanded to account for subjectification and intersubjectification. Both are ultimately

DEMONSTRATIVES				IDENTITIVES	
"1"	"2"	"3"	anaphoric	"self"	"same"
CL HIC	ISTE	ILLE	IS	IPSE	IDEM
VL ISTE	IPSE	ILLE			*MET-IPS-IMUM

Figure 1.2. Shift in demonstratives from Classical to Vulgar Latin (Harris 1978: 69).

dependent on the SP/W – AD/R dyad, and by hypothesis derive from the mechanism of metonymic inferencing combined with rhetorical strategizing in the context of the speech event.

As we saw in 1.2.4, subjectivity is ubiquitous in language synchronically. Subjectification is the semasiological process whereby SP/Ws come over time to develop meanings for Ls that encode or externalize their perspectives and attitudes as constrained by the communicative world of the speech event, rather than by the so-called "real-world" characteristics of the event or situation referred to.[25] Subjectification is very wide-spread, indeed the most pervasive type of semantic change identified to date. Although there is brief mention of it in Bréal (1964 [1900]), subjectification is a relatively new concept in studies of semantic change (see e.g. Traugott 1982,[26] 1989, 1995a, Langacker 1990, and papers in Stein and Wright 1995).

A striking example of subjectification is the shift in demonstrative pronouns that occurred in Vulgar Latin. In Classical Latin, there was a set of demonstratives: *hic* "this near me; close to first person," *iste* "that near you; close to second person," *ille* "that of some other person; close to third person." There was also a set of identitives: *ipse* "self," *idem* "same." In Vulgar Latin forms in this system shifted in the direction of the speaker's deixis; the result was that first person demonstrative was now expressed by *iste* (formerly the second person demonstrative), the second person demonstrative by *ipse* (formerly the identitive "self"), and "self" by **met-ips-imum*, the "self" identity marker *ipse* reinforced by *met* (emphasizing identity, cf. "personally") and -*imum* (the superlative). Harris (1978: 69) represents the shift as in figure 1.2.

---

[25] Contrast Langacker (1990, 1999), who identifies subjectification with attenuation of the subject; cf. comments on his views on subjectivity in 1.2.4 above.

[26] The term "subjectification" is not used in Traugott (1982), but the "expressive" tendency of semantic change identified there is roughly equivalent to subjectification as defined here.

Other examples of subjectification include the development of discourse marker uses of adverbs such as *after all*, performative uses of locutionary verbs such as *promise*, *recognize* (ultimately derived from spatial and mental terms respectively), and a variety of other developments of progressively less truth-conditional and less-referential meanings that have been called cases of "pragmaticalization" (Aijmer 1996) and, in the case of the development of conversational routines, "discursization" (Arnovick 1994). Subjectification draws on cognitive principles but takes place in the context of communication and rhetorical strategizing. It falls directly out of SP/W–AD/R interactions, and the competing motivations of speakers to be informative and of addressees to construe invited inferences. In particular, it is the metonymically based process by which SP/Ws recruit meanings that function to convey information to do the work of communication: to express and to regulate beliefs, attitudes, etc. It therefore inevitably involves intersubjectivity to some degree.

In instances where meanings come explicitly to index and acknowledge SP/W's attitude toward AD/R in the here and now of the speech event, intersubjectification can be said to take place, for example, when non-honorifics are recruited to serve honorific uses. Intersubjectification, therefore, is a change which results in the development of meanings that explicitly reveal recipient design: the designing of utterances for an intended audience (Clark and Carlson 1982) at the discourse level. Note there cannot be intersubjectification without some degree of subjectification because it is SP/W who designs the utterance and who recruits the meaning for social deictic purposes. It is part of the same metonymically based mechanism of recruiting meanings to express and regulate beliefs, attitudes, etc. as subjectification, and can be regarded as a special subtype of the latter.

There has been a tendency, especially in pedagogical circles, to associate explicitness with objectivity. One of the key points in any kind of writing instruction is the importance of being able to make reference clear (e.g. "You (writer) may have the reference clear in your head, but the reader may not be able to access it"). Instruction to be explicit includes providing unique referents, restricting indeterminacies of lexical meaning, and restricting connotative meaning, especially negative ones such as tend to be found in "four-letter" words and swear words, slang, etc. Such instruction is usually accompanied by exhortations to be scientifically objective. It is therefore not surprising that the suggestion has been made that subjectification defined as preemption of old meanings to encode and externalize speaker subjectivity is really objectification (e.g. Diewald 1993, Keller 1995). However, if, as suggested in 1.2.3, objectivity has to do primarily with literal and truth-conditional meaning, and (inter)subjectivity with procedural meanings that make features of the discourse situation manifest, then subjectification and intersubjectification are clearly distinct from objectification.

Subjectification and intersubjectification are typical of "internal" change in the sense that they are natural changes. By contrast objectification is sporadic and largely irregular since it is the highly conscious and deliberately interventive sort of change that comes about when ordinary words are preempted for specific purposes; in other words, it is an "external" kind of change. Therefore, although it is a mechanism of change, it is considered a minor one from the perspective of this book, much as borrowing is. An extreme example of "objectification" is when lawyers seek to constrain interpretations of words. Another is the development of "technical jargon," which involves the stipulative definition of terms by professionals, who seek to construct meanings in ways as immune as possible to personal interpretation. So, for example, when terms like "competence," "performance," "common ground," "subjectivity," or "objectivity" are redefined for purposes of linguistic discourse, objectification occurs. Even though the definitions are the products of individuals and therefore reflect the beliefs of those who construct the definition, the purpose of the definition is to establish a shared, public meaning that can be replicated and used in analytic discourse (scientists often avoid the problem by inventing new words made up of fragments of Latin or Greek), not to make explicit the SP/W's attitude to what is being said. Sometimes the practice of redefinition or of coining new terms is accompanied by a certain amount of linguistic play which may give it the appearance of being less objective, but nevertheless a definite technical meaning is the aim, at least when the term is first used, e.g. "virtual reality," MOOs, MUDDs, etc. All these are cases of "external," "non-natural" change, not of "internal," "natural" change, which is the central concern of historical linguistics.

Since words are used by people in contexts, redefinitions of the kind mentioned above are of course subject to change and may readily undergo de-objectification as the words spread to the market-place of non-technical discourse. For example, current use of *paradigm* in general contexts to mean "major (epochal) new model or approach" (e.g. calling the availability of shopping on the internet *a paradigm shift in shopping*) reflects popularization of a technical use from Kuhn (1996 [1962]); see also *schizophrenia* (Nunberg 1979). Although the public may think that the purpose of a dictionary is or should be to "fix the language" ("objectivize" it), dictionaries can do no such thing, as has been recognized at least from Dr. Johnson's time on. They reflect the language of the time (sometimes with its history, see especially the OED) and the biases of the compilers. They include not only denotations but also connotations, in other words the subjectifications that have come to be fairly wide-spread. Good dictionaries also include extensive material on the contextualization of language.

As characterized here, subjectification (and intersubjectification) results in sema-siological phenomena, i.e. it brings about meaning changes in specific lexical items and constructions. The claim that meaning change is subject to a very powerful and wide-spread tendency on SP/Ws' parts to employ the metonymically based mechanism of subjectification is a claim about the probable history of particular lexemes and constructions. It in no way denies or contradicts the fact that certain large-scale social factors may serve as counterforces. The development of literacy and especially of grammars and dictionaries without question has an objectifying effect on language and language practices. The stylistic choices SP/Ws make either personally or collectively at certain points in history are highly subject to cultural attitude changes; at one point in history an "objective" style may be more highly valued, at another a less objective one, e.g. in the seventeenth century scientific writing underwent a radical shift to a style that demoted the agent of research (and hence interpretation) in favor of "objectivity" as associated with nominalization, passive constructions, and a minimally subjective lexicon (Halliday 1990 (cited in Olson 1994), Thomas and Turner 1994).[27] In a very interesting article Adamson (1995) has discussed the rise of Free Indirect Style. This is the style that represents a consciousness filtered through the perspective of the narrator; its prototype involves third person, past tense, but proximal deictics *now* and *here*, as well as idiomatic speech and exclamations, and modals which report the character's rather than the narrator's conjecture (Banfield 1973, Fludernik 1993), as in:

(16) The sound of wheels while Mrs. Glegg was speaking was an interruption highly welcome to Mrs. Tuliver, who hastened out to receive sister Pullet – *it must be sister Pullet, because the sound was that of a four-wheel.*

(1860 Eliot I, vi [Fludernik 1993: 188])

Here the whole section in italics represents what Mrs. Tuliver, not the reporting narrator, concluded. Free Indirect Style in English is often associated with the development of subjectivity in the late nineteenth century novel, climaxing in Virginia Woolf's writing. But Adamson argues that it originated in *I-was-now* representations of experiential memory as developed in Puritan literature such as Bunyan's. Here interest in the individual self, and in memory of the past "self" as "unregenerate, and of value solely for its exemplification of what it is like to be in a state of sin" became paramount (Adamson 1995: 208). Adamson suggests that the later shift to third person in Free Indirect Style was a case of objectification and a counterexample to Traugott's hypothesis of subjectification. However, this is in an area of style and large-scale preferences for certain modes of representation, not of Ls and their development. Like changes in social practices concerning politeness, such style shifts are outside the purview of IITSC.

---

[27] Note that objectivity in this sense is not identical with our definition of it in 1.2.4; in scientific writing demotion of the agent (the investigator and author) is favored, whereas in our view of objectivity maximally objective language gives overt expression to all participant roles in an event structure.

Likewise, when massive borrowings or word coinages occur, especially borrowings designed to serve the needs of a vernacular language newly validated for use as the vehicle of law or education, of a new technology, or, in the case of medieval feudalism, a new sociopolitical organization, such borrowings and coinages are likely to be used at first in their most objective meaning (Marchello-Nizia Forthcoming). Over time, however, such new coinages are, we predict, likely to undergo subjectification (possibly including intersubjectification).

1.3.2 The Invited Inferencing Theory of Semantic Change model of semantic change

To summarize discussion so far, we assume that at a particular moment in time t_1 the meaning M of a lexeme L is linked to a conceptual structure C. This relationship can be expressed as (ignoring morphosyntactic and phonological Form):

(17) L $\rightarrow$ M

$\updownarrow$

C

At t_1 SP/W, whether child or adult, has acquired a grammar (i.e. a linguistic system) and pragmatic heuristics such as the R-, M-, and Q-heuristics. SP/W and AD/R have available to them both as individuals and as members of the community metaphors, metonymies, and (inter)subjectivities; these provide cognitive constraints on the innovation and therefore actuation of new meanings. They are what Nerlich and Clarke have called "the micro-dynamics of semantic innovation, that is the synchronic process of the actual speech activity, which give rise to constant variation … strategies and procedures of semantic innovation, related to communicative–expressive need" (Nerlich and Clarke 1992: 127). In the on-line production of language SP/Ws use mechanisms such as metaphorization, metonymization (including invited inferencing, subjectification, intersubjectification), and objectification in the context of spoken and written discourses.

SP/W may innovate a metaphoric use of a lexeme in an utterance-token. Creative writers in particular do this. The new use is an instantaneous development for SP/W; it may or may not be gradual for that individual across the speech style and genres he or she uses. Often such uses do not spread to other speakers, but sometimes they do. In such cases the spread across the community may be gradual, but for each individual acquiring the new meaning the change is instantaneous. Most readers will probably recognize their own experiences along these lines with the (metaphorical and playful) innovation "the millennium-bug," coined to refer to the anticipated problem that some computers might not have been able to handle the date change to the year 2000. Alternatively, SP/W may begin ad hoc to exploit a conversational implicature (IIN) that already exists and may even use it innovatively in a new linguistic environment. Such uses may be considered personal features of style and are unlikely to survive and play any part in a particular change unless they come to be endowed with symbolic value. If they do acquire social value and therefore become salient in a community they are likely to spread to other linguistic contexts and to other SP/Ws, in other words, they become GIINs with strengthened pragmatic impact. They are considered GIINs so long as the original coded meaning is dominant or at least equally accessible, but when that original meaning becomes merely a trace in certain contexts, or disappears, then the GIIN can be considered to have become semanticized as a new polysemy or coded meaning: a "macro-dynamic" change (Nerlich and Clarke 1992) has occurred.[28] Again, semanticization of a new polysemy is instantaneous for the individual, but may spread slowly to other speakers.

Different pragmatic meanings can become salient in different communities. Such differences may depend on the context in which the new meanings are primarily exploited. For example, Jurafsky (1996) notes that FEMALE may lead in some cases to augmentative semantics, sometimes diminutive. He shows that these apparently contradictory developments can be quite naturally accounted for in terms of different conceptual structures. MOTHER, when associated with origins and contrasted with CHILD, may lead to "large, important." But WOMAN, perceived as smaller and less powerful than MAN, may lead to "small, unimportant." Note here both the linguistic context (opposition sets) and the social, evaluative contexts are different in each case.

The prime objective of IITSC is to account for the conventionalizing of pragmatic meanings and their reanalysis as semantic meanings. Differently put, historically there is a path from coded meanings to utterance-token meanings (IINs) to utterance-type, pragmatically polysemous meanings (GIINs) to new semantically polysemous (coded) meanings. This is a view of change foreshadowed by some brief and often hesitant statements made in the early 1970s such as "it is probably a fact that, in the course of time, inferences do become references" (Bolinger 1971: 522; see also Geis and Zwicky 1971, Grice 1989 [1975], Levinson 1979; for more details see 2.3.2). But none of the authors involved did a detailed historical study to provide empirical evidence for the hypothesis. As has been widely discussed, change does not originate within language (grammars do not change by themselves), but in language use, i.e.

---

[28] The distinction between individual "micro-dynamic" and communal "macro-dynamic" change is similar to that between "innovation" (which occurs in the individual and may not spread to others) and "change," which involves spread across speakers, communities, and registers (Weinreich, Labov, and Herzog 1968, Milroy 1993).

in factors external to language structure. It is not possible to predict precisely under what circumstances and when a change will take place in historical linguistics (Lass 1980, 1997). But nevertheless there are very strong tendencies that are replicated at the macro-level from language to language and period to period, which suggests certain commonalities of production and perception. Once actuated or initiated, they spread through a community, again in replicable ways, that ultimately lead to cumulative effects and adoption by a community.[29]

As a concrete example, consider the development of *as/so long as* in English. In OE and ME the spatial meaning as in (18) already coexisted with the temporal "for the same length of time as" in (19) (presumably derived in earlier Germanic from the spatial meaning).

(18) þa het   Ælfred cyng timbran   lang scipu ongen ða
      then ordered Alfred king build-INF long ships against those
      æscas;   þa wæron   fulneah tu   *swa lange swa* þa oðru.
      warships they were   nearly twice as   long as   the others
      "then King Alfred ordered long ships to be built to battle the warships; they
      were almost twice as long as the other ships."

(850–950 ChronA, p. 90)

(19) wring þurh   linenne clað on þæt eage *swa lange swa*
      wring through linen   cloth on that eye   as   long as
      him ðearf sy.
      him need be-SUBJUNCT
      "squeeze (the medication) through a linen cloth onto the eye as long as he
      needs."

(850–950 Lacnunga, p. 100)

In (19) temporal coextension of administering the medicine with need for the medicine invites the inference of conditional "provided that." This is because the main clause is imperative, part of a set of procedures to be followed in imaginary situations; in such imaginary situations, the need is construed as contingent and temporary (signaled by the subjunctive). There is even an IIN of "conditional perfection" (the "if and only if" relationship, cf. Geis and Zwicky 1971, van der Auwera 1997), which derives from the projected temporariness of the need together

---

[29] Keller (1994) borrows the "invisible hand" metaphor from the eighteenth century philosopher of economics, Adam Smith, to account for the cumulative consequences at the macro-level of individual acts on the micro-level, particularly those performed without human design. A much-cited example is that of a path that gets cut across grass, the result of people making short-cuts to save time, not with the intention of making a path. On our view, such cumulative acts at the micro-level of language use may or may not be intentional. They include the exploitation by SP/Ws of invited inferences and the interpretation of them as salient by AD/Rs; they also include SP/Ws' preemption of meaning to their own perspective (subjectification).

with the generic distributive aspect ("on all occasions that"). Texts in OE and ME exemplify the use of *as/so long as* primarily with verbs of existence (*be*), living and other event structures that are construed as temporary. Here the conditional reading is available if the temporal clause refers to the future, or is generic, but never seems particularly salient. All examples allow a reading of the type "for the length of time that ... /until X no longer Y," e.g. for (19) "squeeze the medication on the eye for the length of time that he needs it/until he no longer needs it."

In Early Modern English (EMdE), however, examples begin to occur in which the conditional IIN has been generalized to contexts in which the conditional is more salient, i.e. the temporal meaning, though present, is not predominant. The contexts have been extended to event structures involving patterns of reasoning and cognition that are unlikely to change. However, the context suggests that a change is not only possible but would be highly valued, as in:

> (20)   They whose words doe most shew forth their wise vnderstanding, and whose lips doe vtter the purest knowledge, so *as long as* they vnderstand and speake as men, are they not faine sundry waies to excuse themselues?
>
> (1614 Hooker, p. 5)

At this stage we can say the conditional reading has become a GIIN of temporal *as/so long as*. But the temporal is still available ((20) could mean "for the length of time that they understand and speak as men," i.e. "as long as they live").

By the mid-nineteenth century we find examples where the conditional appears to be the only possible meaning. The GIIN has been semanticized as a conditional polysemy of temporal *as/so long as*:

> (21)   a.   "Would you tell me, please, which way I ought to go from here?"
>   "That depends a good deal on where you want to get to," said the Cat.
>   "I don't much care where – " said Alice.
>   "Then it doesn't matter which way you go," said the Cat.
>   " – *so long as* I get *somewhere*," Alice added as an explanation.
>
> (1865 Carroll, chapter 6, p. 51)

> b.   Galligan told the jury that it is proper for police to question a juvenile without a parent present *as long as* they made a "reasonable effort" to notify the parent.
>
> (1990 Aug. 9, United Press Intl.)

Particularly interesting is the fact that there appear to be no examples in which an *as/so long as* clause in Eng. has been saliently associated with an implicature that it is:

> (i)   presupposed true,
> (ii)   adversative; i.e. concessive (meaning *although*).

By contrast, Fr. *tandis que*: "aussi longtemps que" > "pendant que" is attested with the GIIN of concessivity from about 1623 ("au lieu que" according to Wartburg 1928–66; "opposition dans la simultanéité" according to *Robert* 1993). In Late Middle Japanese (LMJ) *hodo ni* "to the (temporal, spatial, or quantitative) extent that" comes to be used in the meaning "because" (a meaning that later fell from use). Thus, from similar semantic beginnings, with similar IINs, different GIINs developed in different contexts (presumably temporal), hence different polysemies.

The overall concept of IITSC is modeled in figure 1.3. This is a model of the mechanism by which innovations may arise in the individual and be affected by community acceptance of salience, etc. For an innovation in the linguistic system of an individual to constitute a change "in the language," the innovation must be spread or propagated through the community: "a change in the output of a single speaker might be regarded as the locus of change in the system, whereas of course a change is not a change until it has been adopted by *more than one* speaker" (J. Milroy 1992; 79; italics original). If SP/Ws innovate, and AD/Rs replicate this innovation, they do so in the role of SP/Ws, i.e. as language producers, not as language perceivers.

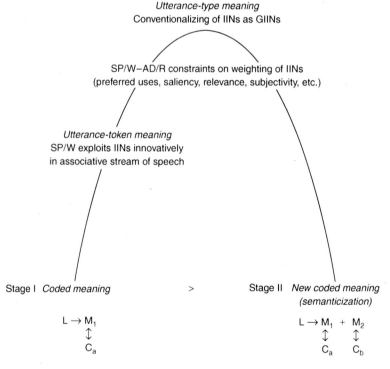

Figure 1.3. Model of the Invited Inferencing Theory of Semantic Change (IITSC; Traugott 1999: 96) (M = Coded meaning; C = Conceptual structure).

Most studies of the role of metaphor in semantic change focus on the bottom part of the model (the relationships between two stages of a lexeme's history in terms of sources and targets, i.e. products, iconicities, and metaphors). Studies of the role of pragmatic inferencing in semantic change focus on the top part of the model and on the processes leading to change (e.g. using language indexically and metonymically). As we have pointed out above, the approaches are not mutually exclusive, but rather mutually enhancing (see also Heine, Claudi, and Hünnemeyer 1991, Andrews 1995); however, they involve significantly different perspectives. It should also be noted that this model, in keeping with the focus of both approaches on the development of new meanings and new polysemies, does not account for loss. Loss is unpredictable and irregular. Development of incremental meaning, however, is largely regular, and this is what the model attempts to account for.

The model in figure 1.3 operates recursively, i.e. M_1 represents any meaning that gives rise to invited inferencing. It may itself be historically derived, by prior invited inferencing, metaphorization, interventive meaning change, etc. In the case of the history of *as long as*, the original M_1 relevant to the development of the temporal meaning was spatial (resulting in M_1 (spatial) $+ M_2$ (temporal)); once we find that the temporal polysemy had arisen, we can "reset" the model so that M_1 is the temporal meaning, which eventually gives rise to the conditional (i.e. M_1 (temporal) $+ M_2$ (conditional)). In indexing the polysemies, it is, however, essential to keep them separate, since older meanings continue to invite inferences and may themselves undergo change, leading to further developments.

It might be asked whether M_1 is an appropriate designation at Stage II. Given a theory of totally discrete change it would not be. Under such a theory, the original M (e.g. temporal) with its various associated meanings would probably be considered different from a later (but also temporal) polysemy because the semantic space would be divided up differently after the new polysemy (e.g. conditional) had been semanticized. This could be captured by a rule such as:

$$(22) \quad \text{M (temporal + conditional inferences)} > \begin{bmatrix} M_1 \text{ (temporal)} \\ M_2 \text{ (conditional)} \end{bmatrix}$$

However, this would obscure the fact that IINs and GIINs from the earlier meaning continue to be available in certain contexts i.e. are stable across time as well as contexts. This is because Ms are always somewhat underdetermined. For example, *since* is sometimes unambiguous in its temporal and causal meanings, sometimes ambiguous, and sometimes indeterminate; temporal *since* still allows causality to be exploited as an invited inference, as in *Since coming to the US, she has been very happy.*

truth-conditional		>		non-truth-conditional
content	>	content/procedural	>	procedural
s-w-proposition	>	s-o-proposition	>	s-o-discourse
nonsubjective	>	subjective	>	intersubjective

Figure 1.4. Correlated paths of directionality in semantic change (in this and subsequent figures, s-w = scope within; s-o = scope over).

The model does not specify the mechanisms by which semantic change comes about: metaphorization and metonymization (including subjectification and inter-subjectification). These are pragmatic processes that lie behind SP/W's exploitation of available implicatures in the flow of speech and writing. It follows from the recursive operation of the IITSC model that meanings become increasingly pragmatic and procedural since the operative constraints are saliency, subjectivity, etc., i.e., constraints that flow from the linking of communicative and cognitive functions that is language. It also follows that there is tendency toward metatextual meaning, or more specifically a shift from *de re* to *de dicto* meaning (see Frajzyngier 1991 for this way of describing shifts from "the world being talked about" to "the speaker's organization of that world in the act of speaking" (Traugott 1980: 47)). Such shifts typically involve increase in scope, from meanings that function at the propositional level (e.g. manner adverbials in event structures), to meanings with scope over the proposition (e.g. sentential adverbials), to meanings with scope over the discourse unit (e.g. adverbials in discourse marker function). These trajectories may be schematized as in figure 1.4.

In this figure we indicate by "contentful/procedural" that if a contentful L acquires procedural meaning, it will usually do so via a polysemy that is both contentful and procedural (for example as long as "if" is contentful with respect to hypotheticality, and procedural with respect to indicating that the clause it introduces is treated by SP/W as a ground for the matrix clause). Although correlated, the individual horizontal trajectories are not necessarily vertically aligned; so different aspects of any one semasiological change may be at some different point on the horizontal trajectory of a particular L. It should be recalled that "layering" always occurs between a first and a second stage, sometimes between all stages. This and subsequent figures of a similar nature show only the changes, not the retentions in meaning.

It should be noted that although we are focusing on what is usually called "internal" change, in the sense defined above as "natural" and largely unconscious change, the mechanisms for change as outlined in this IITSC model of semantic change are external. This is because the mechanisms involve processes of reasoning, mental projection, association, focusing on salient issues (whether driven by social factors or SP/W's own perspective), etc., none of which are part of the language system, but rather are processes brought to bear on this system in language use.

1.4 Child vs. adult acquisition in semantic change

There is currently considerable debate about who innovates: children or adults, so the question might arise, whose acquisition is IITSC a model of. It has long been claimed that child language acquisition is the locus of change: language change, in particular change in grammar or coded structure, occurs because children learn language (imperfectly) (see e.g. Paul 1920 [1880], Meillet 1958 [1905–06]). This view has been central to generative linguistics and was refined as the hypothesis that children can simplify grammars, but adults can only elaborate (see e.g. Halle 1964, Lightfoot 1979, 1991, Kiparsky 1982 [1968]). A particularly strong version of the hypothesis was developed by Bickerton (1984), known as the bioprogram hypothesis, in which it was claimed that evidence from the development of e.g. Hawaiian Creole and especially Saramaccan showed that in the absence of generation-to-generation transmission of language, children would innovate specific semantic and syntactic structures, e.g. highly constrained combinations of Tense–Aspect–Modality, and distinctions between specific and non-specific indefinites.

In the 1970s it was repeatedly suggested that there were matches between child language acquisition of semantics, development of semantics in creolization, and the order of semantic change in the historical data, for example across conceptual structures like SPACE > TIME, TEMPORAL > CONDITIONAL (see especially Slobin 1977; also Baron 1977 and references therein, Shepherd 1981). However, more recently this assumption has been called into question from many sources. For one, the bioprogram hypothesis has been largely exploded because it has been shown that creoles may be developed by adults, but spread and accelerated by children (see e.g. Sankoff 1980, papers in Baker and Syea 1996), and that there is minimal evidence that generation-to-generation transmission of language is absent in creole situations such as Suriname where Saramaccan Creole developed (McWhorter 1997), or Hawaii where Hawaiian Creole English came into being (Roberts 1998). Furthermore, as attention has come to be paid to the discourse processes of acquisition and change, it has become increasingly clear that the task of early language acquisition is considerably different from that of pragmatic extension of the sort arising because of IINs and GIINs. As Slobin points out in discussing the discourse origins of the present perfect in Eng.: "children come to discover pragmatic extensions of grammatical forms, but they do not innovate them; rather, these extensions are innovated diachronically by older speakers, and children acquire them through a prolonged developmental process of conversational inferencing" (Slobin 1994: 130). We assume that most of the changes we will be discussing are not initiated by children, because of the complex inferences involved and the discourse functions in structuring text. As new meanings become available as "currency in the marketplace of cultural meanings," the model of acquisition assumed is one that does not privilege young children, but rather young adults (see e.g. Milroy and Milroy

1985, Eckert 1989) and, especially in earlier times, those carrying the authority of education, law, or political or ecclesiastical and educational power. However, they may well be spread by children and younger adults, who pick up on and extend innovations.

It is frequently pointed out that language-acquirers use various reasoning strategies in the process of learning a language. The most important of these is "common sense reasoning" or "abduction" (see Andersen 1973, Anttila 1992, both building on Peirce 1955 [1898]). The basic idea is that "[a]bduction proceeds from an observed result, invokes a law, and infers that something may be the case." So, for example, a language-learner observes various kinds of verbal activities, construes them as the output of a linguistic system (grammar), uses general principles such as entailment or construal of invited inferences, as well as using heuristics of the type "Say no more than you must and mean more thereby," and guesses at what the system might be. What we assume here in our SP/W-based theory of change is that SP/Ws proceed from a result (the system they have acquired) and invoke and use general principles such as entailments and heuristics to imply that something is the case.

The hypothesis is that innovation and change does not occur primarily in the process of perception and acquisition, but rather in the process of strategic choice-making on the part of SP/W and interactional negotiation with AD/R. Support comes from various sources. One is the textual data in which writers appear to explore new uses in environments that permit the new use to be redundant and therefore easily understood. A second is subjectification. SP/Ws manipulate language for their own ends. AD/Rs recognize this and process the speech/writing of another as at best intersubjective, not based in themselves (as addressees) and their own deictic stance. A third is intersubjectification. As we saw in 1.2.4, politeness marking, hedging, and other intersubjective processes are all ultimately grounded in speakers.

1.5   The hypothesis that ontogeny recapitulates phylogeny

The hypothesis that language change is primarily brought about by child language acquisition has been closely tied to the hypothesis that ontogeny recapitulates phylogeny (acquisition by individuals recapitulates language change). In its generative versions it was a hypothesis designed in part to test "Chomskyan neo-preformationism, with its claim that our faculties of intelligence are endowed innately with a formal mechanism of logic (though the content of intelligence – knowledge – is gradually acquired through ontogeny)" (Gould 1977: 146). This hypothesis that ontogeny recapitulates phylogeny motivated interest in the idea that polysemies are ordered synchronically according to the same "core" > "derived" relationships as they had in their histories (except that some early meanings may have disappeared). It underlies some work by Traugott (e.g. 1986), who suggests that semantic internal reconstruction can be done from synchronic polysemies, given hypotheses about regularities of change. It is also central to much work by G. Lakoff (e.g. 1987), Sweetser (e.g. 1990), and others working with metaphor theory. For example, Heine, Claudi, and Hünnemeyer, in accounting for metaphorical (and grammaticalization) chains such as BODY PART > SPACE relationships, regard the chains as not only diachronic but also synchronic and indeed panchronic (1991: chapter 9).[30] Their examples are like (23) from Kuliak, a language of Northeastern Uganda:

(23) nE′kE cúc sú-o   ím.
      be   fly back-ABL girl

      a. "There is a fly on the girl's back."
      b. "There is a fly behind the girl."

                                    (Heine, Claudi, Hünnemeyer 1991: 249)

Even stronger are claims like the one put forward by Jurafsky with regard to diminutives: "any language with a diminutive with a 'member' sense will have a 'child' sense" (1996: 543). However, attractive as the hypothesis is, there is no principled reason for it to hold. Meanings may, and often do, become reorganized in ways that obscure historical relationships. And we cannot be certain that the early stages were necessarily present even if buried for ever in history.

An example of the failure of synchronic "core" > "derived" relations to match diachronic derivation is provided by the development of meanings of *still* from "quiet." We may suppose that being motionless and quiet invited the inference of continuity, hence of temporality. Its first temporal uses seem to have arisen in the context of verbs that are stative or imply a process of long duration, e.g.:

(24) In tokne ... That sche schall duelle a maiden *stille*.
                               (1390 Gower, 337 [OED *still*, adv. 3a])

As new meanings arose, e.g. the concessive as in (25), the temporal and concessive senses of *still* became dissociated from "quiet, motionless":

(25) Tis true, St. Giles buried two and thirty, but *still* as there was but one of the
      Plague, People began to be easy.
                    (1722 Defoe, 7 [OED *still*, adv 6b]; note the redundantly
                    adversative context of *but* here reinforcing the concessive IIN)

---

[30] Panchrony is an ontologically very problematic concept (see e.g. Newmeyer 1998: 284–288). Although it has the advantage of avoiding a sharp distinction between synchrony and diachrony, and allows for dynamic analyses of language from both atemporal and temporal perspectives, it obscures the fact that over time relationships among constructions can become completely reorganized.

They clustered together in what Michaelis analyzes as a set of scalar polysemies in Modern English (MdE) that are correlated with different syntactic constraints, but share the property of evoking "various types of scalar models: a time line, an 'adversity scale', and graded categorization" (Michaelis 1993: 232). She convincingly shows that synchronically these cannot reasonably be ordered with the temporal meaning as the core meaning, as Lakoff's (1987) radial category model would predict (or, for that matter, Heine, Claudi, and Hünnemeyer's (1991) metaphor chains), because it assumes a polysemy structure that recapitulates the diachronic meaning changes.[31] In conclusion, although it is plausible in many cases to organize synchronic variation in such a way as to replicate diachronic development, the historical validity of the relationship cannot be assumed. It must be tested in each instance.

1.6   The nature of evidence for semantic change

How do we as historians of a language know when an IIN is beginning to be exploited? This must always be a matter of interpretation, on the assumption that IINs are cross-linguistic. Sometimes an IIN may be inferred because the later history by hypothesis requires an earlier stage in which the IIN has operated, but we must always exercise utmost care in projecting such IINs on the textual data. As a working principle, as long as the original coded meaning is accessible, we should assume that the invited inference is just that, a meaning derivable from the semantics in combination with the discourse context. In written records, clear evidence of semanticization of a polysemy typically comes from the appearance of an item in a "new" context in which the earlier meaning(s) of the item would not make sense. At a later time the older meaning may or may not disappear; if it does, this is further confirmation of the earlier coding of the former pragmatically invited inference.

It is a truism that evidence for historical change is skewed – by the cultural value system within which records have been made and kept, and by the happenstance of what has remained despite fire, pillage, and neglect. But nevertheless the evidence is robust enough in some parts of the world, especially Europe, Meso-America, Japan, and China, for strong hypotheses to be made and tested.

Sources of data include dialect differences, past and present. Particularly valuable is evidence from changes ongoing in contemporary linguistic systems since

---

[31] A similar point is made by Goossens (1992) in connection with the development of OE *cunnan* "be (intellectually) able to" into *can*. Dekeyser (1998) gives additional examples in which the original core meaning is either obsolescent or lost and therefore cannot be considered the core meaning synchronically, e.g. *harvest*, originally "third season," then "season for reaping" (metonymic to the salient act in the season), then, again metonymically, "reaping" and "season's yield of any natural product," and *sell*, originally "give," then "give for money."

variation results from change, and change can be detected in progress. This approach is well known from sociolinguistic phonological work (e.g. Labov 1974), and lexicography. An example of work on incipient change in the modal domain is Denison's study of the development of counterfactual *may have* in contemporary Eng. (incipient in the 1980s, now wide-spread), as in:

>   (26)   The whole thing *may* never *have* happened if it hadn't been for a chance
>   meeting.
>
> (1 Nov. 1983, Guardian [Denison 1992: 231, ex. (6)])

Plausible paths of change can be tested against actual paths of change and participant observation of them. In this case Denison assumes the change is not so much internal semantic change but a case of external hypercorrection as *might* (in all its uses) becomes more recessive; in other words, the entry-points here are, on his view, complex interactions involving changes in the available representations of modality, and social factors such as the association of *may* with prestige dialects, etc. Such a study serves as a reminder that the motivations for and processes of change may be much more complex than appears from the relative paucity and homogeneity of historical documentation left to us.

Nevertheless, not all absence should be regarded as a result of skewing. If a later stage of a language consistently uses a lexical item or construction with a meaning that was not associated with it at earlier times, then we can plausibly hypothesize that it was not available at the earlier time (Faarlund 1990: 16–18). If it can be inferred occasionally (and, one finds, often in a redundant context) one can plausibly assume that it was beginning to become available, but that it has not yet been generalized, either in the work of one writer, or in the community (depending on the data base used).

1.6.1   The validity of written data

Except in contemporary situations, our evidence for change is necessarily from written data. Several caveats must be considered in using written data as a window to the spoken language of earlier times (see e.g. Herring, van Reenen, and Schøsler 2000). Written data may reflect conventions of use among a literate group that are not shared by the speech community at large. Reading and writing require at least a modicum of education, and so written language must be recognized as the product of only a segment of a total speech community. In many premodern societies, written communication was conducted primarily among the members of some social elite, e.g. the clergy. The intended recipients of a written text, however, may also include nonliterate addressees to whom texts were read aloud (e.g. sermons, news broadsheets) or performed (e.g. a liturgy or a play).

It follows that due to the relatively lasting nature of respected works of literature, liturgy, etc., written data may reflect a literary standard that differs from the spoken language of any segment of the speech community of a given time. Nevertheless, when writing becomes the primary medium for preservation of knowledge and tradition, written materials can be transmitted for the purposes of validation, a practice often considered to be "objectivizing." It may become a major mode for the production and reproduction of some experiences (for example, the use of Fr. in ME, use of Eng. by non-native speakers for literary practices). And it may take on a life of its own, situated in part in the meaning of other texts (for example, the use of Latin from OE on for legal, religious, and pedagogical practices). Most importantly for historical linguistics, "text provides a model for speech" (Olson 1994: xviii); in part we may "introspect our language in terms of the categories laid down by our script, to paraphrase Benjamin Whorf" (ibid.).

It also follows from the fact that writing has until recently been in the purview of only a few that written data from different periods of a language may reflect different literate communities or different conventions of use; in other words they do not necessarily provide straightforward evidence of a change or preservation shared by the entire speech community. This is particularly so because certain text types or subject matters may become the locus of innovations in certain semantic domains. For example, modal changes are best exemplified in religious, legal, and philosophical texts, discourse markers in rhetorical and academic discourse where signals of metalinguistic strategy are important, speech act verbs in contexts of institutional production such as prayer, legal proceedings, and royal proclamations.

Because written texts can be detached from the original context of their formation and can therefore be planned more consciously and carefully than most speech, they may focus on precision and explicitness, especially in the use of many of the linguistic structures discussed in this book: modalities, illocutionary acts (many of which are practiced in writing rather than speech, e.g. those associated with contracts), epistemic sentence adverbs and discourse connectives. How writers achieve sufficient clarity and explicitness, however, varies according to many factors. As Seidensticker (1980: xii) notes in the introduction to his translation of *Genji*, "It was certainly not impossible in Heian Japan to come right out and name one's agents and objects, but it was considered better form to let elaborately conjugated verbs and adjectives convey the information obliquely." How can we, then, tell what the relationship is between a written text and spoken language? As we trace the histories of words and constructions in the history of languages, we find that they typically have well-attested reflexes in contemporary spoken data, so there is potentially a definite, discoverable connection between written and spoken varieties (Biber 1988).

As in all historical work that relies on editions, we must of course remain aware that editorial practices have led to emendations, and additions of punctuation. Particularly with respect to discourse and other pragmatic markers, there has been a tendency to omit them in editions as "extraneous" (see Blake 1992–93, Jucker

1997). Despite these difficulties, directions and apparent mechanisms of change over time can nonetheless be determined, in broad strokes across text types, and in detail within the confines of particular text types. In general, texts that are drama, personal letters, or trials can be expected to be closer to the spoken language than those that are academic, especially philosophical treatises, or royal proclamations (Rissanen 1986). Therefore, it is important to attempt to find evidence for change from texts of the former kind.

Since the present study makes considerable use of data from the history of the Japanese language, it is important to note that the history of early Japanese is a history of writing practices borrowed from Chinese (Ch.), and that Ch. may have had considerable effect on the texts that have come down to us. Writing was introduced into Japan from China from about the third through the seventh centuries, A. C. (Miller 1967). There were several waves of lexical borrowing, one occurring in conjunction with the introduction of Buddhism in the sixth century, followed by others in the eighth and fourteenth centuries (Shibatani 1990: 120–121). Written Ch. continued to be used in Japan until the modern era for many chronicles and official documents, and was the language of much scholarship and religious writing. Moreover, throughout the recorded history of Japan, written Ch. played an important role as a repository of cultural and literary aesthetics, and as a model behind many collocations, proverbs, and perhaps larger discourse structures. However, geographic and political barriers severely limited direct contact with speakers of Ch., so contact with the Chinese language in Japan came almost exclusively through the written language. This contrasts radically with the influence of Fr. on Eng., which was not limited to written texts.

In addition to being used for writing in the Chinese language, by the early eighth century Chinese characters were used in Japan in order to write extended Japanese language texts. A description of the history of Jp. orthography, including the development of the Jp. phonetic syllabaries (*kana*) from cursive and abbreviated forms of Ch. characters (*kanji*), can be found in Miller (1967) and Seeley (1991) among others. At present, Japanese texts are written in mixed *kanji–kana* style: *kanji* are typically used for content words, e.g. nouns, verb stems, and adjectives, and *kana* are used for function words, such as verb endings and particles. While this style developed over several hundred years, and the history of Jp. orthography reflects several strikingly different models, one consistent characteristic of the orthographic system throughout the recorded history of the language is that it provides considerable flexibility for writers to choose an orthographic expression of an utterance. Writers might, for example, choose between any of several orthographic possibilities for a word in order to (i) achieve a pleasing visual balance between *kana* (especially cursive style *hiragana*) and *kanji*, which are typically more complex symbols and impart a dense appearance to the written page, (ii) mark off word boundaries (as Jp.

is written without spaces between words), or (iii) elucidate the meaning in context of a polysemous word or highlight a double entendre. Writers may even write a word innovatively with the *kanji* for another word in order to calque the sense of both items.

Another influence of Ch. on the history of the Japanese language comes from the practice of *kanbun-kundoku*, which refers to the "reading in Japanese of a text in Chinese." This practice involved transformations of word order and the addition of morphosyntactic elements necessary to convert a Chinese-language sentence into a Japanese-language one. *Kanbun* has resulted in various turns of phrase now found in the Japanese spoken language; moreover, as is discussed in chapter 4, a number of discourse marking elements in Japanese developed from conjunctions used in *kanbun*.

The presence of *kanji* and *kanbun* in the Japanese orthographic system provides the potential for layers of meaning unique to the written text (see e.g. Tamba 1986). Studies of orthographic representations have played a role in exegetic studies of Japanese literature, but a comprehensive analysis of the effects of orthography on language change in Jp. is still needed. Orthography has certainly had an effect on the size and structure of the Jp. lexicon. The presence of *kanji* probably enables the number of homonymous lexical items to be greater than would otherwise be possible. Similarly, many native words have corresponding Ch. loanwords written with the same *kanji*. Therefore, it is sometimes unclear whether a polysemy in Ch. was imported into Jp., or whether it originated after the borrowing into Jp. However, the overall direction of semantic change as evidenced from the meaning of the *kanji* itself to the meaning of the word (written with that *kanji*) in Jp. is consistent with the patterns found in data from other languages. Since we are interested in types of change rather than in the histories of particular languages, it is ultimately not of great importance whether a change originated in Jp. or Eng. or in a donor language.

1.6.2   *The language and data sources for this book*

We believe that to firmly establish types of changes, it is necessary to work with long-term historical textual records. This necessarily reduces the number of languages that can be covered, but it allows for a consistent analysis. The demonstration of regularities across two languages as linguistically and culturally dissimilar as Eng. and Jp., both with textual records extending over a millennium should, with supporting evidence from other languages, dispel skepticism about regularity in semantic change, while at the same time contributing to the theory and method of historical semantics and discourse analysis.

The computerized Helsinki Corpus of the English Texts, abbreviated as HCET (see e.g. Rissanen, Kytö, and Palander-Collin 1993), is the major source of data for Eng., with extensive supplementation from dictionaries and other data bases. Data from the recorded history of Jp. are readily available through modern, annotated editions of premodern literature; the present study focuses on prose literary works that are thought to reflect relatively closely the colloquial language of their time.

1.7 Summary and outline of later chapters

In this chapter we have outlined the assumptions and claims of the Invited Inferencing Theory of Semantic Change (IITSC). The basic idea is that historically there is a path from coded meanings (Ms) to utterance-token meanings (IINs) to utterance-type, pragmatically polysemous meanings (GIINs) to new semantically polysemous (coded) meanings. According to this approach, pragmatic implicatures play a crucial bridging role in semantic change. The system change known as "semantic change" is on this view the result of SP/Ws and AD/Rs negotiating meaning. While the dyadic relationship between SP/W and AD/R is a given of discourse, the main tendency in semantic change from a semasiological perspective is toward greater subjectivity or grounding in SP/W attitude and perspective. This is because SP/Ws are the prime initiators of change. Over time, increased overt attention may be also given semasiologically to addressees, but explicit marking of intersubjectivity presupposes increased explicit marking of subjectivity.

While much remains to be understood about semantic change, work on pragmatics and discourse analysis gives us reason to believe that semantic change not only can be regular, but indeed must be so, if synchronic processes of inferencing and of strategic interaction are replicated from generation to generation.

In chapter 2 we review some earlier and current approaches to semantic change, with particular attention to hypotheses and findings that inform the present work. In the remainder of the book, several empirical studies will be presented of semantic changes from the perspective of IITSC. In chapter 3 we discuss the domain of modal verbs, including "core" auxiliaries (e.g. *must*), quasi-auxiliaries (e.g. *ought to*), most especially the development of epistemic modal meaning. The domain investigated in chapter 4 is that of adverbs like *in fact*, and Jp. *sate* "so," which acquire discourse marker functions via an intermediate epistemic, adversative stage. Discourse marker uses are maximally subjective, and therefore the acquisition of discourse marker function is regarded as a case of subjectification. In chapter 5 we turn to the development of speech act verbs. The development from verbs with spatial meanings (e.g. *promise* < Lat. *pro* "forward," *miss*-past participle of "send") to locutionary verbs to verbs which can be used with illocutionary force illustrates a particular type of subjectification: in many cases, preemption by the speaker for institutional purposes of regulation and power. The last domain to be investigated is that of honorification in Japanese, that is, the development of intersubjective social deixis.

Although the domains that are the central focus of this book might seem rather disparate, they do in fact share several commonalities. The first domain involves modality in a relatively narrow sense. In natural language modals typically express obligation or cast some doubt on the proposition: "The essence of 'modality' consists in the relativization of the validity of sentence meanings to a set of possible worlds" (Kiefer 1994: 2515). More broadly stated, modality expresses a perspective that considers the possibility of things being otherwise than they are. Our view of modality builds on work by Lyons (1977), Coates (1983), Chung and Timberlake (1985), Palmer (1986, 1990 [1979]), Bybee, Perkins, and Pagliuca (1994) where distinctions between "root" (or "deontic") and epistemic meanings are central. Modality can be expressed in different languages in a number of different ways, ranging from main verbs like Gm. *willen*, *mögen* "want" to auxiliary or "light" verbs like *must*, *ought to*, to adverbs like *probably*, and to routinized parenthetical expressions such as *I think* (in other words, it may be more grammaticalized in one language than another). Jp. lacks a syntactically uniform set of items that correspond to Eng. modal auxiliary verbs. Instead, modality in Jp. is expressed by various means, including verb suffixes (e.g. -(*r*)*eru* "potential, the ability to carry out an action"), constructions built around predicate nouns and similar elements (e.g. *hazu* "expectation" and *beki* "obligation"), and periphrastic conditional verb constructions such as *V-nakereba naranai* (lit. "If one does not do V, (the situation) will not become (acceptable)"). Although not usually considered modal on a narrow interpretation, nevertheless on a broad interpretation, certain adverbials with adversative function like *in fact*, *truly* modify the truth of the proposition in partially epistemic ways. Likewise verbs which can be used with speech act functions like *promise* can also be construed as broadly modal. Indeed, many are expressed indirectly by modals, e.g. *promise* by *will*. The directive function of some speech act verbs imposes obligations on individuals like deontic modality, while the representative function expresses degree of commitment to the truth of a proposition somewhat like epistemic modality does. Like modals, some illocutionary verbs illustrate root (directive) > epistemic (assertive) meanings (e.g. "suggest that you do" > "suggest that something is the case").

There are several links between subtypes of modality and deixis. One is that epistemic modal verbs have been argued to have a deictic function, most obviously where they intersect with tense (Lyons 1982, Chung and Timberlake 1985, Frawley 1992, Diewald 1999). Another is that epistemic modal adverbials and discourse markers are deictic in that they index not only SP/W's belief-state toward what he or she is saying/writing, but also SP/W's perspective in terms of distance and proximity (Schiffrin 1990b). A third link is that although honorification is primarily a special kind of social deixis, it has links to modality. For example, certain uses of modals in English such as *You must have some cake* have been argued by R. Lakoff (1972) to serve functions reminiscent of honorification in Japanese. Together, then, the domains to be discussed exemplify various aspects of the developments of modality and deixis broadly construed.

2
Prior and current work on semantic change

2.1 Introduction

In this chapter we outline some of the work and issues to date on semantic change, with particular attention to research focused on regularity and on mechanisms of semantic change that will be developed further in later chapters. No attempt is made to cover research into the history of research into semantic change comprehensively. For some overviews discussing different approaches, see Kronasser (1952: chapter 1), Ullmann (1957: chapter 4), Warren (1992: chapter 1), Blank (1997: chapter 1, 1999), Geeraerts (1997: chapter 3), Fritz (1998: chapter 4).

2.2 Backgrounds to contemporary work

In Europe and America much of the groundwork of semantic theory was laid by Greek and Roman grammarians, who argued at length about the arbitrariness or naturalness of meaning–form pairs, homonymy and polysemy, and by philosophers and logicians especially from the seventeenth century on, who focused on the nature of reference. Likewise, the nature of the lexicon was discussed by dictionary makers, especially from the eighteenth century on. In the nineteenth century the work on language families that led to comparative Indo-European linguistics focused on sound correspondences and plausible sound change, but crucially required a notion of cognate meaning and of plausible meaning changes as well, and triggered the development of more sophisticated views of semantic change. This is particularly true of the major comparative dictionaries that arose out of this work, much of it in the Neogrammarian tradition, among them Pokorny (1959/69), *The Oxford English Dictionary* (1989; the first volume appeared in 1884), Wartburg (1928–66).

Japanese lacks the extensive sets of obvious cognates with related languages that facilitated comparative Indo-European studies, but there have been traditions of dictionary writing in Japan for the purpose of explaining Chinese characters or appropriate word use in poetry since at least 900 AC (see Komatsu 1980: 460–464). Scholarship in Japan on the history of the Japanese language arose out of the *kokugaku* "national studies" movement of the eighteenth century. At present, the native tradition of Japanese language studies is represented by the academic discipline *kokugogaku* "study of the national language" (for a description in English see Hattori 1967). The *kokugogaku* field was directly influenced by the Neogrammarian movement of nineteenth century Germany (see Kakehi 1980: 58–59) and has provided a wealth of descriptive studies of earlier periods of the language. With this emphasis on the description of Japanese rather than on cross-linguistic theoretical issues, it is not surprising that many *kokugogaku* studies still reflect early twentieth century views of semantics and semantic change. At the same time, studies of semantic theory and semantic change within the *gengogaku* "linguistics" discipline in Japan provide contributions to theoretical approaches such as those described in the following sections.

2.2.1 *Bréal*

An early attempt to codify the criteria for semantic change that were developed in the context of work on Indo-European was Bréal's ground-breaking *Essai de Sémantique* (1897), translated into English as *Semantics: Studies in the Science of Meaning* (1900).[1] Our references are to the 1964 edition. His aim in this and earlier work (Bréal 1991 [1882]) was to develop a science of meaning by studying "the intellectual causes which have influenced the transformation of our languages" (Bréal 1964 [1900]: 5), with focus on language as a "human product" (ibid., p. 2) and goal-oriented activity regulated by "laws" (in the sense of tendencies discoverable by empirical investigation).[2] He takes a semantic approach to grammar in general, and therefore his "laws" concern changes in a wide range of linguistic domains, not only lexical items, but also inventories of inflections, and word order.

In addition to general mechanisms like analogy, Bréal outlines several "laws" that are still cited by most handbooks. We discuss these with examples largely from sources other than Bréal. Although he does not explicitly do so, we may divide them according to principles of onomasiology and semasiology. The latter he calls the proper subject of the "science of significations" (p. 99).

The onomasiological changes Bréal mentions are of two types:

(i) *Specialization*: one element "becomes the pre-eminent exponent of the grammatical conception of which it bears the stamp" (p. 15), for example, the selection of *que* as the sole complementizer in French (Schlieben-Lange 1992).[3]

---

[1] Bréal was the first to coin the term "semantique" (Wolf 1991: 3).

[2] These principles are based on his own empirical work in semantic change. In Bréal (1991 [1882]) he had not yet seen a way to articulate "principles" or "laws" of semantic change, and sought only to organize them according to empirically observable trends (ibid. p. 154).

[3] Hopper (1991) refined this concept and privileged it as a principle of grammaticalization.

(ii) *Differentiation*: two elements which are (near-)synonymous diverge. Paradigm examples include, in English, (a) the specialization, e.g. of *hound* when *dog* was borrowed from Scandinavian, and (b) loss of a form when sound change leads to "homonymic clash," e.g. ME *let* in the sense "prohibit" from OE *lett-* was lost after OE *lætan* "allow" also developed into ME *let* (for examples and discussion of the development of homonymy through sound change, see Ullmann 1957, 1964, Geeraerts 1997: chapter 4, Campbell 1999 [1998]: chapter 10).

Both specialization and differentiation may lead to loss or relegation to marginal status of one or more members of the set. They have been thought of as tendencies to avoid dangerous homonymy (Geeraerts 1997: 130 refers to "homonymiphobia") on the one hand and absolute synonymy on the other. Both have been construed as variants of a principle of "one-form:one-meaning" (e.g. Hock and Joseph 1996: 225). One problem with the "one-form:one-meaning" principle is that it focuses on form–meaning pairs out of context. As can be seen from contemporary English, speakers can in fact be tolerant of highly divergent meanings when Ls are used in context (for example, *rent an apartment* may mean "rent from" or "rent to"). Sometimes words can have polysemies that are highly divergent, even contradictory (a phenomenon that Lepschy 1981 termed "enantiosemy"): borrowed in the sixteenth century as a noun meaning "decree," *sanction* came to be extended metonymically first to the penalty enacted to enforce the decree:

(1) The *sanction* and pain of this divine Law being by sin incurred.
(1671 MacWard, 316 [OED])

Later it was extended, also metonymically, to "approval," an attitude that is an appropriateness condition for the issuance of a decree, and therefore an invited inference from such a decree, as in:

(2) [He] told her, this experiment had not only his *sanction*, but warmest approbation.
(1798 Lee, Yng. Lady's T. II, 103 [OED])

This new meaning may also have been supported by the borrowing of the verb *sanction* in the eighteenth century, as either "decree" or "approve," as in:

(3) My own voice never shall *sanction* the evils to which I may be subjected.
(1797 Radcliffe, viii [OED])

Despite the early development of a negative meaning of the noun in some contexts (see (1)), the first negative use of the verb in the OED is dated 1956:

(4) (heading) Let Church *sanction* road killers.

(1956 July 27, The Universe [OED])

and is labeled as "of doubtful acceptability." Both the positive meaning of the verb, "approve," and the negative one, "punish," seem to be widely used at present, though context often disambiguates them:

(5) a. Bush again outlined the sins of the Iraqi leader as decried by the United Nations in an unprecedented series of punitive resolutions, including Thursday's move to *sanction* the use of force if Iraq does not comply by Jan. 15.

(1990 Nov. 30, United Press Intl.; "approve")

   b. Justice Antonin Scalia asked if a state could *sanction* a cigarette manufacturer that printed the surgeon general's warning along with a statement that cigarettes are "good in other respects."

(1991 Oct. 8, United Press Intl.; "punish, impose penalty on")

The notion of homonymiphobia underestimates the multifunctionality of lexemes, hence the availability of polysemies, of idiomatic as well as compositional meanings of the same expressions, and also of pragmatic meanings. Some of these polysemies may be harmonic with each other, but others may be strongly disharmonic; nevertheless, they can all coexist. For example, in Modern Japanese (MdJ) the verb *kotowaru* has meanings that include "refuse, decline" and "apologize." Apparently a compound of *koto* "word, thing" and *waru* "split, divide up (something)," *kotowaru* appears in Old Japanese (OJ) c. 750 AC as a mental verb with the meaning "discern (the right versus wrong or benefits versus disadvantages of something)." In Late Old Japanese (LOJ) c. 1000 the mental verb meaning of *kotowaru* is extended to include an understanding of the inner workings, nature, or reason for something. The word is first found as a verb of speaking meaning "tell a reason, circumstance, or excuse" in Early Middle Japanese (EMJ) c. 1225 and subsequently comes to be used in a variety of speech act verb meanings, including "apologize (by giving a reason)" (from the fourteenth century), "file a document, bring suit" (from the seventeenth century), "deny, refuse (the statements of another)" and "fire, lay off a worker" (both from the late nineteenth century). Although the earlier mental verb meaning has disappeared from the modern language, most of the speech act verb meanings continue to coexist, despite potential homonymic clash, distinguished by the context in which the word is used.

The types of semasiological change Bréal mentions are now familiar: pejoration vs. amelioration, restriction vs. expansion, metaphor vs. metonymy. We discuss these in turn, largely with examples from sources other than Bréal.

(i) *Pejoration*: the tendency to semanticize the more negative connotations of a word. Thus OE *cnafa* "boy" > *knave*; *mistress* "head of household" > "woman in continuing extra-marital relationship with a man"; OE *selig* "blessed, innocent" > *silly*; EMdE *bourgeois* "resembling the French middle class" > "philistine." Bréal attributes pejoration of this type in part to malice and "pleasure in looking for a vice or a fault behind a quality" (Bréal 1964 [1900]: 101). Hock and Joseph (1996) further point out that pejoration affects words referring to "young, innocent persons, young males, and females of all ages" (1996: 244). Bréal also sees it as the result of euphemism, the tendency to veil disagreeable ideas, and to disguise such ideas with new terms that themselves later take on the taboo meanings they were meant to mask (1964 [1900]: 100). For example, in OE *stincan* meant "to smell" (sweet or bad):

(6) Ic *stince* swote.
"I smell sweet."

(*c.* 1000 Ælfric, Grammar, 220 [OED])

In ME it came to be associated with bad smells. The verb *smell* appears in EME (*c.* 1300) in the same positive and negative meanings as OE *stincan*. As it in turn came to be associated with bad smells, new complex predicates with *have* and *be* came into being involving such borrowings as *odor* (*c.* 1300), *scent* (*c.* 1375) and *fragrant* (*c.* 1500), *fragrance* (*c.* 1670). Consider in this connection the difference between the movie title *Scent of a Woman* and hypothetical titles like *Smell of a Woman* or even *Odor of a Woman* (in so far as deodorants "eliminate odors," *odor* is currently becoming pejorative).

Sometimes a pejoration simply involves shift from higher to lower value. A case in point is the tendency of Japanese honorifics to lose high honorific value over time – originally respectful meanings may become devalued through regular application (for euphemistic purposes) to less respected referents. For example, *omae* "you (second person singular)" is used in MdJ only in reference to a close intimate who is a social inferior of the speaker (e.g. by parent to child). The word, however, originates in OJ *oFo-* "great, august" (> honorific prefix) plus *maFe* "location in front of," and was extended to the meaning "in the presence of a god or a great person." *Omae* came to be used as a euphemistic expression for nobles (second or third person reference) in LOJ (*c.* tenth century), and Ohno (1980: 35–37) cites the word as a respectful second person pronoun from the sixteenth century.

(ii) *Melioration* (usually called "amelioration"): the tendency to semanticize more positive connotations: Old French (OF) *ber/barun* "common men, servants" > "servants to the king" > "baron, member of lowest rank of nobility in Britain"; Lat. *nescius* "ignorant" > OF *ni(s)ce* "stupid" was borrowed into English in the French sense, and gradually developed more positive polysemies, specifically "shy, bashful," later "pleasant, appealing" (examples from Hock and Joseph 1996: 241–244). The meanings of MdJ *kawaii* "cute" and *itoosii* "lovable" similarly develop from earlier meanings "pitiful" and "pathetic," respectively. The explanation usually given for the change is that the earlier and later meanings share a sense of emotional concern by a stronger party toward a weaker party (Iizumi 1963: 82–84, 181).

Sometimes the same root may develop an ameliorative meaning in one language and a pejorative meaning in another. Bartsch (1984: 387) cites Dutch (Du.) *knap* "able, fit, clever, good-looking," German (Gm.) *knapp* "narrow, hardly sufficient," both derived from an earlier Germanic meaning of "fitting close, tightly."

(iii) *Restriction/Narrowing of meaning*: OE *deor* "animal" > *deer*, *corn* "grain" > "maize" in the USA (and > "oats" in Scotland according to Geeraerts 1997: 96). Sometimes the narrowing may take place in only one part of speech; e.g. *erection*, which was used of buildings and parts of the body from the sixteenth century on, is not now usually used for a building although the verb *erect* still is, and children get *erector sets* as presents.[4] In the eighteenth century, Jp. *yakuza* "gangster" was a general term that characterized a person as a "good-for-nothing," "ne'er-do-well." Its range of referents included various types of persons (males) who did not make a positive contribution to society, including vagrants, wealthy playboys, gamblers, and various scoundrels. That range has gradually narrowed to participants in organized crime.

(iv) *Expansion/Generalization/Broadening of meaning*: Lat. *armare* "to cover one's shoulders" > *arm*; Lat. *adripare* "reach the river's shore" > "reach a destination"; Gm. *Wand* "wall" < Indo-European (IE) **wendh-* "weave" (walls were woven from branches). Originally meaning "cloth to wrap clothes in, cloth for the head," *toilet* was extended to various items of clothing, and, in the context of "making" or "doing" was extended to grooming and dressing (its use to refer to a lavatory is a case of metonymy and euphemism; see below). *Ejaculate* was originally (in the sixteenth century) used for ejecting fluids from the body, and only later came to be used for locutionary acts, as in:

(7) I could not but with hearty thanks to Almighty God *ejaculate* my thanks to him.

(1666 July 23, Pepys, Diary, IV, 22 [OED])

MdJ *asita* "tomorrow" derives from *ake-sita* "dawning-time." Examples in which *asita* can be interpreted to have the deictic meaning "the following morning" appear as early as OJ, and the word undergoes generalization to refer to the entire day "tomorrow" in Middle Japanese (MJ) (Takemitsu 1998: 26).

---

[4] The examples of *erection* and *ejaculate* (below) appear in Bryson (1991: 72, who cites Robert K. Sebastian, 1989, Red pants, *Verbatim*, Winter issue).

Sometimes the same root may undergo broadening in one language and narrowing in another. Bartsch (1984: 385) cites the example of Gm. *Tier* "animal (wild or tame)," Eng. *deer* "hoofed ruminant animal." In German there was broadening of meaning from a Germanic root apparently restricted to "wild animals" (see OE *deor*), while in English there was narrowing from wild animals in general to a specific kind.

(v) *Metaphor*: the mapping of one concept onto another, e.g. space > time as in *before* "in front" > "earlier," or position > time as in *pending* "hanging" > "until" (Kortmann 1992). For Bréal metaphor is associated with images, and languages are full of metaphors. Indeed, he says "[t]he Indo-European languages are condemned to figurative speech" (1964 [1900]: 3) (presumably also other languages). His examples include the way even "dry grammars" use metaphors like "'clou' ['nail'] *takes an s* in the plural" (pp. 4–5). His use of the word "condemned" (itself a metaphor in the quotation cited above) presumably evokes the pretensions of stylists of his time that scientific discourse was objective, literal, and therefore non-figurative. Jp. *yakuza* "good-for-nothing (person)" > "gangster" originally referred to the worst possible hand in a traditional game of playing cards, i.e. *ya* "eight" plus *ku* "nine" plus *za* "three."[5] The meaning of the word was first transferred from the domain of card-playing to the domain of human characteristics and then underwent narrowing (as in (iii) above).

(vi) *Contagion (Metonymy)*: the association of one word with another, e.g. the association in Middle French of *rien* "thing" and *pas* with the negative *ne* "not," resulting in the eventual semanticization of negative in *rien* and *pas*, and the loss of *ne*. Other metonymies include the association of objects characteristically having the color in question with the color, e.g. orange, gold, silver (Berlin and Kay 1969); or the material with products of that material, e.g. Greek (Gk.) *papuros* "papyrus plant" > "material for writing on" > *paper* (Buck 1949: vii); and IE **wendh-* "weave" > Gm. *Wand* "wall," mentioned in (iv) above; or the object with the purpose for which it is used, e.g. Finnish *raha* "pelt" for "medium of exchange" > "money" (Campbell 1999 [1998]: 169). Other cases involve part-for-whole synecdoche,[6] e.g. Jp. *kuruma*, literally "wheel," was used synecdochically to refer to a variety of wheeled vehicles, including carts and carriages until modern times (see also Eng. *wheels* for "car"). Almost all cases of narrowing and broadening, pejoration and amelioration are cases of metonymic change: shifts in use dependent on context.

---

[5] Closer study may show that *yakuza* is actually a case of metonymy.

[6] We follow Nerlich and Clarke (1999) in distinguishing part-for-whole synecdoche from genus–species synecdoche. The first (e.g. *sail* for *ship*) involves a type of metonymy and is a major factor in semantic change; the second (e.g. *TV* for *color TV*) involves taxonomic shifts from lower to higher or higher to lower in a taxonomy, and appears not to be widely attested in semantic change.

A more complex example of metonymy is provided by Jp. *hootyoo*. Originating in a Chinese loanword comprised of the characters *hoo* "kitchen" plus *tyoo* "servant," *hootyoo* referred in the LOJ period to servants who worked in the kitchen and was later metonymically extended to the work they did: the act of preparing meals. The modern use of *hootyoo* for "(kitchen) knife" apparently results from a shortening in MJ of *hootyoo-gatana*, a compound of *hootyoo* plus *katana* "knife, sword."[7] The latter example illustrates how fine-grained an analysis is required to determine whether a shift is metaphoric or metonymic (see also Goossens 1995a, 1995b). If one compares the modern meaning "(kitchen) knife" directly with the original loanword meaning "kitchen servant," the change may appear to be one of metaphor. Closer study reveals that the meaning shift involves two stages of metonymy: association of the relationship between the kitchen servants and their work, and ellipsis of a term for a specific part of that work.

Nerlich and Clarke summarize the types of metonymy identified within the Bréal tradition as follows:

> the part stands for the whole (also called synecdoche), the cause for the effect, the container for the contained, the form for the function, the material an object is made of for the object, the place for the people who live there, the name of a producer for the product, an article of dress for the person who wears it, the name of an author for his or her work, the object used for the user, the controller for the controlled, the institution for the people responsible, the place for the event, and so on.
>
> (Nerlich and Clarke 1992: 134)

We extend these types of metonymy to include pragmatic associations that arise in the flow of speech (see 2.3.2 below).

Bréal (1964 [1900]) characterizes motivations for such changes as primarily social and psychological. He identifies five types of motivation of which the first three centrally involve strategic use of language for communicative purposes.

(i)   Avoidance of difficulty (p. 60),
(ii) Securing of greater clarity (p. 65),
(iii) Taboo and euphemism (pp. 100–3); these readily lead to generalization (expansion of the meaning of the item used as a euphemism), and concomitant narrowing or even loss of the term referring to a taboo topic. The case of *toilet* illustrates both. At first the meaning "cloth for wrapping clothes/the head" was extended to more and more activities associated with grooming and dressing. Eventually it became

---

[7] *Katana*, a term for "long sharp object," was presumably understood in this compound only in the specialized sense of "long sharp object used for culinary purposes."

58

associated via euphemism with the fixture for disposing of bodily excretions, and the room containing it. But the more the word was used as a euphemism, the less it was used for grooming. Taboo has led *toilet* itself to be replaced by terms such as *restroom*, or *bathroom* (even when no bath is expected or known to be present). Janda (2001) discusses the euphemistic "clipping" or loss of the noun (e.g. "body") after the prepositions *behind* in English, *derrière* "behind" in French and *After* "behind" in German, resulting in the nominalization of the erstwhile prepositions to denote "buttocks." Citing Kluge and Seebold (1995), he says that in Gm. a new noun *After*, also from a preposition, came to be used as a euphemism for "anus," but the taboo associated with the latter led to the early loss of this word.

(iv) Fading and discoloration (p. 103), or loss of semantic content (now also known as "bleaching"), e.g. *awfully* "in a way inspiring awe" > "very," Gm. *sehr* "cruelly" > "very."

(v) External factors such as cultural changes (p. 105), e.g. attitudes to referents of *bourgeois*. These are, however, of little interest to Bréal who focuses instead on language-internal factors in semantic change.

Such lists may seem like sets of irreconcilable principles, and hardly examples of "laws." But Bréal does not treat all equally. With respect to "laws" of semantic change, he suggests that pejoration dominates over melioration, that restriction is language-internal, expansion external; further, that metaphor may be at work in all the other types of changes. With respect to motivations, avoidance of difficulty and attention to clarity are presented as the dominant motivations (pp. 60, 65), ultimately driven by principles of analogy that Bréal considers foundational to the language capacity. These competing motivations have been redefined since Bréal's times in various ways. For example, Langacker (1977) speaks of the competing searches for signal simplicity and for greater informativeness, and Slobin (1977) of "charges to language" including "be quick and easy" and "be clear."

Bréal devotes a whole synchronic chapter to subjectivity, which he sees as arising from speakers developing scenarios in which "we are at the same time the interested spectator and the author of events" (p. 229). He sees subjectivity as particularly associated with moods, but also (p. 230) with what have since come to be known as "stance adverbs" (Biber and Finegan 1988) like *happily* as in *An accident took place yesterday . . . but happily caused no loss of life* (where *happily* means "I am happy to say"). Bréal hypothesizes that "the Subjective Element is the oldest" property of language (p. 237), based on the observation that speech is primarily speaker–hearer based, and "was not made for purposes of description, of narration, of disinterested consideration," but to "express a desire, to intimate an order . . ." (p. 238). Perhaps because he considers it foundational to language, he does not discuss it as a factor in semantic change, although his examples of pejoration and melioration and his interest in change due to the desire to be expressive directly suggest such a role.

Until very recently most authors have largely followed Bréal's characterization of semantic change, but usually without paying any attention to the role that subjectification might be regarded as playing, or to context, which, Bréal points out, can eliminate "obscurity and confusion" (p. 287). Faced with pairs of changes that seemed to cancel each other out, even if one member of each pair is predominant, and with examples taken out of context, many linguists have tended to see semantic change as essentially unstructured. This opinion is still reflected in Hock and Joseph, who, despite acknowledging that "given the right circumstances, semantic change can have very sweeping and systematic effects," nevertheless say that "in the majority of cases semantic change is as fuzzy, self-contradictory, and difficult to predict as lexical semantics itself" (1996: 252). Nevertheless, significant advances have been made, and it is to these we now turn.

2.2.2 The early twentieth century

Two early twentieth century figures of great importance in the development of theories of semantic change were Meillet (see especially 1958 [1905–06]), who emphasized the grounding of meaning change in the structure of society, and Saussure (1996 [1916]), whose interests in comparing synchronic systems ultimately led to work on "semantic fields" (see 2.2.3). It is often forgotten that much of Saussure's work concerned language change, and that his career started with a brilliant reconstruction (1967 [1879]) of Indo-European phonemes that was later known as laryngeal theory. He is now remembered primarily for the profound effect of his interests in the sign as an element in a synchronic system. According to Saussure, change disrupts the system and is process; synchrony is product. Change emphasizes the arbitrariness of language because individual signs are the result of individual changes over time (even though there may be overall regularities such as the exceptionlessness of sound change). "In spite of appearances to the contrary, diachronic events are always accidental and particular in nature" (Saussure 1996 [1916]: 92) and not subject to "laws" in the sense of generalizations that are "imperative" and "general" (ibid. p. 90). Saussure cites the semantic change Fr. *poutre* "mare" > "beam, rafter" as an example, saying that "The change can be explained by reference to particular circumstances" (ibid.). *Poutre* appears to originate in OF *poutrel* "young horse," *poutre* "young mare." Mares carry burdens; analogically, beams carry roofs (Wartburg 1928–66 Lat. *pulliter*). While Saussure's insight is correct that individual signs are the result of individual changes, nevertheless, most are instances of general changes. The "particular" change exemplified by *poutre* is an example of a general process of metaphoric transfer.

One post-Saussurean line of thinking led to emphasis on the arbitrariness of change, particularly as evidenced by change resulting from external factors, such as changes in material culture. Such approaches focused on referential and denotational meaning. Ullmann (1964) provides an example which, he shows, looks quite simple at first. The bread-roll called *croissant* might be thought to have this name because of its shape (we might think the meaning of *crescent* in French was simply extended by metonymy from an early stage of the moon to an object shaped like it). In fact, however, the connection to shape is more complex: the French word is calqued (translated into the native language) from Gm. *Hörnchen* "little horn"; this term was first applied to rolls baked in the late seventeenth century in Vienna to commemorate a victory over the Turks, whose national emblem was and is the crescent (Ullmann 1964: 197, citing Bloch and Wartburg 1960). This is still a metonymic explanation, but it involves social factors and only indirectly visual ones.

Other examples of denotational meaning changes that reflect social and technological change include terms for economic exchange or for living communities. A contemporary *town* has little or no referential connection with an OE *tun* or enclosure beyond designation of a community where people live together, a "population center." In OE times, such a center was no larger, and often smaller, than what we now think of as a village, it was enclosed, and was not on a scale in which "city" or "urban center" played any part. In the present century changes in the nature of aviation or of information technology have changed the denotation of *plane* (from a single-engine plane such as the Wright brothers flew to Boeing 747s, the Concorde, and Stealth planes) and *computer* (from a machine that filled whole rooms to a lap-top). Similarly, Jp. *kuruma* signified "wheeled vehicle" (by metonymy from "wheel," see above), including carts and carriages until modern times. During the early part of the twentieth century, *kuruma* most often referred to rickshaws, but since World War II its default interpretation has come to be "automobile." MdJ *daidokoro* "kitchen" originates in LOJ *daibandokoro*, a compound of *daiban* "portable tray-table" and *tokoro* "place." The *daibandokoro* was a specific room in the Imperial and other palaces of the ninth century and was used for placing (already cooked) food onto portable trays for serving to the nobility. At that time, the room in which the food was cooked was expressed by *kuriya*, but *dai(ban)dokoro* came to be used to refer to this room as well. *Daidokoro* came to be used in MJ for "kitchen" in a different type of architecture, namely the room in samurai houses and large farmhouses in which a large kettle was kept over a fire. *Daidokoro* continues to be used for kitchens in present-day Japan, although Takemitsu (1998: 195) expresses reluctance toward using *daidokoro* in reference to a modern Japanese "dining-kitchen" (*dainingu kittyin*) with various appliances and eating table.

As Meillet 1958 [1905–06]) pointed out, regardless of the extent to which semantic changes may be driven by changes in the nonlinguistic world, they are driven in this way within the framework of linguistic meanings: senses, or conceptual structures. Furthermore, they are subject to the kinds of meaning changes outlined in 2.2.1 above, e.g. *dai*(*ban*)*dokoro* was generalized first from a room specialized for a particular phase of food preparation in Imperial palaces to Imperial kitchens as well, then to kitchens in samurai houses, and eventually to kitchens in general; this kind of generalization also involved a mild kind of pejoration. Takemitsu's reluctance to use the term for a dining-kitchen suggests later specialization.

While changes in material culture are most frequently adduced to support the Saussurean notion of arbitrariness of change in meaning, the most striking examples of such arbitrariness are closely tied to conscious choice and linguistic intervention, or "language planning by decree" (Bartsch 1984: 369). We give two examples, one in the technical realm of scientific research, the other in the realm of social interaction (for others, especially in the realm of oligarchic control, see Hughes 1992). Gould (1977: 28–32, citing Bowler 1975) discusses how the Lat. etymology of the scientific term *evolution* denotes an unrolling of parts that pre-exist. From its earliest uses in English it meant both this and a series of connected events involving growth, even "progress." As theories of preformationism declined, the first meaning fell into disuse. Definitions associated with development by structural differentiation of unstructured material ("epigenesis"), came to be preferred in the mid nineteenth century. Since *evolution* was shorter than the phrase Darwin used in *The Origin of the Species*, "descent with modification," biologists began to prefer *evolution* for organic change leading to greater complexity.[8] In the twentieth century *evolution* was extended from "general progress" to "any genetic change in populations," including "specific cases of adaptation" (Gould 1977: 32). Such changes in meaning have been affected by transmission of biological theories; they have influenced what is deemed worthy of research, and therefore worthy of funding, and have also filtered down into public consciousness, primarily through pedagogical and informational materials, in ways that are not subject to any kind of regularity of the type we are discussing in this book.

Efforts to develop social awareness and "reinscribe" cultural mores have in recent years led to redefinition of terms like *rape* and *harassment*. Like changes in *evolution*, these are changes that are essentially "objectification" in so far as they are attempts to preempt for discussion and eventual regulation behaviors that were

---

[8] Gould (1977: 32) points out that this was, however, not Darwin's own view of descent.

originally conceptualized differently. In recent years *harass* has come to be more and more associated with verbal behaviors, as in:

> (8)   He chose to live with the poor. He chose to argue for the homeless. He chose to embarrass, *harass* and challenge our leadership.
>
> (1990 July 6, United Press Intl.; Jesse Jackson, eulogizing Mitch Snyder)

According to the OED, *harass* was borrowed from French in the seventeenth century. It is defined as:

> (9)   1.   To wear out, tire out, or exhaust with fatigue, care, trouble, etc. Obs. or dial. (the first example is dated 1626)
> 2.   To harry, lay waste, devastate, plunder. Obs. (first example 1618)
> 3.   To trouble or vex by repeated attacks. (first example 1622)
> 4.   To trouble, worry, distress with annoying labour, care, perplexity, importunity, misfortune, etc. (first example 1656)
> 5.   Technical term. To scrape or rub. (first example 1875)

None of the examples in the OED are strictly verbal; all, however, have to do with effect. *The American Heritage Dictionary* defines the word similarly. Verbal uses are alluded to only in the section on synonyms: "*Harass* and *harry* imply systematic persecution by besieging with repeated annoyances, threats, or demands" (*The American Heritage Dictionary* 2000). *Harass* had, however, come to be extended to contexts involving verbal events by the beginning of the nineteenth century. A possible early example is:

> (10)   but was strangely *harassed* by a queer, half-witted man, who would ["wanted to"] make me dance with him, and distressed me by his nonsense.
>
> (1818 Austen, Northanger Abbey, vol. I, 26)

Here *would make me dance* and *distressed me with his nonsense* appear to be reports of verbal acts. In (11), also from Austen, the harassing is clearly verbal, in the sense of self-questioning:

> (11)   while *harassing* herself in secret with the never-ending question, of whether Captain Wentworth would come or not?
>
> (1818 Austen, Persuasion, vol. II, 227)

The contemporary meaning of *harass* appears to be deeply connected with US federal laws including Title VII of the Civil Rights Act (1964) and Title IX of the Education Amendments Act (1972), forbidding harassment of any type, and specifically sexual and racial harassment. Especially influential is the definition of sexual harassment by the 1980 Equal Employment Opportunity Commission (EEOC) Guidelines on Discrimination because of Sex. The by now well-known definition is, in part, as follows:

> (12) Unwelcome sexual advances, requests for sexual favors, and other verbal or
> physical conduct of a sexual nature constitute sexual harassment when (1)
> submission to such conduct is made either explicitly or implicitly a term of
> condition of an individual's employment ...[9]

Verbal conduct is central to this definition. Since the Meritor vs. Vinson case in 1986,[10] efforts to define the hearer's role as interpreter of meanings have led to lengthy legal debate concerning the meaning of "unwelcome," "reasonable person," more recently "reasonable woman," and "hostile environment." As the noun *harassment* and the cognate verb *harass* have come to be used in more and more non-legal contexts, older meanings pertaining to effect of conduct are being replaced by newer meanings pertaining to interpretation, and significant uncertainties as to the meaning of the words have arisen, leading to constant revision of workplace and campus codes of behavior. One thing that is certain, however, is that language plays a far more prominent role in the meaning of *harassment* and *harass* than it did in earlier times, a change that may be attributed not only to changing social expectations, but even more specifically to the 1980 EEOC Guidelines, that is, to interventive change. Interestingly, the interventive change happens to coincide with shifts to "speech act" meaning. Examples (10) and (11) from Austen suggest this change might have been naturally in progress and was merely hastened by intervention.

While much work on semantic change in the years after the publication of Saussure's lectures concerned individual arbitrary change, far more important was the attention paid to the structural oppositions inherent in Bréal's list and to the mutual constraints these oppositions imposed on each other (see Ullmann 1957, 1964: 244).

For example, in his chapter on semantic change in *Language*, Bloomfield built on the traditional classification of semantic change as narrowing–widening, metaphor–metonymy, synecdoche, hyperbole, litotes, degeneration–elevation, but insisted that these types of changes could not be regarded as explanatory. In his view such meaning changes arise out of "a connection between practical things" (1984 [1933]: 428), most especially out of language in use: "Since every practical situation is in reality unprecedented, the apt response of a good speaker may always border on semantic innovation" (1984 [1933]: 443). This leads him to insist on the need to determine contexts of change. Since in many cases the social and political contexts are no longer accessible, a more abstract set of contexts needs to be found: that of the oppositions into which the term enters. To Bloomfield the most important investigation in semantic change is gradual extension from one type of situation to

---

[9] Title VII, Equal Employment Opportunity Commission (EEOC). Guidelines on Discrimination because of Sex. *Federal Register* 1980, 45 (219): 74677.

[10] Meritor Savings Bank vs. Vinson (477 U.S. 57, 1986).

another, with concomitant competition from some other term. For example, of the shift from *meat* "food" > "edible flesh of an animal" he says that while we may "some day find out why flesh was disfavored in culinary situations" (1984 [1933]: 441), linguistic analysis leads us to:

> see that a normal extension of meaning is the same process as an extension of grammatical function. When *meat*, for whatever reason, was being favored, and *flesh*, for whatever reason, was on the decline, there must have occurred proportional extension of the pattern:
>
>   *leave the bones and bring the flesh*   : *leave the bones and bring the meat*
>   = *give us bread and flesh*   : *x*,
>
> resulting in a new phrase, *give us bread and meat*. The forms at the left, containing the word *flesh*, must have borne an unfavorable connotation which was absent from the forms at the right, with the word *meat*.
>
>   (Bloomfield 1984 [1933]: 441; italics original)

Bloomfield, therefore, moved from focus on arbitrariness in semantic change, and change in reference, to the structural issue of extension and obsolescence as consequences of analogies and patterns that operate on structural forms. Without being explicit about directionality in semantic change, he presumably subsumed it in his claim that: "As to change, we have enough data to show that the general processes of change are the same in all languages and tend in the same direction. Even very specific types of change occur in much the same way, but independently, in the most diverse languages" (Bloomfield 1984 [1933]: 20). His chapter on semantic change ends with a comment on the way in which "personal innovations are modeled on current forms" (1984 [1933]: 443), and on the relationship of ordinary to poetic metaphor, a theme that was to survive long after Bloomfield's behaviorist, referential views on language had been replaced by focus on mental, sense constructs, and which was taken up in the context of work on semantic fields. It is to the latter that we now turn.

2.2.3 Semantic fields

     The concept of semantic domains is an intuitive one with a millennium of history. Structuralist interest in oppositions and taxonomies led to the development of the concept of a structured conceptual domain, or "semantic field" (also sometimes called "lexical field"). The term "semantic field" is attributed by Ullmann (1964: 244) to Ipsen (1924). Work on semantic fields shifted attention to conceptual categories and the recruitment of lexemes to these categories, i.e. to onomasiology.

     Among the first major studies of a semantic field was Trier's (1931) study of the development of terms for INTELLECT. According to Ullmann:

Trier elaborated his conception of fields as closely-knit sectors of the vocabulary, in which a particular sphere is divided up, classified and organized in such a way that each element helps to delimit its neighbours and is delimited by them ... In each field, the raw material of experiences is analysed and elaborated in a unique way, differing from one language to another and often from one period to another in the history of the same idiom. In this way, the structure of semantic fields embodies a specific philosophy and a scale of values.

(Ullmann 1964: 245)

Trier tried to show that in Middle High German *c.* 1200 the field of intellect was organized around three terms: *wîsheit* "courtly, chivalric attainments," *list* "non-courtly attainments," and *kunst* "human wisdom in all its aspects, theological and mundane." By *c.* 1300, however, feudalism had fallen apart, and *list* was acquiring the pejorative meanings that lead in Modern German to "cunning, trick," and the field of the intellect was differently organized as *wîsheit* "religious, mystical experience," *kunst* "art," and a new term *wizzen* "knowledge." This is represented by Lehrer (1985) as in figure 2.1. As Ullmann points out (1964: 249) there are problems with such analyses: the neatness of the "mosaic" of meanings, as Trier called it, without overlap is false – meanings are not discrete. If gaps in a field are detected, they are often a function of theory. Trier also gives no role to marginalized senses such as *list*, which persists up to the present day. Matoré (1953) partially solved this problem by introducing the concepts of *mots-témoins* "witness-words" around which semantic fields are organized and *mots-clés* "key-words," words privileged by a society at a particular point in time (discussed in Ullmann 1964: 252–253; see also Williams 1985 [1976]).

Trier's work was largely grounded in social and cultural history. By contrast, Stern (1968 [1931]) took a psychological view of meaning and argued that change within a semantic field could be independent of culture. Particularly interesting is

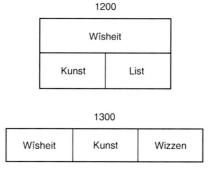

Figure 2.1. German terms of intellect (Lehrer 1985: 284; based on Trier 1931).

his analysis of what he calls "permutation," which is closely related to the type of metonymy involving association (as opposed to the type involving synecdoche, which Stern called "adequation"). His examples involve transfer of "a detail of a total situation" (ibid. p. 351) to some other situation, for example, from prayer to an object associated with it; thus, in his now famous example, *beads* "prayers" was transferred in ME to the balls of the rosary by which prayers were counted (ibid. p. 353). Among other permutations cited is the development of Fr. *cependant* and Eng. *while* from a temporal meaning "during the time which" to an adversative meaning "although." Stern characterized such changes as involving the changes in perception: the "subjective apprehension of the referent" (ibid. p. 351).

A special interest of Stern's was in the type of change evidenced by RAPIDLY > IMMEDIATELY. He claimed that terms for the conceptual category RAPIDLY developed a polysemic meaning of IMMEDIATELY in the context of perfective verbs "denoting the action as a unit" (Stern 1968 [1931]: 185–191). Thus OE *swifte* and *georne* "rapidly" > "immediately" in about 1300. He argued that this change affected words meaning RAPIDLY before 1300; words from other sources that came to mean RAPIDLY or were borrowed with that meaning after 1400, e.g. *fleetly* (1598) and *rapidly* itself (1727), did not undergo this change.

The theoretical interest here is several-fold: Stern aimed to provide evidence that related words (he lists twenty-two) could show parallel semantic changes, and that, like phonological ones, semantic changes can take place over a certain period, and then cease to be in effect so that new words with the original meaning do not undergo the change. He argued that there was an intermediary stage where the two meanings were in variation (A > A ~ B > B; see (10) in 1.2.2). He also suggested that the changes were dependent on the lexical aspect of the verb, *rapidly* being associated with process events (he calls them imperfective events), *immediately* with punctual (perfective) ones; in other words, the change was associative. Most importantly for our purposes, he identified this as a change that was a "permutation," that is, a metonymy leading to a new meaning. He also showed that it was implausible for the reverse change to take place: "it is evident that if a person rides rapidly up to another, the action is soon completed; but we cannot reverse the argument and say that if a person soon rides up to another, then the action is also rapidly performed" (ibid. p. 186). This is an argument for unidirectionality. In our terms it is an example not only of invited inferencing and unidirectionality, but also of subjectification: a shift from a descriptive manner adverb to a deictic one (of time).

Unfortunately, the example seemed at the time so language-specific that his conclusions about unidirectionality and culture-independence were not persuasive. He provides no contextualized examples in the book, and does not account for the other polysemies of the adverbs in question (e.g. OE *georne* meant "eagerly" as well as "rapidly"), or for the loss of some of the adverbs such as *georne*. Although he considers the change to be an example of a general process, his interest in arguing that the change was completed by 1400 significantly undermined his larger objective, which was to show that careful empirical studies could show "laws," i.e. regularities, in change. In actual fact, his finding is indeed an example of a change replicated not only within the semantic field in English, but cross-linguistically. In his chapter on TIME, Buck comments "The majority of words for 'soon' are, or were once, simply 'quickly'" (1949: 964).

Buck refers only to Indo-European languages. But Jp. suggests a similar semantic relationship. In MJ the adverbs *hayaku* (a regular derivational form of the adjective *hayai*), *sassoku*, and *sumiyaka ni* all express both RAPIDLY and IMMEDIATELY. Although written records do not provide direct evidence of the direction of the change in Japanese, the distribution of the semantic fields for RAPIDLY and IMMEDIATELY suggests that the meaning RAPIDLY is primary relative to IMMEDIATELY in this language as well. Most expressions in Japanese that express RAPIDLY also express IMMEDIATELY. Besides these examples, the adjective *tosi* "sharp" (as in a sword blade), "alert" appears in the meanings "rapid" and "immediate" during the LOJ period. *Soosoo* "hastily" likewise appears in the meanings "rapidly," "immediately" from LOJ. However, a few words for RAPIDLY are not used in the meaning IMMEDIATELY, e.g. *subayai* (adverb *subayaku*, a compound of the prefix *su-* "pure(ly), nothing else but" plus *hayai*) expresses only the meaning "rapidly." Similarly, the loanword *zinsoku ni* (made up of two Chinese characters for "speed") appears to mean only "rapidly." In contrast, words for IMMEDIATELY in Japanese tend to be derived and drawn from a number of other concepts as well as RAPIDLY. These include *sugu* (*ni*) "directly, immediately," *tadati ni* "directly, immediately," *niwaka ni* "abruptly, suddenly," and *sokuza ni* "immediately, impromptu." *Sugu* (*ni*) and *tadati ni* both reflect spatial to temporal meaning change, while *niwaka ni* and *sokuza ni* appear to reflect origins in other manner adverb sources.

While work on regularity in semantic change in Europe focused on psychology (e.g. in the decades after Stern, Kronasser's 1952 study of semasiology), the main impetus in the USA was from anthropology, most especially Berlin and Kay's (1969) cross-linguistic study of color terms. Drawing on the notion of semantic field in linguistics and kinship taxonomies in anthropology, they sought to test the "Sapir–Whorf hypothesis" concerning the arbitrariness of the linguistic sign and of the relation of language to thought. Their conclusion was that the "basic" (one-word) color terms of all languages form a maximal set of eleven perceptual foci, and that there is a partially fixed order in which these foci are acquired by children and in semantic development as in figure 2.2. They concluded that such paths of development were universal and motivated by non-linguistic perceptual factors, specifically visual perception, and therefore not arbitrary. The details of the hypothesis were

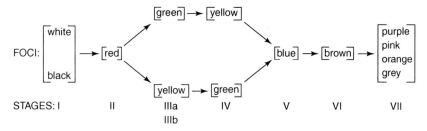

Figure 2.2. The proposed cross-linguistic development of color terms (Kay 1975: 257).

subsequently called into question and much revised and need not concern us here. For studies of semantic change the interest was primarily in the proposal that there were implicational hierarchies of COLOR development such that one could predict that if a language had a term for BLUE, then it would also have terms for YELLOW and GREEN, and the term for BLUE would have developed later than either YELLOW or GREEN.

Implicational universals and hierarchies were being established in a number of areas of grammar in the context of cross-linguistic typological work, much of which is represented in Greenberg (1966 [1963]) and Greenberg, Ferguson, and Moravcsik (1978) (for a detailed summary see Croft 1990). Implicational universals were intended to capture tendencies such as "If a language has property Y, then it will have property X, but not necessarily vice versa," e.g. if a language has nasal vowels, then it will have oral vowels, but not necessarily vice versa. Implicational hierarchies are of similar form but concern probability rankings, such as "Property A is more likely to occur/is more accessible to various linguistic processes than property B." One of the best-known of these hierarchies is the animacy hierarchy (see Silverstein 1976b, Dixon 1979, and several subsequent versions):

(13)   1st, 2nd person pronouns < 3rd person pronoun < proper names < human
       common noun < nonhuman animate common noun < inanimate common
       noun
              (Croft 1990: 113, based on Dixon 1979: 85; here < indicates that the
              preceding term ranks higher in the hierarchy than the following term)

This hierarchy specifies that first and second person pronouns outrank third person pronouns, etc. with respect to certain linguistic phenomena such as morphological distinctions among person pronouns and demonstratives (e.g. Greenberg 1993), nominative–accusative vs. ergative–absolutive morphology (e.g. Dixon 1979), and empathy effects in word order and information packaging (e.g. Kuno and Kaburaki 1977).

Diachronically, implicational hierarchies are to be understood as "If C, then it is likely to have arisen from B, and if B, then B is likely to have arisen from A, but not necessarily vice versa," a weakly unidirectional statement. For example, Greenberg (1978) showed that:

(14)   Definite demonstrative > definite article > gender marker
(here > indicates that the following term is likely to have
arisen from the preceding term)

(Here "gender marker" is to be understood as "noun class marker.") Stated as a diachronic implicational hierarchy, the hypothesis would be that gender markers may arise from definite articles but not vice versa (of course, they may, and often do, arise from other things as well). More specifically, the definite demonstrative is typically a distal, third person deictic (e.g. Lat. *ille/illa*, OE *þæt*); it becomes a definite article when it is used primarily with anaphoric reference (e.g. Fr. *le/la*, Eng. *the*), and a gender marker when anaphoric reference ceases to be its predominant function, and nouns are typically marked by it. In English only a few nouns are of this type, mostly names of places or rivers, e.g. *The Mississippi, The Hague*. In French, however, the definite article is typically used in the absence of other appropriate markers of gender and number, as in *j'aime les livres* "I love DEF-ART books" (Harris 1978: 75–76). English, then, shows the seeds of the development of an original demonstrative into a gender marker; French shows a rather advanced stage of this development.

The work of Berlin and Kay focused on a semantic field and its referentiality (informants made responses to a fine-grained color chart). The prime issue was how many terms were available, and in what historical order lexical semantic differences were encoded. Their study was initially taken to show that external factors such as the physiology of the eye could motivate change within semantic fields. Other semantic field studies focused on the extent to which changes in social attitudes and practices drive meaning changes, or vice versa. Dahlgren (1978), for example, argues that the social construction of kingship over the ages has changed the meaning of *king*. In OE the *cyning* was a "war-lord," then a "chief lord" and, after the Norman Conquest, *king* came to mean "absolute monarch"; the stereotypes associated with "kings in the actual world determined what the meaning was" (1978: 61). An approach from critical and cultural theory (e.g. Crowley 1996), which interprets meanings in terms of the production and reproduction of social relations, would argue that the myths and narratives about kingship were linguistic contexts for such changes; i.e., the "actual world" is in part linguistic. Dahlgren's work, in highlighting stereotype meanings, and in focusing on the language-external influences on linguistic representations, raised issues that were later of central concern

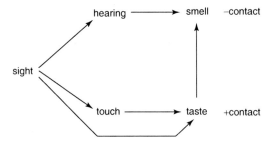

Figure 2.3. Extension of verbs of perception across modalities (Viberg 1983: 147).

to cognitive linguistics, but nevertheless very different from it, in so far as she addressed social rather than cognitive systems.

Implications of semantic fields analysis were also considered in cognitive domains such as INTELLECT. A pioneering work was Derrig (1978) in which she hypothesized with respect to hues that cross-linguistically WHITE was extended metaphorically to innocence (hence sometimes stupidity), BLACK to evil, ignorance, and gloominess, RED to anger and sex, BLUE/GREEN to inexperience and being uneducated, YELLOW to ripeness. She also found with respect to intensity, that BRIGHT was associated with understanding, LIGHT with intelligence, DARK with ignorance and opacity, and CLEAR with alertness. Another pioneering work was Viberg (1983) on PERCEPTION, in which the author hypothesized that meanings associated with one modality may be cross-linguistically extended to cover another modality; sight and hearing, in particular, are subject to extension not only to other sense modalities but also to INTELLECT. Noting that a linear representation of the hierarchy among perception verbs is inadequate to capture the complexity of the paths of extension, he proposed the flow-chart in figure 2.3. Implications of more recent work by Sweetser (1990) in the general area of PERCEPTION and INTELLECT will be discussed in section 2.3.1 on metaphor from a cognitive linguistic perspective.

The findings about semantic fields of INTELLECT and PERCEPTION were directly connected with work on synaesthesia, the metaphorical extension of terms for the five senses onto the domain of other senses and onto social behaviors, language, and so forth (Williams 1976; see also Kronasser 1952). This phenomenon had already been noted by Bréal, who gives as examples of metaphor the mapping of sight onto hearing, e.g. *bright note* and of taste onto language, e.g. *bitter reproach*, etc. (Bréal 1964 [1900]: 130). Williams refined this programmatic kind of observation with a study of synaesthesia in English, from which he hypothesized that the paths of extension were as in figure 2.4. He tested this against IE (as evidenced by Buck's 1949 dictionary of synonyms in IE), and in Japanese, where he found 91 percent

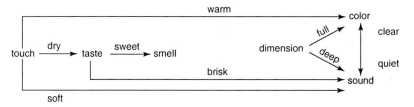

Figure 2.4. Synaesthetic adjectives (Viberg 1983: 159, with examples added to Williams 1976: 463).

correlation with the schema in figure 2.4. Derrig (1978) showed that the directionality proposed by Williams was less firm than he had suggested, but continued to affirm the hypothesis that cross-linguistic evidence could be found for directionality, hence predictability in semantic change. Viberg (1983) noted that while the relation between touch, taste, and smell was the same in both the hierarchy of PERCEPTION and in synaesthesia, the relation between sight and touch was reversed. Whereas vision predominates in extensions across perception modalities, and from PERCEPTION to INTELLECT, touch is the predominant source in synesthesia, with sound as its predominant target (1983: 159).

One particularly fruitful semantic field, especially in cross-linguistic typological work, has been that of BODY PART terms (see e.g. Brown and Witkowski 1983, Wilkins 1996). For example, using a sample of 118 languages, Brown and Witkowski undertook an investigation of the relationship between EYE and FACE. They showed that in "small-scale societies" EYE has a cultural importance ("salience") far greater than FACE and that forms for the former often have polysemies for the latter, but not vice versa. In these languages, EYE is "unmarked" in the sense that it is usually the simple lexical form, whereas terms for FACE may be derived by compounding or derivation from EYE. In such societies SEED and FRUIT are in parallel relationship: "eye and seed are in a sense the centre or core of face and fruit respectively, while face and fruit comprise the periphery of eye and seed. Thus formally speaking, eye and seed are to face and to fruit as centre is to periphery or 'figure' to 'ground'" (Brown and Witkowski 1983: 76). Furthermore, EYE is sometimes extended to SEED and even FRUIT. In other words, not only individual lexical representations have similar directionalities, but parallel ones may as well, given extra-linguistic criteria such as cultural importance (see figure 2.5).

As societies become "large-scale" and urban, cultural importance may shift; indeed, FACE and FRUIT tend in such societies to be as important as or more important than EYE and SEED, and Brown and Witkowski predict that the polysemies illustrated in figure 2.5 will not be found in such societies. They note that in ancient Gk., a single term *ops* was used to designate eye and face; later, complex terms

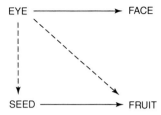

Figure 2.5. Direction of polysemy extensions in the field of eye/face and seed/fruit (Brown and Witkowski 1983: 73).

derived from *ops* came to distinguish the two, and later yet this connection between eye and face was lost (Brown and Witkowski 1983: 83).

Many studies of semantic fields, including those by Derrig, Williams, and Brown and Witkowski discussed above, assume that the basic mechanism of change is metaphor. Sometimes this mechanism has been shown to be deeply connected with evaluation, especially pejoration. Lehrer (1985) investigates the way in which zoological subcategory terms developed denigrating pejorative polysemies in English, e.g. PRIMATE (*ape, baboon, gorilla*) > brutishness; BIRD (*goose, cuckoo, pigeon, coot, turkey*) > foolishness; SCAVENGER BIRD (*buzzard, vulture*) > greed. Similarly, Kleparski (1990) demonstrates the extent to which terms for humans have undergone pejoration cross-linguistically, and also how pejorative terms for humans may be derived from the domain of animals and foods, e.g. Polish *burak* "beetroot" > "country lad"; *grzyb* "mushroom" > "old, unpleasant man" (Kleparski 1990: 130–131).

A semantic field that is more directly related to the concerns of this book is that of verbs of speaking or LOCUTION. In a study of "the linguistic action scene," Goossens (1985) compares MdE *speak, talk, say*, and *tell* with verbs demonstrating similar functions in OE. He argues that, among other things, *speak* and *talk* focus on the linguistic action. He identifies three main types of *speak* with focus on (i) vocalization (*speak loudly*); (ii) establishing contact with a receptor (cf. *speak to you*); and (iii) establishing contact in public ways (*speak at a meeting*). *Talk* is similar in many respects, but treats AD as an interactive interlocutor (*talk to you*) and often specifies the function of speech (*talk business*) (Goossens 1985: 154–155). By contrast, *say* and *tell* focus on the message. *Say* can introduce all types of speech act, and can draw attention to speech properties, e.g. *Just say quietly, "I'm going to leave now,"* while *tell* primarily introduces a narrative. The OE data, however, suggest that there are only three high frequency verbs in OE, *sp(r)ecan, cweþan*, and *secgan*, of which the first focuses on the type of linguistic action, the second and third on the message. *Sp(r)ecan* is most like *speak*, and indeed is etymologically its origin, but is more like *talk* than *speak* with respect to AD, who is treated as an interactor; furthermore, the public pronouncement aspect of *speak* is absent. *Cweþan* frames direct messages and reports messages indirectly, *secgan* primarily introduces indirect ones; in this regard *cweþan* is most like *say*, *secgan* like *tell*. This means that there have been some significant semantic changes: *cweþan* has become obsolete except in archaisms like *quoth*, and *secgan*, the etymological source of *say*, has become generalized. Goossens concludes that in OE "there are no items with the same specificity" as the modern ones (ibid. p. 470); the reorganization of the lexicon occurred in ME with the introduction of *talk* (an early Frisian term) and the focusing of *tell* on verbal action (in OE *tellan* meant primarily "count" (cf. *bank teller*) or recount[11] in sequence, i.e. "narrate"). He suggests that the reorganization is "at least partially" explained by the absence of specificities. Rather than formulating the motivations for change in terms of therapeutic (and hence teleological) "filling of gaps," we might think of the changes in terms of changing practices with respect to discourse and the metalanguage associated with it.

Of particular interest in the domain of verbs of LOCUTION is the development of what Benveniste calls "delocutive verbs": verbs that name formulaic language acts of the type "to say ..." (Benveniste 1971b [1958]: 245). He argues that they derive cross-linguistically (at least among European languages) from discourse, especially ritual, formulae, such as Gk. *khaírein* "to greet" < "say *khaîre*! ('greetings')"; Eng. *hail* "shout 'Hail!'"; Fr. *(re)mercier* "thank" < "say *merci*! ('thanks')." He compares the ability to create such verbs denoting activities of discourse to the ability to create verbs out of responses, e.g. Lat. *negare* "to say '*nec*,' to deny" out of *nec* "no," or *autumare* "to say '*autem*,' to argue, assert" out of *autem* "but." This change is therefore presented as an instance of metonymy, in this case an ellipsis, of a report of a speech act. On first thought it might suggest a counterexample to subjectification: to give a name to the reported act "to say X" would seem to objectify the subjectivity of "X." However, in the cases discussed here we do not have instances of semasiological development within one morphosyntactic category. Rather, the forms have undergone derivation into another morphosyntactic category. Such derivation allows names, morphemes and phrases to be turned into nouns and verbs, cf. *to sandwich* (derived from association with John Montagu, Fourth Earl of Sandwich), *ism* (a derivative word-formation device), *whodunit*.

Being testable and predictive, many hypotheses about semantic fields seemed to promise the potential for finding "laws" of semantic change comparable to those in phonology such as Grimm's Law. Sometimes these were thought of like chain shifts rather than isolated regularities of the sort Stern discussed. For example, Anttila cites briefly a shift of form–meaning pairs "one notch" across a semantic field in Latin legal terminology that is "so regular and far-reaching" that it looks

[11] Note the lexical association of counting with speaking.

like chain shift in the sound system (Anttila 1989 [1972]: 146–147). Unlike most phonological laws, these semantic "laws" were to be understood as statements of patterns: implicational and taxonomic hierarchies that are tendencies not absolutes; furthermore, they were not "exceptionless," as had been posited of sound changes at the time. Therefore, although the analogy with phonological change was attractive, it was also misleading (for a detailed critique, see Hoenigswald 1992). The fact that semantic change does not apply like phonological change to every potential M may have contributed to the continuation of the attitude that semantic change is basically irregular (so, of course, did the late development of semantic theory). Nevertheless, attempts to classify changes on analogy with phonological change were fruitful in so far as efforts were made to come to grips with semantic change in terms of semantic features and types of splits and mergers (see Anttila 1989 [1972]: chapter 7, Kleparksi 1986), or (in generative terms) rule addition and loss (e.g. Voyles 1973). From our perspective, the most important contribution of the kind of work on semantic fields discussed in this section is that it not only laid the groundwork for research on conceptual domains but also suggested ways of organizing lexical commonalities across time and languages in terms of sense units, the networks they enter into, and their hierarchies (Lehrer 1974).

2.3 Major contemporary issues

In this section we review some of the contemporary theoretical issues in work on semantic change that are particularly relevant to this book.

2.3.1 Metaphor

Work began in the late 1970s on an approach to semantic change that drew on various converging threads emerging from studies of language universals (e.g. Greenberg, Ferguson, and Moravcsik 1978), historical syntax and grammaticalization (e.g. Givón 1979), and generative semantics (e.g. McCawley 1968). Most work at this time concerned fields similar to those studied earlier by anthropologists and psychologists, most notably SPACE > TIME (e.g. Traugott 1978), BODY PART > SPACE (e.g. Kahr 1975). Like earlier work, it tended to assume that the major mechanism for change was metaphor, construed as the analogical mapping of a more concrete term from a "source" domain onto a more abstract term in the "target" domain. Like earlier work it also tended to focus on lexical items out of context, and evidence from dictionaries, grammars, and other secondary sources. There were, however, several significant differences about this line of research. One was a move away from taxonomies, often with physical, social, or cultural referents (e.g. EYE and FACE), to the study of conceptual categories and their relations. These relations were not organized as binary features typical of componential analysis, but were conceived as occupying an abstract cognitive domain or "mental space"

75

and could be arranged on a "map" of that mental space (see e.g. Anderson 1982). Furthermore, the focus shifted from lexical semantic change to semantic changes correlated with shifts from lexical to grammatical status; thus the interest in body parts was not so much whether meanings for face derived from meanings for eye or vice versa, but rather what body part terms developed meanings in grammatical domains such as case. For example, Kahr showed that in Papago *wui* "eye" > *wul* "toward," and in Ewe *nkúmè* "face" > "before" (Kahr 1975: 45) (see section 2.3.3 below for discussion of grammaticalization).

But most important of all was a reconceptualization of the role of metaphor in language. In traditions that treat metaphor as figurative and somehow derived, metaphor is inevitably construed as a deviation from literal meaning. One of the prime objectives of Cognitive Linguistics has been to show that metaphor is not derived, superimposed, or deviant. Rather, it is a pervasive mode of thought, a fundamental aspect of human cognizing and of human language, so fundamental indeed that language is virtually inconceivable without it. It is grounded in perception and body movement, and especially in abstract and topological image-schemata based on them (see e.g., Lakoff and Johnson 1980, Talmy 1985, 1988, Lakoff 1987, 1993, and, from a somewhat different perspective, Langacker 1987/91). Cognitive Linguistics led to the refining of two kinds of analysis, diachronic prototype semantics (Geeraerts 1983, 1992, 1997; see also Györi 1996), and diachronic metaphorical analysis (Sweetser 1990).

With respect to prototype theory, Geeraerts points to several characteristics of prototypicality that are relevant to semantic change (Geeraerts 1997: 22–23). Most importantly, since prototype theories focus on the unequal status of polysemies, and on their tendency to cluster in related groupings (see discussion of Jurafsky's work on diminutives in 2.3.3 below), certain changes will be construed as more salient than others, and carry more weight than others. Thus there may be "peripheral meanings that do not survive for very long next to more important meanings that subsist through time" (Geeraerts 1997: 24). Uncertainties regarding the delimitation of a category may result in "the phenomenon that one and the same reading of a particular lexical item may come into existence more than once in the history of a word, each time on an independent basis," a phenomenon that Geeraerts calls "semantic polygenesis" (ibid.). As an example, he cites the use of *verduisteren* by a Dutch song-writer in 1983 as "eclipse, disappear (Vt)," and suggests that it is unlikely that this use was a continuation of a similar use in the sixteenth and seventeenth centuries. He considered it an innovation based on the literal meaning "become dark" (Geeraerts 1997: 63). As was discussed in 1.3.2, we require that for a diachronic change, rather than an idiosyncratic innovation, to take place it must have spread within a community, and therefore we question whether a single use by a song-writer would count as a diachronic change. Nevertheless, Geeraerts' conclusion from examples like this is an important one, and is consistent with our view: "In a prototypical conception of meaning, the more salient readings are among those that are conventionally handed down from generation to generation, while other readings may at any moment be creatively and independently based on those transmitted meanings" (Geeraerts 1997: 68).

With respect to metaphor, since it was conceptualized as involving one domain of experience in terms of another and operating "*between* domains" (Sweetser 1990: 19; italics original), changes motivated by it were conceptualized as primarily discontinuous and abrupt. However, since source and target meanings of metaphors constrain each other experientially, it was hypothesized that aspects of the abstract image-schemata associated with source and target are "preserved across metaphorical mappings" (ibid. p. 59). In a now classic study of the lexical field of intellect, reconceived as involving a mind-as-body metaphor motivated by experience, e.g. VISION/HEARING/TACTILE ACTS > INTELLECT, Sweetser showed how verbs of seeing and grasping can come cross-linguistically to be metaphorized as verbs of understanding, e.g. Gk. *eîdon* "see," perfect *oîda* "know" (cf. Eng. *idea*) (Sweetser 1990: 33; for a detailed study of the development of the Russian lexicon of knowing and believing derived from seeing, see Andrews 1995). She also suggested that in more abstract domains, such as that of modality, there is metaphorical mapping across domains both synchronically and diachronically. Thus *may* can be said to operate in three domains synchronically, for example:

(15)   I   sociophysical world ("content"):   Kim *may* go. ("content modal of permission")

      II   mental world (reasoning):   Kim *may* be tired. ("epistemic modal")

      III   world of speaking (speech acting):   Kim *may* be a nice guy, but I don't trust him. ("speech act modal")

Here the image-schemata involved are barriers (Sweetser 1990: 61, 70, drawing in part on Talmy 1988):

(16)   I   content: X is not barred by some authority from doing Y.

      II   reasoning: I am not barred by my premises from the conclusion Y.

      III   speech acting: I do not bar from our conversational world the statement Y.

Sweetser showed that meaning change is from content to reasoning and speech acting meanings, not vice versa, a macro-level claim that is of fundamental importance to the present work.

Historical evidence for the unidirectional change of content modals > epistemic modals, that is, from Stage I > Stage II (not epistemic modals > content modals) had been firmly established (see Shepherd 1981 for an early study). The question remained whether evidence for a further change from epistemic into speech act modalities could be found. While evidence in the domain of modal auxiliaries has remained elusive, perhaps in part because of the nature of the data, there is abundant support for the hypothesis in other domains to be discussed throughout this book, especially the rise of metatextual discourse markers and of speech act uses of locutionary verbs. These will be discussed in detail in chapters 4 and 5.

2.3.2 *Metonymy and invited inference*

Although Bréal distinguished between metaphor and association (metonymy), and many others have done so since, e.g. Jakobson and Halle (1971), the distinction has often been eroded. For example, Hock and Joseph say that metaphor is "the major vehicle through which words acquire new or broader meanings" (1996: 228), and include within it part-for-whole synecdoche (e.g. use of *hand* for *laborer*), metonymy (association, e.g. use of *bar* [the physical barrier between lawyer and jury] for the *legal profession*),[12] hyperbole (exaggeration, e.g. use of *awfully* as an intensifier), litotes (understatement, e.g. use of *a bit* for *rather*), and euphemism (e.g. *pass on* for *die*). Within Cognitive Linguistics, metaphor took pride of place in the 1980s, even though Lakoff and Johnson (1980) and Lakoff (1987) emphasized the importance of certain types of metonymy, for example the use of a well-known (often salient) aspect of something to stand for the whole, e.g. *Washington* "(a place for) government."

Until recently, metonymy was thought of largely in terms of idiosyncratic usages with external referents, such as *White House* for President of the USA, or elliptic, such as *a Picasso* for *a painting by Picasso*, although as was mentioned in 1.3.1, there has in recent years been a fundamental shift in thinking, most especially in Cognitive Linguistics (see Barcelona 2000a and papers therein, especially Barcelona 2000b, Radden 2000). Among factors that led to this shift was synchronic work on frame semantics; research exemplified by Fillmore (1982) and Lehrer and Kittay (1992) suggested that there are "frame metonymies," in which components of the frame are parts of the whole. For example, in a restaurant frame customers and food are part of the whole; thus the well-known metonymy *The ham sandwich wants a second glass of coke* (Nunberg 1978) involves not just a metonymy from the person who ordered the sandwich to the sandwich, but to the whole restaurant scene and to our mental model of it (Sweetser and Fauconnier 1996). The same may be said for the well-known example in Japanese linguistics *Watasi wa unagi da*, which is structurally "I am (an) eel" but in a restaurant context means "I'd like (the) eel." Of metonymy Langacker has said that its "prevalence would be hard to exaggerate" (Langacker 1995: 28). Indeed, it is fundamental to reference:

---

[12] Note that Hock and Joseph distinguish synecdoche and metonymy, although the former is often considered a subtype of the latter.

"In metonymy, an expression's usual referent (i.e. its profile) is invoked as a reference point to establish mental contact with its intended referent (its target)" (ibid.), for example:

(17)   She bought **Lakoff and Johnson**, used and in paper, for just $1.50.

(Langacker 1995: 28; boldface original)

Here *Lakoff and Johnson* is a salient reference point, metonymically establishing mental contact with the book rather than its authors. Similarly, Croft (1993: 354) writes of metonymy as "the highlighting of an aspect of a concept's profile" in a larger domain or frame.

Likewise in historical work, the focus on metonymy in an extended sense came to be of increasing importance. Attempts were made to establish functional differences between metaphor and metonymy/association. From this perspective, metaphor involves similarity, mapping of one domain onto another, in what is essentially a conceptual mode of analogy, paradigmatic choice, and iconicity. By contrast, metonymy involves contiguity, syntagmatic relations, and indexicality, and shifts within the same domain (Anttila 1989 [1972],[13] Traugott 1988). But as mentioned in 1.3.1, what exactly a "domain" is, or where the locus of change occurs has not always been so clear. Is intensity of speed within the same semantic domain as aspectual phase, or in a different one (see Stern's example of RAPIDLY > IMMEDIATELY (see section 2.2.2))? It would be possible to think in terms of domain transfer and metaphor here: a mapping from the sociophysical world of description (in a rapid manner) to that of temporal deixis, shifting according to the subjective view-point of the speaker (within a time-period proximate to a point of reference, as subjectively construed by the speaker). However, Stern treated the shift as permutation (phrasal association, therefore metonymy), invoking as he did changes in the context of process vs. punctual verbs. Metaphor and metonymy involve different axes but they interact; Goossens has coined the term "metaphtonomy" as a reminder of this interaction (see e.g. 1995a).

In addition to semantic work, especially in Cognitive Linguistics, other lines of work in the pragmatics of presuppositions, implicatures, and inferences, combined with close textual study inspired by discourse analysis, and enabled by the development of computerized corpora, suggested a way to reconceptualize metonymy as a major language-internal force in semantic change.

Some brief and hesitant hypotheses were mentioned in 1.3.2, such as Bolinger's (1971) insight that inferences can become references. Proposals in the same vein included Cole's, in connection with the development of *let's* from *let us*, that conversational meanings "not inherent in the logical structure" of the sentence in which

---

[13] Anttila acknowledges Guiraud (1955).

they occur can come via frequent use to acquire "literal meaning" (1975: 273), and Grice's tentative "it may not be impossible for what starts life, so to speak, as a conversational implicature to become conventionalized" (1989 [1975]: 58). The diachronic shift from conversational to conventional implicature was followed through in some detail in Brown and Levinson (1987 [1978]) and Levinson further proposed that "it is possible to argue that there is a sequence from particularized through generalized conversational implicatures to conventional implicatures" (1979: 216). But probably the most influential work, at least in Traugott's thinking, was a brief paper by Geis and Zwicky (1971) on the "invited inferences" involved in conditional perfection, or the tendency for promises like *I'll give you $5 if you mow the lawn* to be understood as *If and only if you mow the lawn will I give you $5*. In the context of their paper they mention the development of causal *since* out of temporal *since*, saying:

> it seems to be the case that an invited inference can, historically, become part of semantic representation in the strict sense; thus, the development of the English conjunction *since* from a purely temporal word to a marker of causation can be interpreted as a change from a principle of invited inference associated with *since* (by virtue of its temporal meaning) to a piece of the semantic content of *since*.
>
> (Geis and Zwicky 1971: 565–566)

Geis and Zwicky distinguish invited inferences from Gricean conversational implicatures, commenting that Grice's "Relevance" principle does not seem to provide any obvious account of the inference from temporality to causality. However, Grice's Quantity 2 principle (understood as the R-heuristic "Say no more than you must, and mean more thereby," see 1.2.3) combined with the view espoused here of strategic, rhetorical language use, motivates this development: in specifying temporality, SP/W may imply a subjective assessment of connectivity richer than pure temporality.

Focus of attention on the pragmatic meanings that arise in language use opened the way for thinking about "conceptual," language-internal metonymy arising out of the syntagmatic contexts of language use, association, contiguity, and indexicality.[14] Metonymy in its extended conceptual sense came to be seen as a powerful alternative to metaphor, in fact as the key to conceptualizing semantic change in context.

When we look at changes that have been designated as metaphorical, the "metaphor" often appears to be primarily a function of the fact that we are looking at lexical entries in their "before" and "after" stages, and out of context. Consider,

---

[14] However, see Warren (1998) for an attempt to distinguish "inference" and "implication" from metonymy.

for example, the extension of WHITE > INNOCENT, SPACE > TIME, or of *ape* > "brutish person." As soon as we think about change in terms of its syntactic and ultimately discourse contexts, associations arising out of the context can be construed as playing a major role in change (see e.g. Brinton 1988: chapter 5, Traugott 1988). Already extant metaphors that themselves have arisen out of the patterns of language use at earlier times are construed as templates, or mental models constraining the kinds of invited inferences that become salient, and in many cases the outcome of changes arising by semanticization of GIINs (see 1.3, 1.4).[15] Furthermore, the fine-grained "paths" of change can begin to be elucidated, without the need to seek evidence for discrete cross-boundary leaps. The remarkably high incidence of redundancy or at least semantic harmony in the contexts of semantic change can be seen as the textual locus of experimentation by SP/W with the possibilities of invited inferencing. And, most importantly, subjectification can be understood as a type of metonymy – association with SP/W in the strategic course of speaking/writing. We will, however, leave discussion of subjectification to the last section, after a brief survey of issues in the study of grammaticalization and the hypothesis of unidirectionality, since the understanding that subjectification is a major mechanism of change developed largely in the context of work on these issues.

2.3.3 *Grammaticalization and unidirectionality*

Much of the debate in the 1980s on the role of metaphor and metonymy in semantic change took place within the context of the study of grammaticalization (also known as "grammaticization"). As originally conceptualized by Meillet (1958 [1912]), grammaticalization is typically the development of lexemes into grammatical items; Meillet also suggested that change from relatively free to relatively fixed word order is an instance of grammaticalization. In either case, the change is conceived as unidirectional, from A to B, not vice versa. A more recent view has been that it is a shift from discourse > syntax > morphology (Givón 1979; see also Lehmann 1995 [1982]). Givón's formulation was a major catalyst for work on change taking discourse processes into account, an approach that had been briefly touched on in Stern's book with respect to semantic change, but which had not been pursued. Subsequent work on grammaticalization has suggested that it is more properly conceived as the change whereby lexical material in highly constrained pragmatic and morphosyntactic contexts is assigned functional category status, and where the lexical meaning of an item is assigned constructional meaning (van Kemenade 1999: 1006, Traugott, Forthcoming).

---

[15] From a different perspective, Kövecses and Radden (1998) suggest that metaphors like ANGER IS HEAT may arise experientially out of conceptual metonymies; see also Kövecses (2000), Radden (2000).

Although most early work focused on structural properties of grammaticalization, (e.g. Lehmann 1995 [1982], Heine and Reh 1984), attention to lexical or discourse origins naturally also led to exploration of semantic change, both onomasiological (e.g. what terms would give rise to prepositions, complementizers, aspect or agreement markers), and semasiological (e.g. what semantic path did Lat. *cantare habeo* "sing: INF have: 1SG" traverse as it grammaticalized to Fr. *chanterai*?). The literature on these questions is substantial and growing rapidly. Representative examples of work in which semantic change is of considerable importance include Fleischman (1982), Heine, Claudi, and Hünnemeyer (1991), Hopper and Traugott (1993), Svorou (1993), Dasher (1995), Sun (1996), Haspelmath (1997), and Ohori (1998); a lexicon of grammaticalization is provided by Heine et al. (1993). Bybee, Perkins, and Pagliuca's (1994) study is a major investigation of grammaticalization based on materials from a cross-linguistic sample of seventy-six language groups. Most specifically, the authors are concerned with asking whether there are any regularities or commonalities across languages in the meanings expressed by closed-class grammatical morphemes such as affixes, stem changes, reduplication, auxiliaries, particles, or complex constructions like *be going to* in the target domains of tense, aspect, and modality (Bybee, Perkins, and Pagliuca 1994: 2–3). The answer is a dramatic "yes." Since most sources are reference grammars, little discourse data is provided, but text-based studies of particular languages confirm the more general hypotheses concerning sources for the target "grams" (grammatical morphemes).

In the course of this book we will be discussing some data that involves grammaticalization, specifically the development of the modal *must* (chapter 3) and the development of adverbials like *pray* (chapter 6). We outline two examples of grammaticalization here: the development of the future *be going to* in English, and the development of the modal particle *as* in Modern Greek.

The history of *be going to* is well-known (see Pérez 1990; also Bybee and Pagliuca 1987, Hopper and Traugott 1993: 80–86, Tabor 1994a) but we revisit it here because it gives direct insights into the question of analysis in terms of metaphor vs. invited inference. Verbs meaning GO and COME have long been used as a prime example of SPACE > TIME. From the perspective of large-scale onomasiological changes, it is a cross-linguistically widely attested prototype example of semantic change. Often the shift from GO/COME > FUTURE has been treated as an example of metaphor (e.g. Traugott 1978, Bybee and Pagliuca 1987, Heine, Claudi, and Hünnemeyer 1991). But cross-linguistic study at a more fine-grained level of analysis shows that bare GO and COME actually never become FUTURE. Bybee, Pagliuca, and Perkins argue that the change occurs only in highly specific contexts: "along with movement as a component of meaning, the source of such futures includes an imperfective (or progressive) component and an allative component" (1991: 30). This is a constraint that is readily understandable in terms of inferences arising out of language use:

motion toward something takes time (i.e. is imperfective), and one will arrive there only at some time later than the motion starts. It is not clear how such a constraint could be placed on a metaphor, and indeed Bybee, Perkins, and Pagliuca explicitly question the usefulness of a metaphorical approach to the change and propose an analysis that draws on pragmatic intentions and inferences:

> The temporal meaning that comes to dominate the semantics of the construction is already present as an inference from the spatial meaning. When one moves along a path toward a goal in space, one also moves in time. The major change that takes place is the loss of spatial meaning. Here ... the function of expressing intention comes into play. When a speaker announces that s/he is going somewhere to do something, s/he is also announcing the intention to do that thing. Thus intention is part of the meaning from the beginning, and the only change necessary is the generalization to contexts in which an intention is expressed, but the subject is not moving spatially to fulfill that intention.
>
> (Bybee, Perkins, and Pagliuca 1994: 268)

Note that while the semantics of space may be lost or at least recede into the background (a phenomenon commonly known as "bleaching"), this change involves pragmatic strengthening of the temporal implicature (Traugott 1988). The ultimate semanticization of temporality involves the development of a new polysemy which is as rich as the earlier one although more abstract (Sweetser 1988) and also more subjective (Traugott 1988, Langacker 1990).

As a motion verb, *go* occurs very frequently in ME texts. The form *going* is used almost exclusively as a nominal gerund, with imperfective/durative meaning (Peréz 1990).[16] The first plausible example of *be going to* in a temporal rather than motion sense known to us is the much-cited example in (18):

(18) thys unhappy sowle by the vyctoryse pompys of her enmyes
      this unhappy soul   by the victorious displays of her enemies
      was goyng to be broughte into helle for the synne and
      was going to be brought   into hell   for the sin   and
      onleful   lustys of her body.
      unlawful lusts   of her body
      "this unhappy soul was going to be brought into hell in the victorious procession of her enemies because of the unlawful lusts of her body"
                                                                (*c.* 1482 Monk of Evesham, p. 43)

Here the context is not only imperfective. The passive demotes the agentivity of the subject. A modern interpretation suggests strongly that a temporal, not a motion reading is called for, since we do not expect souls to have physical properties. On

---

[16] The progressive construction with *-ing* emerged only late in ME.

this reading, temporality would be a salient GIIN, or possibly even an instance of a newly semanticized "immanent future." However, it is quite possible that the motion verb is to be taken literally, since in this sermon a vision is narrated in which the soul is represented as a very physical entity, tormented in the stomach with darts. On this reading, temporality is only an IIN in (18). Unambiguous examples of the temporal do not occur until the later sixteenth century. An example from the seventeenth century is:

> (19)   *Witwoud*: Gad, I have forgot what I *was going to say* to you.
>
> (1699 Congreve, Way of the World, I, p. 331)

(18) and (19) suggest that in its early stages the change is primarily abstraction (spatial > temporal). Later, in the nineteenth century, we find examples with inanimate subjects ("raising" constructions), at first relatively objective in the sense that anybody could anticipate rain from accessible evidence (20a), later in more subjective senses (20b) based in SP/W's reasoning processes:

> (20)   a. Do you think it's *going to rain*?
>
> (1865 Carroll, chapter 4, p. 146)
>
> b. There *is going to be* a shooting and somebody *is going to get hurt*.
>
> (1894 Doyle, 568)

By the beginning of the twentieth century we find incontrovertible written evidence that temporal *be going to* has been fixed as a unit ("univerbated"), because we begin to find instances of *be gonna*. The form is used only in texts deliberately signaled as colloquial (note in (21) the use of *me and Jeanne, put the skids under*):

> (21)   Me and Jeanne *is gonna have* a flat over in Brooklyn as soon as we put the skids under the Kaiser.
>
> (1918 Whitwer [OED])

Characteristics associated with grammaticalization are:

(i)   a specific construction (in this case imperfective aspect, and direct collocation between *be going* and the purpose clause),

(ii)   bleaching (of the semantics of motion),

(iii) pragmatic strengthening (of the GIIN from the imperfective motion construction followed by a purpose clause), subjectification, and ultimate semanticization as a polysemy (of the motion construction),

(iv)   reanalysis (of open class event structure material as closed class temporal material),

(v)   fixing of the construction (including univerbation of *going to*),

(vi)   phonological attrition (of the univerbated part of the construction).

Characteristics (i)–(iii) are typical of lexical, independently of grammatical, change. The case of *be going to* is an example of grammaticalization because characteristics (iv)–(vi) are closely associated with (i)–(iii).

We balance this very familiar example with a less familiar but partially similar one: the development of a highly polysemous modal particle *as* in Modern Greek. It serves as a hortative "let's," expressing wish ("may it be that"), irrealis, conditionality, and concession (Nikiforidou 1996). According to Nikiforidou, *as* originates at the time of Koiné in *áphes* "allow!," the imperative of the verb *aphiemi* "send away, let go of, let, leave, allow," as in:

(22) adelphè, *áphes*   exbálo   tò kárphos.
      brother   let-IMP-2SG pull-out-SUBJUNCT-1SG the nail
      "Brother, let me pull out the nail."
                    (before 300 AC, Matthew 27: 46 [Nikiforidou 1996: 602])

By the sixth or seventh centuries AC it begins to appear as *as*, no longer as a verb with inflections but as a preverbal particle in a paradigm with *na* "irrealis" and *tha* "future":

(23) elthé   oun   pròs emas kaì *as*
      come-IMP-2SG therefore to   us   and "as"
      lalesomen   tà pròs   eirénen.
      talk-SUBJUNCT-1PL the towards peace
      "Come therefore to us and let's talk about peace."
                    (9th century, Theophanis, Chronographia 387 2 [ibid: p. 605])

Rather than the original meaning of permission we now find suggestion, and later wish:

(24) *as* génetai   parà sou.
      "as" be-do-PFV-NONPAST-3SG by   you
      "May it be done by you."
                    (mid 13th century, Sfrandzis Georgios, Small Chron. [ibid. p. 609])

Later meanings include a conditional and a concessive which Nikiforidou interprets as functioning like Sweetser's kind of "speech act" modal (see 2.3.1), "whether the content of the *as* clause is true or not does not matter. What matters is that for the purposes of the conversation the speaker will accept it as true while she insists on asserting the content of the main clause" (1996: 612):

(25) *as* chionísi   emís tha páme
      "as" snow-PFV-NP-3SG we   FUT go:PFV:NONPAST:1PL
      "We will go, even if it snows"
                                            (ibid. p. 611)

We again find the same six kinds of characteristics as were outlined for *be going to*; together they show that this is a case of grammaticalization.

Semantically the two sets of changes outlined here are instances of generalization: in both cases the original lexical meaning is extended to other meanings. But it was not generalization that made grammaticalization a focal point of interest for researchers in semantic change. What has been a catalyst is the substantial cross-linguistic evidence from studies of grammaticalization for the regularity of such shifts as SPACE > TIME, permission to exhortation, described world to speech world, less to more subjective, not vice versa; crucial too has been the focus of grammaticalization research on discourse contexts for change.

The examples of grammaticalization given here illustrate a strong overarching hypothesis associated with much work on grammaticalization: that of unidirectionality in all the correlated shifts. As a testable hypothesis unidirectionality has been questioned, most especially in the domain of morphosyntax (see Janda 1995 and the references therein, Newmeyer 1998: chapter 5, Lightfoot 1999: 220–225, Lass 2000, among others). One line of argument is that there are ontological difficulties with notions such as grammaticalization "clines," "paths," or "trajectories" like Givón's discourse > syntax > morphology > morphophonemics > zero (Givón 1979: 209). Are such clines assumed to exist? If so where? Are they explanatory linguistic principles or outcomes of non-linguistic factors?

In our view such paths are schemas for observed regularities across time. The categories on the paths (e.g. clitic, affix, or TEMPORAL, CONCESSIVE) do not shift; individual forms come to be associated over time with these onomasiological categories in a predictable, unidirectional way. In other words, the path represents the probable new polysemies of a form if it changes meaning. As models of change constructed by linguists, paths or clines are part of the metalanguage of change. They are metaphors and are therefore necessarily expressed in concrete terms, but that does not mean that they exist as concrete paths or conduits for change. The structural path that a form or construction undergoing grammaticalization takes is motivated by speakers' tendency to seek signal simplicity (hence the tendency for clitics to be reduced and fixed as affixes), just as the path that the meaning of that form or construction takes is constrained by speakers' tendency to recruit referential meanings to less referential functions of language (hence the tendency for concrete spatial terms to be recruited to the function of case or of aspect). The paths are explanatory to the extent that they predict frequently attested directions of change, whether at the semantic level from TEMPORAL > CONCESSIVE or at the morphosyntactic one from clitic to affix. Falsifiers would be frequently attested examples of shifts from CONCESSIVE > TEMPORAL or from affix to clitic. Speakers innovatively use old forms and constructions with new meanings, subject to semantic and pragmatic constraints. If these innovations spread to other speakers the resources available for the category at that point on the path are renewed (Meillet 1958 [1915–16] called this "renouvellement"). The recruitment of these new forms or constructions into extant conceptual categories is motivated by speakers' tendency to seek maximal communicative effect (informativeness, rhetorical strategizing, etc.).[17] In other words, grammaticalization is motivated by the dyadic communicative situation.

One argument against unidirectionality in grammaticalization has been that patterns of shifts from more lexical to more grammatical material or from less morphologically bound to more morphologically bound are not without exception. An example of the strong position on this point is: "I take any example of upgrading as sufficient to refute unidirectionality" (Newmeyer 1998: 263). One of the examples of upgrading that Newmeyer cites (quoting Nevis 1986) is the upgrading of a Finno-Permic abessive case affix *-pta to a clitic postposition *taga* in Northern Saame (Lappish). As indicated in chapter 1, we are concerned with tendencies, not absolutes. Language is a product of human beings. Grammaticalization, like semanticization, involves the interaction of linguistic structure and language use. One would not expect absolute 100 percent regularity from strategic interaction, subject as it always is to human intervention. Under such a view, a small number of falsifiers of a hypothesis does not discredit the hypothesis, but a large number, say a quarter of the instances would certainly do so. To date the number of counterexamples to semantic unidirectionality in grammaticalization remains small.

What is particularly striking for our purposes in this book is that many of the counterexamples to grammaticalization that have been cited show no semantic shift (e.g. the cliticization of *-pta), or show regular semantic shift of the sort described in this book. In other words, even if structural unidirectionality is violated, semantic unidirectionality is not. For example, one of the first papers to discuss a counterexample to the posited structural directionality of grammaticalization, in this case less to more bonded morphology, Yo Matsumoto (1988) showed that an earlier Jp. clause-final postfix -ga "although" came to be a clause-initial conjunction meaning "however" (affix to clitic). Nevertheless, despite structural upgrading, the semantic and pragmatic shift is toward greater subjectification.

As the study of grammaticalization progressed it rapidly became clear that the semantic changes observable in grammaticalization are a subtype of regular changes in the lexicon. What is different is that in grammaticalization semantic changes affect only certain Ls (those with relatively general meaning) and correlate with other changes such as morphosyntactic decategorialization. How true this is can be seen from the study of cross-linguistic tendencies in the development of the semantics

---

[17] See Langacker (1977) for an early formulation of the competing motivations in grammaticalization (he refers to "reanalysis" rather than grammaticalization).

of the diminutive as presented in Jurafsky (1996). Despite saying that "the diminutive function (... defined as any morphological device that means at least 'small') is among the grammatical primitives" (ibid. p. 534), Jurafsky does not frame his discussion in terms of grammaticalization. Rather, he builds on and develops a diachronic dimension to Lakoff's (1987) semantic proposal that many metaphors are organized in complex ways which can be thought of as a radial category with core members linked to extensions represented by a network of nodes. Jurafsky argues that at the core of the diminutive is the notion of CHILD. The shift from CHILD > SMALL, as exemplified by the diminutives *vi*, *-dzai*, *-pil* in Ewe, Cantonese, Nahuatl respectively (Jurafsky 1996: 562), is presumably metonymic (and also a case of grammaticalization). Jurafsky regards many extensions as metaphorical, e.g. from diminutive to female gender specification (contrast Gm. *Junge* "male youth," *Mäd-chen* "female youth," with a diminutive), or to derogatory, marginalized status (contrast Cantonese *nui*^{25} "woman" with *mo*^{25}*nui*^{35}, where *mo*^{25} is a derogatory diminutive). An alternative view might be that these are metonymic to social perspectives, and to the opposition he himself sets up (the female of the species is smaller, less powerful than the male). Be that as it may, Jurafsky sees in the radial category of diminutives evidence for the mechanisms of metaphorization, metonymic inferencing, generalization,[18] and a special type of metaphorical generalization which he calls "lambda-abstraction-specification": "[l]ambda-abstracting takes one predicate in a form and replaces it with a variable. The resulting expression is now a second-order predicate, since its domain includes a variable which ranges over predicates" (Jurafsky 1996: 555).

Jurafsky suggests that lambda-abstraction allows for a single generalization over a number of second order meanings that diminutives develop into, for example picking out individuated forms in a partitive frame, e.g., Yiddish *der samd* "sand," *dos zemdl* "grain of sand" (Jurafsky 1996: 555), or serving as a hedge, e.g., Jp. *chotto* as in:

(26) Taroo wa *chotto* iji   ga   warui.
      Taroo TOP DIM   character SUBJ bad (nasty)
      "Taroo is somewhat/kinda nasty."

(Yoshiko Matsumoto 1985: 145)

At the same time as allowing a single generalization over a variety of shifts to second order predicate status, it also captures an essential feature of semantic changes: only certain aspects of a source lexeme or concept are inherited in the target domain. Which aspects are selected can be accounted for in part in terms of prototype theories

---

[18] It is not clear why this should be regarded as a separate mechanism, rather than as the result of metaphorical and metonymic processes.

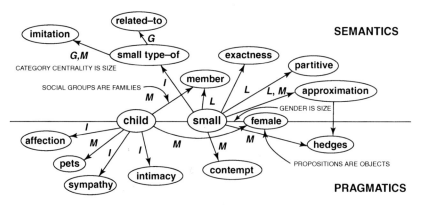

Figure 2.6. Proposed universal structure for the semantics of the diminutive (Jurafsky 1996: 542).

of salience. If the source terms refer to concrete physical entities, size and location may be salient, e.g. what is salient about eyes is not that they comes in pairs (in humans) but rather that they are central to the face and attention-getting (Brown and Witkowski 1983 [see 2.2.3]); what is salient about legs is again not that they come in pairs, but they are the basis on which one stands (the foot of the hill is the base of the hill); what is salient about a mouth is not that teeth and lips are inside but that it is the entry-point of food or the exit-point of language (the mouth of a cave is the entry–exit point) (see Heine 1997). Which aspects are selected can also be accounted for in terms of IINs. These always abstract away from the particulars of the expression in question. Furthermore, they can be accounted for in terms of interlocutors' interaction.

Jurafsky's model of the radial category of diminutive is reproduced here in figure 2.6 as an example of an attempt to combine recent work on semantic change that brings together theories of semantic field, metaphoric change (M), invited inferencing (I),[19] generalization (G), his lambda-extraction (L), and grammaticalization. In addition the changes show evidence, Jurafsky argues, for the often-observed shift from what he calls "real-world reference" (e.g. *child*) to meanings based in purely linguistic categories (e.g. exactness) and speaker-based, discourse meanings (e.g. hedges). This type of change will be discussed in greater detail in the next section.

2.3.4 Subjectification and intersubjectification

Subjectification as a factor in change came to be of particular interest in the context of discussion of grammaticalization. However, it is typical of semantic

---

[19] Jurafsky cites only "(context-induced) inferencing," using the terminology of e.g. Traugott (1989), Heine, Claudi, and Hünnemeyer (1991).

change in general and is not limited to grammaticalization. This is also true of intersubjectification.

As in the case of most contemporary issues in semantic change, the initial work in these areas was synchronic (see especially Benveniste 1971 [1958a], Lyons 1977, and discussion in 1.2.4). The relationship between speakers' experience and grammatical restrictions in Japanese was early identified as a site for the study of encoded subjectivity (Kuroda 1973). Kuroda notes that, in Japanese, speakers make unequivocal declarative statements involving experiencer verbs or similar forms, e.g. desiderative adjectives derived from verbs, only in reference to their own experience or mental state. It is not possible to make such direct statements in reference to the mental state or experience of a second or third person. Consider (27):

(27) a. Watakusi wa sakana o   tabe-tai.
          I   TOP fish   DO eat-DESID
          "I want to eat fish."

      b. *Sensei wa sakana o   tabe-tai.
          teacher TOP fish   DO eat-DESID
          *"The teacher wants to eat fish." (or, if spoken by a student to a teacher:
          *"You want to eat fish.")

(27b) is not acceptable, no matter whether *sensei* is used with second or third person reference. In order to express such an experiencer concept in reference to a second or third person, one must use a grammatical form that embeds that proposition in the speaker's point of view, e.g. by means of a form expressing probability:

(27) c. Sensei wa sakana o   tabe-tai   desyoo.
          teacher TOP fish   DO eat-DESID PROB
          "The teacher/you probably want(s) to eat fish / The teacher/you must
          want to eat fish."

As indicated by the second gloss of (27c), *desyoo* expresses strong epistemic probability from the point of view of the speaker. Professional translators often render predicates containing *desyoo* with phrases such as "I think that . . ."

Such constraints are not unique to Japanese. Consider the following in English:

(28) a. I am thirsty. ??Am I thirsty?[20]

      b. ??You are thirsty. Are you thirsty?

---

[20] (28) is not to be confused with the exclamatory *Am I thirsty!*, which has a variety of different syntactic constraints, as well as a different intonation envelope and a different illocutionary force (see Rosengren 1992, 1994).

The oddity of *You are thirsty* and *Am I thirsty?* can be considered a function of constraints on cognitive access to states of mind and epistemological stances. A speaker does not have access to an addressee's mind, hence it is odd to affirm something about that person's mind unless there is direct evidence such as fainting, or the interlocutor's own admission. On the other hand, a speaker does have access to his or her own mind, so it is odd to question one's own state of mind, except perhaps as a mocking response to a locution like *You are thirsty*, or on awakening from an unconscious daze. Likewise it is more appropriate to say *I think, I guess* than *You think, You guess*, hence the high frequency of the first expression but not the second (see Thompson and Mulac 1991).

Despite their first person pronoun, *I think, I guess* can be used not only to express subjective stance, but also to acknowledge possible intersubjective "image-saving" needs. They may therefore serve in certain contexts as expressions of politeness, hedges, and other mitigators of statements that might be controversial (G. Lakoff 1972), alongside such expressions as *y'know, you see*, which highlight the addressee. Both types of expression are of course fundamentally subjective in the sense developed in this book, as well as intersubjective, because saving the image of AD/R is something only SP/W can choose to do. In other words, hedges are grounded in speakers, however much attention is paid to AD/R.

A well-known example of the operation of intersubjectivity (although not always under this name) is the selection of personal pronouns for attitudinal and social deictic purposes. Obvious examples involve the selection of "polite" or "formal" plural forms for singular second person addressees (*vous* "second person plural pronoun" vs. *tu* "second person singular" in Fr., *Sie* "third person plural" vs. *du* "second person plural" in Gm.), or avoidance of pronouns for first person singular and second person singular in Ch. (see Brown and Gilman 1960, Silverstein 1976a, Brown and Levinson 1987 [1978], Held 1999). But there are other uses that have received less attention, such as care-givers' use of first person plural for second person singular:

(29)   Yes, *we* can take the eye-drops.
                    (Registered male nurse, in hospital emergency room, April 1996)

This style "positions" (O'Connor 1994) the speaker in apparent empathy with the patient, as does the waitress':

(30)   What would *we* like tonight?

At the same time, it implies distance since AD knows that under the circumstances, it is impossible or inappropriate for SP to participate in the situation – the nurse cannot put the patient's eye-drops in his own eyes, the waitress should not decide what the client will choose to eat, unless invited to do so.

Example (31) provides an interesting case of the way in which speakers can shift attitudinal positions. The speaker, an agent in an insurance company, projects herself onto the client being addressed in the role or position of first, second, and third person:

> (31)   So say *I* put in 100 a month, *you*'re going to take out $5 a month of that, 5% of the premium. *They*'ll also take out $5 a month administrative charge. And then the mortality cost which will vary depending on how old *I* am and how much insurance *I*'m buying.
>
> (Lewis 1996: 2)

This agent hypothetically positions herself as a client or potential buyer of life insurance, such as AD (*say I put in 100 a month*), switches to the company, but refers to it as *you* (*you're going to take out $5 a month of that*, implying a generic, therefore common practice, and perhaps implying that the addressee is directly engaged in it), then refers to the company in the third person, distancing herself from it in this instance (*they'll also take out $5 a month*), and back to the buyer (*depending on how old I am*), all within the space of three consecutive sentences.

First person (*I*) for second person (*you*), second and third person for first person (*you, they* for *we*), and so forth are all projected from the basic SP/W – AD/R dyad. In this dyad, first person, proximal deixis is the norm for SP/W, third person (often) plural in distal space for others not in the context and above all for anaphors (Silverstein 1976a: 38; and, with a historical perspective, Greenberg 1985). Second person can be associated with first person in proximal space, or with third person in distal space.

Positioning is a strategy that SP/Ws use, drawing on the normative deictic meanings of first, second, and third person. In many languages pronominal forms may also have specially coded meanings that index social space, e.g. the use in Gm. of third person plural *Sie* for polite address to a single second person. Some of these coded meanings may historically have arisen through optional positioning.

A fundamental distinction among politeness markers has been made since Comrie (1976), Levinson (1983: 90), and Brown and Levinson (1987 [1978]). They may be broadly divided into:

(i)   Items that index a participant referred to in the described event, or addressed in the utterance. These are known as "referent honorifics."[21]

(ii) Items that index a participant in the speech event (SP/W or AD/R) without representing that participant as directly involved

---

[21] The term "referent" is used without regard to truth-conditional considerations. The term merely indicates a participant in the described event.

in the described event. Brown and Levinson call these "addressee honorifics."[22]

Brown and Levinson make a further important division between:

(i) Items that convey social attitudes of politeness through usage conventions and conversational implicatures, but which do not encode politeness directly.

(ii) Items that in at least one of their polysemies are procedural and function primarily to signal simple deictic systems of social proximity and distance. In one of the first works to explore Grice's insight that implicatures may be conventionalized as new meanings, Brown and Levinson conceptualize such items as frozen conversational implicatures, "grammaticalized outputs of politeness strategies" (1987 [1978]: 23).

Given these distinctions, terms of address and terms for first, second, and third persons who are participants in the described event (type (i)) serve "referent" functions. Some participants are implicated, and are not coded for politeness. For example, as a term of address, a speaker may use any of various third person expressions in Eng., including last name plus title (*Ms., Mr., Professor, Dr.*) versus first name (*Elizabeth, Richard*) versus familiar name (*Liz, Dick*), as well as the pronoun *you*. In themselves these forms do not convey politeness, but social conventions may motivate their use in ways that convey degrees of such politeness, depending on situation, including the social relationships between participants in the speech event. By contrast, if a T-V system exists in a language (extended sometimes, as in the case of German, to a third person form: *du-ihr-sie*), the *vous* does not refer to more than one addressee (in this meaning); its function is to deictically signal politeness (social distance). It is conventionalized. Although T-V second singular person pronouns refer to AD/R, they are used as referent SDs; such pronouns can index the social status of AD/R only by making reference to him or her as a participant in the described event. In Modern Standard English there is no pronominal referent SD, but in earlier stages of English a T/V contrast between *thou* versus plural *ye* (for polite singular reference) was a standard feature of the language.

In chapter 6 we build on Brown and Levinson's primarily synchronic work and exemplify how erstwhile "politeness" implicatures can come to be conventionalized as referent honorifics, and how referent honorifics can in turn become conventionalized

---

[22] A third type, bystander honorifics, that index relationships to bystanders or overhearers as in Dyirbal "mother-in-law language" (Dixon 1972) will not concern us here.

as addressee honorifics. We will further argue that these changes crucially involve subjectification and intersubjectification.

Like many other aspects of language use, subjectivity and intersubjectivity were first discussed with reference to synchronic attestations. More recently it has become evident that coded subjective meanings arise out of less subjective meanings, and that coded intersubjective meanings arise out of subjective ones.

In the 1980s attention was drawn to the fact that in semasiological change there is a strong tendency toward increase in "expressiveness," which can be understood as subjectivity. An early formulation is to be found in Traugott's hypothesis that meaning change in early grammaticalization is unidirectional, and may proceed along the path in (32) but not in the reverse direction:

(32)   propositional > (textual >) expressive

(Traugott 1982: 257)

This hypothesis was based on Halliday and Hasan's (1976) proposal that there are three functional domains of language, which they call the "ideational," the "textual," and the "interpersonal" components, respectively. The term "propositional" was chosen to draw attention to expression of "content" rather than "context of culture" which Halliday and Hasan include within "ideational" (1976: 26). The term "expressive" was chosen partly to leave open the question of how "*inter*-personal" Halliday and Hasan intended the component to be, since they define it as concerned: "with the social, expressive and conative functions of language, with expressing the speaker's 'angle': his attitudes and judgments, his encoding of the role relationships in the situation, and his motive in saying anything at all" (Halliday and Hasan 1976: 26–27). The choice of the term "expressive" was also intended to leave open the questions of whether all changes are "interpersonal" as well as subjective, in so far as they involve AD, and whether interpersonal meanings were earlier or later than subjectification historically. "Expressive" was roughly equivalent with "affective," "attitudinal," and "emotive" and was regarded as relevant to semantic as well as pragmatic meaning (see Lyons 1995: 44).

Example (32) proved to be a useful hypothesis since it was strong and testable. It provided overwhelming evidence for increase in expressiveness/subjectivity and is the basis of much of what follows in this book. But the ordering appeared to be too strong (see e.g. Powell 1992a, Brinton, 1996: 225 *passim*). To address the problem of ordering, the hypothesis in (32) was revised as a set of tendencies that may overlap:

(33)   Tendency   I: Meanings based in the external described situation >
              meanings based in the internal (evaluative/perceptual/cognitive)
              described situation.

Tendency II: Meanings based in the external or internal described situation
> meanings based in the textual and metalinguistic situation.
Tendency III: Meanings tend to become increasingly based in the speaker's
subjective belief state/attitude toward the proposition.

(Traugott 1989: 34–35)

Tendency I subsumes many changes from concrete > abstract, most especially from physical to mental, e.g. OE *felan* "touch" > "experience mentally," or *agan to* "have for" > "obligation," "ought" (see also the shift from the sociophysical world to the world of reasoning discussed in Sweetser 1990); Kakouriotos and Kitis (1997) discuss the development from Homeric Gk. *phobomai* "be put to flight" > Modern Gk. "fear," and point to similarities in Germanic, where "fear" is related to Old Saxon *far* "ambush." In MdJ *kowai* means both "be (physically) stiff, tough" as in *kowai gohan* "hard boiled rice," and "fearsome, be fearful." This adjective developed from OJ *koFasi* "(physically) stiff"; in LOJ *kowai* (*kohasi*) came to be used with a variety of meanings, all of which involve stiffening of the muscles or psychological tension; these include "exhausted," "painful," "feeling (physically) sick," "piteous," and "embarrassed," as well as "fearsome, be fearful" (Iizumi 1963: 153, Ohno 1980: 35b). As the meaning "fearsome, be fearful" became semanticized, the two meanings of *kowai* came to be distinguished in written texts with different Chinese characters, but the semantic link between the polysemies remains clear.

Tendency II subsumes changes of the type evidenced by the development of *while*. An adverbial phrase in OE, *þa hwile þe* "the time that," in which *hwile* serves as the noun meaning "time," was reduced by grammaticalization to a temporal connective, and later a concessive polysemy arose. Tendency II was intended to cover not only the development of connective (text-linking) meanings, but also "metalinguistic" (or more properly "metatextual"[23]) change – shifts to meanings that reflect on language, e.g. the development of performative meanings of locutionary verbs such as *I recognize* and of adverbials with discourse marker function, e.g. *anyway* as a marker of SP/W's return to a prior topic. An example in Jp. is OJ *sunawati* (< *sunaFati*), a temporal nominal phrase meaning "(just at) the time (when ...)" > EMJ "immediately after, precisely, surely" > LMJ discourse connective "namely." In other words, "textual" covered both contentful and procedural connectivity. As discussed in 1.2.1, *so* may be contentful and introduce a clause of reason, as in:

---

[23] "Metatextual" is preferable since it refers to the act of using language in negotiating meaning through explicit mention of the discourse being undertaken. Use of this term (suggested by Dancygier 1992) allows "metalinguistic" to be reserved for the kinds of corrections that mention prior text typified as "'I object to *U*,' where *U* is crucially a linguistic utterance rather than an abstract proposition" (Horn 1985: 136), as in: *I didn't manage to trap two monGEESE – I managed to trap two monGOOSES.* (Horn 1985: 132; the form of the plural is being objected to).

(34)   She left *so* she could get to Bella Johnson's talk on time.

or it may be primarily pragmatic, and serve to express the speaker's attitude to the textual strategy being adopted, as in (35) ((8b) in chapter 1):

(35)   *So*, our speaker tonight is Bella Johnson.

The important point is that semasiologically where L has an M_1 that does not serve a connective function, and an M_2 that does, then the M_2 can be predicted to have developed later. Furthermore, as we shall see in considerable detail in chapter 4, if L has a connective meaning that is primarily contentful (e.g. *so* "therefore"), and another that is primarily pragmatic, then the pragmatic one can be predicted to have developed later, as a function of increased embedding in the discursive practices of SP/W–AD/R, and most especially as a function of the force of subjectification in preempting material to SP/W's own rhetorical uses in the speech event itself.[24]

Tendency III is the dominant tendency. It involves "self-orientation" (Seiler 1983) and "subjectification," as exemplified by the development of epistemic modality, scalar particles like *even*, concessive from temporal meanings, as in the case of *while* (and, in contemporary English, *meanwhile*). Harkins has suggested that perhaps "the subjectification process has its basis in the human ability to think and say things that are beyond the bounds of the speaker's knowledge; and to talk about things like future events as if one knows they will happen" (Harkins 1995: 275). From this perspective, subjectification is indexical to the speaker's cognitive processes. But subjectification can also be social. As Dasher (1995) notes, the acquisition of socially deictic meaning by non-honorific lexemes and constructions in Japanese likewise represents subjectification (as well as intersubjectification): the point of view (social status and distance) of SP/W relative to AD/R and to referents becomes an intrinsic part of the meaning structure of such items. For example, the verb *agaru* is attested since OJ in various meanings (e.g. "float up, be lifted up") that can be grouped together as "move from a low position to a high position." In MJ, *agaru* is additionally found with meanings that can be characterized as "move toward a (generally) respected location," e.g. (in Kyoto) "go/come in the direction of the Imperial Palace" and (in Osaka) "go/come toward the castle." From the nineteenth century *agaru* became used as a humiliative honorific for "visit (the place of) (SP/W's) superior" (Dasher 1995: 170). In using *agaru* in this honorific meaning, it is SP/W who personally recognizes or awards the status of social superiority to the human referents associated with the place visited.

---

[24] Positing a fourth tendency along the lines of "Increase in metatextual and illocutive meaning" as Wegener (1998) suggests seems unnecessary.

As indicated in 1.3.2, we consider subjectification to be the major type of semantic change. Intersubjectification is subordinate to it, since it cannot occur without subjectification. In our view subjectification is associative and metonymical to the SP/W's act of communication, most especially to SP/W's attitude. This attitude may be toward other referents, as in the case of pejorations and ameliorations (see 2.2 above). Linguistically more interesting is expression of attitude toward the factuality of propositions (marked by e.g. epistemic modality like *probably* and evidentiality like parenthetical *I hear*), and toward the argumentative rhetorical stance being taken (marked by e.g. discourse markers like *in fact*).

Furthermore, in 1.3.2 we claimed that subjectification typically involves making SP/W attitude explicit. While recognizing the importance of subjectification in semantic change, Langacker (1985, 1990, 1999) developed an alternative theory of subjectivity more directly related to Benveniste's distinction between the "syntactic subject"/"sujet d'énoncé" and the "speaking subject"/"sujet d'énonciation." In contrast to our perspective, objectivity, according to Langacker, is associated with placing participants in an event "on-stage" as foci of attention, that is, explicitly, whereas subjectivity is associated with elements of the "ground" (the speech event itself, and its participants) that are unprofiled, unexpressed, "off-stage":

(36) a. Vanessa jumped across the table.
      b. Vanessa is sitting across the table from Veronica.
      c. Vanessa is sitting across the table from me.
      d. Vanessa is sitting across the table.

(Langacker 1990: 17–20)

(36a) is maximally objective according to Langacker because *across* profiles movement without regard to speaker–hearer position, (36b, c) more subjective because the conceptualizer (speaker) traces a mental path to locate the trajector with respect to a reference point, and (36d) most subjective because the (off-stage, i.e. zero) reference point is the speaker. Similarly, Langacker regards (37) as subjective because the earthquake is not directly controlling the event, but rather the (off-stage) speaker is foretelling the event's occurrence (1990: 23).

(37) An earthquake is going to destroy that town.

Langacker's is an approach from Cognitive Linguistics, with attention to situation types, specifically event structures and associated argument structures, i.e. the interface between conceptual and syntactic subject (and object). Most of the examples are constructed out of context. Central to his theory is a "conceptual structure" which involves a subject and an object of conception. The subject is an "implicit locus of consciousness" or "perspective point." "It is construed with

97

maximal *subjectivity* when it remains offstage and implicit, inhering in the very process of conception without being its target" (Langacker 1999: 149; italics original). Not only is the maximally subjective conceptualizer implicit, it is also unaware of self: "maximal subjectivity characterizes an implicit conceptualizer whose attention is directed elsewhere and who thus loses all self-awareness" (Langacker 1993: 451). As a result, event structures, and most particularly choice of syntactic subject, as in the raising construction, are fundamental to Langacker's view of subjectification.

By contrast, our approach is from discourse and from an array of linguistic choices, including modals, deictics, and adverbials, not those restricted to event structure. In our view, subjectivity will have different manifestations in different parts of the linguistic system and may be shown to function differently in strategic discourse than in decontextualized conceptual structure. What seems objective out of context, e.g. active declarative, may be so only by virtue of the value attached to it in discursive modes including academic writing and linguists' constructed examples. Most frequently an expression is neither subjective nor objective in itself; rather the whole utterance and its context determine the degree of subjectivity. This means that from our perspective a sentence such as (36d) is structurally neutral, not maximally subjective as Langacker (1990: 20) argues. He regards the construing subject as the speaker, who is "off-stage," i.e. unexpressed. However, in the context of, say, a phone conversation in which someone is describing a seating arrangement at dinner:

> (38) Max is sitting next to Bill, and Bill is sitting next to Martha. Vanessa is sitting *across* the table.

the inference is not necessarily to the speaker; it could be to Martha. If we imagine the same locution in the context of stage-directions the audience, not the speaker, is the point of reference.

It is true that in relevant linguistic constructions the "objectively profiled subject" may well be attenuated in the process of subjectification. For us this is a matter of construction change (raising) that is consistent with the directionality of semantic change discussed here (less > more subjective); however, it does not pertain to semasiology or onomasiology. In our view, if subjectification occurs, some lexeme L is semiologically enriched, resulting in explicit expression of the newly semanticized subjectivity. Thus in (37) the subjectivity lies in our view not in the absence of overt reference to the speaking subject, but in the explicitness (marked by *is going to*) of the strength of SP/W's commitment to the likelihood of *At some future time, an earthquake destroy the city*. Langacker's theory of subjectification can provide no principled way of accounting for the fact that intersubjectification arises out of subjectification. As mentioned in 1.3.2, in our view there can be no intersubjectification without some degree of subjectification. This is because SP/Ws display points of view in the ongoing interactional negotiation of discourse production; when these encoded points of view come to signal particular attention to AD/R, intersubjectification occurs. Therefore, although Langacker's and our views on the ubiquity of subjectivity coincide, we are using the term "subjectification" to refer to substantially different phenomena, and from different perspectives on theory and methodology. Therefore the issue is not "purely terminological" as Langacker (1999: 150) has suggested.

2.3.5 *Historical pragmatics*

Although most work on metaphor, metonymy, and subjectification within Cognitive Linguistics has been grounded in semantics, pragmatics has never been out of sight. Sweetser's (1990) book, which is foundational for thinking on the role of metaphor in semantic change, nevertheless is entitled *From Etymology to Pragmatics*; in other words, discussion of metaphor is contextualized within discussion of pragmatics, especially of the validity of pragmatic as well as semantic ambiguity (see from a different perspective also Horn 1985).

Other, related strands of work have been conceptualized primarily in terms of a historical pragmatics that focuses on the interface between linguistic structure and its discourse meanings, for example Traugott's three Tendencies (1989; given in (33) above), and her perspective on subjectification (1995a). So has work to be discussed in more detail in chapter 4 that draws heavily on narrative theory, conversational analysis, and especially discourse analysis as developed by Schiffrin (1987). Here the focus has been on foregrounding and backgrounding of material in the narrative story-line (e.g. Hopper 1979, Fleischman 1990), and on markers that signal narrative structure (e.g. Brinton 1996).

To what extent there is a substantive difference between historical pragmatics and historical discourse analysis remains unclear at the time of writing. Both are concerned centrally with investigation of language use over time. We have chosen the term historical pragmatics to describe our work primarily because IITSC is grounded in neo-Gricean pragmatics. Overviews of historical pragmatics from various perspectives are presented in Jacobs and Jucker (1995) and Foolen (1996), and of historical discourse analysis in Brinton (Forthcoming).

Jacobs and Jucker (1995) distinguish two main types of historical pragmatics: "pragmaphilology" and "diachronic pragmatics." These distinctions are based on the type of discourse phenomena investigated. Pragmaphilology is the study of text types seen in terms of religious, legal, pedagogical, and other norms of text production and reproduction. Research along these lines poses anthropological and cross-cultural or intercultural questions. Diachronic pragmatics, by contrast, focuses on the interface of linguistic structure and use, for example, the development of discourse markers (see chapter 4), performativity (see chapter 5), or of politeness markers (see chapter 6), and is primarily linguistic in orientation. Jacobs and Jucker distinguish two approaches within diachronic pragmatics, the one involving "form-to-function mapping" (primarily semasiological), the other "function–form mapping"; the latter is primarily onomasiological, with speech act function as the focus of attention. The present book is a study of diachronic pragmatics in Jacobs and Jucker's sense, with particular attention to form-to-function mapping.

Much historical pragmatics builds on Gricean work. Essential to the debate around what is known as Neogricean pragmatics is discussion of whether there should be a division of labor between the Maxim that he called Quantity1: "Make your contribution as informative as is required (for the current purposes of the exchange)" and Quantity2 ("Do not make your contribution more informative than is required") (Grice 1989 [1975]: 26). Relevance theorists argue that no such division of labor is necessary (e.g. Sperber and Wilson (1995 [1986]). By contrast, the division of labor was upheld, though somewhat differently conceptualized, by Atlas and Levinson (1981) and Horn (1984), among others. Here we outline some of the issues Horn (1984) raises, especially in his work on the logical system of contraries and contradictions, since he explicitly relates it to semantic change.

Invoking Zipf's (1965 [1949]) recognition that much of language use can be accounted for in terms of the competing forces of speaker economy vs. hearer economy, Horn reduces Grice's Maxims of Quantity, Relation, and Manner, and their subparts, to two principles, Q(uantity) and R(elation). These are:

(39)   a.   The Q Principle (Hearer-based):
            MAKE YOUR CONTRIBUTION SUFFICIENT (cf. Quantity1).
            SAY AS MUCH AS YOU CAN (given R).
            Lower-bounding principle, inducing upper-bounding implicata.

       b.   The R Principle (Speaker-based):
            MAKE YOUR CONTRIBUTION NECESSARY (cf. Relation, Quantity2, Manner).
            SAY NO MORE THAN YOU MUST (given Q).
            Upper-bounding principle, inducing lower-bounded implicata.

                                                            (Horn 1984: 13)

(39a) is to be understood as "a speaker, in saying '... p ...,' implicates that (for all she knows) '... at most p ...'" (Horn 1984:13); for example, in saying *Some of my friends are linguists*, I imply that not all my friends are linguists. This is a lower-bounding principle, since, under a principle of Quality, or truthfulness, in saying this sentence I am committing myself to the claim that I have at least some friends who are linguists. It has upper-bounding implicata ("at most p") which are pragmatic and defeasible, since they can be canceled by such explicit phrases as *if not all*, as in *Some, if not/in fact all, of my friends are linguists*. By contrast, (39b) is to be understood as "(a) speaker who says '... p ...' may license the R-inference that he meant '... more than p ...' " (ibid. p. 14); for example, in saying *Can you pass the salt?*, I imply that I want more than a yes/no answer. In saying *I broke a leg*, I imply it was my leg that broke. Geis and Zwicky's (1971) prototype invited inference, conditional perfection: – "if p then q" + > "if not-p then not-q" – is another example of an R-inference.

Horn goes on to suggest that historically there are two types of lexical narrowing that reflect the operation of the Q- and R-Principles, though these may be "synchronically indistinguishable" (1984: 34). An example he gives of Q-based narrowing is *rectangle* on the assumption that "rectangle" primarily refers to any four-sided figures with right angles, including squares. Horn considers the use which excludes squares to be a case of Q-based narrowing, and suggests that such Q-based narrowing is the result of filling a gap in a subpart of a lexical field by a more specific use of the general term (ibid. p. 33, referring to Kempson 1980). An R-based narrowing, however, Horn suggests, is a shift from a set denotation to a subset of the general category; examples given include *undertaker* "one who undertakes" > "mortician" (p. 32); by contrast, broadening is always R-based, e.g. *Xerox*, *Kleenex* (p. 35); here the salient exemplar, e.g. *xerox*, of a wider class, e.g. copy-machines, is generalized to denote the wider class. Attractive as these suggestions are, the historical data do not strongly support the Q-based narrowing hypothesis. Absent any contextual data or time-depth, we cannot be sure in what context or when the narrowing is supposed to have occurred. For example, the first example of *rectangle* cited in the OED is (40), which suggests that the meaning was narrow to start with (i.e. excluded squares), at least in the history of English:

(40)   If one side containing the right Angle, be longer than the other containing
       side, then is that figure called a *Rectangle*.

(1571 Digges, 1 [OED])

As mentioned in 1.2.3, we suggest a different approach to the difference between Q-based and R-based heuristics: Q-based change retards change and is related to standardization. When a narrowing is externally imposed, e.g. by institutional fiat in the case of *harass*, then this kind of narrowing appears to be Q-based. In either case the change is not "natural" since it is acquired through relatively conscious means of transmission.

Horn (1989) makes a particularly interesting hypothesis regarding the operation of the Q- and R-heuristics in an attempt to account for the (near) universal lack of lexical items that denote the negation of the weaker member of a scaled pair.

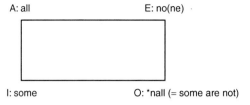

Figure 2.7. The logical square of quantifiers (based on Horn 1989: 254).

He points out that, like English, most languages do not lexicalize O in the logical square of oppositions. This is modeled in figure 2.7 using the square of quantifiers as an example.[25] Likewise, there is no *nalways*, or *noth of them*. Likewise, too, in evaluative lexical fields we typically find *true–untrue–false*, but not *unfalse*, *friendly–unfriendly–hostile*, but not *unhostile*. Horn proposes that the reason for such structural gaps is that negative O would be uninformative and therefore would violate the R-Principle (make your contribution necessary). For example, *some are* implicates that *some are not*; these two representations are informationally (though not communicatively) interchangeable; hence the presence of *some* blocks *nall* (Horn 1989: 245), because it would be redundant and uninformative.

Horn and, building on his work, Van der Auwera (Forthcoming) have shown that while quantifiers and connectives cross-linguistically tend not to have lexical forms of O, modals are somewhat different. In the lexical field of modality, distinctions between E and O may be distinguished syntactically by word order, as in the French example of possibility in (41):

(41) a. Tu *ne peux pas* manger de la viande.
          You not can not eat   of the meat
          "You can't eat the meat." (E: not possible that you can)

      b. Tu *peux ne pas* manger de la viande.
          You can not not eat   of the meat.
          "You can not eat meat." (O: possible that you can not)
                                            (Van der Auwera Forthcoming: 1)

Alternatively, E and O may be distinguished lexically, e.g. in English:

(42) a. John *must not* eat his soup today. (E: It is necessary that not)

      b. John *need not* eat his soup today. (O: It is not necessary that)
                                            (ibid. p. 2)

---

[25] A = universal, I = particular, E = universal negative, O = particular negative (Horn 1989: 11), as in A: *Every woman is happy*, I: *Some woman is happy*, E: *No woman is happy*, O: *Not every woman is happy*.

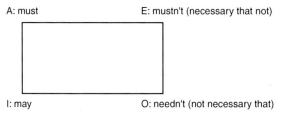

A: must   E: mustn't (necessary that not)

I: may   O: needn't (not necessary that)

Figure 2.8. The logical square of *must* of obligation (based on Horn 1989: 259–260).

This can be shown in the logical square of modality represented in figure 2.8 which models the square of obligation modals.

Historically, in the conceptual structure of obligation /necessity, even though O may be expressed, the representation of E is often derived from that of O. For example, in fourteenth century French

(43)   Il *ne faut pas* que tu   meures.
        it not must not that you die
                                    (Horn 1989: 262; Van der Auwera Forthcoming: 8)

could mean either:

(44) a. It is necessary that you not die. (E)

       b. It is not necessary that you die. (O)

According to Horn (1989: 261–262, citing Tobler 1921 [1882]), in the fourteenth century, although the word order remained the same, the main reading available came to be that of (42a). Basing his study on twenty-nine languages of Europe and India, Van der Auwera (Forthcoming) found that the lower right-hand corner is systematically asymmetric for both necessity and possibility. The distinction may have become vague, as in the case of Fr. *ne pas falloir* illustrated in (43), or a form may have been recruited from a different lexical set, as in English (*needn't*). The important observation for us here is that the hypothesis is that "not necessary that" "may drift towards" "necessary that not" meanings; this is a unidirectional claim; furthermore, it is based on the assumption that the R-heuristic predominates, i.e. there is an enriching implicature from "not necessary that" + > "necessary that not" "which process either renders them vague or gives them a new meaning, with the implicature ousting the original" (Van der Auwera Forthcoming:12). In the following chapters we will show that the R-heuristic predominates in semantic change.

2.4 Conclusion

We have outlined several approaches to semantic change, starting with Bréal's taxonomies of competing changes, and moving on to theoretical approaches that have all contributed to current thinking on semantic change. These include the development of semantic field theory, and advances in work on metaphor, metonymy, grammaticalization, subjectification, and historical pragmatics. We consider the present book to be a contribution especially to the interface between historical pragmatics and historical semantics, building on the various approaches we have sketched in this chapter, especially Neogricean pragmatics.

We now turn to our first detailed case study: semantic change in the domain of modal auxiliaries and particles.

3
The development of modal verbs

3.1 Introduction

Focal points for many of the case studies in this book are modality and deixis. We start in this chapter with selected examples of the development of epistemic from deontic meaning within the domain of modality relatively narrowly construed. Themes are developed that will be shown in later chapters to be relevant to modality more broadly construed.

There is little agreement on exactly how to define modality, beyond the observation quoted in 1.7: "The essence of 'modality' consists in the relativization of the validity of sentence meanings to a set of possible worlds" (Kiefer 1994: 2515). In work on logic, the fundamental types of modality are necessity and possibility in so far as they relate to the truth or falsity of the proposition. In work on linguistics, two related types, deontic (obligation) and epistemic (conclusion), have received most attention, but at least one other is also recognized: ability/capacity (see e.g. Leech 1971, Lyons 1977, Palmer 1990 [1979], 1986, Coates 1983, Sweetser 1990, Bybee, Perkins, and Pagliuca 1994, Kiefer 1994, 1997, Van der Auwera and Plungian 1998). Some brief working characterizations of the three types of modality[1] follow; more detailed discussion of deontic and epistemic modality is provided in 3.2:

(i) *Deontic modality* (from the Gk. *deon* "what is binding"); also widely known as "root" modality (e.g. Coates 1983, Sweetser 1990). This centrally involves

---

[1] Other taxonomies have been proposed because the set of terms "deontic, epistemic" and even "ability" may not be universally generalizable across languages, at least in their traditional logical sense (see Palmer 1986: 20), and because it does not fully account for all aspects of modality. Coates (1983), for example, uses the term "root" for both deontic and ability modalities. Bybee (1985 and subsequent work) has used the super-set "agent-oriented" modality to encompass "all modal meanings that predicate conditions on an agent with regard to completion of an action referred to by the main predicate, e.g. obligation, desire, ability, permission, and root possibility" (Bybee and Fleischman 1995: 6). The category "agent-oriented" has been a major catalyst for cross-linguistic work on modality (e.g. Bybee, Perkins, and Pagliuca 1994, Heine 1995). Nevertheless we do not use this categorization here, because we are not focusing on the main reason for it: the morphological findings associated with grammaticalization.

obligation or compulsion. In his ground-breaking study of modality in language Lyons identified several characteristics of deontic modality. It is "concerned with the necessity or possibility of acts performed by morally responsible agents . . . What it describes is a state-of-affairs that will obtain if the act in question is performed" (Lyons 1977: 823). Also, it "typically proceeds, or derives, from some source or cause" (ibid. p. 824), such as moral or social norms, a person in authority, or some "inner compulsion." Deontics typically involve "language as action" (Palmer 1986: 121):

> (1) Jane *must* go. ("I require Jane to go.")

or, more weakly, permission, e.g.:

> (2) Jane *may* go. ("I permit Jane to go.")

Although the paraphrases suggest that the meanings in (1) and (2) are performative (see Boyd and Thorne 1969, Sweetser 1990), as will be discussed in chapter 5, in our view modals are only indirectly performative. Note that the clauses in (1) and (2) may be reportative as in (3):

> (3) a. Jane *must* go, the boss requires it.
>
>   b. Jane *may* go, the boss said so.

Another kind of weak deontic is advisability. It includes the sense that the action sought of the subject is not only normatively wished for but is also beneficial to the subject, e.g.:

> (4) Jane *ought* to swim if she wants to keep fit. ("It would be advisable for/I advise Jane to swim if she wants to keep fit.")

Although not often mentioned in discussions of deontic modality, advisability plays an important role in the development of some modals in English and is typical of some Japanese constructions that have been considered functionally equivalent to English modals (see 3.5 below).

(ii) *Epistemic modality* (from Gk. *episteme* "knowledge"). This is largely concerned with knowledge and belief (as opposed to fact). Epistemic expressions qualify the truth of the proposition. Most specifically they are used to express the speaker's degree of commitment (short of complete) to the truth of the proposition, e.g.:

> (5) Jane *must* be tired. ("The evidence suggests to me Jane is tired/I conclude that Jane is tired.")

or, more weakly:

> (6) Jane *may* be tired. ("I think it is possible that Jane is tired.")

Epistemic modality shares certain characteristics with deixis, particularly with respect to interactions with tense (Lyons 1977: 819). If the proposition is thought of as an expressed world (the "described event") which is related to an actual referenced world, then epistemic modality can be said to index the degree of distance from the actual world (Frawley 1992: 387–389, drawing on Chung and Timberlake 1985; see also Diewald 1999). *Must* expresses confidence in the close proximity of *Jane is tired* to the actual referenced world, but only the declarative *Jane is tired* expresses SP/W's belief that the proposition coincides with the actual world and is truly "proximal" to it. *May* indicates less confidence than *must* in a direct match between the proposition *Jane is tired* and the actual world, and *might* even less confidence, in other words, it expresses greater distance from the actual world than *may*.

(iii) *Ability/capacity*[2] This is usually construed in terms of absence of barriers to or constraints on events and states of affairs, e.g.:

> (7) Jane *can* swim. ("Jane is able to swim/Nothing prevents Jane from swimming.")

Languages vary considerably with respect to the morphosyntactic categories that regularly express modality, and how many modal expressions, if any, serve both deontic and epistemic functions. With respect to category, in English modality is usually thought to be expressed primarily by auxiliary verbs (the "core" set *can, could, may, might, shall, should, will, would, must*, which has been the basis of most historical work on modality), quasi-auxiliaries (*be to, got to, have to, had to, ought to, need to, dare to, be supposed to, (had) better*), and adverbs and adverbials (*probably, possibly, necessarily, supposedly, in fact, indeed, actually, truly*). If we extend beyond a restricted definition of modality, there are also main verbs, including illocutionary directive and assertive verbs (*to will, require, suggest, insist that*, etc.), and parentheticals (*I think, I guess*) (Perkins 1983, Halliday 1994 [1985]). There are also modal clauses, such as conditional (*if*), conditional concessive (*even if*) and concessive (*although*) clauses which themselves may be expressed in a variety of ways. Even in closely related languages, not only the grammatical categories but also the precise polysemies available within any one cognate category may differ; an example is provided by *may* in English and its cognate *mag* in Dutch. In English *may* can be used in both (8a) and (8b):

> (8) a. You *may* leave now. (permission)
>
>   b. To get to the station you *may* take bus 66. ("It is possible to take bus 66 to get to the station.")

---

[2] Ability/capacity are also known as "dynamic" (Palmer 1990 [1979], Plank 1984) or "facultative" (Goossens 1987a) modality.

However, in Dutch only the first meaning is possible:

(9) a. Je *mag* weggan nu.
      you may leave   now

   b. *Om   naar het station te gaan, *mag* je   bus 66 nemen.
       in order to   the station to go   may you bus 66 take

(Van der Auwera 1999: 57)

It is hardly surprising then that languages that share little or no history may vary even more. Nevertheless, at the macro-level distinct similarities can often be detected. Specifically, if epistemic modality is polysemous with the other types of modality it appears to have developed later in the history of the language (e.g. Shepherd 1981, 1982, Traugott 1989, Kytö 1991, Bybee, Perkins, and Pagliuca 1994, Van der Auwera and Plungian 1998). Also, if a language or language variety allows a sequence of modal expressions, such as "double modals" (e.g. *might could, might ought to*), the epistemic modal meaning will be further away from the main verb, the deontic one closer (e.g. Shepherd 1981, Bybee 1985, Montgomery and Nagle 1993).

As Palmer (1986: 123) points out, "there is no immediately obvious reason why the same forms should be used for expressing the speaker's degree of commitment to truth and for getting other people to do things." The prime purpose of this chapter is to account, from the perspective of IITSC, for how the same forms can come to be used for epistemic as well as deontic modality, with focus on English *must*, and very brief discussion of *ought to*. We will also pay particular attention to changes in the scopal properties of the modals (the range over which the modals operate), to the degree of subjectivity adopted by the speaker over time, and to the question why past tense forms of the verbs in question might have come to be generalized to present tense.

3.2   Some more detailed distinctions relevant to deontic and epistemic modality

In this section we elaborate further on distinctions between deontic and epistemic modality that we will be drawing on in our discussion of the development of modal meanings. We start by commenting on some of Lyons' criteria cited in 3.1 above. Specifically we consider the claim that deontics involve agents and explore the nature of the source of compulsion (in its varying degrees). We then discuss claims about differences between deontics and epistemics in terms of generalized necessity and possibility, scope, (inter)subjectivity, and temporality. We end with some comments on similarities in degree or "scale" of strength within each domain.

3.2.1   *Subjects of modals*

The characterization of deontic modality as involving acts performed by morally responsible agents ("obligees") serves as a prototype definition:

normally, a speaker asked to give an example of an obligation expression would choose one in which (in English) the semantic subject is an animate, typically human, agent capable of controlling the activity to be performed, as in:

(10) "You *must* play this ten times over," Miss Jarrova would say, pointing with relentless fingers to a jumble of crotchets and quavers.

(Coates 1983: 34)

However, less prototypical uses do occur. For example, in (11) the subject is human but not an agent, and no act is obliged/allowed to be performed; instead, the subject is semantically an anticipated possessor (of *respect*), and the verb (*have*) is stative:

(11) You *must* have respect for other people's property.

(Coates 1983: 34)

Subjects of deontics are sometimes not even human, as in:

(12) Clay pots *must* have some protection from severe weather.

(Coates 1983: 35)

In MdE deontic and epistemic modals, unlike main verbs, impose no selectional restrictions on their subjects or the verbs that follow them. Subjects may be animate or inanimate, and syntax may be active or passive; these modals are neutral to *there*-constructions, and other characteristics associated with main verbs.[3]

3.2.2 *Conceptual sources*

The conceptual source of obligation/permission in prototypical deontics is human: "[t]here is some force that is characterized by an 'element of will'" (Jespersen 1924: 320–321), i.e., that has "an interest in an event either occurring or not occurring" (Heine 1995: 29). (10) is a prototype example; Miss Jarrova is the source of the obligation; she is trying to impose her will directly when she says "*You must play this ten times over*," as well as expressing her interest in perfecting her pupil's skills. But in a less prototypical example such as (13):

(13) Parents *must* obtain a social security number for their children.

although *parents* are the "agents" who are obliged to bring about the event of obtaining a number, the "force" is presumably government regulation. Any "element of will" associated with this "force" is only indirect; government regulation results from the will of persons, and is exercised through the will of persons, but it in itself

---

[3] However, some modals of intention, e.g. *dare*, *will*, do appear to impose some subject-selection; see Warner (1993: 16–17) for a summary of the issues.

does not have will. In the case of (12), not only is the subject (*clay pots*) not an agent, but the source of obligation (norms of prudent behavior) is also covert and has no discernible element of will.

Sources of deontic modality may be external or internal to the obligated subject; in (10)–(13) the source is clearly external – someone other than *you* in (10) and (11) and other than *clay pots* in (12). Some modal verbs strongly favor internal sources, such as *can* (in the sense of internal ability/capacity), and *need* (internal necessity), see (14a); others favor external ones, such as *may* in the permission sense, and *ought to*, see (14b):

> (14) a. Boris *needs* to sleep ten hours every night for him to function properly.
>
> (Van der Auwera and Plungian 1998: 80)
>
> b. Boris *ought to* sleep ten hours a day to regain his strength.

By contrast, the source of epistemic modality is usually the speaker, who concludes from evidence whether the proposition is true or not, as in (5) and (6).

One influential view of the relationship between deontic and epistemic modality and their conceptual sources has appealed to a "force-dynamics" metaphor. Talmy (1988: 53) suggested that fundamental to deontic modality is the concept of source as a sentient "force" controlling as an Agonist or "focal force entity." The Agonist is typically the Agent in a "psycho-social" interaction (ibid. p. 79); sentences with inanimate subjects such as (12) are said to have an unexpressed (demoted and backgrounded) Agonist, such as *people*. Building on Talmy's theory of force-dynamics, Sweetser suggested that modality crucially involves intentional forces (authority) affecting choices (Sweetser 1990: 52). In the case of obligation modals, choices are restricted by the imposition of barriers; or, in the case of ability and permission modals, choices are expanded by the lifting of barriers. With respect to *must*, in examples like (12) and (13), the modal indicates that SP/W represents the subject's alternatives (whether or not to obtain a social security number, whether or not to cover clay pots in bad weather) as highly restricted. By contrast, in the case of *She can go*, the modal indicates that SP/W either asserts that there are no barriers, physical or legal, to her going (the ability reading), or lifts such barriers as there are (the permission reading); as a result she can exercise alternatives to go or not.

Sweetser further proposed that the epistemic domain should be understood in terms of a metaphorical mapping from the sociophysical world of obligation (the "root"/deontic domain) to the world of reasoning (the epistemic domain). In the case of *must*, evidence compels the subject to the conclusion expressed in the proposition. For example, in the following pair, the relationship in the sociophysical deontic world of (15a) is mapped onto the mental epistemic world in (15b):

(15) a. You *must* come home by ten. (Mom said so.)
       "The direct force (of Mom's authority) compels you to come home by ten."

(Sweetser 1990: 61)

b. You *must* have been home last night.
    "The available (direct) evidence compels me to the conclusion that you were home."

(ibid.)

The subject's reluctance to act implied by deontic *must* is not present in the epistemic *must*. Sweetser attributes this to the nature of reasoning and the value we attach to it.

Despite the attractiveness of such analyses, there are reasons to doubt that the forces and barriers metaphor is a key to the semantic development of either deontics or epistemics. For one, the lexical sources of the modals show little evidence of the semantics of forces and barriers (see 3.3). For another, while extant metaphors resulting from prior developments of epistemic out of deontic meaning may play a role in enabling shifts from deontic to epistemic, nevertheless metaphorization does not appear to be crucial to an understanding of the processes behind semantic change as revealed by the textual evidence (3.4).

3.2.3 *Generalized deontic and epistemic necessity and possibility*

Among non-prototypical deontic sentences with *must* are general objective expressions like (16) meaning "it is necessary for X to do/be Y":

(16) The simple truth is that if you're going to boil eggs communally they *must* be hard. "it is necessary for the cook to boil eggs hard"

(Warner 1993: 14)

Similarly, there are generalized *must*-expressions that are epistemic, like (17) meaning "the only possible conclusion is that/it can't not be that":

(17) All scientific results *must* depend on a rather specialized form of history. "scientific results can't not depend"

(Palmer 1990 [1979]: 32)

In the realm of modal possibility examples such as (18) have been shown to have both deontic and epistemic readings:

(18) or the pollen *may* be taken from the stamens of one rose and transferred to the stigma of another.
     a. "it's possible for the pollen to be taken" (root)

     b. "it's possible that the pollen will be taken" (epistemic)

(Coates 1995: 62)

In these kinds of general modal statements, the source of authority is usually unspecified (Warner 1993: 15); it is always external. We call these general root/deontic necessity (16) and possibility (18a) and general epistemic necessity (17) and possibility (18b).[4] Root/deontic necessity comes close to the kind of necessity logicians have in mind when they speak of deontics as being "alethic" (involving "necessary truths" about some possible world); however, the conditions for the necessity and possibility need not be universally quantified as in alethic modality.

Coates has pointed out that the polysemy between root and epistemic possibility such as is illustrated by (18) is often "problematic" (i.e. undecidable), especially in writing, and has suggested that there is a "merger" of the two in many instances: "instead of having to choose one meaning and discard the other (as with ambiguous examples), the hearer is able to process *both* meanings" (Coates 1995: 61; italics original). By contrast, she suggests that the polysemy between root and epistemic necessity is "unproblematic" (Coates 1995: 56). However, in earlier work she cites (19), which appears to be as undecidable as (18):

(19)   and anyway I think mental health is a very relative thing – I mean, mental
       health *must* be related to the sort of general mentality or whatever other word
       you use of the community you're living in.
          (Coates 1983: 47; she paraphrases these as "it's essential that mental
          health is related to . . ." (root) or "it's inevitably the case that mental
          health is related to . . ." (epistemic)[5])

General root/deontic possibility and necessity appear to have been pivotal in the development of modal meanings in English (see Bybee 1988, Nordlinger and Traugott 1997, Goossens 2000). In each case the earlier modal was underspecified with respect to distinctions between possibility and necessity or deontic and epistemic readings.

3.2.4   Scope

An issue of some debate in modality is "scope," or range over which the modal applies. A distinction between narrow and wide semantic scope goes back to the Stoics. Narrow scope applies only to a subpart of the proposition, while wide scope applies to the whole proposition. In recent years scope has been discussed

---

[4] Not all authors require such constructions to be general, although they require some evidence
that general conditions apply, e.g. Bybee, Perkins, and Pagliuca define "root possibility" as modal
expressions which report "on general enabling conditions" (1994: 178), but cite a very particularized example with *could*: *I actually couldn't finish reading it because the chap whose shoulder
I was reading the book over got out at Leicester Square* (from Coates 1983: 114).
[5] Intonational diacritics have been removed. Coates uses "or." However, "+>" would be more
consistent with our view.

primarily in connection with adverbs (e.g. Jackendoff 1972), negation, quantifiers, and modals (e.g. Horn 1972, 1984, 1989). An example in the domain of negation is the ambiguity in:

(20) All the girl scouts did*n't* attend.

This can be understood as:

(21) a. Some of the girl scouts attended, but not all. [girl scouts, attended (NOT all)] (narrow scope)

b. None of the girl scouts attended. [NOT (all girl scouts, attended)] (wide scope)

A similar scope distinction can be seen in:

(22) a. She ran *happily*. (narrow scope; *happily* modifies the verb *ran*, and is subject-oriented: "She was happy.")

b. *Happily*, she ran. (wide scope; *happily* modifies the proposition *she ran*, and is speaker-oriented: "I am happy to say she ran.")

A correlation has sometimes been made between deontics and narrow scope on the one hand and epistemics and wide scope on the other (e.g. Bybee 1988). However, general root/deontic necessity and general root/deontic possibility expressions involve wide scope (Nordlinger and Traugott 1997). Thus deontic *must* in (10) has narrow scope over the agent *you*, whereas deontic necessity *must* in (16) has wide scope. They are repeated here with a scope analysis:

(23) a. "You *must* play this ten times over," Miss Jarrova would say. [(MUST you) play this] (narrow scope "it is required of you you play this")

b. The simple truth is that if you're going to boil eggs communally they *must* be hard. [MUST(eggs be hard)] (wide scope "it is required, eggs boil till hard")

In 3.4.1 we will show that the development of wide scope root/deontic necessity meanings is one factor that enabled the development of epistemic meanings, in other words, wide scope deontic uses developed before epistemic meanings became semanticized.

3.2.5 *(Inter)subjectivity*

Sometimes narrow vs. wide scope appears to be conflated with low vs. high subjectivity (see e.g. Palmer 1986, Gamon 1994). Subjectivity is, however, not the same as scope (Nordlinger and Traugott 1997). Modals, whether deontic or epistemic, can express more or less subjective viewpoints depending on the extent to which they represent the attitudes, opinions, or conclusions of the speaker (Lyons 1977: 797ff.).

Although logicians have long been concerned with objective necessity and possibility, in natural languages modality is strongly bound up with subjectivity. For example, building on Lyons (1977: 452), Palmer proposed that: "Modality in language is ... concerned with subjective characteristics of an utterance, and it could even be further argued that subjectivity is an essential criterion for modality" (Palmer 1986: 16). But as his use in this quotation of the modal *could* implies, Palmer cautions that not all modal utterances are subjective. *You must leave at once* could be a subjective insistence by the speaker or a general (relatively objective) comment on an inescapable state of affairs over which neither speaker nor addressee has any control (ibid. p. 17). Some linguistic deontics do express universal truths (at least as construed by speakers), e.g. *All men must die*, and, as we have seen, deontic necessity and possibility can concern general conditions. Furthermore, the modality of ability is not subjective (Hoye 1997: 43), and there is a considerable conceptual distance between weakly subjective modals that appeal to norms and regularities and strongly subjective epistemic modals that are based solely on the speaker's opinions and beliefs. Finally, even epistemics that are based in speaker judgment rather than general truths can range from less to more subjective. Sanders and Spooren (1996), for example, suggest a complex cline for epistemic subjectivity in Dutch based on two kinds of evidence: knowledge-based and observation-based. Later in this chapter we will see how meanings have become increasingly subjective over the history of both deontic and epistemic *must* and *ought to*.

With respect to deontics, there is a cline of subjectivity from objective (the source of obligation is universal) to subjective (the source of obligation is the speaker). According to Myhill there is in addition what in our terms is an intersubjective use of many deontic modals that deserves attention. Basing his studies (1995, 1996, 1997) on dialog in late nineteenth and twentieth century American plays, he suggests that there is a set of "group-oriented" uses of modals which can be used "as a rhetorical device to try to convince the listener that there really is general agreement from other people, so that the listener ought to agree" (Myhill 1997: 9). He argues that this intersubjective meaning is often associated with *ought to* in the plays, whereas *should* is associated with individual, subjective opinions. For example, although the uses of *ought to* and *should* might on first thought appear to be interchangeable in (24), they actually reflect acknowledgment of the interlocutor and agreement that the Far East is "where everything's happening" in the first case and a subjective opinion on a different matter, in the second:

> (24) Norman: Are you doing anything relevant?
>
> Dick: You can't get more relevant than Far Eastern studies. Ask me anything about the Far East and I'll tell you the answer. That's where everything's happening. China, Vietnam, Japan, Korea. You name it.

Norman: I guess I *ought to* know more about those things. I don't know, I
keep thinking there's a lot of things I *should* know about.

(1970, Weller p. 131 [Myhill 1997: 3])

Myhill suggests that during the twentieth century, at least as evidenced by plays, there has been a shift away from "group-oriented" (intersubjective) uses of the modals like *must*, *ought to*, and intentional *will*, to more individualized uses of modals like *got to*, *should*, and *gonna*. The tendency Myhill observes in American English is borne out by statistics on use of *have got to/gotta* in spoken contemporary British English. Krug (2000) found that these forms were one and a half times more frequent than *must* in the British National Corpus despite prescriptive warnings against them. To what extent these shifts are a function of particular ideologies expressed in plays, or of social changes as a whole remains to be determined. In any event they are shifts in norms of use rather than semasiological shifts in the meanings of individual modals and are subject to different motivations from those that are the focus of this book.

A particular kind of (inter)subjectivity may be associated with epistemics, especially *may* and *can*. For example,

(25)   She *may* jog.

can mean not only that she is permitted to jog (deontic: something a doctor might say at some point after surgery) or that it is possible that she will run (epistemic: something a coach might say about a team member who is on the list of potential runners), but also:

(26)   I acknowledge that she jogs.

The type paraphrased in (26) seem to be restricted to complex clause constructions, such as:

(27)   She *may* jog, but she sure looks unhealthy to me.

Here the first clause is concessive and presupposes that the interlocutor or someone has said that she runs ("although she may jog, as you say ..."). The speaker grudgingly accepts this, and then goes on to draw some conclusion that does not directly follow from the modalized proposition. Pointing out that it may be used metatextually to relativize the form of the communicative act itself, Sweetser (1990) calls the type of modal use in (27) the "speech act" use (see 2.3.1). To what extent speech act uses of modals are cross-linguistic is not clear at this point. Nor does the textual evidence give precise insight into what historical path individual modals have undergone to reach this stage. However, by hypothesis, since the metatextual meanings are the most (inter)subjective, they are probably the latest to develop semasiologically. Bybee, Perkins, and Pagliuca (1994: 240) treat concessive meanings in general as later stages of modality. This is echoed by Van de Auwera and Plungian, who cite Dutch *mag* "may" in a speech act/concessive sense, pointing out that in Dutch *mogen* "does not have any epistemic meaning (any more)" (1998: 93). Furthermore, as we shall see in the chapter on discourse markers, sentence adverbs that have adversative epistemic meanings give rise to metatextual discourse marker meaning, not vice versa.

3.2.6   Temporality

Prototypical agentive deontics involve an event that is projected or obligated to occur later than reference time. Therefore the reference time of *You must/may leave* is future of the time of utterance. By contrast, prototypical epistemics have present time reference.

(28)   They *must* be reconciled.

is future-oriented in its deontic meaning (obligation), but present (utterance-time)-oriented in the epistemic meaning. However, the correlations are far from uniform. In English, general root/deontic necessity as in (18) has generic present as its reference time. And epistemicity can be future-oriented as in the case of probability:

(29)   The storm *should* be clear by tomorrow.
       (Bybee, Perkins, and Pagliuca 1994: 180)

It has often been noted that historically, deontics often give rise to futures (e.g. Fleischman 1982, Bybee, Pagliuca, and Perkins 1991). They are most likely to do so if they have agent-oriented meaning, such as "desire" or "obligation." A prototype example in work on grammaticalization is the development of Late Lat. *cantare habeo* "sing-INF have-1stSg" > Fr. *chanterai* "I will sing." Here *hab-* "have" acquires an obligation meaning and subsequently comes to serve as the future suffix (for various approaches see Benveniste 1968, Fleischman 1982, Pinkster 1987).

Past reference time is available for epistemics. In English it is usually expressed by *have* + past participle following the modal as in:

(30)   They *must have been* reconciled.

Here the speaker's subjective viewpoint is from the present, but the reference time is prior to the time of utterance. (30) cannot be deontic. There is, however, a lexically differentiated deontic of obligation *must* with past reference:

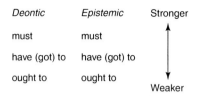

Figure 3.1. Relative modal strengths of *must, have (got) to, ought to* (based on Coates 1983: 19, 26, 31).

(31)　They *had to* be reconciled.[6]

The *had to* modal is less subjective in the sense that the source of obligation is much less likely to be SP/W than in the case of deontic *must*. Since the speaker cannot be the source of the compulsion in a past tense deontic, the less subjective equivalent is used to express past reference.

3.2.7　Scales of modal strength

　　　　The last property of modals to be discussed here is the degree of intensity or "strength" of the requirement or likelihood expressed by a modal. Where ambiguity between deontic and epistemic exists, there appears to be a regular relationship between the degree of obligation and the degree of likelihood that the expressed world/described event is related to an actual referenced world. Thus Horn (1972) points to synchronic matches between deontic and epistemic *must, should,* and *may*, and Coates (1983) to matches between deontic and epistemic *must, have (got) to,* and *ought to,* on a scale of greater to lesser closeness to the actual referenced world. The latter situation is schematized in figure 3.1. Similar matches have been shown to occur cross-linguistically (Steele 1975, Bybee, Perkins, and Pagliuca 1994, especially p. 195).

　　Such matches are further borne out by modally harmonic collocations with adverbs (Lyons 1977: 807, citing Halliday 1970: 331). For example, *must* (but not *ought to*) collocates with *absolutely*, while *ought to* (but not *must*) collocates with *perhaps* (Hoye 1997).[7] Other harmonic collocations involve verbs to which a modal clause is subordinated; for example, *grant* and *request* collocate (in formal contexts) with *may*, but not *must*:

(32)　I request that she *may/*must* leave.

We will see how harmonic relationships of this kind develop over time, not always in tandem, although the outcome, from the general perspective of MdE, is parallel.

---

[6] In some contexts, e.g. embedded in a past tense report on a cognitive state, such as *I thought that . . .*, this could be construed as epistemic, but only with pluperfect ("past in past") meaning.

[7] See especially Hoye's index of modal expressions. Sanders and Spooren (1996) discuss harmonic collocations with Dutch epistemic modals according to degree of subjectivity.

MEANING	Languages
i. NEED	Basque (*–tu bear*)
WANT	Tucano (*ro + ia*)
ii. BE	Abkhaz (*r*), Chepang (*sa*), English (*be to*), Slave (*woleani*)
BE, SIT, STAND	Buli (*bo–*)
FALL, BEFALL	Baluchi (*əg kap*)
iii. POSSESS	English (*have to, ought to*),
BE, HAVE	Chepang (*sa, haŋ*)
GET, OBTAIN, CATCH	Lahu (*ɣa*), Temne (*ba kə*)
OWE	Cantonese (*ying goi*), Danish (*skulle*, English *shall*)
iv. BE FITTING	Lahu (*cɔ*), Mwera (*wandicila*)
GOOD	English (*'d better*), Palaung (*la*)
METE (MEASURE)	Danish (*mätte*, cog. English *must*)

Figure 3.2. Some possible sources of modals of obligation (based on Bybee, Perkins, and Pagliuca 1994: 182–183).

3.3 Semantic sources of deontic and epistemic modals

Before presenting our case studies, we will briefly outline some of the major cross-linguistic sources of modals. Bybee, Perkins, and Pagliuca (1994: chapter 6) provide a detailed study of the larger class of deontic/agent-oriented modality, with particular attention to both the semantic source (they call it the "lexical source") and the target morphology (free or bound element), as evidence for the semantics and morphosyntax of grammaticalization. Here we will highlight only a few points concerning the semantic sources of deontic and epistemic modals, and concerning some typological claims about their paths of development.

Bybee, Perkins, and Pagliuca's data base, much of it synchronic, reveals a number of relationships between source "gram" (grammatical morphemes) and "target" modals of obligation.[8] In figure 3.2 we have selected from their findings and supplemented them with material from English. We have also organized them according to the main source semantic fields involved:

(i)   future-oriented need and desire,
(ii) being or coming into being,

[8] See 2.3.3 for brief mention of their data base and overall aims.

MEANING	Languages
i. FINISH, ARRIVE	Morowa (*golleh*), Guaymí (*reb*) Lahu (*gà*)
ii. BE	Lao (*bpe:n*), Lahu (*phɛ*)
iii. GET, OBTAIN	Lahu (*ɣa*), Mandarin (*de*)
iv. KNOW (HOW TO)	Motu (*diba*), Danish (*kunne*), Mwera (*manya*), Nung (*shang*), Tok Pisin (*kæn, sævi*), Baluchi (*əga zan*)

Figure 3.3. Some possible sources of modals of ability, root possibility, and permission (based on Bybee, Perkins, and Pagliuca 1994: 188).

(iii)   possession, including owing,
(iv)   positive evaluation.

Types (ii) and (iii) are closely interconnected, since there is a cross-linguistic relationship between possessive (*have*), existential (*be*) (and locative (*be at*)); cf. Lyons (1968), Clark (1978).

It is striking that in the sources of obligation modals that Bybee, Perkins, and Pagliuca cite there are no examples in which a barrier appears to be entailed, such as one might expect if Talmy (1988) is correct that forces and barriers are fundamental conceptual structures for modals (see 3.2.2). Furthermore, the examples in figure 3.2 do not entail an active energetic willful force, despite the fact that prototypical deontics have agents as subjects (see 3.2.1).[9]

Ability, root possibility, and permission have partially similar sources according to Bybee, Perkins, and Pagliuca (1994). Verbs of knowing (how to) are especially predominant (note that in English *can* derives from *cunnan* "to have the mental ability" (cf. *know, cognize*), *may* from *magan* "have the physical ability" [cf. *might* "strength"]). In figure 3.3. we organize the source grams into four main semantic fields:

(i)   completion,
(ii)   being,
(iii) possession,
(iv)   knowing,

and add Mandarin *de*, since we will be discussing its development in 3.4.3.

Not all epistemic modals derive from deontics or modals of ability. For example, Bybee, Perkins, and Pagliuca (1994: 205–210) suggest that in some cases verbs of

---

[9] Occasionally an agent-related source is attested, e.g. Italian *and*- "go," which has deontic readings in the present tense, future, and conditional. It is noteworthy, however, that the deontic reading of *and*- emerged only in contexts with inanimate subjects (Giacalone Ramat 2000: 134–135).

befalling, becoming, etc. may become epistemic directly, without an intervening obligation or ability stage. However, in many European languages the sources of the meanings of epistemic modals are typically deontic and ability modals. Bybee, Perkins, and Pagliuca (1994: 195–196, 203–205) note that Abkhaz, Baluchi, Basque, Guaymí, and Lao are among other languages in which epistemics (not always strictly modals, but also moods and conditional markers) have forms cognate with deontic modals (often in a different tense, and greatly reduced by grammaticalization).

Bybee, Perkins, and Pagliuca (1994) develop schemata for development from such pre-core modal meanings as are illustrated in figures 3.2 and 3.3, to core modal meanings (deontic and epistemic), and to post-core modality-related meanings, such as are found in a variety of subordinate clauses, for example "concessive speech act" uses such as (27) above. These schemata are testable hypotheses outlining possible paths of development of polysemies. They form the basis of several more elaborated schemata or "lexical maps" in Van der Auwera and Plungian (1998); in the view of these authors, the dimension of internal or external source is key to modality (see 3.2.2 above), and it figures prominently in their models under the names "participant-internal" and "participant-external" modality. Noting "vagueness" or at least overlap between what we call general deontic possibility and necessity, they suggest that these two are historically bidirectional (however, everything else in their model is unidirectional).

Figure 3.4 draws on their integrated maps of epistemic and deontic developments, with particular attention to the dimensions relevant to this chapter. The prediction from this figure is that elements will develop unidirectionally in the direction of the arrow-head. This will be illustrated by the case studies below. A significant change to Van der Auwera and Plungian's modal map is the arrow from possibility to necessity. We hypothesize that this is unidirectional, since to date we have found no examples of weakening from deontic necessity to permission or ability, although the reverse, strengthening of permission to deontic necessity, is well attested, and illustrated below. Another significant difference from their map is that we treat participant-internal vs. participant-external meanings as overlapping on the margins of prototypical possibility and necessity, rather than as separate meaning types, because the historical record is not always clear that the one type definitively preceded the other. For purposes of this map, subjectification is ignored since it is a mechanism rather than a change in modal meaning. How subjectification correlates with the developments in figure 3.4 will be discussed below.

3.4   The development of epistemic meaning
3.4.1   *English* must

In MdE *must* is a core modal in the syntactic sense of being an auxiliary and in the semantic sense of having both deontic and epistemic meanings; these

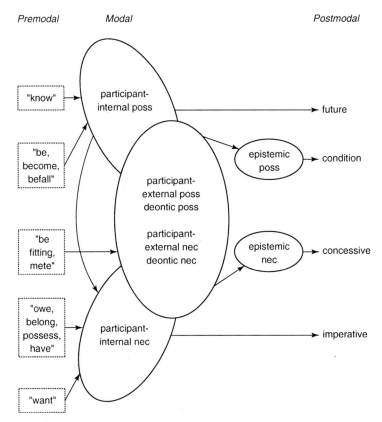

Figure 3.4. Schema for the development of modal polysemies (based on Van der Auwera and Plungian 1998: 98, 111) (in this and subsequent figures, poss = possibility; nec = necessity).

meanings are high on the scale of obligation/certainty. According to Coates, deontic and epistemic meanings were found with approximately equal frequency in her PDE data base: 53% : 47% (1983: 24) respectively. The situation in OE was very different. Syntactically it was originally a main verb. Semantically it expressed ability and permission in earlier OE, obligation only in later OE (*c.* 1000 AC). The epistemic meaning is very rare in OE texts and does not develop fully till *c.* 1300. Therefore epistemic meanings of *must* are considerably less frequent in earlier periods than at present. The broad outlines of the development of *must* are well known (see e.g. Visser 1969, Denison 1993, Warner 1993, from a primarily syntactic perspective, and OED, MED, Goossens 1987a, 1987b, 1999, 2000 from a primarily semantic one) and will only be sketched here. The focus will be on three questions:

(i)   What were the contexts for the development of the deontic out of the ability meaning?

(ii) What were the contexts for the development of epistemic meanings?

(iii) What were the contexts for the generalization of the past tense form *must*?

The OE precursor of *must* was OE *mot-*[10] meaning "be able, be permitted" ("may"). Like other pre-core-modals in English, except *will-* "will," it was originally a preterite-present verb, that is, it expressed completed action resulting in present state ("have come to be able"). Its origins are in IE **med-* "take appropriate measure, be fitting/mete" (cf. *medical, modal, modify, commodity,* etc.), and the OE meanings were inherited from Gothic and Early Germanic *mot-* "ability, measure, have room for." It therefore appears originally to have had a primarily participant-internal (ability) semantics. By the time of Early Germanic a participant-external meaning of permission had arisen, presumably out of the invited inference that what is internally unrestricted may have been made so by some external force or regulation, whether divine or social. The result was a generalization of meaning.

Stage I: must₁*: ability, permission*

Examples of the premodal "ability" meaning of *mot-* in OE are rare. One that reflects the putatively original Germanic participant-internal ability meaning is (33):

(33) Wilt ðu, gif þu *most,*[11] wesan usser her aldordema,
      will you if you able:are be-INF our   army leader
      leodum   lareow?
      people-DAT teacher
      "Are you willing, if you are able, to be the leader of the army, the teacher of the people?"
                                                    (8th century, Genesis, 2482)

More common are examples like (34) with participant-external ability:

(34) Ic hit þe þonne gehate þæt þu on Heorote *most*[12]
      I it you then promise that you in Heorot will:be:able
      sorhleas   swefan.
      anxiety-free sleep
      "I promise you that you will be able to sleep free from anxiety in Heorot."
                                            (8th century, Beowulf, 1671 [Visser: 1969:
      1791])

In (34) Beowulf promises to be the enabler of sleep. One could think of him as

---

[10] The infinitive form of *mot-* is not attested.

[11] *Most* here is second person singular present tense.

[12] Ditto.

promising to be the external remover of barriers to sleep. In this sense he is also "permitting" sleep. We have here at least an IIN of permission; on the other hand, we may also have indeterminacy between the older and the newer reading.

Unambiguous permission and prohibition uses are far more frequent than ability uses (Goossens 1987a). Aelfric uses *mot-* to translate Lat. *licere* in his Latin Grammar, e.g. *licet mihi bibere – mot ic drincan* "I am allowed to drink" (Warner 1993: 146). Examples of the OE permission use of *mot-* in textual data are:

(35) a. þonne rideð ælc hys weges mid ðan feo & hyt
 then rides each his way with that money and it
 motan habban eall.
 be:permitted have-INF all
 "Then each rides his own way with the money and can keep it all."

(c. 880 Orosius, p. 21.4 [Traugott 1989: 37])

 b. he ne *mot* na beon eft gefullod.
 he not may not-at:all be again baptized
 "It is not permitted for him to be baptized again."

(c. 1000 ÆLS I, 270.142 [Denison 1993: 425])

(35a) comes from an account of the burial customs of the Estonians; the source of authority is custom. (35b) comes from a sermon by Aelfric; the source of authority is Christian belief. Both examples refer to general situations. But *mot-* is also used in more particularized contexts, most notably in questions where the speaker is asking permission of the addressee (i.e. the subject of *mot-* is participant-external) as in:

(36) *Mot* ic nu cunnian hwon þinre fæstrædnesse, þæt ic
 may I now test a-little thy fortitude that I
 þonan ongietan mæge hwonan ic þin tilian scyle & hu.
 thence judge may whence I thee provide ought and how
 "May I now inquire a little about your fortitude, so that I can judge from what source and how I should provide for you?"

(c. 880 Boethius 5, 12.12 [Traugott 1989: 38])

The permission meaning of *mot-* survived through the ME period, but became increasingly restricted, especially in later ME, when it appears primarily in formulae for prayers, blessings, curses, and oaths, e.g. *so mot I then* "so may I thrive," *cristes curs mot thou haven* "may you have Christ's curse" (MED *moten* 9–12). During the later OE and ME periods, the permission meanings of *mot-* were slowly replaced by *may* < *magan* "have the physical ability."

Stage II: must₂*: obligation/deontic*

In later OE and especially EME a new obligation meaning of *mot-* arose alongside the ability and permission meanings. Some examples are:

(37)   a.   Hit   is halig restendæg;   ne   *most*   ðu   styrigan þine
           it   is holy rest-day   NEG   may/can/must thou   move   thy
           beddinge.
           bed
           "This is a holy rest-day; you may/must not move your bed."
                          (*c.* 1000 ÆCHom II, 42 [Goossens 1987b: 33])

       b.   we *moton* eow   secgan eowre sawle   þearfe, licige
           we must   you-DAT tell   your   soul-GEN need   please
           eow   ne   licige eow.
           you:DAT   not   please   you:DAT
           "we must tell you about your soul's need, whether it please you or not."
                  (*c.* 1000 ÆCHom I, 17 (App) 182.240 [Goossens 1987b: 32])

       c.   Ac ðanne hit is þin wille ðat ic ðe   loc   ofrin *mote*.
           but then   it   is thy will   that I   thee sacrifice   offer must
           "But then it is Thy will that I must offer Thee a sacrifice."
                    (*c.* 1200 Vices and Virtues 85.5 [Warner 1993: 175])

       d.   Ær   ic *moste* in ðeossum atolan æðele   ʒebidan.
           before I   had   in this   black   territory stay-INF
           "Before/earlier I had to stay in this dark place."
                  (*c.* 1000 Fallen Angels 108 [OED *must* v[1] I., 2])

(37a), being negative, collapses distinctions between "not permitted to" and "obliged to not."[13] (37b) explicitly excludes any possibility that the addressee has options (i.e. excludes a permission reading). In (37c), *mot-* is embedded in the NP "God's will" and expresses a high degree of obligation. In (37d) a past obligation is represented. There are no options available to the subject in any of the examples in (37).

How might this scalar strengthening from relatively weak permission to deontic obligation have come about? One factor that has been suggested is that in the context of denied (negative) permission (*you may not*) as in (35b) and (37a) there was an inference (in our terms an invited inference) of "obligation-not-to" (Goossens 1987b: 34). Another is that in the contexts of authorizations such as granting permission for something that is not desired or is regarded as unwelcome an invited inference of obligation arose (ibid.) as in (37b). However, what is unwelcome to one participant may be welcome to another, as in the case of (38), where the permittees (the advisors) presumably welcomed the permission, but Equitius, the individual on who they were permitted to act, presumably did not.

---

[13] This is in keeping with Van der Auwera's (Forthcoming) claim mentioned at the end of 2.3.5 that there is a regular unidirectional shift among modals from e.g. "not necessary that" > "necessary that not"; this change is itself an example of increase in the scope of the modal.

(38) swa þa lærendum   þam   preostum   se papa geþafode
      so   then advising-DAT those-DAT priests-DAT the pope granted
      þæt Equitius *moste* [MS vr. sceolde] beon gelæded to Romebyrig.
      that Equitius should   be   brought to Rome
      "so then the pope granted to those priestly advisors that Equitius should be
      brought to Rome."

      (*c.* 1000 GD 35.19 [Warner 1993: 161])

This suggests that the constraint that the permission granted is unwanted is too restrictive. With reference to PDE, Leech says that examples of event predications in past tense such as *He allowed me to borrow his car* "seem[] to compel the inference 'and moreover I did borrow it'" (1970: 206). It is likely that in OE reports of permission to act invited the inference that the instruction was performed, or that the action granted was fulfilled, thereby reducing the options available both to the permittee and to the subject of the subordinate clause, especially where the authority is all powerful (God in (37c)), or almost so (the pope in (38)). Note that in (38) the request is granted that Equitius be brought to Rome. The textual variant *sceolde* suggests that the intention here is not only that Equitius might be brought to Rome but that he indeed would be; i.e. he is left no options. Because the clause is subordinate to "grant," this is not the kind of strong deontic of necessity or compulsion that could be translated as "so that Equitius had to be brought." It is therefore not a case of obligation but of possibility, cf. "made it possible for Equitius to be brought to Rome." Nevertheless it is by inference higher on the scale of obligation than permission.

Given the number of early participant-external examples of deontic *mot-* and the proposals above concerning the origins of the deontic meaning, we hypothesize that the new deontic meaning of *mot-* developed in the context of participant-external uses such as (38). Few clear examples of participant-internal deontics occur until later ME:

(39) I *moste* han of the perys that I se, Or I *moot* dye.
      "I must have some of the pears that I see, or I will die."

      (1395 Chaucer, CT, Merchant, p. 167, l. 2331 [MED *moten* 3])

Note that *moste* in (39) is not only participant-internal but also first person. This is a more subjective use than most earlier examples, in so far as no social, religious, or other normative force is specified or implied. But not all subjective uses of *must* require a first person subject, or even a participant-internal subject. If it is SP/W who is obligating the non-first person subject, then the source is external to the subject, as in *You must go, I demand it*, but the deontic is subjective because it has been preempted to the subjective self of SP/W. Given the largely homiletic and historical texts of the crucial period of the development of deontic polysemy at the end of OE and beginning of the ME period, it is difficult to tell to what extent subjectification operated on deontic *must* in the early part of the period; however, the examples in the Helsinki Corpus suggest that more subjective uses increased over time during the later ME period. Goossens underscores the unidirectionality of the shift to subjective *must* by showing that whereas in the Helsinki Corpus some 70 percent of examples of participant-external *must* are non-subjective in ME, the reverse is true of the Brown Corpus (a corpus of written American English). Equilibrium was reached in the period 1500–70 (Goossens 2000: 165).

Often subjectivity is masked as more objective obligation. (40) is a particularly interesting example of this masking. Although by inference we understand that the speaker, the Lord Chief Justice, is the human agent who could open the gap, he distances himself from the possibility of acting in this way by using an agentless passive, an indefinite subject (introduced by *there*), and embedding reference to himself within a modalized conditional (*if we should grant this*).

> (40)   *Ld. Ch. Just.*:   There *must* not such a Gap be opened for the Destruction of the King, as would be if we should grant this. You plead hard for your self, but the Laws plead as hard for the King.
>
> (*c.* 1603 Raleigh, p. 1213)

In earlier ME examples of obligation *mot-* involve an obligee that is human or at least a body-part (e.g. *heart*, *hand*, metonymically used for some aspect of human cognition or behavior), but in the later ME period the deontic *mot-* is extended to contexts in which the obligee is inanimate:[14]

> (41)   nota þæt euery centre *mot*   ben also smal   as a nedle   &
> note that every center must be   as   small as a needle and
> in euery equant *mot*   be a silk thred.
> in every equant must be a silk thread
> "Note that every center must be as small as a needle and there must be a silk thread in every equant."
>
> (*c.* 1392 Equatorie of the Planets, p. 26)

In sum, the deontic polysemy arose in OE, and was widely used by the earliest ME period. The development of strong obligation *must* out of weaker permission was a complex process probably involving:

(i)   invited inferences of obligation arising out of the granting or willing into being of projected enabling conditions (38),

(ii)   development of participant-external uses (37a, b), (38).

---

[14] Syntactically this is a case of raising.

Once the deontic polysemy was firmly established, further developments involved:

(iii) extension of participant-external necessity to participant-internal necessity (39),
(iv)   extension of participant-external necessity to nonanimate subjects (41),
(v)   further subjectification.

Stage III: must₃*: epistemic*

A few possible examples of epistemic *must* appear in OE. One context in which epistemic readings are possible or even likely is impersonal constructions (Denison 1990, Warner 1990) and especially impersonals in conditional clauses (which are themselves epistemic), e.g.:

(42) &   raðe   æfter ðam, gif hit *mot* gewiderian, mederan settan.
      and quickly after   that   if   it may be:fine   madder plant
      "and quickly after that, if the weather may be fine, [one can] plant madder."
                                        (950–1050 LawGer 12, 454 [Denison 1993: 300])

Such impersonal examples are rare. If epistemic, they are relatively objective.

Other contexts are general statements, which could be examples of general deontic necessity (with a wide scope reading), but can also be understood as epistemic. Out of context, the following early example might be construed as deontic ("it is necessary for all of us to die"):

(43) Ealle we *moton* sweltan.
      all   we must   die
      "We must all die."
                                        (?8th century Exodus, 12.33 [Warner 1993: 162])

However, Warner (1993: 162) shows that the context is contingent to a particular situation, so epistemic conclusion about an inevitable future is also possible (this could be paraphrased as "it is necessary/it can't not be that we all will die"). Warner describes the situation as follows: "The Egyptians force the Jews to leave Egypt, saying: If you Jews do not leave Egypt, we Egyptians will all necessarily die." If an epistemic reading is correct here, it is presumably one of epistemic futurity, arising out of invited inferences of futurity from deontic obligation.

Examples like (43) in which the subject involves a generalized quantifier are similar to some that in PDE Coates (1983, 1995) has suggested undergo "merger" (see 3.2.3), that is, they are cases in which both root and epistemic readings are equally possible, and perhaps both intended. They invoke general sources, both social and cognitive, and hence wide scope readings. With respect to the history of

English, the term "merger" is clearly inappropriate since in ME the distinction was still emerging.

Constructions which are indeterminate between deontic and epistemic meaning can be considered key to the emergence of semanticized epistemic meaning. Goossens (2000: 161) cites the shift "from participant-external" to "general objective use" as the "first stepping stone" to epistemic readings of *must*, and cites (44a) as an example; another example is provided in (44b):

(44) a. why burieth a man his goodes by   his grete avarice,
           why buries   a man his goods   by ("because of") his great avarice
           and knoweth wel   that nedes   *moste* hy dye? For deeth
           and knows   well that necessarily must   he die   for death
           is the ende of every man.
           is the end   of every man
           "why does a man bury possessions because of his great avarice, when he knows well that he must necessarily die? For death is the end of all men."
                  (1386–90 Chaucer, CT, Melibee, p. 234, l.12 [Goossens 2000: 161])

      b. ho-so   hath with him godes grace: is dede *mot* nede
           who-so-ever has   with him god's   grace his deed must necessarily
           beo guod.
           be   good
           "he who has god's grace necessarily is required to be/we can conclude is good."
                          (*c*. 1450 Life of St Edmund, p. 440)

As Goossens (2000) notes, (44a) is not only potentially epistemic; it also has a form of the adverb *nedes* "necessarily";[15] the same is true of (44b). The collocation of *mot-* with a form of *nedes* is rare in OE, but frequent in ME and EMdE. The MED even devotes several subsections of *moten* to this collocation. It is reasonable to believe that *nedes* played a key role in the semanticization of epistemic *must* (see also Goossens 1999). If SP/W explicitly states that some event is necessarily obliged or compelled to occur in the future, especially if the source is God's authority, law, spiritual awareness, or logic, the inference is readily invited that the state of affairs represented in the proposition not only will be true in the future but is virtually present.

(45) Ah heo *mot* nede   beien, þe mon þe ibunden biδ.
      but he   must necessarily submit the man that bound   is
      "But he who is bound ought necessarily to submit/necessarily submits."
                    (*c*. 1225 (?1200) Lay Brut, 1051 [MED *moten* 2c])

From the perspective of MdE, at least, not only *mot-* but *nede* in (45) are indeterminate between a deontic (it is necessary for a man to submit if he is fettered) and

---

[15] The most frequent forms are *nedes* and *nede*.

an epistemic (it is logically necessary/one would necessarily conclude that a man submits if he is fettered), particularly in a generic context such as this one.

Some unambiguous examples of epistemic *must* appear by the middle ME period, as illustrated in (46).[16] In (46b) epistemic conclusion is explicitly mentioned (*I have concluded*), in (46b, c) *nedes* is used, and in (46c) the subject is generic:

(46) a. He *moste* kunne muchel of art,
            he must know much   of art (cunning)
            ðat þu   woldest ʒeve   þerof   part.
            that you would   yield thereof part.
            "He must know much of art since you are willing to give part of it."
            (*c* 1300 (?1250) Floris (Cmb), 521 [MED *moten* 4])

       b. I have wel concluded that blisfulnesse and God ben the sovereyn good; for
            whiche it *mote* nedes be that sovereyne blisfulnesse is sovereyn devynite.
            "I have properly deduced that blissfulness and God are the supreme good;
            therefore it must necessarily be that supreme blissfulness is supreme divinity."
            (*c*. 1389 Chaucer, Boece p. 432, l. 124)

       c. For yf that schrewednesse makith wrecches, than *mot* he nedes ben moost
            wrecchide that lengest is a schrewe.
            "For if depravity makes men wretched, then he must necessarily be most
            wretched that is wicked longest."
            (*c*. 1380 Chaucer, Boece, p. 447, l. 47)

Examples in (46) illustrate epistemic necessity. They are also relatively objective. Over the later EMdE period we find examples of increasing subjectivity. These do not invoke general opinion as (46a) does, nor are they contextualized in logical reasoning (as for example in philosophical argumentation such as (46b, c), in a trial, or a report of scientific experiment), but simply express the speaker's confidence in the inference being made at the moment. Early examples of genuinely subjective uses of epistemic *must* appear to be:

(47) a. There ys another matter and I *must* trowble you withall . . . hit ys my lord
            North. . . . surely his expences cannott be lytle, albeyt his grefe *must* be more
            to have no countenance at all but his own estate.
            "There is another matter that I must trouble you about . . . It is my Lord North
            . . . surely his expenses can't be small, although it must be an even greater
            grief to him that he has no standing other than his own estate."
            (1586 Apr. 30, Dudley)

       b. *Lady Touchwood:* Don't ask me my reasons, my lord, for they are not fit to
                                           be told you.

---

[16] Goossens (1999, 2000) calls examples of this kind "inferential" rather than fully epistemic.

> Lord Touchwood: (*Aside*) I'm amazed; here *must* be something more than
> ordinary in this. (*Aloud*) Not fit to be told me, madam?
>
> (1693 Congreve, Double Dealer, III, p. 154)

In sum, like the deontic meanings, the epistemic ones appear to have arisen in several contexts. These include:

   (i)   impersonal constructions in which there is no controlling subject, and use in conditional clauses (42),

  (ii)   the invited inference from obligation to act at some generic time that is future of reference time to present probability (45).

The chief one, however, as far as our textual evidence suggests, is

  (iii) wide scope generalized deontic necessity (43).

Here the generalized source of authority as well as the tendency to use generalized subjects invited the inference that what is necessarily obliged to happen in the future is also obliged to happen in the present.

Also noting multiple sources for the development of epistemic *must*, Goossens (2000) suggests that the development illustrates "partial schematicity" or "partial sanction" (Langacker 1987/91: vol. I, p. 69). In our terms, the partial sanctions follow from the IITSC – certain implicatures become salient, but not all, in any kind of semantic change.

The development of *must* discussed here conforms to the predictions in figure 3.4. The particular semantic development of *must* is modeled in figure 3.5. Were we to have clearer data about the pre-Germanic development of $must_1$, we would presumably be able to show the development from premodal "take appropriate measure, be fitting/mete" to participant-internal ability ("ability" $must_1$) directly. Since this had already occurred by OE, we here mark this phase of development indirectly by a broken arrow.

Apparently basing their hypotheses on PDE, Bybee, Perkins, and Pagliuca claim that "[the] contexts in which *must* has an obligation reading and the contexts in which it has an epistemic reading are mutually exclusive" (1994: 200), specifically, *must* has an obligation sense only in future contexts, and an inferred certainty sense in the present with a stative verb or Progressive and Past. Furthermore, they say, "the obligation does not imply the inferred certainty sense," and they conclude that because "*must* arises in contexts with aspectual interpretations distinct from the obligation uses," therefore "the conventionalization of implicature cannot be the source for the epistemic sense" (1994: 201). Instead, they propose a metaphorical source, a shift "from the domain of social obligations and physical necessities applied to an agent, to the epistemic domain that speaks of the necessary conditions

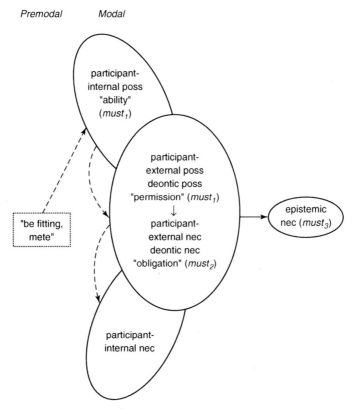

Figure 3.5. Schema for the development of *must₁* to *must₃* (- - ► = reconstructed development).

under which a proposition can be true" (ibid.). An example they give to argue their point is PDE:

(48)   He *must* understand what we want. (or we'll never get it; deontic)

(we've told him so many times; epistemic)

(Bybee, Perkins, and Pagliuca 1994: 201)

In (48) the deontic reading requires that "he" understand in the future (implying that "he" does not understand now), whereas the epistemic reading is stative and present (implying that he does understand now).

Projection from present-day examples of ambiguity to potential loci for change in the past is a useful first-pass methodology, but it cannot lead to definitive recon-struction of mechanisms, particularly in historical semantics, since the outcomes of change via invited inferences can so easily appear to be metaphorical synchronically (see 2.3.2). This is particularly true when the synchronic analysis itself is subject to

	Meaning	OE	LOE	ME	EMdE	MdE
must₁	V of ability/permission	——————————				
must₂	Narrow scope deontic		—————————————			
	Wide scope deontic		- - - - -—————————			
	More subjective deontic		→——→——→——→—			
must₃	Epistemic (wide scope)		- - - - -—————			
	More subjective epistemic			→——→—		

Figure 3.6. Time-line for the development of *must* (in this and subsequent figures, — = attested as semanticized, and continues to period specified; --- = in sporadic use, probably not fully semanticized; ——>— = increase in strength of change).

question. While not rejecting a metaphoric analysis for some synchronic examples, Goossens has argued that there may nevertheless be "a metonymic underpinning (stated differently: in certain contexts the epistemic meaning may be an implicature of the root meaning)" (Goossens 1996: 38, 2000). As an example he cites (19) from Coates, given in 3.2.3 above. On this account, even in PDE there is no necessity for a metaphorical analysis in all cases. As we have seen, several examples in ME suggest that there are areas of indeterminacy or at least overlap between deontic and epistemic *must*. The textual data for the development of the epistemic out of the deontic *must* do not require a metaphorical account of the mechanism of change involved. Indeed, the indeterminacies strongly disfavor such an account although, as is so often the case, general conceptual metaphorical mappings no doubt constrained and enabled the invited inferences to become GIINs and then be semanticized.

Figure 3.6 summarizes the main changes discussed so far across time. It adds to Figure 3.5 the dimensions of scope and subjectification (a broken line indicates highly restricted and probably not yet fully semanticized use; a line with arrows indicates increase in strength over time).

So far we have not addressed the problem of tense. How could it be that the past tense form was generalized, and in fact became the nonpast form in most uses? The past is now periphrastic: *had to* is the usual form of the past tense deontic, and *must have* for the epistemic.

As was mentioned at the beginning of this section, *mot-* was historically a preterite-present form like most premodal verbs in OE. In other words, like *ag-* "possess," *durr-* "dare," *scul-* "owe, be destined/obliged to," *mag-* "be able" (and some non-premodals like *wit-* "know"), *mot-* was a verb that in its origins belonged to a class of verbs that refer to states that come into being as a result of an event, with emphasis "on the state attained and not on the action of which it was the result"

(Prokosch 1938: 188).[17] This class was, according to Prokosch (ibid.) preserved to a far greater extent in Germanic than in other Indo-European languages, and was probably increased in Germanic times (he cites the form of the premodal *cunn-* "can," related to Lat. *gno-* "know"). These verbs, including *mot-*, had etymological past forms in the "present" (i.e. nonpast) tense, and for most, the past tense was innovatively formed in Germanic with a weak (*-t-*) stem.

In OE *mot-* was used for nonpast, *most-* for past time reference. In (37d) past tense agrees with *ær* "earlier, before now." In PDE it would have to be expressed by *had to*. In (38) *moste* is past tense because it is embedded in a report of a past event (granting that Equitius be brought to Rome). This situation continued in ME, but increasingly the past tense form came to be used for nonpast reference, as in (46a) from the thirteenth century, and (49) from about 1400. Lear laments that his daughter told him the truth, but he refused to believe her, and let her go away:

(49) *now wote* y neuer what forto fone, seþ my ij
      now know I not   what to   do   since my two
      doughtres *have* me þus *desceyuede*, þat y so michel louede;
      daughters have me thus deceived   that I so much loved
      now *moste* me   nedes   seche here that *is* in oþere land.
      now must 1sg-DAT necessarily seek her who is in another land
      "Now I do not know what to do, since my two daughters whom I loved so
      much have deceived me in this way; now I am forced to/I have to seek her
      who is in another country."

                                                         (*c.* 1400 Brut, 1333)

Striking here is the present tense context marked by *now*, and the present tense forms of *wote, is,* and the present perfect *have desceyuede* (all italicized in (49) for ease of reference). Lear is commenting on the situation/resultant state he finds himself in, given his past actions. *Moste* seems to be being used at least as an inchoative and perhaps once again like a preterite-present – a past form used to express a present obligation contingent on past actions.

Bybee (1995) has analyzed the generalization of *would, should, might,* and *could* as markers of present or future hypotheticality as in:

(50) If you had that job lined up, *would* Fulbright then pay up?
                                        (Bybee 1995: 503, citing Coates 1983: 211)

She argues that the past forms of the OE modals *scul-* "be destined, obliged to" and *will-* "intend," when used to express future in the past, for example, in subordinate clauses, "offer two areas of vagueness: (i) whether or not the predicate event was

---

[17] Warner (1993: 145) provides a useful list of recorded nonfinite forms of the major preterite-present verbs in OE.

completed; and (ii) whether or not the modality remains in effect" (Bybee 1995: 506). One example is:

> (51) Næs   þæt forma sið þæt hit ellen-weorc æfnan *sceolde.*
>   NEG-was that first   time that it valor-deed perform had:to
>   "That was not the first time that it (a sword) had to perform a deed of valor."
>   (8th century, Beowulf 1464 [Bybee 1995: 505])

At this point in the epic, it has not been stated whether or how the sword was to be used (though addressees probably knew the story already, and we have been told that the sword "never betrayed anyone who used it"). Bybee suggests that in various contexts, most especially in conditional constructions, the continuation of the modality into the present could be implied, as in:

> (52) Quat! hit clatered in þe clyff, as   hit cleue *schulde.*
>   what! it clattered in the cliff as:if it cleave would
>   "Lo! There was a clattering in the high rocks as if they would break in two."
>   (after 1345, Gawain, 2201 [Bybee 1995: 510])

Unlike in the case of the modals Bybee discusses, the past form *must* came to be the only one available, so that we have no pair such as *must–moot* in Standard English on analogy with *should–shall*. The same thing came to be true in the case of *ought to*, as we will see below. It is of course interesting to note that *shall* is coming to be almost entirely recessive, leaving only *should*. The only obligation modal that still retains a fully productive past–nonpast pairing is *have to*, and it has not developed a "hypothetical present" with past form.[18]

As far as *must* is concerned, it is clear that when it meant permission, the embedded past tense uses were of the type Bybee adduces – they left open the question whether what was enabled did indeed occur (see (38)). However, in the context of God's will and other sources of strong obligation, any implicature that what was required might not have been fulfilled is only very weak, and easily cancelable by an adverb like *nede(s)*.

Two factors suggest that the generalization of past form *most-* for nonpast obligation meaning was not parallel to that of *would, should,* etc. as proposed by Bybee (1995):[19]

---

[18] On the other hand, of the pair *might–may*, the hypothetical *might* of possibility and low probability is coming to be replaced by *may* (see Denison 1992). Again, however, a single form predominates.

[19] Other hypotheses are also problematic, e.g., Visser's suggestion that the extension of the past tense form was "fostered" by the fact that the second person singular of the present tense was *most* (Visser 1969: 1805); see (33), (34), (37a). For this to have been a major factor in the development would require that second person singular context predominated in the use of *mot-*. Skeat's suggestion (cited in Visser 1969: 1805) that Scandinavian may have had some effect because Swedish *maste* is used for present and past only pushes the question of origins onto another language. Neither hypothesis provides any insight into similar developments of past-in-present use for most of the modals (cf. *could, might, should, would, ought to*).

> (i) the frequent collocation with *nedes* makes a GIIN of the kind "it is unknown whether the required action occurred" unlikely,
>
> (ii) in the earliest examples, the obligation expressed by *most-* is the result of a new condition.

Factor (ii) is especially clear in (49) – Lear's earlier assessment of his daughters has brought him unexpectedly to the situation where he has to seek out the daughter he had rejected. The context for (46a) *He moste kunne muchel of art* suggests that the speaker concludes "he must know a lot about art" on the basis of newly acquired evidence "you are willing to give part of it." We propose that in the case of *must*, the particular history of the development of strong obligation out of permission led to the salience of coming to be obliged (i.e. present state resulting from some action or condition such as God's or a king's command or will). The scalar strength of the obligation that is expressed by *nede(s)* reinforced the nonpast orientation of the verb.

Evidence that *nedes* is one of the relevant contexts not only for the development of epistemic *must*, but also for the crystallization of the past form is provided by the Helsinki Corpus. All examples of this modal with *nedes* after 1420 have the past tense form *must*, although in other data there continue to be some examples of *mot-* without *nedes* until the early sixteenth century.[20] A late fourteenth century example in which *mot-* and *most-* both appear with *nedes* is (with superscript letters to aid discussion that follows):

> (53) But here þese blynde heretykes, þat ben vnable to conceyue sutilte
>   but here these blind   heretics   that are unable to conceive subtlety
>   of holy writ, schulden furst lerne þer owne wordis. Soþ hit is þat
>   of Holy Writ should   first learn their own words true it is that
>   alle þingus *mote^a* nede   come as God haþ ordeyned, and so
>   all things must necessarily come as God has ordained and so
>   eche dede of Crist *mut^b* nede   be doon as he dide hyt. And
>   each deed of Christ had:to necessarily be done as he did it   and
>   þus, ӡif men schulde not sewe Crist her, fore   he *muste^c*
>   thus if men should not follow Christ here because they would
>   neede   suffre, noo cristene man   schulde sewe   Crist in noo
>   necessarily suffer no Christian person would   follow Christ in any
>   þing þat he dyde, for   alle þe þingus þat Crist did *musten^d*
>   thing that he did because all the things that Christ did had:to
>   nedly   comen as þei cam. And so suche heretykes *musten^e*
>   necessarily come as they came and so such heretics must

---

[20] Elly van Gelderen (p.c.) has drawn our attention to instances of *mote needes* and *needs mot* in the later sixteenth century in the writings of Spenser (e.g. 1596 Fairie Queene Bk. V, vi, 36.9 *That if two met, the one mote needes fall ouer the lidge* ("ledge")); however, Spenser is well known for using archaisms in this text, and these are possibly to be understood as such.

nede   sewen anticrist   and be dampned wiþ hym for
necessarily follow Antichrist and be damned   with him because-of
defawte of here byleue.
fault   of their belief
"But here these blind heretics, that are unable to conceive the subtlety of Holy
Writ, should first learn their own words. The truth is that all things must
necessarily come to be as God has ordained. So each of Christ's deeds had to
be done as he did it. And thus, if men choose not to follow Christ here,
because they think, if they did so, they would necessarily suffer, no Christian
person would follow Christ in anything that he did, because all the things that
Christ did had to occur as they occurred. And so such heretics must
necessarily follow Antichrist and be damned with him because of their belief."

(c. 1400 English Wycliffite Sermons, 416)

Mote[a] and *mut*[b] are in a present context ("true it is that"); they pertain to universal truths and are indeterminate between deontic and epistemic necessity: what is
necessarily expected to occur can be concluded to be true of the present as well as
the future. It can also be true (epistemically in the present) of actions deontically
required in the past, and *mut*[b] appears to be interpretable as having wide scope
("each deed Christ did, necessarily he had to do it"). If so, here is a present form
with implied past reference. *Muste*[c] is embedded in a conditional and is harmonic
with *schulde*. *Musten*[d] might be regarded to follow on in conditional mode, or
could be seen to be in variation (excluding agreement markers) with *mut*[b], since
it is a past form that this time appears to refer to deontically required past action, while inviting the inference of present epistemic certitude. Finally *musten*[e]
is a past form with a clearly present reference. Note that, as in many discussions of predestination, deontic requirement and epistemic truth are inextricably
related.

Although this passage is heavily quantified with *all*, nevertheless it is not only
about universal truths but also about the necessity of coming into being. With respect
to *mote*[d], *musten*[d]: all things, including Christ's deeds, must necessarily come into
being/happen as God has ordained (note the use of *com-* "come"); *muste*[c]: people
are conceived of as avoiding Christianity in case they should come to suffer for
their faith; and *musten*[e]: they are predicted to come to be followers of Antichrist as
a consequence.

The number of examples of past form for nonpast meaning is small in the early
part of the fourteenth century but increases from the earlier to the later fourteenth century, especially in sermons and texts on religious subjects. This is true
of both deontic and epistemic *must*. It is favored, but, as (53) shows, not obligatory in the Wycliffite sermons, which must have had a significant influence on
English.

By the fifteenth century examples of *must* begin to appear in Modal–*have*–V–Past Participle constructions. *Have*–Past Participle is the marker of past tense after a modal (as in MdE *She must have left*), and therefore examples of this construction unambiguously demonstrate that *most-* was no longer understood as marked for past tense. Most examples of *must have* in ME are in counterfactual conditionals, as in (54a); in EMdE they begin to be found in other contexts, especially when *must* is epistemic, as in (54b) (its modern use):

(54) a. yf the kynge wolde have take   any execucyon a-pon   hyt
          if the king   would have taken any action   against it
          he *moste have* take   hyt a-pone alle the hoole   schyre.
          he must have taken it   against all   the whole shire
          "If the king had taken any action against it, he would have had to take it
          against the whole shire."

                                                             (1475 Gregory, p. 195)

     b. *Loveless:*   Sure this addition of quality, *must have* so improv'd his Coxcomb,
                       he can't but be very good Company for a quarter of an Hour.
                       "Surely this new honor (a title), must have improved his coxcomb
                       so much that he will have to be very good company for quarter of
                       an hour."

                                                             (1697 Vanbrugh, II.i.145)

In sum, uses of the past tense form *must* appear to have evolved in situations that replicated the old preterite-present inchoative contexts. In the case of *must* the particular history of the development of strong obligation out of permission appears to have led to association of this type of obligation with coming to be obliged (i.e. present state resulting from some action or condition such as God's or a king's command or will). The "necessity" involved in deontics is the necessity of coming into being, as in (49), or in the case of epistemics of coming to a conclusion, as in (46a). *Must* became the default form for both deontic and epistemic *mot-* by the early part of the fifteenth century (at least in the Helsinki Corpus data) primarily in the context of an adverb harmonic with its high rank on the scales of obligation and possibility (*nedes*).

3.4.2 *English* ought to

We turn very briefly to *ought to* to demonstrate how similar its semantic history is to that of *must*, despite its somewhat different syntax[21] (for a fuller study, see Nordlinger and Traugott 1997). In PDE *must* is usually considered to be a core

---

[21] Much of section 3.4.2 is based on Nordlinger and Traugott (1997), which provides a fuller account of the history of *ought to*.

modal, while *ought to* is quasi-modal since syntactically it does not have all the properties associated with core modals, e.g.

(i) *to* is present in most dialects (in speech it is usually bonded with *ought*, expressed as *oughtta*),

(ii) in some dialects it triggers *do*-support, e.g. *Did she ought to go?*,

(iii) in some dialects it disallows negative reduction; these dialects require *She ought not to do that* (however, others allow *She oughtn't to do that*).

Also, as Coates (1983: 70) points out, "[c]ompared with the other modal auxiliaries, OUGHT occurs relatively infrequently, particularly in written language." In Coates' PDE corpus, epistemic uses are outnumbered by 8 to 1 by deontic uses compared with almost even numbers for *must* (1983: 32, 77) (see 3.4.1).

In PDE *ought to* typically expresses a moral or social obligation on the subject to bring about the state of affairs described by the predicate, and is deontic. Epistemic uses indicate a probabilistic conclusion to be drawn about the likelihood of an event, often on the basis of widely held beliefs. One of the characteristics of *ought to* that has been noted is that the epistemic and nonepistemic uses are often indeterminate. As Coates (1983: 78) suggests, speakers may exploit this possibility in their use of *ought to*, intentionally conveying both an epistemic inferential meaning and a deontic moral meaning in one utterance. An example is:

(55) There may be evidence that day-care or short-stay surgery is just as effective, but of lower cost, than traditional surgery... Therefore providers *ought to* be able to agree to contracts for these services at a lower price.
(after 1978, British National Corpus B2A 1199 [Manfred Krug p.c.])

Meanings of moral obligation in which the subject is animate are at the stronger end of the deontic continuum, but there are a number of weaker uses of nonepistemic *ought to* in PDE that are weaker since they involve meanings such as "it is proper/fitting that," or "it is advisable that." The latter is illustrated in (56):

(56) "I'll make it clear to President Gorbachev that he *ought to* view this outcome of the summit very positively," Bush said.
(1990 July 12, United Press Intl.)

Stage I: ought$_1$*: possession*

Ought to originates in OE *agan*. The form in ME is *ouen* (OE "long a" became "long o" in early ME, and velar $/\chi/$ (spelled g/h) became $/w/$ in the environment of back vowels). This is usually translated as "have, own, possess" (premodal). Its most frequent use is as a transitive verb; the complement may be property, wealth, glory, power, etc. Typical examples include:[22]

(57) se   cing let   geridan   ealle þa   land   þe   his modor *ahte*
      that king caused bring-INF all   those lands that his mother had
      him   *to* handa &   nam of   hire eall þæt heo *ahte* on golde...
      him:self in control and took from her   all   that she   had in gold
      "the king caused all the lands that his mother owned to be brought under his
      control and took from her everything she had in gold . . ."
                        (1042 Chron A [DOE *agan*; Nordlinger and Traugott 1997: 305])

Agan also occurs with nonfinite complements; semantically they are close to
"owe" and involve implied possession and obligation:

(58) tuoege scyldgo woeron sume   ricemenn   an *ahte to*
      two   debtors were   certain:DAT rich-man-DAT one had to
      geldanne penningas fif hundra oðer fifteih.
      pay   pennies   five hundred other fifty
      "there were two debtors to a rich man; one had 500 pennies to pay/had to pay
      500 pennies, the other 50."
                        (late 10th century Lindisfarne Gospels, p. 81 [DOE; Nordlinger and
                        Traugott 1997: 306])

In order to pay off the debt the debtor will have to possess (temporarily) the pennies
due, but at the time at which the debt is outstanding possession is only an implied
obligation. Cases like this are semantically intermediate between the type *have my
house to let* (possessive; the object "house" is referential) and the type *have a letter
to write* (obligation; the object "letter" does not yet exist, and is therefore nonreferential).[23] In cases like (58) the debt is referential, but the pennies to pay it off
are not (yet). Where the object may not yet exist (like the pennies) and especially
where it does not yet exist (like the non-written letter) the semantics of possession is
bleached, and the pragmatic inference of obligation strengthened. Semanticization
of the obligation has clearly occurred when the object is no longer physical, only
cognitive or experiential, as in (61) below.

Stage II: ought₂: *deontic*

By the end of the tenth century or the early eleventh century some
instances occur which, according to DOE (*agan*), "shade into auxiliary uses." From
a semantic point of view, they are shading into deonticity. In one construction the

---

[22] Many of the OE examples cited here are to be found classified and discussed in the *Dictionary
of Old English* (DOE) ed. by Healey et al. (1994) *agan* (entry compiled by Shigeru Ono).

[23] On constructions of the type *have a letter to write* vs. *have to write a letter* and hypotheses about
their semantic development see e.g. Benveniste (1968), Fleischman (1982).

subject is defined in the DOE as "the person to whom the obligation is due." i.e., the subject is in the semantic recipient role as in:

(59) þe eorl ... benam   him al ðæt he *ahte*   *to* hauen.
      the earl ... deprived him all that he ought to have
      "the earl ... deprived him of all that he ought to have had."
          (1140 ChronE [DOE *agan* A.2.b; Nordlinger and Traugott 1997: 306])

In constructions of this type the obligations are secular rights accompanying kingship or other high status. *Agan to habenne* appears to have been an idiom in late OE that might be the equivalent of PDE "have/get the right to." The rights of kings are to obtain taxes, own lands, etc. on a regular basis into the future, and to keep them. In so far as there is a modal implicature in this type of construction, the inference is invited that there is a potential controller of a situation that may not yet have taken place but under normal circumstances has a probability of doing so at a later time. In other words, the construction is weakly deontic, at least by implication.

Another type of construction that "shade[s] into auxiliary use" according to the DOE, involves a subject which is "the person bound by the obligation" (the obligee). This obligation may be social or moral:

(60) ic eow   wylle eac eallswa cyðan, þæt man *ah*
      I you-DAT wish also similarly say-INF that one ought
      seoce men *to* geneosianne and deade bebyrian.
      sick   men to visit-INF   and dead bury-INF
      "I also want to say to you that one ought to visit sick people and bury the dead."
          (early 11th century HomU, 46 [DOE *agan* II A.2.a; Nordlinger and Traugott 1997: 307])

Here the subject is human, and therefore a willful controller, and generic. The source is general social obligation. Since possession is virtually ruled out, (60) appears to be an example of participant-external general root/deontic necessity, newly polysemous with *ought$_1$*.

By the beginning of the thirteenth century we begin to find examples of the type in (61) with participant-internal subjects, e.g.:

(61) Sire ich wes of swuch ealde æ   ic *ahte* wel *to* habben
      sir I   was of such   age that I ought well to have
      wisluker   iwite   me.
      wisely-COMPAR guarded me
      "Sir, I was of such an age that I certainly ought to have conducted myself more wisely."
          (*c.* 1230 Ancrene Wisse, p. 163 [Nordlinger and Traugott 1997: 307])

The deontic meaning of *agan/ouen*, attributing moral or legal obligation to its animate subject, remained its primary modal function in ME. Most uses are only weakly subjective in that the speaker is merely reporting an obligation which is imposed by a conventionalized, accepted set of rules and expectations (such as the Church or the Law).

Around 1300 a new construction is found, one in which the subject can be inanimate as in:

(62) Goddys seruyse *owyþ to* be doun.
      "God's service ought to be done."
                    (1303 Robert of Brunne, Handling Synne 1024 [Visser 1969: 1815;
                    Nordlinger and Traugott 1997: 309])

The wide scope associated with general participant-external root/deontic necessity shows its effect on the construction, motivating increased use with inanimate subjects. These uses focus only on the necessity that the situation represented in the proposition will come to be true, given the moral or legal frame which the speaker assumes to be generally valid. The conceptual properties typically associated with *ought to* in ME (and beyond into MdE) are as follows: the force is social and moral, the obligee is plural, generic or nonspecific, and the event probable. From its beginnings it evokes "universal/societal principles" and is "group-oriented" (Myhill 1997). Possible inferences that individual internal deonticity might be intended can easily be defeased, as in this interchange (where *may* expresses ability, and *will* intention):

(63) *1st Citizen:*   Once if ["If indeed"][24] he do require our voices, we *ought* not
                       to deny him.

      2nd Citizen: We may, sir, if we will.

      3rd Citizen: We have the power in ourselves to do it, but it is a power that
                       we have no power ["no moral right"] to do.
                       (1607–8 Shakespeare, Coriolanus II. iii. 1–5 [Nordlinger and
                       Traugott 1997: 311])

Note *must* would be inappropriate here since its strength cannot be defeased.

In our earlier texts *ought to* is used in only weakly subjective ways; appeal to external values predominates. By the beginning of the sixteenth century we begin to find examples that suggest the speaker is identifying with these values, and is presenting him- or herself rather than society as the force behind the obligation:

(64) they vse to haue a chylde, to go in the forowe before the horses or oxen . . .
      and he taketh his hande full of corne, and by lyttel and lytel casteth it in the

---

[24] This and the gloss below are provided in *The Riverside Shakespeare.*

> sayde forowe. Me semeth, that chylde *oughte to* haue moche dyscretion.
> "they customarily have a youth walk in the furrow in front of the horses or
> oxen, . . . and he takes a handful of corn and slowly casts it in the said furrow.
> It seems to me that that youth ought/needs to have much discretion."
>
> (1534 Fitzherbert, p. 40 [Nordlinger and Traugott 1997: 311])

In other words, later examples of *ought to* can involve greater subjectivity than
earlier ones.

Stage III: ought to₃: epistemic

In later ME there are one or two examples with inanimate or pleonastic
subjects that might be interpreted as having an epistemic reading. But it is not until
late in the EMdE period that we find the first clear epistemic constructions, and even
then they are infrequent. Among the earliest unambiguous examples of epistemic
uses of *ought to* in the Helsinki Corpus is:

(65) For the Attrition having caus'd an intestine commotion in the parts of the
      Concrete, the heat or warmth that is thereby excited *ought* not *to* cease, as
      soon as ever the rubbing is over, but to continue capable of emitting Effluvia
      for some time afterwards.
      (1675–76 Boyle, Electricity, pp. 12–13 [Nordlinger and Traugott 1997: 312])

Being scientific, the context suggests that here we have *ought to* in the epistemic
sense of "can logically be expected to." The EMdE and most MdE examples are
at best weakly subjective, and most tend to be at least potentially ambiguous with
deontic meanings when the subject is animate, as in (66):

(66) these merciless Tyrants murder'd them by wholesale . . . This was a Practice
      so inconsistent with Humanity, that all the People of the World *ought to* have
      resented it; as having much more reason to declare the Spaniards to be
      Enemies to Mankind, than ever the Roman Senat had to declare Nero to be
      such.
                                            (1699 Pola, l.83 [Lampeter])

In (66) the preferred reading is epistemic: "one could conclude that . . ."; however,
moral directive cannot be ruled out. When the subject is inanimate, however, *ought
to* can be clearly epistemic:

(67) If General Motors has a worse credit rating than Toyota, its borrowing costs
      ought to be higher. They are, so there is no surprise there.
                  (British National Corpus ABJ 3828, written data [Manfred Krug p.c.])

More strongly subjective examples grounded in the speaker's personal expectations
rather than those of a wider group are rare. A probable example is (68):

(68) *Q:* And what do they pay you?

    A: Well, they pay, they pay, they are paying me a little bit, I think it *ought to* go up in price a bit.
                (British National Corpus KBX 95, spoken data [Manfred Krug p.c.])

The prediction is that epistemic *ought to* will increase in frequency and in subjectivity over time.

The development of the meaning "owe" into deontic and epistemic "ought" is in broad strokes similar to that of Lat. *debere* "owe" into Fr. *devoir* "ought." In one respect, however, it is significantly different: Fr. *devoir* participates in the full tense–aspect system, but Eng. *ought to* is a frozen form used with past and nonpast meaning. Warner notes that *ouen/ought* came to be associated with *to* by the sixteenth century despite the fact that it had in ME been used with the bare infinitive. It therefore did not become a member of the core modal group. He suggests this is "because it retained the possibility of past time reference and its preterite was interpreted as formed according to the full verb schema of *bought, brought, fought . . .*" (1993: 204). While it is certainly the case that present tense forms occur throughout ME and in the earliest part of the sixteenth century, nevertheless there are several instances even in EME of *ouen* with past tense form but present or future meaning, such as (69):[25]

(69) *Hvte* we nu þankin and herien ure hlauerde.
     ought we now thank and praise our lord
     "We ought now to thank and praise the Lord."
                (*c.* 1200 Vices and Virtues (1) 151/15 [MED *ouen* 5.c])

We hypothesize that, like *must, ought to* had the potential in the ME period to become the default form for nonpast, as in the case of the modals Bybee (1995) discusses in contexts where present results of past actions or conditions are at issue. In (61), for example, if the past tense refers to obligations at the time (*ich wes of swuch ealde*), it also invites the inference that the obligation persisted into the present of t_u. As would be expected for a modal expressing advisability rather than strong obligation, it did not collocate with *nedes* and the present tense forms continued to be quite robust in LME. Given its association with norms it also does not appear to have been strongly associated with preterite-present contexts, which tend to be individualized instances of coming into being. As *owe* came to be specialized to largely financial obligation ("be obliged to (re)pay") it came to replace the older meaning of *scul-* "owe," leaving *shall–should* and *ought to* with primarily modal meanings. What role, if any, *must* may have played in this reorganization of the semantics and form of *ought to* remains to be investigated.

---

[25] See also MED *ouen* 4a(c), 4b(b), 4c(b), 5c–j.

We turn now to a modal development in a non-European language, Chinese, to show the generalizability of aspects of modal development discussed above.

3.4.3 *Chinese* de

In Modern Mandarin (MdMand)[26] there is a lexical verb "obtain" as in:

(70) *De* le   jiangxuejin.
      get PERF scholarship
      "X got a scholarship."

(Chao 1968: 741)

and an auxiliary *de* meaning "be able, be possible, be permitted,"[27] as in:

(71) a. Nan   *de*   qu kan dianyinger.
          difficult get:to go see movie
          "X hardly gets to see a movie/rarely goes to a movie."

(Chao 1968: 742)

      b. *De* weituo daibiao chuxi.
          may entrust proxy attend
          "X may delegate a proxy to attend the meeting."

(Ibid. p. x)

      c. Wo de   xie xiu *de*   liao ma.
          I POSS shoe fix possible well Q
          "Is it possible for my shoe to be fixed well?"

(Yang 1989: 129)

(71c) is an example of *de* used as an "infix" (Chao 1968, Sun 1996), where it is usually translated as "be possible"; however, most examples, including (71c), are of the ability/root possibility type, not, as such a translation might suggest, of the subjective epistemic type. The latter is expressed in MdMand by *keneng*,[28] for example:

(72) Ta *keneng* lai   le.
      3Sg possible come PERF
      "S/he probably has come."
      *"S/he is permitted/allowed/able to come."

De can be found as a lexical verb meaning "obtain" in Pre-Archaic Chinese, as represented by oracle bones (c. 1300–1050 BC), bronze inscriptions, the Books of Odes, and the Book of Documents. In these works Chinese "*de* has not yet acquired the modal usage," according to Chou (1953: 226). The concrete, physical nature

[26] We are grateful to Nina Lin for her extremely helpful research for and comments on 3.4.3.
[27] The permission meaning is found primarily in legal language (Nina Lin p.c.).
[28] Also by other forms not discussed here, e.g. *yinggai* (see Cantonese *ying goi* in figure 3.2).

of the original verb is reflected in the written representation: "The shape of the character *de* in oracle bones depicts a hand holding a shell. The cowry shell is an ancient means of exchange, and it represents things of value. So [*de*] means to obtain or to acquire. There is also the extended meaning of coveting" (Li 1992: 59). Li's description suggests this verb may have had a modal coloring, at least as a GIIN from early on. *De* was borrowed into Jp. with this extended meaning of desire (Nelson 1962).

According to some scholars, *de* "obtain" developed modal meanings in the Late Archaic Chinese period: "*De* is used as a modal to express ability or permission and is often seen in texts and documents of the Spring and Autumn period and later texts" (Chou 1953: 226). For example, in Mengzi *de* is used in the original meaning "obtain, get":

(73) er *de* tianxia.
      and obtain world
      "and have the kingdom."

(300 BC Mengzi, Gongxun Chou [Sun 1996: 112])

and also with a second verb in the participant-external meaning of "allow":

(74) qi *de* bao bi min zai.
      how allow oppress DEM people EXCL
      "How (could he) be allowed to oppress the people?!"

(300 BC Mengzi, Wanzhang [Sun 1996: 113])

According to Sun (1996), "obtain" appears to have been grammaticalized to a modal in this two-verb construction. This would seem consistent with developments in other languages, including English in which *get to* has the modal meaning "can" (see for example, Bybee, Perkins, and Pagliuca 1994: 188, referencing Matisoff 1973, who cite "obtain" as a source for "ability, root possibility and permission"). However, other scholars have questioned the etymological connection with *de* "obtain."[29] (75) below is an example that allows both the permission and the epistemic reading:

(75) wu *de*   you qi yi yi man qi er.
      how allowed/possible[30] possess this one with despise these two
      "How is it allowed/can it be/is it possible that the person who possesses one of these (properties) despises the one who possesses the other two (properties)?"[31]

(300 BC Mengzi, Gongxun Chou [Sun 1996: 113])

---

[29] Alain Peyraube, p.c.

[30] Sun translates *de* as "all right."

[31] The translation given is "How can the possession of one of these (be presumed on) to despise the one (who possesses) the other two?" (from Legge 1984: 214). However, Chaofen Sun and Nina Lin (p. c.) agree that the one given here may be more accurate, given the context.

Such ambiguous examples are either interrogative like (75) or negative, i.e. they occur in contexts that are modalized. In Mengzi the only examples of *de* that appear to be primarily epistemic occur in the context of an already modal verb *ke* "be able/be possible." Since in Archaic Chinese the syntactic subject is often unexpressed, the distinction between ability and possibility is very difficult to determine, and translations often differ. For example, (76) is translated by Lau (1970: 102) with an ability reading as: "Only then were the people of the Central Kingdoms able to find food for themselves" and by Legge (1984: 251) with a possibility reading as: "It became possible for the people of the Middle kingdom to cultivate the ground and get food for themselves."

(76) ranhou   zhong guo   *ke*   *de*   er
     and:only:after:that middle kingdom able/possible able/possible then
     shi   ye.
     eat/feed PTC
     "Only then were people of the Middle kingdom able to have food/Only then was it possible for people of the Middle kingdom to have food."
                                                        (300 BC Mengzi, Gaozi)

In fact, the ambiguity of *de* still survives, and the epistemic reading appears still to be a GIIN that occurs only in already-modalized contexts, such as negatives and questions.

Although a more detailed study of the historical record is needed, if it is correct that *de* "obtain, get" > *de* "can, be possible," it appears that the history of *de* can be summarized as in figure 3.7.

One example of *de* in Mengzi that strongly favors an epistemic reading is:

(77) guo   yu   zhi   *ke*   *de*   hu?
     kingdom desire govern able able Q
     "One may wish for the kingdom to be well governed, [yet] is it possible?"
                                                        (300 BC Mengzi, Gaozi)

Here the epistemic reading is favored because (77) refers to the possibility of the situation desired happening rather than to the king's own ability to make it happen. The compound *kede* is not used in MdMand to denote either "ability" or "possibility." It was, however, superseded by another compound *keneng* from about the Early Mandarin (EMand) period on. In almost all of its occurrences *keneng* is interpreted unambiguously as an epistemic modal of "possibility/probability"; see (72) above for a modern example, and (78) below for an early one:

(78) *ke   neng* tong   shang   yueyang lou.
     able able together ascend Yueyang tower

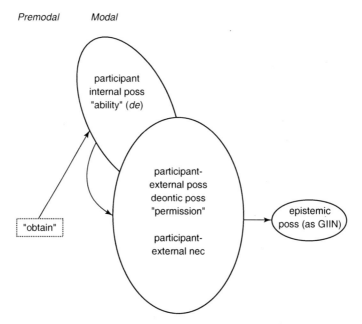

Figure 3.7. Schema for the development of Chinese *de*.

"Is it possible [for us] to ascend the Yueyang Tower together?"
(1200 AC Zhuzi Yulei Scrolls)

Epistemic *kede* derives from *ke* "be able, be permitted/required" + *de*, and epistemic *keneng* from *ke* + *neng* "be able, permitted, willing" (< N *neng* "talent"; see Peyraube 1998). Note that both compounds involve the development of epistemic meanings from verbs that at an earlier time were independently not epistemic; one may hypothesize that the compounds were used to rhetorically reinforce the GIINs that were already in operation, and to make explicit SP/W's subjective doubt with respect to particular situations.

3.5 Conclusion

Not all languages have modals in the strict sense of grammaticalized (auxiliated or otherwise morphosyntactically specialized) verbs. Of those that do, not all have deontic–epistemic polysemies. But for those that do, we have confirmed earlier findings that:

  (i)   deontic > epistemic, not vice versa,
  (ii)   narrow > wide scope, not vice versa,
  (iii) root possibility/necessity > epistemic, not vice versa,
  (iv)   subjectification increases within each domain.

premodal	>	*deontic*	>	*epistemic*	
content			>	content/procedural	
s-w-proposition	>	s-o-proposition			
D-nonsubjective	>	D-subjective			
		E-nonsubjective	>	E-subjective	

Figure 3.8. Correlated paths of directionality in the development of epistemic modals (D = uses in the deontic domain; E = uses in the epistemic domain).

These correlations are summarized in figure 3.8. We have also shown that there is strengthening from possibility to necessity (but not weakening from necessity to possibility), and that the kinds of contexts in which epistemic meanings can arise strongly point to a process that originates with invited inferencing rather than metaphorization (although metaphoric relationships may frame and constrain the favoring of the IINs, then GIINs, in question and may appear to be the result of the semanticization of the GIINs).

The historical development of modals conforms to the regular tendency for semantic change to follow a path to increasingly nonreferential and increasingly speaker-oriented meanings, not vice versa. Like other changes to be discussed later in this book, the acquisition of modal meaning involves the acquisition of procedural in addition to content meaning.[32] These changes are consistent with (but not necessarily projectable onto) what Cinque (1998), drawing on Bybee (1985) and others, has proposed as a universal hierarchy of functional heads for modality/mood from which the linear order can be predicted (in (80) the hierarchic ">" has been replaced by linear " – "; for head-final languages the order is in reverse):

(79) $Mod_{epistemic} - Mod_{necessity} - Mod_{possibility} - Mod_{volition} - Mod_{obligation} - Mod_{ability/permission}$

(based on Cinque 1998: 81)

Our view of Universal Grammar is too parsimonious to endorse Cinque's position that the modal hierarchy justifies positing an innate functional make-up rich enough to include (79). Nevertheless, (79) serves useful descriptive purposes. Synchronically, the whole of the sequence is not found overtly in languages, but varieties of English that allow multiple modals, and many other languages evidence many of the positions. For example, in the following example from Hawick Scots, *will* expresses future (epistemic), *might* possibility, and *could* ability:

---

[32] As mentioned in Chapter 1, see Groefsema (1995) for discussion of modals in terms of procedural meaning (1.2.2), and Nicolle (1998) for the importance of recognizing that forms can have both contentful and procedural meaning (1.2.1).

(80)   He'*ll might could* do it for you.

Historically, the development is *grosso modo* from right to left. Typologically, the semantic–pragmatic motivation for the cross-linguistic onomasiological picture is the tendency to recruit meanings into increasingly subjective semantics (non-modal > deontic > epistemic), wider semantic scope (narrow > wide), and more abstract syntactic structures (control verb > raising verb).

Among the many developments that deserve further study is the role of "preterite-present" semantics in the history of modal verbs in English. We have suggested that it may have been a significant factor in the crystallizing of the forms of *must* by the fifteenth century. Preterite-present is by no means limited to *must*, for it found explicit expression in the modal *have got to* (*have* expresses present perfect, and signals "present relevance of past action/state of affairs"). Derived from *have got* of possession (note the origin in possession again), it came in the nineteenth century to compete with deontic *have to* (which had developed in later ME and especially EMdE), especially in representations of informal speech:

(81)   "Never did sir!" ejaculated the beadle. "No, nor nobody never did; but now she's dead, we'*ve got to* bury her."

(1837/38 Dickens, Oliver Twist [Krug 2000: 62])

In the twentieth century *have got to* acquired an epistemic meaning:

(82)   This *has got to* be some kind of local phenomenon.

(1961 Brown Corpus, Science Fiction MO4: 165 [Denison 1998: 173])

Despite its later development than *have to* as a modal of obligation, (*have*) *got to* in its current spoken form *gotta* has more auxiliary properties than *have to* (Coates 1983: 52) and therefore is a more prototypical model for emerging modals with *to* such as *be going to, want to, need to, ought to* (Krug 2000: 236); also, unlike *have to*, (*have*) *got to* often expresses subjectivity (Coates 1983: 53). More importantly for the present discussion, it has come, especially in informal spoken English, to be used in the form *got to/gotta* (past form for nonpast meaning), presumably as a result of elision and subsequent loss of *have*, obliterating a past–nonpast distinction:

(83)   "I don't know," said Dickie, "but we *got to* do it som'ow."

(1909 Nesbit, 105 [Denison 1998: 173])

However, not all verbs that develop deontic meanings necessarily do so in the past tense, let alone generalize the past form to nonpast meaning. For example, Giacalone Ramat (2000) points out that in Italian although the verb *andar* "go" has deontic meanings in some tenses, it does not have such meanings in the simple past and in compound tenses. The constraints imposed on modal developments by certain tenses and persons for specific verbs in specific languages need to be far better understood.

Another question to be explored is the extent to which languages cross-linguistically express the extremes of deontic scales illustrated in figure 3.1, and hence how universal the strengthening of modalities of obligation to extreme height on the scale may be. As mentioned above, not all languages have (partially) grammaticalized epistemic modal verbs such as have been discussed here that are derived from nonepistemic ones. Indeed, not all languages have grammaticalized modal verbs. Japanese is one such language. However, as Akatsuka (1992) has shown, there are other resources in the language for expressing non-epistemic and epistemic modality. She argues that concessive conditional constructions of the type "S1 *temo*, S2" are analogs of permission auxiliaries in English. For example, requests for granting of permission are expressed as follows:

(84) *A:* Tabe-*temo* ii   desu ka?
      eat-even:if good is   Q
      "Is it all right even if I eat?/May I eat?"

      B: Aa,   tabe-*temo* ii   yo.
      Yeah, eat-even:if good PTC
      "Yeah, it is all right even if you eat/Yes, you may eat."

(Akatsuka 1992: 6)

Obligation is expressed in a more complex fashion: by a double negative in a conditional construction expressed by either "S1 *tewa*, S2" (85a) or, in more formal styles, by "S1 *ba*, S2" (85b):

(85) a. Tabenaku-*tewa* ikenai.
          eat:NEG-if   no:good
          "You must eat."

      b. Tabenakere-*ba* ikenai.
          eat:NEG-if   no:good
          "You must eat."

(Akatsuka 1992: 7)

Akatsuka argues that rather than being defined in terms of necessity and possibility, these (concessive) conditional constructions should be defined in terms of desirability, i.e. of subjective affect rather than of truth and falsehood. She has also argued that the conditional marker -*tewa* itself underwent a semantic change from perfective auxiliary (fifth–eighth centuries) > conjunctive particle (early eleventh century) > negative conditional (twentieth century), a shift from clause-internal to connective to "discourse interactive" meaning (Akatsuka 1997: 331). This is a shift consistent with the larger set of changes that are the topic of this book.

It appears unlikely that strong deontic meanings such as English speakers associate with *must* or even *ought to*, are attested cross-linguistically. Rather, a weaker conceptual category such as DESIRE would appear to be universal. Akatsuka's (1992) analysis of conditional constructions as equivalent to English modals of desirability suggests links to work on putative semantic primes in terms of Natural Semantic Metalanguage (e.g. Goddard and Wierzbicka 1994). Most particularly it suggests links to Harkins' (1995) cross-cultural study of DESIRE. Harkins (1995) notes that in the Australian language Kayardild, the inflectional suffix *-da*, which is readily translated into English "should," is a desiderative[33] (DESID) or perhaps conditional, as in:

(86)   Dathin-a dangka-a dali-*d*.
        that-NOM man-NOM come-DESID
    a. "I want that man to come."
    b. "That man should come."
    c. "It would be good if that man comes."

(Harkins 1995: 141)

At the same time, the changes discussed here underscore the fact that "primitiveness" of some of the primes posited in Natural Semantic Metalanguage must be understood at the general experiential and cognitive level, not at the linguistic level since lexical representations in individual languages are typically derived. The proposed primes include WANT, MAYBE/CAN, the latter in the sense of ability/possibility (Wierzbicka 1994, 1995). Some sources for ABILITY/POSSIBILITY are given in figure 3.3, sources for obligation in figure 3.2. For WANT Wierzbicka (1994) notes that there are also polysemies/homonymies with body parts in Arrente (*ahentye* "want, throat") and Mangap-Mbula (*lele-* "want, insides").

We turn now to another set of changes related to modality broadly construed: the development of discourse markers out of manner adverbs via an epistemic, typically adversative, meaning to a confirming/additive discourse marker.

---

[33] Harkins attributes the term to Evans (1994).

4
The development of adverbials with discourse marker function

4.1 Introduction

In this chapter we move to the development of pragmatic meanings of adverbials (ADVs). The main function of the subclass of ADVs in question, e.g. *in fact, after all, so, then, well,* Jp. *sate* "well," *sunawati* "namely, in other words," in some of their uses, is to signal an aspect of the speaker's rhetorical stance toward what he or she is saying, or toward the addressee's role in the discourse situation. They have little conceptual semantics, and do not contribute significantly to the truth-conditional meaning of propositions, hence some researchers have considered them a subset of "pragmatic markers" or "metatextual particles." However, they mark the speaker's view of the sequential relationship between units of discourse, that is, they serve as connectives between utterances. They are widely known as "discourse markers" (Fraser 1988) or "discourse connectives" (Blakemore 1987).[1] The ones of primary interest to us here have modal properties, in that they reflect aspects of the speaker's epistemic (information and belief-state) stance toward the sequencing of the discourse; they also have deictic properties in that they index the speaker's viewpoint on the proximity or distance within the world created in the text, and do both anaphoric and cataphoric work (Schiffrin 1990b).

There are several other types of pragmatic markers, including those that signal narrative structure. Works on earlier English that are particularly relevant to the present chapter include Hopper (1979) on word order, *þa* "then," and aspect as narrative structuring devices in OE Chronicles; Enkvist and Wårvik (1987) on the role of *þa* in the hierarchical structuring of story, episode, and subepisode also in OE narratives; Brinton (1996: chapters 5 and 6) on *gelamp* "happened, befell, came to pass" in OE, and on *bifel* that replaced them in ME – both *gelamp* and *bifel* signal change in a shift in scene, often temporal, but also spatial; and Manoliu (2000) on the development of discourse markers from proximal temporal adverbials.

---

[1] A survey of the very varying terminology used in connection with DMs is provided in Pons Borderia (1998).

Yet other kinds of pragmatic markers include epistemic parentheticals like *I know*, *I guess*, *y'know*, *I think* (see Thompson and Mulac 1991 for a synchronic account; Brinton 1996: chapters 7 and 8, Aijmer 1996 for a diachronic account); *I promise you* (see chapter 5); and evidentials that indicate the source of the speaker's information, e.g. *I hear* (see Chafe and Nichols 1986). Yet other pragmatic markers are "politeness" markers, which express not attitude to the discourse content but to the participants in it, e.g. *Sir*, *boy*, *love*, *please* (see chapter 6). There are also "focus particles" like *only*, *merely*, *even* (see König 1991, Kay 1997) which foreground and background constituents within clauses, but do not mark sequential relationships unless the constituent is clausal (e.g. *even if*).

Taxonomies of different types of MdE pragmatic markers are given in Fraser (1988, 1990, 1996); Brinton (1996: Appendix A, B) provides extensive bibliographic information on prior work on the specific pragmatic markers she investigates, as well as on typologies of pragmatic markers in MdE. Synchronic accounts of various types of discourse markers in French can be found in Hansen (1998), for German in Abraham (1991), for Latin in Kroon (1995), for Spanish in Schwenter (1999) and for Japanese in Maynard (1993), to cite just a few examples. The major historical study of various pragmatic markers in English is Brinton (1996); Blake (1992–93) discusses a range of pragmatic markers in Shakespeare's work. In Japanese, much of the historical work on discourse particles has concerned the development of topic and subject markers (e.g. Hinds, Maynard, and Iwasaki 1987, Fujii 1991, Shibatani 1990, 1991), but there has also been work on the development of pragmatic markers with a more modal function, such as concessive *ga*, from subordinate clause marker to main clause marker (Yo Matsumoto 1988), and concessive conditional *demo* (Onodera 1995); Suzuki (1999) focuses on the development of quotative *-tte*, and *wake* "you see." Diachronic studies on other languages include Lehti-Eklund (1990) on Swedish; and Abraham (1991), König (1991) on "modal particles" in Gm.

A common thread in the diachronic studies of pragmatic markers is that they are either demonstrably or by highly plausible hypothesis derived from terms that served primarily contentful rather than procedural functions. Not all languages use adverbs; fewer yet use them polysemously in the way we discuss below (see Ramat and Ricca 1998, Swan 1997), but if they do, there is an overwhelming tendency for them to develop from clause-internal or "predicate adverbs" to sentential adverbs, and ultimately to discourse markers or "connecting adverbs" (see Traugott 1995b, Ramat and Ricca 1998: 248 on the languages of Europe). For example, in the context of discussion of grammaticalization, Abraham suggested the following specific path of development for German "modal particles" such as *denn* "after all" < "then":

(1)   (LOCALISTIC) > (TEMPORAL) > LOGICAL > ILLOCUTIVE/
      DISCOURSE FUNCTIONAL
      (Abraham 1991: 373; parentheses added to show that the stage is optional)

4.2   Discourse markers

In a ground-breaking work building on Östman (1981), and Schourup (1985), among others, Schiffrin analyzed certain functions of *and, because, but, I mean, now, Oh!, or, so, then, well, y'know* and showed that they can serve as "discourse markers" (DMs) or "sequentially dependent elements which bracket elements of talk" (Schiffrin 1987: 31). Such brackets may function "locally" between contiguous utterances, without imposing a discourse hierarchy on those utterances, or "globally," in which case they mark episodes, and impose a hierarchical structure (Schiffrin 1992, Solomon 1995). Schiffrin showed that such markers are not, as used to be claimed, "meaningless." Their meanings may be hard to grasp (Longacre 1976 called them "mystery" particles), but they are essential to the rhetorical shape of any argument or narrative. While some of these pragmatic markers (e.g. *y'know*) are restricted to talk or highly colloquial representations of it, many are used in a variety of discourse types, including highly literate expository prose (e.g. *in fact, then*). In Schiffrin (1990b) she showed how certain DMs, for example, *then* as in (2), which is an excerpt from a conversational sequence on academic careers, can serve to express the speaker's attitude to the sequential relationship between the preceding discourse and what is to come:

(2)   The money part of it isn't eh: anything, is it.
      [confirmation and elaboration by addressee]
      Oh I see. And *then* say you wanna get married. Cause it makes it hard.
                                                              (Schiffrin 1987: 253)

Here *then* looks back anaphorically to prior discourse and forward cataphorically to upcoming discourse (in this case that of the addressee, as well as her own), marking it as a subtopic within the larger topic of academic careers. In other words, it is "discourse deictic" (Schiffrin 1990b). It also "creates a bridge" (Schiffrin 1987: 253) from prior discourse time to immediately upcoming discourse time, while primarily serving not a temporal function but a discourse function of bracketing off subtopics as members of a list.

It is the subset of pragmatic markers that create a bridge pointing both backwards and forwards, whether at a local level (as in (2)) or at a global episodic level that has now come to be defined as discourse markers (DMs). For example, referring to spoken discourse, Fraser characterized them as follows: "[DM's] signal a comment specifying the type of sequential discourse relationship that holds between the current utterance – the utterance of which the discourse marker is a part – and the prior discourse" (Fraser 1988: 21–22); "They are expressions which signal a relationship across rather than within utterances, and contribute to the coherence of the discourse" (Fraser and Malamud-Makowski 1996: 864). Because DMs are pragmatic markers signaling local connectivity that connect individual utterances in ways that are anaphoric and cataphoric at the utterance level (Blakemore 1987), they are to be distinguished from what have been called "speech act adverbials" (Swan 1988) or "stance adverbs" (Biber and Finegan 1988), such as *frankly* in:

(3)   *Frankly*, I didn't enjoy that movie at all.

Like many DMs, stance adverbs make explicit the attitude with which SP/W claims to utter or write what follows. However, unlike DMs, they do not link back directly to a prior utterance. Contrast:

(4)   *In fact*, I did not enjoy that movie at all.

where the DM *in fact* evokes a prior comment.

Even though utterances marked by local DMs need not be adjacent, there must be some immediate relationship of the content of an utterance p to a subsequent utterance q in terms of condition, cause, justification, elaboration (e.g. additivity), contrast (adversativity), topic shift (for some typologies of clause types, see Lehmann 1988, Matthiessen and Thompson 1988). By contrast, DMs signaling global connectivity connect larger chunks of discourse, and impose hierarchy on the sequence, typically a narrative one.

DMs are clearly subjective and procedural in that they indicate SP/W's rhetorical, metatextual, stance towards the cohesiveness of the discourse being developed – elaboration of or counter-argument to what preceded, continuation of or change in topic, background, or foreground in narrative. In addition they also often convey conviction, uncertainty, or unwillingness to take responsibility for the truth of what is said, etc. (Brinton 1996), and are in that broad sense modal. Some are oriented almost completely to the speaker and the rhetorical strategy being engaged in, e.g. *indeed, in fact*. Others are more intersubjective in that they have the double function of signaling the type of rhetorical strategy being used (*so* may signal "Listen up: I am going to start the expected discourse"), and at the same time expressing concern for the addressee's "face" – these are usually called "hedges," or "mitigators" and are exemplified by some uses of *well, actually, y'know*, and in earlier Eng., *hwæt*. Brinton (1996) discusses how *hwæt* in verse[2] is typically followed by information about the poet or quoted interlocutor's sources; it signals that what follows is to be

---

[2] Its occurrence in prose is less frequent than in the poetry but, according to Brinton, its function is similar.

regarded as part of the shared knowledge, or common ground, of poet and audience, and it makes explanatory material salient. Alternatively, when *hwæt* is addressed to a second person, it may serve as a reminder of what has been said, or of something that is evident or generally true (Brinton 1996: chapter 7). An example is:

> (5) *Hwæt*! Ic þysne sang siðgeomor fand
> what I this song travel-weary found
> on seocum sefan, samnode wide.
> with sick mind gathered widely
> "What!, I, weary of travel, discovered this song, with a sick mind gathered (it) widely."
>
> (*c.*1000 Fates of the Apostles, 1–2 [Brinton 1996: 182])

This *hwæt* appears to have originated from the interrogative pronoun of the same form, perhaps in a process that we can recapture from the rise in MdE of *Know what?*, which also serves an attention-getting, intersubjective function.

Many discourse markers occur in syntactically marginal positions in the clause; whether it is the right or the left margin depends in part on the word order of the language in question. In Eng. they tend to occur on the left margin (though they can occur in other places as well); in Jp. they may be on the right or the left. In other languages such as Gk. they occur in what is often referred to as "Wackernagel's position," as the second element of the clause.

DMs are highly language-specific in their distribution and function. But nevertheless there seem to be quite similar paths of development at the macro-level. When their histories are accessible to us, they typically arise out of conceptual meanings and uses constrained to the argument structure of the clause. Over time, they not only acquire pragmatic meanings (which typically coexist for some time with earlier, less pragmatic, meanings) but also come to have scope over propositions. If they link discourses on a hierarchically similar level, i.e. if they function at the local level, they can be called "connectives." They may also come to have global functions, marking larger structures, for example episode units in narrative (e.g. *then*), or, in conversation, conversational turns (e.g. *so*). Some may not require any prior discourse, or at least no obviously connected one. For example, *so* may be used to start a meeting, to introduce a speaker, etc. In this use it serves as an attention-getter and a signal that the speaker has something to say of import to the discourse expectations.

We will illustrate the development of DM *indeed* in English, and follow that by a brief discussion of two similar, but, we will show, rather different DMs: *actually* and *in fact*.[3] We then go on to summarize work on the history of *well* (Jucker 1997), which illustrates the development of a primarily intersubjective DM. Finally

---

[3] Thanks to Lisbeth Lipari, who first made the history of *in fact* exciting territory for Elizabeth Traugott.

we turn to the history of Japanese *sate* "thus," which acquired episode marker functions similar to *well (then)*, *so*.

4.3 The development of discourse markers signaling local connectivity

The DM uses of *indeed*, *actually*, and *in fact*, are to various degrees polysemous with other, earlier uses of the same lexeme/construction.[4] For example, *in fact*, the most recent of these adverbs, has three distinct uses in PDE. Consider:

> (6) Humanity, comfortably engaged elsewhere in the business of living, is absent *in fact* but everywhere present in feeling.
>
> (1997 May, UA Hem. Mag. [Schwenter and Traugott 2000:11])

Here the adverb is in a lexical set with *in feeling*, *in law*, etc. and functions as a clause-internal adverb of "respect (to something)." By contrast, in:

> (7) Humanity is *in fact* absent.

in fact is a sentential adverb which may occur in various positions in the clause, and overlaps with epistemic ADVs like *probably*, and concessive ones like *however*. Despite having epistemic modal meaning, it does not contribute much if anything to truth conditions since the truth of the proposition is expressed by the declarative. It is a procedural, expressing SP/W's strong commitment to the proposition *Humanity is absent*, and at the same time introduces a polyphonic perspective: the perspective of an opposing point of view such as *Humanity is not absent/Humanity is present* (see Anscombre and Ducrot 1989, Nølke 1992). The opposition is to something previously either said by another speaker, or by the same speaker. The latter is particularly common in argumentative discourse in which one position is put forward as a "straw argument" and then knocked down. Occasionally, out of context, as here, it simply evokes opposition. Such opposition is usually termed counterexpectation or adversativity. "Counterexpectation" is a term that is often used for propositions that present counters to normative view-points characterizable as "People say/think that X" (Heine, Claudi, and Hünnemeyer 1991: 192–204). It is also sometimes used to refer to the "novelty factor" that is so fundamental to most discourse. For example, in speaking of narrative, Chafe says: "Topics are verbalized when they are judged interesting, which usually means that the speaker judges them to conflict in some way with normal expectations" (Chafe 1994: 135). "Adversativity" is, however, more often used for specific markers that SP/Ws use to signal that they are expressing beliefs or points of view contrary to their own or the interlocutors' expectations regarding the states of affairs under discussion, and we use the term in this sense

---

[4] Section 4.3 is based on parts of Traugott (1995b, 1999b).

(see König 1991, Schwenter and Traugott 1995, Schwenter 1999). In the case of adversative *in fact*, it is one of a large class of pragmatic markers including *actually*, *indeed*, *certainly*, *really*, *in truth*, *truly* (and, in Biblical context, *verily*).[5] It can be said of all of them that they are only called for when "expression is a remarkable and thus highly unlikely value for a propositional schema" (König 1991: 138).

The third use of *in fact* is as a discourse marker the primary function of which is to indicate that SP/W considers that the upcoming proposition is a more precise formulation than the one he or she has used immediately before; in other words, it is monologic. It is conceptually additive rather than adversative. Consider the rather artificial:

(8)   Humanity is not often present. *In fact*, it/humanity is usually absent.

Out of context, the written form *In fact, humanity is usually absent* is ambiguous: it could evoke either adversativity to or an elaboration of something that preceded. In speech, *in fact* in both meanings may have a typical disjunct intonation with a sharp rise and fall; however, impressionistically, the elaborative use (*in fact₃*) can be relatively unstressed, whereas the adversative use (*in fact₂*) cannot. The distinctions between the various polysemies will become clearer as the historical development of this and the other discourse markers is outlined below.

As has long been noted, the position of an adverb is correlated with difference of meaning (e.g. Greenbaum 1969, Jackendoff 1972, McConnell-Ginet 1982, Ernst 1984, Quirk et al. 1985, Cinque 1998, to mention only a few). Allerton and Cruttendon (1974), Aijmer (1986), and Ferrara (1997) further discuss correlations with intonation, a factor that must have been important in the history of the DMs,[6] but which we do not have ready access to in our written texts and therefore cannot discuss here. In (6) *in fact* appears at the right margin of the clause. In this position it serves as a verb-phrase-internal adverb within the semantic scope of the adjective (*absent*) and ultimately the subject (*humanity*). *In fact* in (7) occurs adjacent to the tensed verb, but it can also appear at the left margin of the clause, following complementizers like *that*, *if*. As we have seen, in this position it serves as a sentence adverb, with a modal epistemic function: absent any further context, we know that the truth of the proposition *Humanity is absent* is somehow in doubt and counter to SP/W's expectation. In (8) *in fact* is outside the clause (though it can follow *and*, *so*, and other discourse connectives). It occupies a syntactic position that has been identified in several languages as available for expressive markers of various types

---

[5] Fraser and Malamud-Makowski (1996) use the term "contrastive markers" for this subclass of DMs.

[6] See also Ormelius-Sandblom (1997) on German. The synchronic intonation patterns of most of the adverbials discussed in this chapter deserve special attention.

or for focused constructions (see e.g. Aissen 1992).[7] Since our prime concern is semantics, not syntax, we will not explore this issue further here, except to note that even though most material in this position on the left margin of the clause is pragmatic and procedural, it unquestionably belongs to syntax and grammar.[8]

4.3.1 *English* indeed

Indeed has its origins in oblique uses of a full lexical noun in OE. *Dede* is ultimately derived from the verb to *do*; specifically, it is derived from a deverbal form of IE **dhe-* "set, put."

Dede is first encountered as a full lexical noun in OE, as in:

(9) nis   hare   nan   þe ne ... gulteð ilome oðer i
    NEG-is they-GEN NEG-one that not ... sins   often either in
    fol   semblant oder *in vuel dede.*
    foolish display or   in evil deed
    "there is none of them that does not ... sin greatly either in foolish display or
    evil action."

(c. 1225 Sawles Warde, p. 167)

As a lexical noun it can be modified, as here, by adjectives, or by demonstratives and quantifiers.

Stage I: indeed₁*: adverbial of "respect in which"*

The earliest example of the bare prepositional phrase (PP) in action/practice (*indeed₁*) in the Helsinki Corpus is (10) from *c.* 1300. It answers the question "With respect to what?" and will here be called a respect adverbial (RA).

(10) "Vuolf," quod þe vox him   þo, "Al þat þou hauest her
     Wolf   said the fox 3sg-DAT then All that you   have   here
     bifore I-do, In þohut, in speche, and *in dede,* In euche
     before done in thought in speech and in action in each
     oþeres   kunnes   quede, Ich þe   forȝeue."
     other-GEN kind-GEN evil   I   thee forgive
     "'Wolf,' said Fox to him then, 'All that you have done before this, in thought,
     in speech, and in action, in evil of every other kind, I forgive you for it.'"

(c. 1300, Fox and Wolf, p. 34)

---

[7] Following Banfield (1973), she calls this the E[xpression]-node (Aissen 1992: 47).

[8] This point has frequently been made by Fraser, who argues that DMs "are members of a separate syntactic category" (1990: 386). We leave open the question whether there is a syntactic category of DMs, or whether they belong to a larger set of discourse connectives that occur in the syntactic position in question.

In ME this bare PP is often used in a contrast set with other PPs (typically referring to words and thoughts), but now this usage is rare except in phrases like *in deed as well as name*; however, it lasted well into the nineteenth century.

In a formula like that in (10) *in dede* "in action" could invite the inference that the event was observable. The fallacy "seeing is believing," which draws on the view that what is physically/empirically accessible is true, allowed *in dede* to be endowed with evidential (epistemic) modal meanings ("in action/practice" > "in actuality, certainly"). In this context it was often used contrastively as in:

> (11) ofte in storial   mateer scripture rehersith the comune
> often in historical matters scripture repeats   the common
> opynyoun of men, and affirmeth not, that it was so *in dede*.
> opinion   of men and affirms   not that it was so in actuality
> "often where matters of history are concerned, scripture repeats men's
> common opinion, but does not affirm that it was so in actuality [rather than
> opinion]."
>
> (*c*. 1388 Purvey, Wycliffe, 56)

Note the adverb in this kind of utterance could be intended and understood as having either narrow or wide scope. In the latter case, the potential contrast would be not with an adverb like *in opinion* but with a modal adverb such as *certainly, for sure, truly*. The next example shows well how invited inferences can arise and be exploited.

> (12) For as moche as rumour ... is amonges some men of the Citee that vitaillers
> foreins, bringyngge fissh to the Citee of london to selle, shulde be restrained
> ... of hire comyngge to the citee ... to selle it freliche, which thyng nas neuer
> the Maires wille ne the aldermens ne hire entente, as semeth openlich *in dede*,
> but that alle swiche vitaillers foreins, that bryngeth fissh ... to the same Citee
> to selle, mowe come and selle hire forseid fissh ... Wherfore the Mair and
> aldermen comandeth ... that no man ... ne destourbe, lette ne greue *in dede*
> ne in word ne in non other manere no maner straunge vitailler bryngynge
> fissh.
> "Whereas there is rumor ... among some men of the city that foreign food
> merchants, bringing fish to the City of London to sell, should be restrained ...
> from coming to the city ... to sell it freely, and whereas such restraint was
> never the will or intent of the Mayor or aldermen, as is openly evident in deed,
> but the intent was that such foreign food merchants that bring fish ... to the
> same city to sell it, may come and sell their foresaid fish ... Therefore the
> Mayor and aldermen command ... that no man may disturb, prevent, or
> harass in action or in word or in any other manner any foreign food merchant
> bringing fish."
>
> (1383–84 Appeal London, p. 32)

The first *in dede* contrasts covert will and intent with overt action. The second contrasts action with speech. The first *in dede* occurs in the context of a parenthetical clause concerning evidence (*semeth*). SP/W could mean simply "in action," or could also invite enrichment of the inference that actions of the Mayor and aldermen reveal the strength of their intent and the veridicality of the proposition *which thing was neuer oure wille ne intente*, despite rumors.

A similar indeterminacy is detectable in:

(13)   "Purs is the ercedekenes helle," seyde he,
        But wel I woot he lyed right *in dede*.
        "'The purse is the archdeacon's hell,' he said, but I know well that he lied
        right in the act (of speaking)/in truth, wholly certainly."
                                        (1387–95 Chaucer, CT, Prolog, p. 34, l. 659)

Interestingly, both MED and Benson's Riverside Chaucer gloss *in dede* in this example as "in truth," but it could conceivably still be "lied in the act" (of saying *Purse is the ercedekenes helle*). At a very minimum, the epistemic meaning is a GIIN in (13), strongly invited by the context of lying, and in (12) by the context of will and intent.

Stage II: indeed$_2$: *epistemic*

Unambiguously abstract uses of *in dede* meaning "in truth" (*indeed$_2$*) appear by the mid fourteenth century. At first it appeared in clause-final or medial position; by the sixteenth century it also began to appear clause-initially, where it clearly had sentential scope (see (18) and (19) below). *Indeed$_2$* is an epistemic modal adverbial (EA) expressing SP/W's commitment to the truth of the proposition:

(14)   a.   and sworn vpon a bok to sey the playn trouth and
            and sworn on   a book to say the plain truth and
            nouȝt to mene   it with eny ontrouth for hate or
            not   to mingle it with any untruth   for hate or
            euel will neiþer for loue ner fauour but plainly
            evil will neither for love nor favor but plainly
            report as it was *in dede* nouȝt sparing for no persone.
            report as it was in fact   not   sparing for no person
            "and was sworn on a book to say the plain truth and not mix it with any
            untruth because of hate, evil will, love, or favor, but plainly report it as
            was in actuality, not sparing anyone."
                                        (1437 Documents Chancery, p. 168)

        b.   The men of þe town had suspecion to hem, þat her tydyngis were lyes (as it
            was *in dede*), risen.
            "The men of the town, being suspicious that their reports were lies (as was
            certainly true), rose."
                                        (1452 Chronicle Capgrave, p. 216)

161

(14b) is unambiguous because the singular *it* shows that the writer is assessing the whole proposition, not the preceding subject, which is plural (*tydyngis*). Since the invited inference from *indeed₁* was one of strong veridicality, this newly coded meaning *indeed₂* is automatically high on the epistemic scale (preserving the former GIIN).

Like all epistemic markers high on the scale of certitude, *indeed₂* in its earliest uses invites the inference that the proposition over which it has scope (q) is to some degree in contrast with a prior proposition (p), explicit or evoked. This arises from the M-heuristic: "marked expression warns pragmatically special situation" (see 1.2.3): marking declarative signals some doubt about the truth of that declarative. Thus *as it was in dede* is presented as being in contrast with *mene with ontrouth* in (14a), and with *had suspecion* in (14b). However, as these examples illustrate, it is a characteristic of *indeed₂* that it always signals some element of agreement (with *trouth* in (14a) and with the whole proposition p in (14b)). In later developments the adversativity is lost in some contexts.

Adversativity alongside of confirmation is most clearly maintained in non-initial position, as illustrated by the PDE example in (15). In this example Defense Secretary Cheney acknowledges the possible negative aspects of the budget proposal. He then goes on to introduce the positive ones (with the dismissive *having said that*), and intensifies the affirmative aspects of the proposal with *does*. He further moves to confirmation of the government's commitment to retaining a nuclear capability. His own expressed commitment and its intensity despite problems are signaled by *indeed*, and later *certainly*, thus invoking the M-heuristic several times over. The latter and other intensifiers are italicized:

(15)   "It is not perfect by any means," Cheney said of the rescission bill, "It will create some difficulties in terms of what we do in the department . . ."
  "Having said that," he added, "I think on balance it *does* achieve the level of savings that we were looking for when we sent the rescission package up. It *does* resolve a number of issues that have been outstanding for some period of time."
  "We do *indeed* want to retain the capacity to produce nuclear submarines," the defense secretary said, "the money that Congress approved in the rescission package will *certainly* be put to that use."
                                                      (1992 May 22, United Press Intl.)

There is, however, one extension of *indeed₂* in non-initial position that has lost its adversativity: the use of *indeed* as an "emphatic" degree adverb. This appears in clause-final position modifying adjectives (16) and adverbs (17). In respect of this meaning development, *indeed* is like *very* < *verily* "in truth," *truly, really*, all of which became intensifiers; however, it is the only one of these that was conventionalized to a post-adverbial and post-adjectival position. An early example is:

(16)   This sleep is sound *indeed*.
        (1600 Shakespeare, 2Henry IV, IV.v.35)

In this scene Prince Hal is contemplating the burden of kingship as his ailing father lies sleeping, dead, Hal thinks – the sleep is not just truly sound but *too* sound, so the Manner-heuristic is at work, calling the proposition *The sleep is sound* into question. In (17) Deloney presumably chose to use *indeed* to highlight the exaggeration of the "prattling" woman's false assurances:

(17)   Now assure you quoth shee (lisping in her speech) her tongue waxing somwhat too big for her mouth, I loue your mistresse well *indeed*, as if she were my owne daughter.
        (1619 Deloney, p. 79)

Today this use as an emphatic is found almost exclusively in formulae like *very much indeed*.

When *indeed$_2$* first appeared in clause-initial position it was favored after adversatives like *but*, or *though*, suggesting that early uses were intended as discursively adversative. In (18) Elyot is discussing educational practices, particularly practices designed to enhance the self-esteem of "noble" children who might not have been as intellectually smart as some of their less highly born peers:

(18)   [teachers] somtyme purposely suffring ["allowing"] the more noble children to vainquysshe, and, as it were, gyuying to them place and soueraintie, thoughe *in dede* the inferiour chyldren haue more lernyng.
        (1531 Elyot, p. 21)

Even when *but* or *though* are not present, initial *indeed* still retains some element of contrast during the sixteenth century. In (19a) Gaunt hints that his interlocutor, his nephew the young King Richard, has violated expected norms of address (compare how the Queen addresses Gaunt in the first line). In (19b) the interlocutor's doubt or need to ask a question is being gently countered.

(19)   a.   *Queen:*   How fares our noble uncle Lancaster?
             K. Rich.: What comfort, man? How is't with aged Gaunt?
             Gaunt: O how that name befits my composition!
                          Old Gaunt *indeed*, and gaunt in being old.
                          (1597 Shakespeare, Richard II, II.i.71)

       b.   *Dan.:*   Is it any trouble of conscience for sinne? If it be,
                          that may turne to good.
             Sam.:   O, no, no. I know no cause why.
             Dan.:   Why, what is it then, if I may be so bold, I pray you tell me. I
                          thinke you take me for your friend.
             Sam.:   *In deede* I haue alwaies found you my very good friend, and
                          I am sure you will giue me the best counseil you can.
                          (1593 Witches, p. A4V)

Nevertheless, some examples of initial position *indeed₂* with a primarily confirmatory meaning roughly equivalent to *Yes* begin to appear in conversation before the end of the sixteenth century, as in (20). Although it is not adversative it may be considered a subtype of *indeed₂* at least in its beginnings because it is epistemic, equivalent to "that's true":

(20) a. *Shal.:* I dare say my cousin William is become a good scholar. He is
                  at Oxford still, is he not?
          Sil.: *Indeed*, sir, to my cost.

                                    (1598 Shakespeare, 2Henry IV, III.ii.9)

      b. *Euans:* Why, this is lunaticks: this is mad as a mad dog.
          Shal.: *Indeed*, Master Ford, this is not well, *indeed*.
          Ford: So say I too Sir, come hither Mistris.

                    (?1597 Shakespeare, Merry Wives of Windsor IV.ii.124)

Stage III: indeed₃*: DM*

By the end of the sixteenth century *indeed₂* had been recruited to clause-initial DM function (*indeed₃*). Here epistemic meaning is only marginal. Its prime function is to signal additivity, somewhat like *what's more*. *Indeed₃* signals that SP/W views what follows (q) as adding to rhetorical argument, being a more appropriate statement for the circumstances at hand than something that preceded (p). It arises out of the IIN (later GIIN) from the epistemic *indeed₂* that if SP/W indicates commitment to the veridicality of q, then he or she is committed to the belief that the expression (verbal form) of q is better, more appropriate, etc. than the form of p.

(21) is a transitional example. The epistemic meaning "certainly" may be primary (note *most true saying*); but being in initial position, *indeed* also invites the inference that a discourse move is taking place, one in which the writer is summing up his rhetorical argument ("and furthermore"):

(21) a certaine repyning enuious man, being full gorged with a malicious rayling
      spirit . . . reported that the aforesaid plaister (*De Ranis*) was dangerous vnto
      the patient . . . and picked phrases, like as young Children vse to doe, when
      (in mockery) they counterfeite a strange kinde of language . . . *In deed* it is a
      most true saying: *That fish which is bred in the durt will alwaies taste of the*
      Mud.

                                          (1602 Clowes, p. 16)

Examples of the semanticized *indeed₃* are in (22). The adverb signals that what follows is not only in agreement with what precedes, but is additional evidence being brought to bear on the argument:

Meaning	1300	1450	1600	1850	2000
indeed₁ "in the act" (RA)	————————————				
+> "in truth"					
indeed₂ "in truth" (EA)		————————————			
+> "in addition"					
indeed₃ "what's more" (DM)			—————————		

Figure 4.1. Time-line for the development of *indeed* (RA = respect adverbial; EA = epistemic adverbial; DM = discourse marker).

(22) a. any a one that is not well, comes farre and neere in hope to be made well: *indeed* I did heare that it had done much good, and that it hath a rare operation to expell or kill diuers maladies.

(1630 Taylor, Penniless Pilgrimage, p. 131.C1)

   b. For he that has been used to have his will in every thing as long as he has been in coats, why should we thinke it strange that he should desire and contend for it still when he is in breetches. *Indeed* as he grows more towards a man, it shows his faults the more, soe that there be few parents then soe blinde as not to see them, soe insensible as not to feele the ill effects of their owne indulgence.

(1693 Locke, p. 51)

This use is currently widely attested in newspapers and academic prose:

(23) a. The idea of the Constitution as a living document, written so it can adapt to changing social and political times, is a major theme in U.S. judicial history. *Indeed*, it is the Constitution itself that allows those dissatisfied with Supreme Court rulings to turn to the amendment process.

(1990 June 16, United Press Intl.)

   b. Besides the problems noted by Sadock for nondetachability as a diagnostic for (content-based) implicata, it would appear that *any* means of linguistically canceling or suspending an implicatum . . . . is ipso facto a means of detaching that implicatum. *Indeed*, how could it be otherwise?

(1991 Horn, p. 316)

The chief stages of development of *indeed* are summarized in figure 4.1

4.3.2 *English* in fact [9]

We turn now to a rather briefer outline of the history of *in fact*.[9] Like *dede*, *fact* is ultimately derived from IE **dhe-* "set, put." *Fact* was borrowed in the

[9] Parts of section 4.3.2 draw on Traugott (1999a) and Schwenter and Traugott (2000); the latter emphasizes the scalar properties of *in fact₂* and *in fact₃*.

sixteenth century from Latin, and is a lexeme formed from the past participle of *fac-* "do." In the earliest texts we find *fact* meaning "deed, action":

> (24)   For the whiche noble *facte*, the kynge created hym afterwarde duke of
>   Norfolke.
>   (1543 Grafton, 603 [OED])

Stage I: in fact₁: adverbial of "respect in which"

Fact begins to appear in the Helsinki Corpus as an RA by the late seventeenth century in a bare PP as the object of *in*, where, like *in dede* before it, it is favored in coordinate constructions such as (25a) or lexically contrasting contexts like (25b). It seems to be favored in relatively high style texts, perhaps because it is a borrowing that competes with an already extant *indeed* (and *actually*; see below):

> (25)   a.   But it is evident *in fact* and experience that there is no such universal Judge,
>   appointed by God over the whole World, to decide all Cases of temporal Right.
>   (1671 Tillotson, p. 445 [Traugott 1999a: 185])
>
>   b.   This company, therefore, have always enjoyed an exclusive trade *in fact*,
>   though they may have no right to it in law.
>   (1776 Smith, Bk V.i.e, p. 744 [Traugott 1999a:185])

In these kinds of constructions, *in fact* came to be endowed with evidential meanings ("in practice/reality/actuality") that assess something as physically accessible, empirically attested, real, true, and ranked high on the epistemic scale. (25a) cites *fact* (action, performance) and experience (as opposed to speculation) as sources of evidence, (25b) cites it as the pragmatic and experiential locus of daily transactions, as opposed to abstract legal right.

While this kind of coordinate construction is still used in PDE, more loosely structured contrast sets are also evidenced (in the following *in fact* is contrasted with *(in) sensationalism*):

> (26)   "Many of my friends have urged me to issue a point-by-point denial of the
>   book's many outrages. To do so would, I feel, provide legitimacy to a book that
>   has no basis *in fact* and serves no decent purpose," the former president said.
>   "I have an abiding faith that the American people will judge this book for
>   what it really is: sensationalism whose sole purpose is enriching its author
>   and its publisher," said Reagan.
>   (1991 April 8, United Press Intl.)

Stage II: in fact₂: epistemic adversative

Uses such as those in (25a, b), analogous to the extant EA meanings of *indeed* and *actually*, as well as independent developments in the philosophical and scientific construals of "fact," are likely to have contributed to the recruitment of *in fact* to the class of ADVs that are potentially epistemic modals, specifically those that are redundant with epistemic certainty. Consider this example from the philosopher Berkeley, which uses *fact* in two ways:

(27) You were pleased before to make some reflexions on this custom, and laugh at
      the irresolution of our free-thinkers: but I can aver for matter of *fact*, that they
      have often recommended it by their example as well as arguments . . . In
      whatever light you may consider it, this is *in fact* a solid benefit. But the best
      effect of our principles is that light and truth so visibly spread abroad in the
      world.
                    (1732 Berkeley, ii. sect.24, p. 105 [Schwenter and Traugott 2000: 16])

First the imaginary addressee's point of view regarding free-thinkers is acknowledged (*you were pleased to* . . .). Then Berkeley expresses a contrasting opinion, emphasizing his position with a speech act verb commenting on his rhetorical strategy, even while hedging it with *can* (*I can aver for a matter of fact*); the addressee's opinion is again invoked, but concessively (*in whatever light you may consider it*), and then Berkeley's own view of the truth is given (*this is in fact a solid benefit*). As a fixed ADV phrase in the post-finite verb position exemplified by (27) *in fact* appears to have had pragmatically ambiguous wide (sentential) as well as narrow (clause-internal) scope. Thus the narrow scope reading *This is a solid benefit in fact (rather than imagination)* is possible, though at least from our modern perspective the wide scope reading seems more likely: *in reality, this is a benefit*.

The wide scope reading enabled *in fact* to be used unambiguously as an EA in clause-initial post-complement position almost from its first introduction, and extensively by the mid-eighteenth century. Often it occurs in the already contrastive environment of *but*. Almost invariably it occurs in contexts that are highly contrastive, as exemplified by (28). From an informational perspective, this kind of development might appear to be redundant. However, from a discourse perspective, cooccurrence with an already contrastive term or use in a highly dialectic context serves to emphasize the contrast.

(28) That the Turkey Merchants do Ship out much Cloth, I deny not; but as true it
      is, that they have Shipt out more Yearly since the great encrease of the
      East-India Trade, and since themselves have made this Complaint, than they
      did in former Years. So that *in Fact* it doth not follow that the encrease of the
      East-India Trade, and particularly of their Importation of Silk, doth hinder or
      diminish the Exportation of Cloth to Turkey, but rather the contrary.
                                              (1681 ecb l. 33 [Lampeter])

The extent to which *in fact*, *indeed* and other terms discussed here continue to be used in semantically and pragmatically similar environments over time is quite striking, and suggests that despite the appeal to objective-seeming "facts," the type of discourse in which they are preferred is typically rhetorically highly charged:

> (29) there is no agreement on what constitutes the class of contrastive discourse
> markers, if *in fact* there is a class at all.
>
> (1996 Fraser and Malamud-Makowski, p. 865)

In the eighteenth century, unambiguous clause-internal wide scope uses often involve collocation of *in fact* with *actually*:

> (30) When we look about us towards external objects, and consider the operation
> of causes, we are never able, in a single instance, to discover any power or
> necessary connexion . . . We only find, that the one does *actually, in fact,*
> follow the other.
>
> (1748 Hume, Pt 7, p. 63 [Schwenter and Traugott 2000: 16])

In (30) note the contrastive force of *only*. *Actually* and *in fact* are used to contrast possible expectations readers might have with regard to the subject-matter. In one sense the collocation with *actually* might appear to be redundant. However, on closer inspection, we can see that it provides a scalar intensifying function of the contrast. Furthermore, since it has epistemic wide scope meaning, *actually* ensures that *in fact* is also understood as having wide scope. Just as in the case of the modals discussed in the preceding chapter, it appears that extant patterns were drawn upon to motivate and provide redundant contexts to disambiguate new uses, in this case epistemic adversative wide scope with scalar properties.

Stage III: in fact$_3$; *DM*

The first example in our data base of the DM use of *in fact* occurs in a novel by Jane Austen, in dialogue. Here the function is quite different. The earlier epistemic use pertains to the truth despite contrary expectations regarding the proposition. In the new DM use, *in fact* functions at the discourse level to express the speaker's attitude to the appropriateness of the discourse itself. In (31) *in fact* introduces justification of what has just been said, in other words, self-corrective elaboration which is contrastive not in terms of truth but of appropriateness of expression:

> (31) a. I should not have used the expression. *In fact*, it does not concern you – it
> concerns only myself.
> (1816 Austen, Emma, vol. III, chapter 10, p. 393 [Traugott 1999a: 186])
>
> b. Thus in various ways ethical questions lead inevitably to psychological
> discussions; *in fact*, we may say that all important ethical notions are also
> psychological.
> (1886 Sidgwick, chapter 1, p. 5 [loc. cit.])

Note that in both instances, the context explicitly refers to language use (*expression, discussion*). In both the SP/W's rhetorical stance toward his prior expression is strengthened.

In more contemporary examples, *in fact₃* is no longer restricted to locutionary contexts, though a negative is often preferred in p:

> (32)   Not a bad ride on South 880. *In fact* it looks pretty good.
>
>   (Radio traffic report, April 10th 1996)

4.3.3   *English* **actually**

Yet another adverbial, *actually*, has a partially similar history, although its structure, not being a PP, is somewhat different.

Stage I: actually₁*: actively, effectively*

The adjective *actual* was borrowed in the early fourteenth century from French in the senses "active" and "real." *Actually* was coined in English as an adverb of manner (MA) in the fifteenth century.

> (33)   To cure it *actuale* whilez it is introduct but ys not confermed.
>   "To cure it effectively while it is in initial stages but is not yet confirmed."
>   (?1425 Chauliac (1), IIIb [MED; Powell 1992a: 85])

There is an IIN from "active" > "real": what is done is implied to be evident, verifiable, and therefore real (cf. *in fact, indeed, in the act*).

> (34)   For-whi þe feruour of þe affeccioun, wheþir it
>   therefore the fervor of the emotions   whether it
>   be sett *actuely* in God or in man is oftsiþes
>   be set actively in God or in man is often
>   myȝtier, moore egre and moore maistirful, þan is þe
>   mightier, more eager and more tyrranous than is the
>   wisdom of discrecioun of þe soule.
>   wisdom of discretion of the soul
>   "Therefore the fervor of the emotions, whether set actively (+> in reality) in
>   God or in man, is often mightier and more tyrannical that the wisdom of the
>   soul's discretion."
>   (*c.* 1450 Hilton, p. 25)

Some seventeenth century examples suggest influence of the French temporal meaning of *actuel* "of the moment." Here too there is an invited inference of reality:

> (35)   I know the King is my Sovereign, and I know my Duty to him, and if I would
>   have ventured my Life for any thing, it should have been to serve him, I know

it is his due, and I owed all I had in the World to him: But tho' I could not
fight for him my self, my Son did; he was *actually* in Arms on the King's side
in this Business; I instructed him always in Loyalty, and sent him thither; it
was I that bred him up to fight for the King.

(1685 Lisle, 123C1)

Actually here can be interpreted as meaning "actively," and also "at that time,"
as well as "really" (see "to vouch for (a) statement(s) which seem(s) surprising,
incredible, or exaggerated" [OED *actually* 5]).

Stage II: actually$_2$: epistemic adversative

By the mid-eighteenth century the invited inference of epistemic certainty despite expectations otherwise has become semanticized. An early example
has already been given in (30), where *actually* is collocated with *in fact*. A nineteenth
century one is:

(36)　Mr. Perry had been to Mrs. Goddard's to attend a sick child, and . . . found to
　　　his great surprise that Mr. Elton was *actually* on his road to London, and not
　　　meaning to return till the morrow.

(1816 Austen, Emma, vol. I, chapter 8, p. 68)

Stage III: actually$_3$: DM

In the early nineteenth century we find DM uses which are additive
rather than adversative and epistemic. In (37a) *actually* confirms *fully intended* and
introduces specific evidence of that intention (was *looking around*):

(37)　a.　It was now his object to marry. He was rich, and being turned on shore, fully
　　　　　intended to settle as soon as he could be properly tempted; *actually* looking
　　　　　around, ready to fall in love with all the speed which a clear head and quick
　　　　　taste could allow.

(1818 Austen, Persuasion, vol. I, chapter 7, p. 61)

　　　b.　In the middle of the complaint I started to worry that maybe I shouldn't be
　　　　　saying anything. And *actually* I said to myself, "boy, I sound like a
　　　　　complainer." You know, when a person complains a lot, that bothers me.
　　　　　When 'm down I tend to complain more. But I said, "I'm really tired of
　　　　　working with these people." *Actually* I even embellished the complaint.

(1993 Boxer, p. 123; transcript)

4.3.4　Comparison of the three adverbials

From a macro-perspective, the three ADVs underwent similar changes.
Each functioned as a clause-internal adverbial at Stage I, as an epistemic sentential
adverbial at Stage II, and as a DM at Stage III. Each had its origins in a clause-
internal adverbial (RA or MA). Each developed an EA polysemy with wide scope

Adv Type	*indeed*	*actually*	*in fact*
RA	1300	1425	1670
EA	1450	1750	1680
DM	1600	1815	1815

Figure 4.2. Approximate dates of development of *indeed, actually, in fact.*

serving a polyphonic adversative function; and each further developed a DM function indicating that q is argumentatively related to p as an elaboration or clarification. The approximate dates of development are shown in figure 4.2. But at the same time, each construction has its own history at the micro-level, and the coexistence of the forms with each other (and other ADVs like *really, in truth,* etc.) ensures that some differences persist, on an assumption that no two Ls mean exactly the same thing (Haiman 1980: 516).

The two PPs are most obviously similar in their histories, having the same syntax. The chief differences between them are that:

(i)   The original lexical *deed* is now largely restricted to such phrases as *deeds of valor,* whereas no such restriction applies to *fact.* Strengthened versions such as *as a point of deed* are therefore not available, though they are for *in fact,* as in *I don't think that in point of fact there is a distinction.*

(ii) The original bare PP *in deed* is now restricted to formulae like *in deed and word* (or *in word and deed*), whereas *in fact₁* is not.

(iii) *Indeed* can signal agreement (despite counterexpectation) to a prior utterance or implicature, which *in fact* cannot.

(iv) *In fact* cannot be used in the sense of *Yes,* whereas *indeed* can, as exemplified in (19).

(v)   Being confirmatory, *indeed₂* invites the inference that though the information may be new to AD/R, nevertheless SP/W had it in mind before. By contrast, *in fact₂* presents material in q as new information: *What in fact is going on/What is in fact going on?* is a good question, but not **What indeed is going on/What is indeed going on?*

This distinction is made particularly clear by (38), which is the beginning of a newspaper article titled "Murder Suspect Competent for Trial":

(38)   A Superior Court judge has ruled that a man accused in the 1996 murder of a prostitute is *indeed* mentally competent to stand trial.

   In a 10-minute hearing Wednesday at the Hall of Justice, Judge Lenard Louie ruled that Chung Chiu, 41, understands the charges against him and can rationally assist his defense attorneys . . .

> The ruling stems from a competency hearing last December in which two
> of the three court-appointed psychiatrists testified that Chiu suffered some
> mental illnesses, but was not legally incompetent.
>
> (1999 Jan. 21, San Francisco Chronicle)

In this example *indeed₂* invokes the question "Is Chiu mentally competent to stand
trial?," and answers in the affirmative. That a question of this type had been posed
earlier and had been answered affirmatively is shown by the later paragraph that
summarizes the prior ruling (this later paragraph interestingly requires *indeed* to be
reinterpreted not only as affirmation but also as confirmation). Had *in fact₂* been used
here, a different prior discourse would have been invoked, for example, "This man
is not mentally competent to stand trial," and *in fact* would have contradicted that
proposition (as a result the paragraph on the ruling would then have been incoherent).

Consider another example, this time one in which both ADVs are used. Here
President Clinton for the first time acknowledged publically a liaison that he had
formerly denied:

(39)   As you know, in a deposition in January, I was asked questions about my
       relationship with M. L. While my answers were legally accurate, I did not
       volunteer information.
       Indeed, I did have a relationship with M. L. that was not appropriate.
       In fact, it was wrong.

(1998 Aug. 18, TV speech)

Indeed here is *indeed₂*, referring back to *I was asked questions about my relationship*, and confirming the validity of the questioners' assumptions that there was a
relationship. *In fact* is *in fact₃*, strengthening (and confirming) *it was not appropriate*, and signaling that this is new information.

But if the two adverbs are switched as in (40) the effect is rhetorically quite
different:

(40)   As you know, in a deposition in January, I was asked questions about my
       relationship with M. L. While my answers were legally accurate, I did not
       volunteer information.
       In fact, I did have a relationship with M. L. that was not appropriate. *Indeed*
       it was wrong.

In fact would be possible here, but rather than inviting inferences of agreement with
the questioners, it suggests opposition to *I did not volunteer information*. *Indeed
it was wrong* would not signal new information, but rather some agreement with
unspecified critics. Therefore this sentence is only a weak addition to what preceded,
not a "confession." In other words, *indeed* and *in fact* are on a scale of strength,
with *in fact* the stronger member of the pair.

Actually is similar to *in fact*. Like *in fact*:

(i) *Actually* cannot be used in the sense of *Yes*.

(ii) *Actually$_2$* invites the inference that the information in q is new: *What actually is going on/What is actually going on?* is a good question. Substituting *actually* for *indeed* in (38) is incoherent in the context of the larger discourse, just as it would be in *He is in fact mentally competent*. But it seems less incoherent than *in fact*. This is presumably in part because *actually* is weaker on the epistemic scale, as evidenced by the order *actually, in fact*, not **in fact, actually*, and by substituting *actually* for *in fact* in (40).

Another way in which *in fact* and *actually* are similar is that both may be used in spoken language to serve as hedges or softeners, though as one might expect from the fact that *actually* is the weaker of the two, it is more likely to be used this way. Basing her data on the London–Lund and Lancaster–Oslo–Bergen corpora, Aijmer (1986) studied PDE uses of *actually*. She says that a characteristic use in spoken language is to "create contact with the listener" or "rapport," e.g. "I am telling you this in confidence" (Aijmer 1986: 128); in this meaning it often occurs clause-finally. Examples include:

(41) a. No, I don't think I was. No, I was determined to get married *actually*.
> (Aijmer 1986: 126)

b. Trump himself seemed exhilarated by the marathon negotiations that preceded the bridge loan agreement.
"I enjoyed it, *actually*," said Trump, author of "The Art of the Deal."
> (1990 June 27, United Press Intl.)

D. Robert Ladd (p.c.) provided a striking example of the hedged use of *actually* for politeness in Scottish English. On one occasion in a post office he had put a package on the scale to be weighed oriented in a direction which made the mailing address hard for the clerk to see. The clerk said: "Where's it *actually* going?" If *actually* here were *actually$_2$*, it would be the sender of the packet who might be questioning (somewhat rudely) the ability of the post office to deliver mail correctly. Spoken by the post office clerk, however, Ladd interpreted it as "clearly an apology" for not being able to see the packaging label.

In her article on *actually*, Aijmer in passing also points out that *in fact* can be used in this way too in spoken discourse, also usually in clause-final position:

(42) Funny. We really quite enjoyed it *in fact*.
> (Aijmer 1986: 128)

4.4 Subjectification and intersubjectification

The development of the EA meanings of *indeed, in fact*, and *actually* is in each case an example of subjectification. SP/W uses the adverbials to make explicit his or her commitment to the truth of the utterance. The further development of the DM meanings is a case of increased subjectification since SP/W is now making the rhetorical strategy explicit. This new DM meaning has nothing to do with literal deeds or acts, and cannot be directly derived from the RA or MA uses.

This is borne out by examples in Japanese. For example, in her discussion of the development in Japanese of *wake*, a post-VP "extended predicate" marker meaning "it is (the reason/case/situation) that," Suzuki (1998) claims that at the latest stage "the speaker seems to invite the hearer (or impose on the hearer) to accept that there is a logical relationship between the *wake* clause and its preceding discourse" (Suzuki 1998: 80) and suggests the translation "you see" (ibid. p. 68). In its earliest uses, *wake* derived from the verb *waku* meaning "divide." This verb gave rise to two nouns which were represented by different Chinese characters, one "division," "left over food," etc., the other epistemic and concerned with "distinguishing and understanding differences," "logical consequence" (Suzuki 1998: 80, fn. 3, referring to NKD). In the 1830s the noun *wake* meant "reason"; in the late nineteenth century it developed a polysemy as a pragmatic particle with DM function, linking p and q, and signaling that SP/W regards q is related to p as an alternative (or better) formulation, roughly equivalent to "in other words, that means ..." (ibid. p. 74). This meaning can be seen in instances in which a logical relationship between the *wake* clause and preceding discourse (or other aspects of the speech act situation) is not evident, but in which SP/W wants AD/R to assume or construe that one exists. The intersubjective meaning is not only more recent than the epistemic one, but could presumably not have developed had the epistemic one not already been available.

As we have seen, *actually* and *in fact* in some of their uses are intersubjective in the sense that they mark not only connectivity between p and q (a subjective rhetorical device with the intersubjective purpose of conveying to the addressee what sort of textual connectivity is implied) but also function as a "DM hedge" to soften or mitigate what is said with the purpose of acknowledging the addressee's actual or possible objections (see 1.2.4). The question is whether these hedged meanings derive from the textual DM *actually₃, in fact₃*, or from *actually₂, in fact₂*. It would appear that the immediate source is the adversative, *actually₂* and *in fact₂*, since the hedge implies a kind of concessive, e.g. "I am confiding in you, even though you might not believe what I just said/even though you might not approve." The typical position for concessives like *anyway* is clause-internal, or even-final, as in Aijmer's examples (41a) and (42). Furthermore, hedged meanings, which include *I think*, *I guess*, *you know*, *you see*, are often associated with expressions of epistemic attitude.

4.4.1   *English* well

An example of a lexeme that has clearly developed intersubjective meanings is *well*. This adverb appears in OE as a manner adverb meaning "in a good manner." OED relates *well* to the IE verb *wel-* "to will, wish," and states that the adverb derives from "in accordance with a good or high standard of conduct or morality."

In the earliest OE texts we find a compound intersubjective construction *wella* "well + la" which appears to function as an attention-getter "listen up." In his study of the history of *well*, Jucker (1997) points out that in this function it is rather like OE *hwæt*; however, it does not seem to have the same function as *hwæt* of introducing the material as known, or of signaling the narrator's move to an account of his sources (see 4.2 above). Being a compound, *wella* presumably has a different history from *well*, though it is a closely related one.

Well is attested in OE in clause-initial position with an epistemic function, approximately "certainly, definitely," a subjectification of the manner adverb:

(43)   Cwæð he: *Wel* þæt swa mæg, forþon hi   englice ansyne
       Said   he well that so   may, because they angelic faces
       habbað.
       have
       "He said: 'Well that may be so, since they have the faces of angels.'"
       (?900 Bede, ii.i. (Schipper) 110 [Jucker 1997: 100])

Note that in (43) *well* is in a quoted speech, and follows the "inquit" "said he."

In ME as represented by the Helsinki Corpus and Chaucer's works, Jucker finds *well* used clause-initially only in highly restricted contexts: in direct reported speech at the beginning of turns in conversation, followed by "inquits" (Jucker 1997: 98–100). Jucker regards this use as a "frame-marker" and "text-sequencing device" (ibid. p. 99). However, as he acknowledges, "in many cases it may also indicate an acceptance of a situation that has been expressed or indicated" (ibid.), and may be substituted by "if this is so/OK then" (ibid. p. 100) as in (44):

(44)   "Ye sey welle," sayde the kynge, "Aske what ye woll and ye shall have hit and
       hit lye in my power to gyff hit." "*Well*," seyde thy lady, "than I aske the hede
       of thys knyght that hath wonne the swerde."
           "'You say well,' said the king. 'Ask what you will and you shall have it if it
       lies within my power to give it.' 'Well,' said the lady, 'then I ask the head of
       the knight who has won the sword.'"
       (before 1471 Malory, Morte Arthur, 48 [Jucker 1997: 99])

(Note in this example the manner adverb use in *Ye sey welle.*) Occurring as they do in direct speech quotations, these clause-initial DM uses of *well* are ascriptions by the narrator to the quoted speaker, i.e. ascriptions to the subjectivity of the persona, but not to the narrator (SP/W).

In the EMdE period *well* comes to be used in monolog, where it clearly may be anchored in SP/W. The monologs occur in texts normally regarded as close approximations of speech (sermons, plays, transcripts of legal depositions):

> (45) Moyses was a wonderful felowe, and dyd his dutie being a maried man. We lacke such as Moyses was. *Well,* I woulde al men would loke to their dutie, as God hath called them, and we then shoulde haue a flourisyng christian weal.
>
> (1549 Latimer, 29 [Jucker 1997: 100])

Here the preacher uses the proposition p "We lack such as Moses was, people who do their duty as married men," to develop an argument q that the situation in p should be changed; however, the shift to q is a moderated one, granting that q may not be achievable or even agreed upon by AD/R (contrast *(But) in dede/(But) in fact* here). In dialogs *well* appears to have primarily this hedging function since it tends to be used in situations of conflict:

> (46) *Tom:* Yes, you must keep a Maid, but it is not fit she should know of her Masters privacies. I say you must do these things your self.
>
> *Ione: Well* if it must be so, it must.
>
> (1684 Tom the Taylor, 268 [Jucker 1997: 102])

As in the case of other Ls we have discussed in this chapter, when *well* appears with DM meanings, the contexts in which it occurs are quite limited; it is then generalized to more contexts. At first it is anchored in the speech of others than the narrator; then it comes to be preempted to the narrator/speaker/writer's perspective, and finally it develops meanings with strong orientation to AD/R's face.

4.4.2   *English* let's

The developments of hedging *well, actually,* and Jp. *wake,* in which the intersubjective meanings are not present at the earliest stages, do not appear to be fundamentally different in kind from those in which some degree of intersubjectivity is present from the beginning, at least in the historical record of the language in question. For example, in English, there is an imperative construction *let us X* "permit us to X" that is intersubjective from the beginning by virtue of the argument structure: the utterance has illocutionary force; SP and AD are participants in the projected event since the construction is imperative (addressed to a second person) and refers to AD's projected action with respect to SP. This kind of construction is attested from OE to the present day.

In the imperative construction the second person is profiled as separate from the speaker and companions, who are construed as syntactic objects of permission as well as subjects of *go*. Out of this construction, which can be expanded to *Let us go, will you!*, arose a speaker-oriented polysemy *let us* (> *let's*), known as the "hortatory" *let's*. Here first and second person together are syntactic subjects of both *let* and *go*, as in *Let us go, shall we?*, which is attested from Chaucerian ME on. This is more subjective in that the speaker includes him or herself in the exhortation. It is also more intersubjective in that the addressee is now conceptualized as acting with the speaker. Furthermore, an exhortation is a mildly mitigated form of an imperative.

The original verb *let* "allow" in the imperative (with a full NP object) and hortative *let us* cooccur in the following few lines from Chaucer, together with the subjunctive expression *go*, of the type that *let's* in part replaced:

(47) Com doun to-day, and *lat* youre bagges stonde ...
What, *lat us* heere a messe, and go we dyne.
"Come down today and let your bags stand (leave your bags) ... Let us hear a mass and let us go dine."
(*c.* 1387 Chaucer, CT, Shipman, p. 205, l. 220 [Traugott 1995a: 37])

More recent uses of *let's* show a further increase in intersubjectivity, presumably via positioning of first person pronoun for second person (see 2.3.4). Examples include locutions such as one finds addressed to patients or to children, like (48) in which SP is presumably not going to participate in the pill taking:

(48) *Let's* take our pills now, Johnny.

The kind of positioning in (48) strongly mitigates the intention, which is imperative (*Take your pills now, Johnny!*), and therefore explicitly marks intersubjective attention to AD's image needs.

The development of *let's* illustrates not only increases in intersubjectivity but also once again a shift from content meanings based in argument structure at the clausal level to pragmatic procedural meanings at the discourse level. Imperative *Let's go* can be analyzed syntactically as biclausal (*allow us to go*), hortatory *let's go* as a modalized single clause (*may we go!*), and the kind of construction in (48) (*let's take our pills*) as a single clause with a pragmatic marker *let's* functioning somewhat like *well* (though *well* does not allow the pronominal positioning in this meaning: **Well, take our pills now*). The semantic compositionality of *let us* in the imperative is clear, that of the hortatory *let's* less so, but in the case of (48) it is obscured.

We turn now to the development in Japanese of a pragmatic marker that shows many of the characteristics exemplified by the English examples that have preceded.

4.5 The development of a discourse marker signaling global connectivity: Japanese *sate*

In MdJ *sate* is a global discourse particle that typically signals a topic shift. In this its function is similar to some of the functions of English *so*: *sate* appears at the beginning of the first sentence of the new topic of discussion. In the modern colloquial language, *sate* may also carry expressive value as a mild hedge, and is translatable as *well*. A characteristic common to both functions is that speakers use *sate* in speech event contexts in which (they think) their conversational turn is required, as illustrated by:

(49)
    A: Sensee, doo nasai-masu-ka?
    teacher how do (RESP)-POL-Q

    B: Sate! . . . (doo si-masyo-o)
    well . . . how do-POL-PROB

    "*A:* What will you [respected teacher] do?
    B: Well! . . . (What shall I/we do . . .)."

In (49), B's response of just *sate* can stand alone as an utterance, but in other contexts it often introduces B's response (or confirms that there is difficulty in responding) to A's question. Both as a hedge and as a global DM introducing a new topic, *sate* is a procedural with no truth-conditional or contentful meaning. Unlike English *so* and *well*, *sate* in MdJ only rarely occurs in clause-internal position, and it appears to have lost its original meaning, which is that of a deictic manner adverb "thus, in that (sort of) way."

Stage I: sate₁: "thus"

The earliest recorded uses of *sate* are as a deictic adverb; examples go back to OJ (see e.g. NKD v. 9, p. 88). The word apparently originates in a preliterary Japanese second person distal demonstrative element *sa* "that (manner)" plus *te*, which is usually classified as the ADV or adverbializing form (*ren'yookei*) of a predicate suffix *tu* that expresses perfect aspect. The demonstrative element *sa* is the base for a number of adverbs found in OJ and subsequent periods of the language. In addition to *sate*, derivatives that survive in the modern language include *saraba* "if so" and *sayoo* "(in) that way," which is a more formal equivalent of *sono yoo* "(in) that way." An OJ example of *sate* is:

(50) Yuki sabu-mi /[10]   saki- ni   Fa[11] saka- nu /
snow cold-REASON bloom- COP TOP bloom- NEG
ume no   Fana / yosi[12]   kono-koro Fa /
plum- ASSOC flower as-is (ADV) for-a-while TOP
sate mo   aru ga-ne
thus INCL-FOC be- CAUS
"O plum flower that does not bloom because of the coldness of the snow, for a
while it is all right (=as is) that you may be *thus*."
    (before 759 AC, Man'yooshuu X, 2329 [Takagi et al. 1957–60, v. 3: 147])[13]

In (50), *sate* enriches the conceptualized described event by expressing the manner
of the verb *aru* "be." It does so by referring back to the condition of the plum tree
flowers, i.e. not yet open in bloom (the phrase *saki-ni-Fa sakanu* is an emphatic collocation for *saka-nu* "not bloom"). By linking the described event anaphorically with
the absence of blossoms, *sate* additionally provides structure and cohesion to the ongoing discourse from the point of view of SP/W in the conceptualized speech event.

Stage II: sate$_2$: *connection between p (as a whole) and q*
    Although (50) is an example in clause-internal position, *sate* is found
most frequently in clause-initial position already by LOJ. Already in LOJ *sate* no
longer refers to the particular manner of an action in p. For example, in the "Waka-
murasaki" ("Lavender") chapter of *Genji Monogatari* (approximately 880 lines of
text), *sate* appears ten times,[14] of which nine examples are in clause-initial position.
In only three of the examples can *sate* be interpreted as retaining its original manner
adverb meaning. In other examples in this and other LOJ texts, *sate* appears to signal

---

[10] Slashes (/) indicate divisions between metrical units (lines) of the poem, whose form is 5-7-5-7-7
   syllables.
[11] For the phonetic value of F, see Conventions (iii). The particle *Fa* developed into the MdJ topic
   particle *wa*; for convenience it is glossed throughout this section as TOP(IC), although its range
   of meanings included "contrast" and "emphasis." Fujii (1991) provides a detailed diachronic
   study of this item.
[12] The word *yosi* "(you may be) as is" is an adverbial used in OJ to indicate permission or recognition of the action or judgment of another party, or SP's own intention.
[13] Takagi, Gomi, and Ohno (1957–60) provide the reading *sika-ni* "in that way" for the two Chinese
   characters in the original text that correspond above to *sate*. NKD however, cites this poem in
   their entry for *sate* with the reading *sate* for those characters. The metrics of the poem seem to
   prefer the reading *sate* (two syllables, not three), but there are some apparent metric liberties in OJ
   that may reflect contracted pronunciations. (Perhaps, for example, *sika-ni mo* was pronounced
   sikan-mo.) Takagi, Gomi, and Ono are themselves inconsistent. In their note on Poem 2244
   (Takagi, Gomi and Ohno 1957–1960: 131), they quote the poem in (50) (no. 2329) with *sate*.
[14] These instances include three instances of *sate-mo* (a form which indicates inclusive focus) and
   one instance of *sate-ha* (which indicates exclusive or contrastive focus). Other common forms
   built on *sate* in LOJ include *sate-koso* (which indicates strongly exclusive or contrastive focus).

that the whole proposition p, not just a constituent of it, is to be taken as a condition, reason, or even simply the basis for further argument.

An early example in which *sate* introduces q as having a cause–effect relationship to p can be seen in (51):

(51) Kono koyasu-gahi   ha asi-   ku
      this safe-birth-shell (amulet) TOP bad/poor- ADV
      tabakari-te   tor-ase-tamahu-nari.
      fashion (devise)-GER take-CAUS-RESP-COP
      Sate   ha e-tor-ase-tamaha-zi.
      for-that-reason TOP POTEN-take-CAUS-RESP-NEG
      "It is that [you] have had [the men] use clumsy methods to take the amulet.
      For that reason, [you] are unable to have [them] get it."[15]
                (early 10th century, Taketori Monogatari [Matsuo 1961: 146.1])

Although it is possible to interpret *sate* in (51) as having its earlier deictic adverb meaning "thus, in that way," the so-called extended predicate construction (verb-plus-copula *tor-ase-tamahu-nari*) in the preceding sentence supports the interpretation that *sate* expresses a cause–effect relationship between the entire proposition p and following q. The extended predicate construction in Japanese overtly expresses that there is an argumentative reason for stating the proposition p in the particular context of the speech event (see e.g. Kuroda 1973). Here the extended copula predicate indicates that the poor methods used to take the amulet (p) are being presented as the reason for q; *sate* overtly introduces q (failure of obtaining benefit from the amulet) as the consequence of p. Thus, in this use, *sate* takes the entire proposition p as the anaphoric ground for q.

In example (52), *sate* likewise introduces an event in q as being linked to the occurrence of the event previously described in p. Here, however, it refers back to an event the occurrence of which is offered merely as a hypothetical possibility; *sate* signals that the eventuality of q depends on the eventuality of the condition in p:

(52) Nasake-naki hito   nari-te   yuka-ba,   *sate*
      heartless   person be(come)-GER go-CONDIT in:that:situation
      kokoro   yasuku-te   si-mo,   e-okitara-zi
      heart/spirit be:gentle-GER although POTEN-put:aside-NEG
      wo-ya   nado ihu   mo   ari.
      EMPH-Q etc. ones:who:say INCL-FOC be

---

[15] While the verb form *ase-tamahu* is interpreted as CAUS-RESPECT in (51) (see Matsuo 1961: 146, ft. 2), it is alternatively possible to interpret this construction as an intensified honorific that indexes the highest degree of respect toward the imperial family (without causative meaning). In this interpretation, the sentence would be translated as, "It is that [Your Highness] is using clumsy methods to take the amulet. For that reason, [your Highness] is unable to get it." In this example the NP marked with TOP *ha* is best understood as grammatical object.

"There were also those who said: 'If a heartless person takes over as the next
governor], then [the current governor] could hardly put aside [his duties],
gentle though he is,' and so forth."[16]

(*c.* 1006, Genji Monogatari [Abe et al. 1970: 278.14–15])

In this use, *sate* fulfills a function similar to that of English *then* in an *if–then* construction, that is, it marks q as more likely to be true, given the condition in p, than default hypotheticality would imply. *Sate* is not necessary to the expression of the logical relationship between p and q (which is indicated by the conditional form *yuka-ba*)
but it strengthens the nuance of q as the inevitable outcome of what has just been
said. As an expression of SP/W's attitude toward the instantiation of q, the meaning
of *sate* here is more subjective than the original deictic adverb meaning of the word.

A weaker linking function of *sate* in LOJ is to express an additive relationship
between p and q:

(53) Kiyoge-naru   otona hutari   bakari,
       elegant-looking-COP adult   two:people just/only
       sate   ha   warahabe zo   ide-iri-asobu.
       and (*in addition*) TOP children- EMPH go:out-go:in-play

       "[There were] just two elegant-looking adults, also children were playing
       running in and out [of the room]."

(*c.* 1006, Genji Monogatari [Abe et al. 1970: 280.6])

Here, as in (51) and (52), *sate* links back to the previously described situation as a
whole. There is no action or event internal to p that would serve as an anaphoric
referent to which *sate* in (53) could refer as a manner adverb. Instead, *sate* here
indicates that the new information introduced in the following clause is to be added
to the totality of the described event in p. Note that (53) should be considered to
contain an ellipsis of a "be" verb (e.g. *ari*) immediately after *bakari* "just/only"; such
ellipsis of "be" verbs is not unusual in Japanese. The particle *ha* (which developed
into the well-known topic particle *wa*) here probably has a contrastive meaning that
reinforces the nuance that the description of the children playing is the only addition
to the situation p.

A common characteristic of these new uses of LOJ *sate* is that they point back
not to an internal characteristic of p, but rather to p as a whole, inviting the inference
that p serves as condition or ground for q. This ground may be temporal, logical
(51), (52), or situational (53).

---

[16] Depending on the identity of the implicit subject of the first clause, this sentence can also be
interpreted as "If (his daughter) goes on and becomes heartless (=countrified), (the current
governor) could hardly put aside [his worries], gentle though he is."

Stage III: sate₃: *scene-shifter*

Already in LOJ, *sate* exhibits patterns of occurrence that indicate not only local connectivity, but also a more global association with discourse structure. One of the five occurrences of *sate* in *Taketori Monogatari* begins a major new topic of discussion, which is set off in modern annotated editions as a new chapter:

(54) *Sate*   Kaguya-hime   katati no   yo   ni
at that time [Kaguya]-princess form   ASSOC world DAT
ni-zu   medetaki   koto wo   mikado kikosimesi-te...
resemble-NEG(ADV) magnificent thing ACC emperor hear(RESP)-GER.
"At that time, hearing that Princess Kaguya's beauty was more magnificent than the world had seen, the emperor ..."

(early 10th century, Taketori Monogatari [Matsuo 1961: 159.1])

Except for a general temporal connection, the content of the section that begins with (54) bears little connection to the event described in the preceding text, which is an account of Princess Kaguya's sadness at the death of the Lady Chunagon. Similarly, in the *Kageroo Nikki* (*Diary "The Gossamer Years,"* mid-tenth century) *sate* appears frequently at the beginning of narrative sections with the meaning "at that time" and serves to mark an episode boundary not unlike OE *gelamp* "it came to pass" (see 4.1).

Sometimes the interpretation of a particular instance of *sate* depends on how a passage is edited. For example, in "Waka-murasaki," a retainer of Prince Genji describes the lifestyle of the governor of Harima Province. After mentioning near the beginning of his narrative that the governor lives alone with his daughter, the retainer describes the history of the governor, his reasons for leaving the capital, and the magnificence of his residence. Genji responds with a question:

(55) ...to   moose-ba ...
QUOT say (HUMIL)-when
sate   sono   musume ha   to   tohi-tamahu.
well/so that/his daughter TOP QUOT ask-RESP
"When [the retainer] said ... Genji asked '*So* [what about] the daughter?'"

(*c.* 1005 Genji Monogatari [Abe et al. 1970: 277.12–13])

If *sate* is interpreted as being included within the quotation, then its function here seems to be similar to MdJ usage – to deflect the conversation to a new discourse topic.[17] However, it is also possible to interpret *sate* in this example as standing outside of the quotation to modify the verb *tohu* "ask"; in that case *sate* probably has the meaning "at that time" and signals that the narrator is returning to the earlier topic of the narrative.

---

[17] This is apparently the interpretation taken by Seidensticker (1980: 86), who translates Genji's question as "'And the daughter?' asked Genji."

An examination of *sate* in the EMJ text *Tsurezure-gusa* (1330, *Essays in Idleness*) reveals a pattern of distribution in which *sate* plays a pronounced role as an opener for new sections of discourse. Of a total of sixteen occurrences of *sate*,[18] nine introduce a new discourse section (a new discourse topic or a return to an earlier topic following a digression). In an additional four instances, it introduces elaborations that may be considered minor changes in topic. In some instances, e.g. (56), there is little or no evidence that *sate* provides a deictic link to what precedes. Rather, its primary function is to indicate that the following section of text represents a new discourse unit.

(56) *Sate* huyu-gare no   kesiki koso,
      so   winter-decay ASSOC scenery EXCL-FOC
      aki   ni   ha   wosa-wosa otoru-mazi-kere.
      autumn DAT TOP scarcely   be:inferior-NEG:PROB-PAST[19]
      "So, the scenery of winter decay is hardly inferior to that of autumn."
      (*c.* 1330, Tsurezure-gusa [Tokieda 1967: 24.11])

In Tokieda's annotated text, the preceding paragraph starts out with a description of the deepening of autumn, beginning with the Tanabata summer festival and progressing through a description of harvest activities. The author/narrator then digresses, pointing out that it is unnecessary to write of such things, because they have already been written about in famous works such as the *Genji Monogatari*. He goes on to justify his "selfish" desire to put brush to paper, saying that "it is not something for people to read." Then, with (56), the narrator returns to his description of the seasons, but with new content about the winter season (which is first mentioned here). *Sate* announces the return to the main flow of the discourse from that digression, but it is difficult to find a deictic link to an event in p: the event in q does not occur at the same time as the one in p.[20] Similarly, there are no grounds for positing a cause–effect relationship with p. Cohesion with the previous topic of discussion is accomplished through the comparison of the seasons, and through the use of *sate*, which apparently functions primarily to signal a change in scene.

By the period of LMJ the discourse functions of *sate* are clearly established, as is evidenced by Rodriguez' (1604–8) treatment in his grammar. He includes a few sentence-internal occurrences in which *sate* appears to be interpretable in its old deictic adverb meaning *sate₁* "in that way" (e.g. Doi 1955: 94, 470). He also

[18] These examples in *Tsurezure-gusa* include two examples of *sate-ha*, one example of *sate-mo*, and one example of *sate-mo-ya-ha*, which contains the question/dubitative particle *ya*.

[19] Here, *kere* (citation form *keri*) may function as an exclamation rather than as a past tense marker.

[20] Since the expected flow of seasons is maintained, the passing of time itself may constitute the ground of an anaphoric reference. Nevertheless, this ground is not specific to a point in the preceding CDE.

cites *sate* in lists of conjunctions meaning "for that reason" (ibid. pp. 425, 476–477), "and (so)," and "furthermore" (*sate₂*) (ibid. p. 489). In addition, a number of example sentences scattered throughout the book begin with *sate*; in these, the word is probably to be understood as a colloquial-sounding sentence-opener and scene shifter (*sate₃*) since there is no preceding discourse context, as in (57):

> (57) *Sate* sono fitoua   vooxuuno   giuuninca?[21]
> *Sate* sono hito   wa   (w)oosyuu   no   zyuunin ka
> so   that person TOP [place name] ASSOC resident Q
> "So, is that person a resident of the Northern Provinces?"
>
> (1604–8, Rodriguez [Doi, tr. 1955: 339])

It should be noted that some (but not all) of Rodriguez' examples are taken from Japanese literary works, and so they may have been removed from a context in which there was a deictic anaphoric relationship to a previous proposition.

Stage IV: sate₄: exclamation (and hedge)

Also in LMJ, *sate* comes to be attested as an exclamatory lexeme. Rodriguez includes *sate* and the derivatives *sate-sate*, *sate-mo*, *satemo-satemo*, and *sate-wa* (which reflect morphological patterns for expressing emphasis or focus) in his lists of LMJ exclamation words (Doi 1955: 298, 458, 465–466). NKD cites the use of *sate* in this function from the time of Noh plays (latter half of the fourteenth century). The acquisition of affective meaning by *sate* was probably enabled by contexts in which the word was not an essential part of the expression of the relationship between p and q; i.e. by some of its uses as a connector (*sate₂*) as well as its scene-shifter meaning (*sate₃*). Examples such as (58) appear to represent pivotal uses between *sate₃* and the exclamatory meaning (*sate₄*):

> (58) Ge-ni omosiro-ku   mo   nobe-rare-tari,
> truly enjoyable-ADV INCL:FOC tell-RESP-PERF
>
> *satesate* nani no   yoo   yaran?
> (and)so   what ASSOC matter PROB-Q
> "Truly you have told it well; *so* what is your business here?"
>
> (14th century, Shizen koji [Yokomichi and Omote 1960: 100.11])

In such uses, *sate* (here the emphatic derivation *satesate*)[22] may call special attention to q and to the emotional state of the speaker at the time of utterance, regardless

---

[21] The first line in (57) uses the orthographic representation in Rodriguez' grammar; however, long vowels are here shown with double vowels, not with a macron as in the original. The second line is the transcription of the Jp. forms according to the conventions of this book.

[22] The possible role of emphatic derivations such as *satesate* in promoting the acquisition of affective meaning by *sate* itself awaits further study.

of whether or not there is a deictic reference back to a p in the text. (58) may additionally function as a mild hedge in the ongoing dialog in which SP seeks to preserve AD's face as SP begins to pose a direct question. Expressive meaning may also be posited in occurrences of *sate* at the beginnings of conversational turns or major discourse episodes, such as (59). In the context preceding (59), which occurs near the beginning of the Noh play *Eguchi*, an itinerant monk (the *waki* central character of the play) has just asked a villager (an *ai* minor character) about a pile of stones; the villager explains that they are a memorial to the lord of Eguchi. The dialog between *waki* and *ai* is in polite speech style (which makes use of the verb-ending *sooroo*) and takes place near rear stage-left. Then the *waki* returns to center stage, faces the audience, and states:

(59) *Sate* ha   inisihe   no   Eguti no   kimi
     so   TOP past-time ASSOC Eguchi ASSOC lord
     no   ato   nari-keri.
     ASSOC memorial COP-PAST (=EXCLAM)
     "So, this is a memorial to the lord of Eguchi from olden times."
                        (14th century, Eguchi [Yokomichi and Omote 1960: 51.1])

In (59), the phrase following *sate-ha* contains a repetition of the explanation by the villager, but in plain (not polite) speech style. *Sate* thus begins a brief (five line) monolog in which the monk expresses to himself and to the audience his feelings of gratitude at being able to visit this spot. In such uses, one can treat the word as having a global pragmatic marker function plus additional expressive value.

In EMdJ, *sate* gravitates toward the two overlapping functions found in the present day language: pragmatic particle marking global "discourse chunking" functions, and exclamation. An examination of *sate* and its derivative words in two plays of Chikamatsu (1703–4, Mori, Torigoe, and Nagatomo 1972: 57–113, about 830 lines of text) yielded a total of seventeen occurrences, of which six indicate primarily global pragmatic particle marker function and four are exclamations. Not surprisingly, some of the examples are ambiguous between global pragmatic particle and exclamation functions. In three occurrences, the lexeme links q deictically to a p with a meaning such as "for that reason," "at that time" ($sate_2$). In the remaining four examples, *sate* appears in presentations of items in series. In this usage, *sate* occurs in a long list, e.g. feudal lords in a procession, in a pattern such as *A, B, C, sate D, E*, which can be translated as "A, B, C, and in addition D, E." This use thus appears similar to the LOJ use discussed in (53) above. No examples were found of $sate_1$.

Stage V: $sate_5$: epistolary formula

From evidence in Rodriguez' early seventeenth century grammar, it appears that *sate* has not yet acquired a formulaic use, found in MdJ, to mark the

Meaning	OJ	LOJ	EMJ	LMJ	EMdJ	MdJ
$sate_1$ "thus"	——————— – – –					
$sate_2$ "then (conn)"		——————————— – – –				
$sate_3$ "scene-shifter"		– – – ———————————————				
$sate_4$ "exclamation"				—————————		
$sate_5$ "epistolary formula"						———

Figure 4.3. Time-line for the development of Japanese *sate* (conn = connective).

beginning of the body of a written letter (whether business or personal). Rodriguez includes an entire chapter on how to write a letter in Japanese (Doi 1955: 678–711). In it, he notes that *sate-mata* (*sate* plus *mata* "again") is the (colloquial) equivalent of *somosomo* "now, in the first place, to begin with," which is listed as one of three formal (literary) words used to signal the beginning of the body of a letter following the initial formal greeting (ibid. p. 697). Otherwise, *sate* is absent from this chapter. Nowadays, however, *sate* is one of the standard formulaic expressions used to mark the beginning of the body of a letter immediately after a sentence of formal greetings (typically containing a stylized reference to the season), which is written as a separate, one-sentence paragraph. The function of *sate* as marking topic-shift is especially clear in this use. It also has an intersubjective function since, by using it, the writer is following communicative norms of the genre that affect the reader's "face."

In summary, the semantic history of *sate* can be divided into five stages (see figure 4.3):

Stage I: *Deictic manner adverb.* Here *sate* signals that an event in q is linked to a (manner) characteristic of a previously described event in p (e.g., (50)). It is usually clause-internal.

Stage II: *Discourse marker connective.* It introduces q as being deictically linked to the instantiation, time, or logical consequences of p (e.g., (52)). It is usually clause-initial, and functions at a local discourse level.

Stage III: *Pragmatic particle signaling the beginning of a new topic,* even when there is no deictic referent in the preceding discourse (e.g., (54)). It functions at a global discourse level.

Stage IV: *Exclamatory lexeme.* It expresses special emotional involvement by SP/W in regard to q or (as a hedge) toward AD/R in addition to fulfilling global pragmatic marker function (e.g., (60)).

Stage V: *Epistolary formula.*

Sate illustrates increase in discourse pragmatic function over time, including increased scope; originating in a clause-internal adverbial function it comes to have

ADV_{manner}	>	$ADV_{adversative}$	>	$ADV_{elaboration}$	>	ADV_{hedge}
content	>	content/procedural			>	procedural
s-w-proposition	>	s-o-proposition	>	s-o-discourse		
nonsubjective	>	subjective			>	intersubjective

Figure 4.4. Correlated paths of directionality in the development of DMs.

the whole clause in its scope, and then discourse chunks. Each stage of development is a case of subjectification. Its acquisition of functions as a hedging device and epistolary formula further represents an increase in intersubjective meaning, after the epistemic functions have arisen.

4.6 Conclusion

In this chapter we have shown that, as in the case of modals, epistemic adverbs and particles arise out of nonepistemic ones. In particular, we have shown that they develop metatextual meanings that make explicit SP/AD's rhetorical purposes and attitude to what is being said. Some of these polysemies may develop intersubjective meanings; depending on the saliency of markers of intersubjectivity in a speech style or in the community as a whole, intersubjective meanings may develop more or less rapidly. The correlated paths of directionality are schematically presented in figure 4.4.

At the end of chapter 3 we mentioned Cinque's (1998) cross-linguistic hierarchy of verbal modals. This hierarchy is supplemented by a cross-linguistic hierarchy of modal ADVs (Cinque 1998: 106). A schematic hypothesis for a cross-linguistic hierarchy of ADVs with modal properties, based on Cinque's ADV hierarchy that would include the DM types discussed here, is presented in (60).[23] His hierarchy has been expanded to include a position for hedges that is further left (for head-initial languages) than the left-most ADV position he proposes, since it precedes the "speech act" type like *frankly (speaking)*.

(60) $Mod_{DMhedge} - Mod_{DM} - Mod_{speech\ act} - Mod_{evaluative} - Mod_{evidential}$
       $- Mod_{epistemic} - T_{past} - T_{future} - Mod_{irrealis} - Mod_{necessity} - Mod_{possibility}$
       $- Mod_{volitional}$, etc.

---

[23] Cinque's hierarchy starts with speech act adverbials like "frankly." He calls speech act, evaluative, evidential, irrealis adverbials "mood" adverbials, despite the fact that they are often expressed by independent elements, not bound morphology. We have used the term Modal here. Cinque also presents a far richer hierarchy than the one in (60), since he includes a large number of aspectual adverbials such as "usually," "completely," "again," "often," all of which occur to the right of the adverbials given here.

	OE	ME	MdE	PDE
Truth/modal ADV	292	816	987	1336
Evaluative ADV	44	91	103	303
Epithetical ADV	230	170	164	85
Speech Act ADV			4	39
Total	566	1077	1258	1763

Figure 4.5. Number of English initial sentence adverbials by class over time (based on Swan 1991: 412) (MdE here = 16th–19th centuries; PDE = 20th Century).

Examples of each ADV category are: "well" $Mod_{DMhedge}$, "then" Mod_{DM}, "frankly" $Mod_{speech\ act}$, "fortunately" $Mod_{evaluative}$, "alleged" $Mod_{evidential}$, "probably" $Mod_{epistemic}$, "once" T_{past}, "then" T_{future}, "perhaps" $Mod_{irrealis}$, "necessarily" $Mod_{necessity}$, "possibly" $Mod_{possibility}$, "intentionally" $Mod_{volitional}$. Not all languages will allow all positions to be occupied sequentially.

As in the case of our discussion in 3.5 of Cinque's hierarchy of verbal modals, in adapting his ADV schema we do not thereby espouse the hypothesis that all positions are present in Universal Grammar. (60) is a useful description of the cross-linguistic facts as they are known, and provides an empirically testable grid for the study of modal ADVs in languages through time and space. The semantic–pragmatic motivation for the cross–linguistic onomasiological picture is the tendency to recruit meanings into increasingly subjective semantics (non-modal > deontic > epistemic), and into increasingly larger structures (control verb > raising verb) and wider semantic scope (narrow > wide). In our view this semantic–pragmatic motivation appears to be sufficient to account for the hierarchy in (60) (and the modal hierarchy in 3.5). Therefore no innate and "particularly rich functional make-up of the sentence" (Cinque 1999: 140) need be postulated to account for it.[24]

Likewise, different languages may favor different kinds of ADVs at different times in their histories, but the direction of change involved in the recruitment of members of one adverb type into another is unidirectional. For example, in a discussion of the proportion of initial sentence ADVs by class in the history of English, Swan (1991) shows that the subtypes of sentence adverbial used have changed. According to her data, in MdE there are modal adverbs like *possibly*, evaluatives like *surprisingly*, epitheticals like *wisely*, and speech act ADVs like *frankly*. In OE, however. there were only truth intensifiers like *witodlice* "truly," epitheticals like *wislice* "wisely," and evaluatives like *wundorlice* "surprisingly." Speech act ADVs like *briefly, happily (speaking)* do not appear until the seventeenth century, and not in large numbers till the present day; see figure 4.5. The direction of change is, however, entirely regular,

---

[24] Thanks to Nigel Vincent for pointing out this conclusion.

specifically from verb-modifier to sentence-modifier, from relatively concrete to relatively abstract and nonreferential, from contentful to procedural. We expect that comparable differences in frequency of use and of innovation will be found cross-linguistically among classes of ADVs and DMs, dependent on the text types and discursive practices of speakers at the time.

We turn now to the development of performative meanings of verbs. Here marking of the discourse act being engaged in is of paramount importance.

5

The development of performative verbs and constructions

5.1 Speech act and performative verbs

Among the areas of interface between semantics and pragmatics that have attracted particular attention are "speech act verbs" and "performativity." Nevertheless, there is not yet a great deal of convergence about how to approach them, nor is there extensive understanding of cross-cultural differences with respect to speech acting (but see Blum-Kulka, House, and Kasper 1989). This naturally raises significant methodological questions for historical semantics (Papi 2000). In order to allow for comparison across time and across languages and cultures we have chosen to take a restricted view of the problem, and to focus on the semasiological questions of how certain expressions acquire "speech act" and "performative" meaning over time. Here we outline our assumptions about the domain under investigation.

There is a large number of verbs of speaking in English and Japanese. Some of these refer to ways of speaking, e.g. *whine, simper, drawl*, Jp. *donaru* "yell (angrily)," *sasayaku* "whisper"; these are verbs of "locution." Some refer to acts of speaking (*claim, say, command, threaten*, Jp. *syutyoo suru* "insist," *happyoo suru* "announce (in public)"); these are "speech act verbs" (SAVs). A subset of SAVs are "performative" ("illocutionary") verbs: verbs which, under specific conditions can be used not only to report on sayings but to have the force of a doing (Austin 1962). For example, of the set *claim, say, command, threaten*, in PDE only *claim* and *command* are typically used performatively; in Jp. *happyoo suru* "announce" is used performatively, but *syutyoo suru* "insist" is descriptive of a manner of speaking only.

Linguistic conditions for explicit performative use are (typically) first person present tense, indicative, active. However, some institutional speech acts, for example acts of Parliament, Supreme Court rulings, etc., may be plural, even third person, and passive. Performative use also involves nonlinguistic conditions such as the right of SP/W to do the act named, institutionalized social norms, etc., all of which serve to warrant the appropriateness of the action. A standard example of a verb used in performative and nonperformative functions is (see Searle 1965):

(1) a. I *promise* to go.
     b. I *promised* to go.

(1a) "counts as" or "has the illocutionary force of" a promise given certain contextual assumptions; whoever says (1a) puts him- or herself under some obligation to go in the context of an interlocutor's utterance such as *I want you to go*. A speaker may be sincere or not in making a promise, and may speak appropriately or not (one cannot appropriately promise to go somewhere if one is jailed, for example), but that (1a) is a promise is hardly true or false: a promise takes place in the saying of (1a). This performative use of SAVs is clearly procedural as well as contentful. By contrast (1b) is a report, and may be true or false: *promised* is contentful, not procedural, with respect to its SAV function.

Explicit performative verbs have discourse deictic properties in that they are self-reflexive and point to the act being performed (Verschueren 1995, 1999). In other words, they are self-deictic. Note that the word "deixis" is coined from the IE root *deik-* "show, say" and is cognate with Lat. *dic-* "say," Eng. *teach*. Meillet (1958 [1905–6] and later Benveniste (1973: 387) argue that the primary meaning of IE *deik* was showing not merely by pointing but by issuing legal proclamations (i.e. a speech act activity): in Gk. *dike* meant "accusation, judgment"; in Roman times the judge would *dicere ius* "say/show/pronounce the law solemnly," thereby creating and recreating the law. An illocutionary act is an act IN saying. Performative verbs are deeply embedded in the social deixis of the SP/W–AD/R pair (a speaker typically promises an addressee to do something), and their overt form usually reflects this. For example, in actual use, performative expressions in Jp. typically have not only first person subject referents but are also marked with humiliative forms, e.g. (*kaikai o*) *sengen itasimasu* "I humbly declare (do a humble declaration) (that the meeting is open)," *o-iwai moosiagemasu* "I/we humbly say (polite) congratulations" (="I/we send our congratulations"). Even according to Japanese standards, such forms are especially richly marked for social deixis and provide special highlighting of the SP/W–AD/R relationship. Both in Japanese and in English, some verbs in institutional performative acts take first person plural or third person forms (*We, the people of the United States/The people of the State of California do enact* . . .).

Explicit performative verbs also have properties similar to modals, a point that has been particularly clearly brought out by Searle in his discussion of the "direction of fit" between performative and world (Searle 1976, 1979). Searle distinguishes performative verbs that match world to word from those that match word to world.[1]

---

[1] The subclassifications alluded to here are based on Searle (1976); all classifications are problematic (see e.g. Mey 1993); our purpose here is only to make broad distinctions that provide semantic underpinnings to patterns of historical change.

(i) Among those that match word to world are "assertives" of various kinds, including representatives: illocutionary acts that undertake to represent a state of affairs, e.g. *state, claim, hypothesize, insist/suggest/swear that X is the case*, and verdictives: illocutionary acts that deliver a finding as to value or fact, e.g. *assess, rank, estimate*. Both representatives and verdictives have semantic properties somewhat similar to epistemic modals. They are acts designed to express SP/W's knowledge or belief or create similar knowledge or belief in AD/R.

(ii) Performative verbs that match world to word are "directives." Searle distinguishes between those directives that get others to do things (he limits the term "directive" to these), e.g. *request, command, insist/suggest that someone do X*, and those that commit oneself to do things (these he calls "commissives"), e.g. *promise, vow*. Both kinds of directives have semantic properties somewhat similar to root/deontic modals since they impose various degrees of obligation.

(iii) There is a third kind in which the direction of fit is bidirectional in that the act named comes into being with the naming (the fit is from word to world and from world to word). These are called "declaratives": illocutionary acts that bring about the state of affairs they refer to, e.g. *baptize, bet, arrest, marry*. Declaratives are the prototype examples of ways in which language brings about "the linguistic construction of social facts" (Mey 1993: 146), and of the self-deictic properties of speech acts.

Similarities between performative verbs and modality emerge not only in direction of fit, but also in the fact that modals may be used to convey performatives (Boyd and Thorne 1969). Thus an alternative to (1a) is:

(2) I *will* go.

Similarly, in the directive/deontic domain we find:

(3) a. I *order* you to go.
     b. You *will* go! (in a context such as *You will go, I insist on it!*)
     c. You *must* go! (in a context such as *You must go, I require it!*)

These modals are less direct than full performative verbs, partly because, being auxiliaries rather than main verbs, i.e. being more grammatical, they are syntactically more constrained and pragmatically more subject to contextual interpretation. Note, for example, that they cannot cooccur with *hereby* (*I hereby command you to leave* is acceptable, but **You must hereby go* is not).

Another way to express directives is mood, as in:

(4) *Go!* (compare *Go, will you!*)

Here the imperative serves as a short-hand for the full explicit performative verb construction in (3a).

Some speech acts are typically not explicitly marked at all, but nevertheless can have performative force. In English, these include acts of saying with its attendant conditions of right to speak, appropriateness of the speech content, etc. Thus utterances like *The sun is shining* have performative force as representatives, but no overt marker of performativity. (*I say unto you that* ... is regarded as appropriate primarily in Biblical contexts. Note that here it is typically not purely representative: Christ commits himself to the truth of his parables, prophecies, and other discourses, while also investing authority in himself.[2])

As noted in chapter 3, Jp. lacks a grammatical category that corresponds to the English modal verbs, although modality is expressed through various constructions in the language. Many performative acts that in English would be expressed by a performative verb or a modal are expressed in everyday conversational Jp. without an explicit verb or modal, e.g. equivalents of *I* (*promise, demand, urge, find, request, etc.*) *that* ... Instead, the form of the verb and context of utterance indicate the speech act function intended. For example, as a one-word utterance *yameru* "(unspecified subject) will quit (it)" will typically be understood as an indirect performative (promise or similar commitment by SP) to cease some action, usually one known from context. With question intonation, *Yameru?* will similarly often be understood as a request from SP to AD of the sort "Will you (please) quit (it)?" Although grammatically well formed, the explicit commissive with complement *Yameru yakusoku o suru* "(I) promise that (I) will quit" may sound anomalous if used as a performative, at least in certain speech situations.[3] In contrast, the nonperformative use of *yakusoku suru* "make a promise" in reporting a past action (*Yameru yakusoku o sita* "I made a promise to quit") is easily acceptable.

The relative infrequency in ordinary conversation of complement-plus-performative verb constructions in Jp. most likely reflects a cultural preference for indirect speech acts that is in keeping with universal strategies of politeness (see Brown and Levinson 1987 [1978]; also Blum-Kulka, House, and Kasper 1989). At the same time, this phenomenon demonstrates that, although languages may have similar materials to express a function, e.g. a directive, verdictive, or declarative

---

[2] When Wierzbicka uses "I say" in her metalinguistic analysis of speech act verbs, she is apparently not using it performatively, but rather as an indefinable semantic "primitive" without pragmatic, procedural force (e.g. Wierzbicka 1985b, 1985c). In doing so she seeks to capture the fact that speech act verbs, as names for specific speech events, have the potential to have performative value in first person present tense contexts, and are usually used to attribute "certain first person attitudes" to those who have spoken them (1997: 16). But *I say* is only one of many other potential factors.

[3] The following conversational exchange does, however, sound quite plausible:

> *A: Yameru.* "(I'll) quit."
> *B: Yakusoku suru?* "(Do you) promise?"
> *A: Yakusoku suru.* "(I) promise."

speech act, one must keep in mind that different speech communities may have different attitudes toward which mode of expression is appropriate in a particular speech situation. These different attitudes may or may not have an effect on which generalized invited inferences (GIINs) are available to take part in semantic change.

Nevertheless, in expressing directive and commissive concepts, speakers of Jp. make extensive use of socially deictic verbs of giving and receiving, which they suffix to verbs to express the proposition as constituting a favor given or received by SP/W (Martin 1975: chapter 10), e.g.:

(5) Yame-te kudasa-i.
quit-GER give:RESP-IMP
lit. "(You = socially higher) give (me = lower) the favor of quitting."
"Please quit."

(6) Yame-sase-te itadaki-masu.
quit-CAUS-GER receive:HUMIL-POL
lit. "(I = socially lower) will receive the favor (from AD = higher)
of being allowed to quit."
"I will quit."[4]

Besides being marked deictically for much greater politeness between SP and AD than is *Yameru* alone, (6) brings into focus the SP–AD relationship by means of the causative form and the suffixed donatory verb *itadaku* "(subject = socially lower) receive(s) (from indirect object referent or AD = higher)." Jp. honorifics are discussed in detail in chapter 6.

Other explicit performative verbs and constructions in Jp. are for the most part found in formal registers, which in Jp. include public speeches and most missives. It is highly characteristic of such genres to contain declarative performative expressions to identify the speech act function of the discourse both at its beginning and its end. For example, most public occasions include a speech of formal greetings by a distinguished speaker; these are usually at least several minutes in length. At or very near the beginning of such a speech, the speaker will typically say a phrase such as the following:

(7) Hitokoto go-aisatu moosiage-masu.
one-word HONP-greetings HUMIL:say
"I (SP = lower than AD) will express briefly (polite) greetings."

The speaker will typically end the speech with an expression such as:

---

[4] There is no morphological future tense marking in Jp.; however, the utterance is understood to refer to future time and to function as an indirect performative.

(8) Izyoo, kantan de-wa   gozaimasu ga,
     above simple COP-FOC VPOL   but
     go-aisatu   to   itasi-masu.
     HONP-greetings GOAL HUMIL:do-POL
     "The above is simple, but I will make it into [i.e. hereby conclude] my
     greetings."

Similar discourse bracketing is performed by other declarative performative phrases
in personal letters. Such explicit expression of the performative thus plays a global
discourse marking function in Jp., as well as naming the function of the text, but
Jp. does not always require declaratives to bracket the text in that way. As is shown
in (7) and (8), many Jp. performatives consist of an action noun that names the type
or content of the speech act plus a verb for "say" or a pro-verb "do." Other common
items found in such patterns include *iwai* "congratulations," *mimai* "inquiry (into
one's health)," and *rei* "thanks, gratitude."

The focus of the present chapter is on the semasiological development of verbs
into performative verbs; we will also investigate a verb + noun construction in Jp.
The overall claim is that verbs with speech act meanings are typically derived from
verbs with non-speech act meanings. Once this meaning shift has occurred, a SAV
that reports some event or state of affairs, often an event of speaking or cognizing,
can be used to perform that same act or a related one, given the appropriate conditions for performativity, including use in the appropriate linguistic construction.
We will also discuss briefly some aspects of the "post-performative" history of performative verbs, and also of the development of modals into indirect expressions
of performativity. But first we need to consider some problems that historians of
performativity must keep in mind as they do their research, such as the extent to
which performativity is a function of cultural norms, including register, and how to
interpret textual evidence in this domain.

5.2   Some issues for studies of the development of performative verbs

One of the major problems we find in doing historical work on lexical
performative expressions is that little research has been done from a (post-)Searlean
perspective on the types of speech acting available at any one period in the past.
Hence the role of particular expressions and the subset that appear to have been
available for performative use is not well understood. However, a number of studies
of earlier speech events or activity types such as cursing have begun (see e.g. Jucker
and Taavitsainen 2000, Culpeper and Semino 2000). There are also some studies
of particular types of verbal expressions, among them Schlieben-Lange (1983) on
verbs of chronicling and passing judgment in Medieval French; Goossens (1985)
which summarizes a variety of studies investigating the OE SAVs *cweþan, secgan*, and *sp(r)ecan*, and their rough equivalents in PDE, *say, tell*, and *speak* (see

2.2.3); Justus (1993) on prayer petitions in IE; and Arnovick (1994) on promises in English. Work on Jp. speech acts has, however, not enjoyed such attention. This is partly because OJ and MJ literary texts present various philological problems in interpreting point of view represented by quoted conversation, especially in regard to speech of the Emperor and the highest ranking nobility at court, who may have "spoken" through heralds. Moreover, linguistic studies of the history of the Japanese language to date have tended to focus on premodern literary texts, both in Japan and elsewhere, due to the historical roots of the discipline itself. Japan has a rich history of other types of *komonzyo* "old documents" that record the spoken language, including religious documents such as written vows (*kisyoomon* and *rakusyo-kisyoo*[5]) and formal records of dreams, as well as court proceedings (*senmyoogaki*) (Amino 1991), but these are typically not available in modern annotated editions with standardized orthography.

A crucial problem in this work is how to interpret the acts being performed. They often emerged from and legitimized rather different cultural conditions from those of modern times. It has frequently been pointed out that the specifics of performativity are far from universal. Rosaldo (1982) discusses the speech act practices of the Ilongots of Northern Luzon, Philippines, and shows that in their culture personhood is shaped in ways very different from those in English-speaking cultures; specifically, the Ilongots do not have uniquely identifiable expressions for personal commitment such as *I promise* (Rosaldo 1982: 207), although they have many for directives and declaratives. Wierzbicka (1985b) discusses the untranslatability of speech acts cross-culturally. Therefore, we cannot assume that earlier verbs that appear to have speech act functions necessarily had performative functions, or the same performative functions that we recognize today.

It appears, for example, that IE speakers conceptualized what we think of today as promises (commissives) or prayers (polite directives), as reciprocally negotiated interactions between man and god, rather than as centered in the first person subject (Benveniste 1973). This is in part because the first person form was often not used in the prayers and petitions that have come down to us in Hittite, Homeric Gk. and earlier Lat. (Justus 1993); second person imperative is typical instead. An example in Hittite is:

(9) {ANA DUMU.SAL.GAL = ma = kan anda assuli namma *neshut*
     to   daughter-great = PTC = PTC to   please again turn-2SG-IMP

---

[5] The latter term typically refers to a vow to a god that one has been truthful in one's testimony about a crime to which no suspect would confess. After all the *rakusyo* were posted in public places, the criminal was picked out by secret ballot. The *rakusyo* were regarded as reflecting the will of the gods (Amino 1991: 20–21).

```
n = an      kez      GIG-za      TI-nut            nu = ssi    eni
PTC = her this-ABL sickness-ABL save-2SG-IMP PTC = her this
GIG      awan arha  namma *tittanut*}
sickness ADV away  again    set-2SG-IMP
```
"Please turn again toward the Great Princess, save her from this sickness, again take this sickness completely from her"

> (Mursili II's prayer, CTH 380 Obv. 16'-17 [Justus 1993: 134])

By later Lat. first person indicatives ("I pray") with subordinate subjunctives begin to appear, as in (10).

(10) Mars pater,   te   *precor   quaeso*que   uti   sies
      Mars father, you-ACC   pray-1SG beseech-1SG-and that be-2SG-SUBJUNCT
      uolens propitius mihi   domo   familiaeque   nostrae
      wishing propitious I-DAT house-DAT family-DAT-and our-DAT
      "Father Mars, I pray and beseech you that you be favorable and well disposed to me, our house, and family"

> (1st century BC, Cato, 1412 [Justus 1993: 138])

Of this kind of use of first person Justus says: "The indicative Latin speech act verbs, 'pray, ask,' contrast with the Homeric second person imperative of 'give, grant.' The Homeric construction is of the type 'Give/grant, Apollo, (that) they pay,' ... while Cato's [subordinate ECT/RD] subjunctive illustrates the 'I pray that you, Mars, be propitious' type" (Justus 1993: 138). Here we find a shift from focus on the addressee as participant in some future event being negotiated to focus on the speaker as actor in the speech event itself, directly indexing the "here" and "now" of the act of speaking. Once this discourse strategy had been established, and norms had developed for the speaker to self-identify (by using first person) at the same time as act-identify (by using an SAV performatively to index the discursive act), the particular Ls chosen could come to undergo further semasiological change such as intersubjectification and use as epistemic parentheticals (see 5.4.1) and politeness markers (see 6.3.2). One question for the historical linguist must be to what extent such observed differences between Hittite and later Latin should be interpreted, as here, in terms of modern views of speech acting, with the conclusion that in the early texts there was no fully explicit performativity in terms of an explicit *I X you Y* expression, or whether we should conclude that the nature of performativity was different. We take the position that as linguistic form is related to linguistic meaning, it is reasonable to investigate whether and how certain structural features of performativity such as person and tense came to be expressed over time. While acknowledging that the reasons for the changes over time are social and not linguistic, we argue that the mechanisms whereby the changes were enabled are, however, largely cognitive–communicative and therefore linguistic.

Although our focus here is not on cultural reasons for changes in speech acting, we cannot ignore the fact that one of the major cultural changes that has affected the meaning and lexical resources for speech acting is unquestionably writing. In her study of the development of historiography in fifteenth century French, Schlieben-Lange (1983) has shown that new concepts of the purposes of writing led to changes in the inventory of speech acts verbs pertaining to narration. For example, whereas in the thirteenth century, the typical term used was *conter* "to tell," by the fifteenth century terms that evoked collecting of material already available and organizing it were prevalent, many of them borrowed from Latin, e.g. *compiler* "compile, gather up," *composer* "put in order" (Schlieben-Lange 1983: chapter 6). When, in the ME period, English began to gain ground as a language of institution, there was a tremendous influx of borrowed performative verbs, many of them themselves relatively new in French. This was presumably due to the need to find a vocabulary for the production and reproduction of feudal society, including its laws and literary genres. It was a period of political and social upheaval in which new SAVs were needed, whether for claims on French territory in the Hundred Years War, for claims against feuding warlords in the Wars of the Roses, or for translating French literary works, such as the *Romaunt of the Rose* (translated by Chaucer). It was a period of rapid increase in commerce, hence the need for language related to contracts and the new bureaucracies, and of the rise of universities, and hence the need for language related to academic exercise.

The tendency for explicit speech act expressions to occur in institutional texts is likewise true of Japanese, except that here there is the additional complexity that many official documents were written in *kanbun* (Ch. or quasi-Ch., see 1.6.1) throughout much of the recorded history of Japan. Although the speech act expressions in such texts are mostly performatives that appear to have been institutionalized in writing, the fact that they are in *kanbun* obscures their path of development in Jp. Moreover, some speech act expressions may have been translated from written Chinese institutional text genres through *kanbun* (*kanbun* supplied linguistic materials to other domains also, e.g. DMs). Most of the SAVs in use in MdJ rose during the LMJ period (fourteenth and fifteenth centuries). Although this was a period of great turnovers in the vocabulary of many semantic fields, it may be no accident that this vocabulary appeared during a time that also saw the rise of a monetary economy and the emergence of a major social class engaged in commerce (see Amino 1991 for a discussion of such language-external factors).

A second significant problem is the fact that the written documents that have come down to us may not be of the type that favor first person present tense indicative forms. In other words, they fail to allow the formulae typically identified with performativity. In OE times, for example, Latin was by and large the language of education and of institutional documentation, although some Anglo-Saxon wills have come down to us; therefore we have few relevant OE documents for investigating performative expressions. At this time the king, as formal head of the political community, referred to himself in the third as well as first person. A well-known example occurs in the letter by King Alfred that accompanied a copy of the translation of the *Cura Pastoralis* that he had authorized:

(11) Ælfred   kyning *hateð*   gretan   Wærferð biscep his wordum
      Alfred   king   bid-3SG greet-INF Werferth bishop his words:DAT
      luflice &   freondlice   &   ðe cyðan   *hate*   ðæt
      lovingly and in friendly fashion and you know-INF bid-1SG that
      me com   swiðe oft   on gemynd ...
      me came very often to mind
      "King Alfred greets Bishop Werferth lovingly and in friendly fashion; and I ask
      you to know that it often came to my mind that ..."

(*c.* 880 Alfred, Preface to Cura Pastoralis, p. 3)

In (11) *hateþ* is third person, *hate* first; both are present and indicative. Is the third person clause to be understood performatively? Probably, considering that the prototypical first person act of Austin, Searle, and other researchers in performativity is in fact often third person in institutional settings. Some first person representation occurs in speeches in poems like *Beowulf*, and in translations of dialogues such as Boethius' *Consolation of Philosophy*, but for the most part first person forms are relatively infrequent in the OE prose corpus, except in wills.[6] In ME times, French acquired institutional prestige, in addition to Latin. An effort was made to establish English as the language of law and education in the mid-fourteenth century, but English was not widely used for either till the sixteenth century (Tiersma 1999). Absent many documents with first person present tense performative verbs, we often have to rely on third person past tense reports of what appear to be performative acts.

A related problem is that, as has been alluded to in 5.1, many explicit speech act expressions are formal in register. They may be part of academic style, e.g. *In this paper I claim/hypothesize that*; of religious ceremony, e.g. prayers and blessings (see Justus 1993); of legal affairs such as contracts, guarantees, and court rulings (see Kurzon 1986, Tiersma 1986); and of institutions of power generally (see Bourdieu 1991). Poetry has its own speech act conventions; when Virgil starts the Aeneid with *Arma virumque cano* "Arms and the man I sing," or Whitman writes *I sing the body electric*, they performatively bring into being the conventions of sacral poetic

---

[6] Danet and Bogoch (1994: 112) point out that although OE wills were intended as a record of an oral ceremony and could well have been written in third person, nevertheless many were rendered close to verbatim, in the first person.

acts. Given their association with registers that tend to be formal, institutional, and ritualized, it is hardly surprising that despite the generic term "speech act verbs," they are very largely, at least these days, acts that are specified in writing. In many cases, relatively indirect modal or even nonexplicit forms of performativity are preferred in ordinary language. It is also hardly surprising that explicit performative verb functions may be associated with borrowed vocabulary. When rhetorical styles, laws, institutions, or cultural practices are borrowed or imposed by conquest, the language associated with older practices may be deemed inappropriate or illiterate, and whole-sale replacement may occur. In Eng., Lat. roots, often borrowed via Fr., and Gk. roots tend to predominate. Similarly, in Jp., many performatives are formed around Sino-Japanese nouns (plus a verb for "say" or a pro-verb meaning "do"), e.g. *sengen suru* "declare," *nintei suru* "determine, find," *handan suru* "judge." Many such forms, regardless of whether they are built around Sino-Japanese loanwords, originate from scholarly or religious registers, e.g. *o-iwai suru* "congratulate" (<"perform a religious ritual to ask for blessing"), *aisatu suru* "give a (formal) greeting" (<a Zen Buddhist term for mutual question-and-answer that leads toward Enlightenment). As historians of performativity we must be aware of these register differences, and of their "learnedness."

A glimpse into the different social and rhetorical functions of borrowed and native SAVs and explicit performativity is provided in Bergner's (1998) study of speech styles in the ME mystery plays. He points out that certain characters, typically God, Jesus, Mary, Abraham, use primarily "vertical style" – they have predetermined socioreligious roles; their speech is monologic rather than dialogic; "it supplies important information, foretells, preaches, interprets, and harmonizes the atmosphere of the discussion" (Bergner 1998: 77). In the York Cycle, Jesus speaks only twice in the Crucifixion scene; his words, which are typical of the "vertical style," include not only native directive SAVs like *bid*, *beseech*, but also the borrowed commissive *obblisshe* "commit, contract (oneself)," all within the space of six lines:

(12) þou *badde* þat I shulde buxsom be
    you asked that I should willing be
      For Adam   plyght for to be pyned.
      for Adam's plight for to be crucified
    Here to dede I *obblisshe* me
    here to death I commit   myself
      Fro þat synne for   to saue mankynde,
      from that sin for   to save mankind
    And soueraynely *beseke* I þe
    and devoutly   beseech I thee
      That þai for me may fauoure fynde.
      that they for me may mercy find

"You asked me to be willing to be punished for Adam's sin; here I commit
myself to death to save mankind from that sin, and I fervently beg you that
you will grant them mercy on my behalf."

(*c.* 1373 York Plays, l.51 [Bergner 1998: 78])

By contrast, shepherds, soldiers, and others who are characterized as of low birth
and ignorant engage in a "horizontal style," largely characterized by "approval and
agreement" and "empty verbal gestures" (Bergner 1998: 81). Many of these "empty
verbal gestures" are exclamations, parentheticals, conventional greetings, and other
markers of intersubjectivity:

(13) *2 Pastor:* How, Gyb, goode morne! Wheder goys thou?
      Thou goys ouer the corne! Gyb, I say, how!
   1 Pastor: Who is that? – John Horne, I make God avowe!
      I say not in skorne, Ihon, how farys thou?
      "How now, Gyb, good morning! Where are you going? You are
      walking across the corn! Gyb, I say, hey!"
      "Who is that? – John Horn, I swear. I say without jest, John, how
      are you?"

(*c.* 1450 Wakefield Plays, 82 [Bergner 1998: 81])

However, when the shepherds see the Christ child they shift to a style closer to the
vertical.

We turn now to the lexical resources from which new institutional meanings were
created in English and Japanese (or their donor languages).

5.3   Precursors of performative verbs[7]

Fraser (1975) lists some 275 "speech act verbs" in PDE (some, like
figure, are only rarely used performatively; some, like *aver*, are rarely used at all).
The large majority is borrowed from Fr. or Lat. Sources of performative verbs in
Eng., especially those that were borrowed, frequently involve presence or motion
in space; so do several in Jp. In other words, they reveal many of the characteristics
Reddy (1993 [1979]) has associated with what he calls the "conduit metaphor": the
metaphor of language as an object that can be manipulated, transferred along paths
or through a container of some sort.[8] Among such terms we may note:

(i)   Position in space: *insist* < Lat. *in* "in, on" + past participle of *sta-*
      "stand,"

---

[7] Section 5.3 is drawn in part from Traugott and Dasher (1987) and Traugott (1991).

[8] For a critique of Reddy's pessimism regarding the conduit metaphor, and for discussion of the broad
variety of terms used in contemporary English to express metatextual, including performative,
meaning, see Vanparys (1995); Pauwels and Simon-Vandenbergen (1995) discuss in particular
the extension of body-part terminology to Ls for linguistic action.

(ii) Motion through space: *concur* < Lat. *con* "with" + *curr-* "run"; *concede* < Lat. *con* "with" + *ced-* "go away, withdraw,"

(iii) Transfer along a path: *suggest* < Lat. *sub* "under" + past participle of *ger-* "carry"; *suppose* < Lat. *sub* + past participle of *pon-* "put"; *assent* < Lat. *ad* "to" + *sent-* "go, head for"; *admit* < Lat. *ad* + *mitt-* "send" (see also many other derivatives of this root, some of them past participial, such as *promise, dismiss, permit, submit*); Jp. *ukeireru* "assent, grant (a request)" < *ukeru* "receive" + *ireru* "send in, insert"; *tataeru* "praise, extol"[9] < OJ *tataFu* "fill to overflowing."[10]

It has been suggested that the metaphoric extension of spatial terms into metalinguistic ones naming speech events is a function of literacy (e.g. Ong 1982), since it is only with literacy that language is objectified in visual space. However, the conceptualization of speech acts in terms of concrete objects manipulable in space seems to be possible in preliterate societies as well. For example, in discussing lexical fields for metalinguistic terms in Eipo, a language of West New Guinea, Heeschen says: "The semantic fields that seem to be most effective in creating metalinguistic terms are those of carving and cutting, and of laying bare the edible part of a fruit. Longer bits of information, conversation, and tales are conceived as acts of enumerating names, or tying together or accumulating words" (Heeschen 1983: 172 [Traugott 1991: 403]). This having been said, it is nevertheless probably true that literacy favors the widespread use of spatial terms for markers of discourse moves, e.g. signaling topic shift, outlining what is to be said/written, etc. Fleischman (1991), for example, citing Perret (1982), suggests that the shift from use of French as an oral medium in the twelfth century to a written one by the end of the thirteenth century is correlated with a shift from the use of temporal markers for discourse flow to spatial ones. Specifically, there was a shift in discursive practice from *or* "now" as "the predominant traffic-signal for marking the current position in the discourse" (Fleischman 1991: 304) to *cy* "here."[11] Hardly surprisingly, in the thirteenth century both often cooccur not only in the same text but even in the same sentence, as is typical in periods of transition:

(14) *Or* se taist *cy* l'ystoire des deux chevaliers.
now REFL breaks here the-story of:the two knights

[9] *Tataeru* is used performatively in Jp. Christian hymns and similar text types.

[10] Similarly, in MdMand: *ti* "suggest" < Archaic Chinese "lift a hand"; *ju* "recommend" < "elevate with hands" (Shiao-Wei Tham, p.c.).

[11] It should be noted, however, that the OE Chronicle uses *her* "here" to mean "in this year/at this point in the calendar," even in texts supposed to be oral in origin, e.g. the entry for 775 (in the Chronicle entry *her* might of course be a frame provided by the chronicler, not part of the original narrative).

"Now the story of the two knights breaks off here."
(13th century [Fleischman 1991: 304])

In addition to performatives derived from spatial terms that may be favored by literate communities (though not limited to them), there are others, for example those which are derived from terms for:

(iv) Visual perception e.g. *advise* < Lat. *ad* + *vis-* "watch, observe" < *vid-* "see"; *argue* < IE *arg-* "shine, white" (see *argent* "silver"); Jp. *mitomeru* "recognize" < MdJ *miru* "see" + *tomeru* "stop (something)"; *kokuhaku suru* "confess" < *koku* "(give a) report" + *haku* "white."

Space and sight are by no means the only sources for performative verbs. Even among verbs borrowed into Eng. from Lat. or Fr. Other sources include terms for:

(v) Vocalization, including speaking, calling, and shouting, e.g. *advocate* < Lat. *ad* + *voc-* "toward call"; *deplore/implore* < Lat. *de* "from", *in* "in" + *plor-* "wail"; OE *swer-* "swear," *andswer-* "answer" < IE *and-* "against" + *swer-* "speak,"

(vi) Mental state including: cognitive states like *acknowledge, recognize* < IE *gno-* "know"; OE *acyðan* "announce, confirm" (< OE *cuþ* "known" < IE *gno-* "know"); emotive states like *volunteer* < Lat. *vell-* "want,"

(vii) Manipulation of a concrete object: OE *bidd-* "ask, order" (< IE *bedh-* "bend"); *read-* "advise, explain" (<IE *ar-* "fit together"); Jp. *kotowaru* "refuse, make conditions on (the validity of) a statement" < *koto* "word, thing" + *waru* "split (something)."

The sources of SAVs that are used for performative purposes provide further evidence for the shifts that are the theme of this book: from non-speech oriented to speech oriented meaning, from nonsubjective to subjective meaning. Even if the self is institutional, there is a preemption of meanings to that self, and to the discursive event. They also illustrate in a domain other than that of DM a semantic shift from an expression with content semantics to one that has a dual content–procedural function, specifically a discourse deictic function.

(15) event verb > speech act verb > performative (discourse deictic) verb

We would not expect use of *recognize* in an expression like *I recognize that I was wrong to do that* to appear before the mental state verb *recognize*, or for a verb like *argue* to come to mean "shine."

5.4   The development of performative function

Our case studies involve examples of the development of directives, and declaratives; in particular we discuss the development of commissives meaning PROMISE, a Chinese expression for GUARANTEE, and a Japanese expression for GREET.

5.4.1   *Some directives: PROMISE in English*

In this section we look at the commissive PROMISE, and aspects of how it came into being as a SAV and how it developed beyond its SAV meaning.[12] "Commissive" acts are those illocutionary acts whose point is to commit SP/W, and sometimes also AD/R, in varying degrees to some future course of action. Of commissives, Searle has said that "[t]he direction of fit is world-to-word and the sincerity condition is Intention. The propositional content is always that the speaker S does some future action A" (Searle 1979: 14). Commissive verbs in MdE include *promise, vow, pledge, guarantee, swear*. In OE they include *gehat-* and *behat-* "pledge (oneself)."

Commitment "in varying degrees" is a caution that in different cultural traditions, and at different times, commissives may be more or less self-reflexive. This seems to be especially true of the English-specific representation of PROMISE that Searle (1979) treated as the prototype performative: PDE *promise*. In PDE a promise is above all an individual act, for which no reciprocal act is anticipated (barring some stated condition, as in "If you do X, I promise to do Y"). In some cultures the notion of *promise* is hardly known (as in the case of the Ilongots cited in 5.2 above). Or it may be a very serious act, closer to a "vow" than what we tend rather loosely to call a "promise" these days (Arnovick 1994). Benveniste (1973) suggests that in Indo-European times vowing and swearing were not so much acts by an individual swearing or vowing that he or she would do such and such but rather interactive negotiations between man and gods. The gods were expected to respond favorably, and therefore to vow was to consecrate oneself in anticipation of support from the gods. We will see that the verbs which *promise* replaced had more of the reciprocal qualities that Benveniste identifies than *promise*.

Discussing *promise*, the seventeenth century philosopher Hobbes, in an early precursor of speech act theory, saw it as primarily the expression of "purpose or intention":

> Another use of speech is the expression of appetite, intention, and will; as the appetite of knowledge by interrogation; appetite to have a thing done by another, as request, prayer, petition; expressions of our purpose or intention,

---

[12] Parts of section 5.4.1 draw on Traugott (1996).

as PROMISE, which is the affirmation or negation of some action to be done
in the future; THREATENING, which is the promise of evil.
(1650 Hobbes, Elements of Law, Pt. 1, chapter 13, p. 67; caps original)

Like many others since his time, Hobbes paired *promise* with *threaten*. For example, of commissives, Palmer has said that "the only difference between" threats
and promises "seems to be in what the hearer wants" (Palmer 1986: 115). However, *promise* can be used performatively, while *threaten* cannot, as noted by Searle
(1979: 7), and before him, Hobbes: "Even amongst men, though the promise of
good, bind the promiser; yet threats, that is to say, promises of evil, bind them not"
(1651 Hobbes, Leviathan, Pt. 3 chapter 38, p. 456).

Furthermore, promises are institutional, and must be communicated, but threats
and warnings "to the extent they are speech acts at all" need not be (Sperber and
Wilson 1995 [1986]: 145). In other words, *threaten* is not a performative verb,
though it can be an SAV; it pairs with *promise* only in the latter's nonperformative
uses. This casts doubt on the appropriateness of trying to predict historical changes
for THREATEN based on an assumed parallel with PROMISE, as do Traugott
(1996) for Eng., and Verhagen (2000) for the equivalents in Du.: *beloven* "promise"
and *dreigen* "threaten."

The noun *promise* was borrowed into late ME shortly after 1400 (i.e. after
Chaucer's time) from Fr. A deverbal noun in Lat., it was ultimately derived from
the past participle of the spatial verb *pro-mittere* "to send forward," i.e. a promise
was something "sent forward." In Lat. *promittere* was used not only as a verb of
transmission but also as an SAV "vow" and, usually with inanimate subjects, in
the epistemic meaning "portend." It was specialized in Late Lat. exclusively in the
nonspatial senses, as reflected by a split in the root forms: *-mitt-* was restricted
to PROMISE, *-mett-* to SEND. Nevertheless, in early Fr. *-mitt-* was analogized to
-mett- "send," so the form *promettre* was found in Fr. from very early times. This
PROMISE verb was largely restricted to religious contexts. It appears that in the
history of Fr., the speech act meaning preceded the "portend" meaning (*Robert* 1992
cites the locutionary meaning *c.* 980 and the portend meaning *c.* 1160, and comments that the latter was replaced by *prédire*). Since both meanings were already
available in Lat. and therefore both might have been expected to appear at the same
time in OFr., this suggests that the "portend" meaning was derived anew in Fr. If
so, this development again involves the deontic > epistemic shift. As we will see,
the same sequence of development was replicated in English (in two different sets
of lexical representations of PROMISE).

A few instances are cited in the MED of the French verbal form *promit* in ME,
but the most frequent form *promise* seems to have been coined in English from the
noun. As a verb, *promise* is found in the Helsinki Corpus at first with a sentential

complement (either a *that*-clause or a *to*-clause) primarily to report what we must assume were illocutionary acts. Typically we find third person past or even passive examples:

(16) a. vn-to þe day whech he had *promysed* to come a-geyn.
           unto the day which he had promised to come back
           "to the day on which he had promised to return."

(after 1438, Kempe, 57 [Traugott 1996: 186])

      b. that the seid Pilgrymage was avowed and *promysed* for
           that the said pilgrimage was sworn and promised for
           the greet periles and combrous occupacions that be
           the great dangers and onerous occupations that by
           liklynesse at diuerse tymes myght haue falle.
           likelihood at various times might have happened
           "that the said pilgrimage was sworn to and promised in anticipation of the
           great dangers and difficult tasks that might have been expected to happen."

(1441 Documents Chancery, p. 167)

First person present examples that appear to be performative first occur in the later part of the fifteenth century in drama. In (17) Herod has just ordered Watkyn to engage in the activity now known as the Slaughter of the Innocents, and Watkyn responds:

(17)   We wylle let for no man ...
               we will stop for no man
        For your knyghtes and I wille kylle them alle, if we can! ...
        for your knights and I will kill them all, if we can
        An *this I promyse you*, that I shalle neuer slepe,
        and this I promise you, that I shall never sleep
        But euermore wayte to fynde the children alone.
        but always wait to find the children alone.
        "We won't stop for anyone ... your knights and I will kill them all if we can
        ... and I promise you this, that I will not sleep but wait till I find the children
        alone."

(*c*. 1500 Digby Plays, p. 102)

A different type of expression arises in LME: a formulaic epistemic parenthetical construction *I promise you*. Like other epistemic parentheticals it is speech-time, not future oriented (see Thompson and Mulac 1991, Aijmer 1996). It indexes SP/W's degree of certitude about the utterance, whatever the tense of the described event. In this sense it is subjective and modal in character. At the same time there is some intersubjectivity, because its use suggests SP/W recognizes there may be some doubt in AD/R's mind about the veracity of what is being said. The parenthetical function is clearest after the main clause. Here it is noncommissive and seems to serve primarily as an assurance or a hedge.

(18) He losyth sore   hys tyme her, *I promyse yow.*
      He wastes badly his time here I promise you
      "He is wasting his time badly here, actually."

(1469 Paston I, 542 [MED])

It can also precede the main clause without a complementizer. Here it appears to serve as a comment on the utterance that follows, somewhat like epistemic speech act adverbials *truly* (*speaking*), *for sure.* As in clause-final position, it presumably serves interpersonal functions:

(19)   *Pinchwife:*   I tell you then, one of the lewdest fellows in town, who
                          saw you there, told me he was in love with you . . .
       Mrs. Pinchwife: Was it any Hampshire gallant, any of our neighbours? *I*
                          promise you, I am beholding ["grateful"] to him.
           Pinchwife: *I promise you*, you lie; for he would but ruin you, as he has
                          done hundreds.

(1674/75 Wycherley, II.i.109)

Did this derive directly from the performative or from some other source? As Brinton (1996: chapter 8) points out, a class of epistemic parentheticals, especially those with first person and a verb of cognition, e.g. *I woot wel* "I know well," *I wene* "I think," *I undertake; I guess*, came to be widely used in ME, especially in the works of Chaucer, perhaps to suggest oral style. While these may have served as partial models, they are different in many respects. They do not have speech let alone performative meaning in any of their uses; the second person pronoun is not part of the formula. Another characteristic that is not shared by *I promise you* parentheticals is that, according to Brinton, their precursors include constructions of the type *I Verb so*, e.g. *I wene so*, with anaphoric *so* referring to a prior clause. The closest parallel to the latter kind of construction attested with *promise* appears in examples in which the SAV is nonperformative and has a direct object, as in:

(20)   and there asked hym a gyffte that he promysed her whan she gaff hym the
       swerde. "That ys sothe," seyde Arthure, "a gyffte I *promysed* you, but I have
       forgotyn the name of my swerde."

(before 1471 Malory, Morte Darthur, p. 48)

But *I promised you so* does not appear in the data. Because of this and the other two differences alluded to it appears that *I promise you* parentheticals probably had a different origin from those with a verb of cognition.

207

The most likely source of the epistemic parenthetical *I promise thee/yow* is in the illocutionary use of *promise*. If derived from illocutionary uses, then the speech-time oriented meaning is presumably conventionalized from the speech-time commitment that is a condition for the future orientation of the performative. As we will see below, earlier verbs in English representing PROMISE also became epistemic parentheticals; here too there does not appear to be a viable analogy with the verbs of cognition. We therefore hypothesize that the performative formula was the origin in this case of verbs of promising.

The transitive *promise* illustrated in (20) appears to have given rise in the late sixteenth century to yet a different kind of epistemic use. It is not an SAV in meaning, nor is it parenthetical; rather it means "can be expected to provide/portend." This new epistemic use is future-oriented. It appears to involve an extension from the basic use of *promise* (as a lexical representation of speaking/language that raises expectations) to use as a lexical representation of states of affairs (rather than agentive persons) that raise expectations:

(21)   a.   Yf any man all this can gett, shall he haue the greatest felicitie, shall he fynde
           her in these that we haue shewed you, *promise* more than they giue?
           "If anyone can acquire all this, will he have the greatest happiness, will he
           find it in these things [honor, glory, and pleasure] that, as we have shown
           you, promise more than they give?"

           (1593 Queen Elizabeth, p. 57 [Traugott 1996: 187])

       b.   As the morning *promised* a fair day we set out, but the storm coming up again
           we were obliged to come to.

           (1784 Muhl [Traugott 1996: 187])[13]

The epistemic transitive type in (21) seems to be a precursor for the development in the eighteenth century of nonperformative raising uses with nonfinite complements. Here the meaning is "portend," a meaning that, as we have seen, had developed in Fr. for *promettre*, but apparently came into being independently in English. The SP/W views the proposition as likely to occur in the future, based on experience ("I expect X"), and evaluates it positively (hence collocations with terms of approval, such as *extraordinary, handsome*, as in (22) below). Early examples suggest that the complements are limited to inchoative events with the verb *be* (understood as "turn out to be"):

(22)   a.   *Mirabell:*   I have seen him. He *promises* to be an extraordinary person; I
                       think you have the honour to be related to him.

                       (1700 Congreve, *Way of the World*, Act I, p. 329)

---

[13] Examples (21b) and (22b) are from *A Representative Corpus of Historical English Registers
1650–1990* (ARCHER), provided by courtesy of Douglas Biber and Edward Finegan.

    b.   The Capitol *promised* to be a large and handsome building, judging from the part about two thirds already above ground.

                      (1795 Twin [Traugott 1996: 188])

By the end of the nineteenth century we find the construction extended to a variety of other stative verbs, as well as to weather-constructions such as (23). Here it signals primarily future. In these cases, the thematic role of the subject is demoted or nonexistent, and the raising is more canonical:

(23)   The weather was hardening into what *promised* to be half a gale.

                (1891 Eng. Illustr. Mag. Oct., 65 [Higgins 1990])[14]

It is in examples like this that Langacker's and Traugott's views of subjectification come closest, though different conclusions are reached regarding explicitness.

    This sketch of *promise* suggests that it has undergone subjectification on two different paths, depending on the linguistic as well as the socially interactive context. In the first person present tense, when introducing a sentential complement, it could presumably be used as a performative verb; as a performative, it expresses speaker's appropriation of authority as an actor attempting to match world to word. A probable further outgrowth of the performative use was the epistemic parenthetical, which is an instance of intersubjectification since it explicitly pays attention to AD/R's image needs in the here and now of the speech event. Like the development of *in fact*, it evidences a shift to increasingly pragmatic, discourse-based meanings, as well as to more subjective meanings. Recruiting a verb designating a certain kind of locution (itself ultimately derived from an originally spatial lexeme) to performative use involves recruiting it from the domain of content semantics to function also as a procedural indexing the kind of discourse being engaged in. Recruiting this verb (in construction with the SP/AD pronouns) to the class of epistemic parentheticals involves recruiting it to a primarily procedural class, the chief function of which is not so much to express epistemic modality, but to comment on the statement being engaged in, and to acknowledge at the discourse level that AD/R might have doubts about SP/W's message.

    The second path of development discussed here occurred primarily in third person contexts: development to an epistemic raising verb via generalization of the transitive verb with NP object to nonfinite complements with *be(come)* verbs. The development of epistemic meaning here too is a case of subjectification because the verb is recruited to express SP/W's belief-state about the future explicitly. In this case, however, there is no increase in procedural meaning.

---

[14] Higgins (1990: 10) points out that the kinds of developments discussed here (which are analyzed in his paper as a shift from control to raising verb status) "are not shared by other verbs in the same semantic field, that of commissives ... or undertakings ... such as pledge, swear, vow."

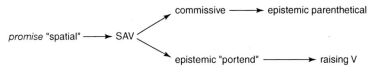

Figure 5.1. The development of *promise*.

These two paths of development are summarized in figure 5.1.

At this point we may compare a study of the development of Dutch *beloven* "promise" by Verhagen (2000). *Beloven* has since the nineteenth century had a polysemy between the speech act ("X says that X will") and epistemic ("be likely to") meanings such as are attested in English in (17) and (19) respectively. Examples are:

(24) a. Hij *beloofde* de grondwet te verdedigen.
        he promised the base-law to defend
        "He promised to defend the constitution."

      b. Het debat *beloofde* spannend te worden.
        the debate promised exciting   to become
        "The debate promised to be exciting."

(Verhagen 2000: 201)

In a variant of Langacker's theory of subjectivity, Verhagen distinguishes "character-subjectivity" (descriptive properties associated with the reported subject) from "speaker–hearer subjectivity." Thus when someone reports (24a) character-subjectivity is attributed to the third person (*he* performed a positively oriented subjective act of promising); there is also speaker–hearer subjectivity, because the speaker aligns him- or herself positively to the act (and "echoes" it by using *beloven* rather than a negatively oriented word like *dreigen* "threaten"). Verhagen goes on to argue that the development of epistemic meaning in (24b) from (24a) is not an increase in subjectivity, but rather loss of descriptive aspects of meaning, including character-subjectivity, while speaker–hearer subjectivity is maintained. Loss of descriptive aspects of meaning is a way of describing a shift from "control" to "raising" construction status (assuming that control is a gradient phenomenon, as suggested by Dowty 1985 and Higgins 1990 on a continuum from full control to noncontrol). Whatever the case in Du., the Eng. data suggest that a different path of development occurred. For one, epistemic uses of *promise* did not arise directly out of control constructions (see (21)). If the only change at issue in Eng. was the loss of character subjectivity, it would be difficult to account for the development of those epistemic polysemies that are not necessarily positively oriented (see (23)), or of epistemic parentheticals, which involve speech-time rather than future orientation (see 18)). It appears that for English at least increased subjectification, given different constructions, is what occurred.

Since *promise* was borrowed, a natural question is whether it replaced an older term and if so why. In OE times there is no question that there were commissives roughly equivalent to *promise*. The verb root most often used was *hat-* (originally a locutionary verb of bidding and naming), and especially its derivatives *gehat-*, *behat-*. Somewhat more like oaths and vows than MdE promising, they were used primarily in contexts of considerable social significance and evoked social and spiritual contract. During the ME period they began to be used in more general contexts, as epistemic parentheticals, and, at the end of the period, with inanimate subjects, i.e. with a very similar historical trajectory to *promise* several centuries later.

In *Beowulf*, the eponymous hero swears several things to Hroþgar, whose kingdom has been ravaged by the monster Grendel, among them that Hroþgar will be able to sleep in his hall, Heorot, without fear (example (34) in chapter 3, repeated here as (25)):

(25) Ic hit þe   þonne *gehate*,   þæt þu on Heorote most
     I it you then   promise   that you in Heorot may
     sorh-leas   swefan.
     anxiety-less sleep
     "I promise you this, that you will be able to sleep free from anxiety in Heorot."
     (8th century Beowulf, l. 1671)

In a charter bequeathing land to the bishop, earl, and others in Norfolk and Suffolk, King Edward says:

(26) Eadward cyningc gret   Ægelmer biscop ... freondlice.
     Edward king   greets Aylmer Bishop... friendly-ADV
     ic cyæ   eou   þæt hic *gehate* be   fullan hæse þæt Sancte
     I announce 2PL-DAT that I promise by   full   behest that Saint
     Eadmundes inland   sy   scotfreo fram heregelde.
     Edmund's inland[15] be-SUBJUNCT exempt from war-tax
     "King Edward greets Bishop Aylmer ... cordially. I declare to you that I pledge
     that that part of St. Edmund's land that belongs to me shall be exempt from
     taxes."
     (1075 Charter (Harm.), 15)

Here *ic gehate* seems closer to "pledge" than to "promise" in the modern sense. It is a solemn vow.

Charters (or "wills") are an especially rich source of information about OE commissives, and give us insight into developing legal practices. In addition, they show how speech acts that were originally spoken came to acquire new meanings in the context of writing (see Danet 1997 on the shift from oral to written styles in a variety

---

[15] An "inland" was a part of a domain retained by a lord, as opposed to "outland" over which he did not have direct control.

of ritualized discourses, including legal discourse). In OE a will was a written representation of an oral act of committing and contracting: "individuals contracted with the Church to look after their souls after death, in exchange for transfer of property" (Danet and Bogoch 1994: 106). Since the oral act, even when written down, was not held to be binding, many OE wills end with a curse on whoever might try to go against the wishes of the testator, or a blessing for those who carried them out. By the seventeenth century wills became unilateral acts, binding declarations in their written form with respect to bequeathing property, etc., but also, according to Bach (1995), for stating religious beliefs at a time of religious uncertainties (and wars). What is important for us here is the observation that, despite their deep embedding in the context of social practices, individual SAVs nevertheless underwent similar historical changes.

In the case of *gehatan/behatan*, as the nature of commitments changed over time, especially in the context of feudal England, the old Germanic term came to be strongly associated with vowing and swearing to do something, as evidenced by such reports as (27) in which the verb collocates with *vow* or *swear*:

(27) a. þis light þey han *hoten*   and a-vowed to kepen.
      this light they have promised and vowed to maintain
      "they have promised and vowed to maintain this light."
                                      (1389 Nrf. Gild. Ret, 14 [MED])

     b. þough ye han sworn and bihight to perfourne youre emprise.
        though you have sworn and promised to perform your enterprise
        "though you have sworn and promised to perform your task."
                           (1386-90 Chaucer, CT, Melibee, p. 220, l.1065)

One could of course swear falsely. In Margery Kempe's autobiographical story, she warns a priest that a certain visitor is not to be trusted; the priest learns that her intuition is right when the visitor prevaricates about a book that he says he has for the priest, and promises to bring it within the week:

(28) "Sere, I hope to be her a-geyn þe next woke &   bryng it wyth
     sir,   I expect to be here again the next week and bring it with
     me &, ser, I *be-hote* ȝow ȝe schal haue it before any oþer
     me and sir I promise you you shall have it before any other
     man . . ." . . . but þe man wold neuyr comyn at þe preste aftyr.
     man   but the man would never come to the priest after
     "'Sir,' I hope to be back again next week and to bring it [the book] with me,
     and, sir, I promise you will have it sooner than anyone else . . .' . . . but the man
     was never to come back to the priest again."
                                        (after 1348 Kempe, 58)

The *hat-* "promise" verbs are all attested in later ME as epistemic parentheticals, just as *promise* was later. Examples are:

(29) a.   Min herte takth,   and is thorghsoght
           my heart pays:heed and is resolved
           To thenken evere   upon that swete
           to think   always on   that sweet:one
           Withoute Slowthe, *I you behete.*
           without   Sloth   I you promise
           "My heart takes notice and is resolved always to think about that sweet one,
           without indolence, I promise you."

$$\text{(after 1393 Gower, 318)}$$

      b.   To Engelond been they come the righte way,
           to England are   they come the right way
           Wher as they lyve in joye and in quiete.
           where as they live in joy and in quiet
           But litel while it lasteth, *I yow heete,*
           only small time it lasts   I you assure
           Joy of this world, for tyme wol nat abyde.
           joy of this world for time will not wait
           "They came to England right away, where they live in joy and peace; as for joy
           of this world, it lasts only a small time, I assure you, for time will not wait."

$$\text{(}c.\text{ 1390 Chaucer, CT, Man of Law, p. 103, l.1130)}$$

One other use worth mentioning here, though not attested in the Helsinki Corpus or in Chaucer, is with subjects that are inanimate.[16] The meaning is "portend," and the verb seems well on the way to having raising syntax:

(30)   It *byhoteþ* deth or comynge aȝen of þe trauaille.
       it portends death or coming   again of the adversity
       "It portends death or the return of adversity."

$$\text{(}c.\text{ 1420 Chauliac (2), 44a [MED *bihoten* 4.c.])}$$

MED points out that in this use *byhoteþ* in (30) glosses Lat. *promittit.* What is interesting is that despite raising analogs in Latin, neither the *hat-* verbs, nor later *promise,* came to be used until relatively late in their histories with inanimate subjects. This suggests that the epistemic meaning developed independently in English.

In sum, the *hat-* verbs underwent almost the same history as *promise* did later. As is often the case when a borrowed word comes to be used in the historical texts that remain to us, *promise* appears early on paired with the older native lexeme:

---

[16] MED *bihoten* 4.c cites an example from Chaucer with *Fortune* as the subject; this is, however, clearly a personification.

(31)   he wolde perfourme and do as he hadde *hight* and *promised*.

(c. 1418 Appeal London, p. 95)

This kind of doubling appears to have been deliberate, in effect a redundancy to ensure that the new word will be understood. In this sense it is much like the recruitment of old words in new meanings in redundant contexts that was pointed out in chapter 4 in connection with discourse markers.

5.4.2   *A declarative: Chinese* bao

Here we look briefly at the development in Ch. of the declarative use of *bao*.[17] Although few explicit performatives seem to have developed in Ch.,[18] nevertheless Ch. data concerning the verb *bao* reveal a very clear historical trajectory. In Late Archaic Ch. (LAC) the verb *bao* is used for physical defense:

(32)   shan gong zhe dong yu jiu tian zhi   shang gu   neng zi
       good attack one move at nine sky ASSOC above thus can   self
       bao   er   quan sheng ye.
       defend and full   victory EMPH
       "The one who is adept at attack strikes as if from the heavens, and thus is able
       to achieve self-defense/protection and total victory."

(5th century BC Sunzi, Xing pian)

By Early Middle Chinese (EMC) it appears to have a speech act meaning, i.e. to refer to defense by linguistic means:

(33)   xian   sheng he   suo tan? zhi   mie   neng bu   you.
       virtuous holy   what OBJ seek reach extinguish can   not   worry
       shui sheng *bao*   ci   shi   chu   chou ling wu huan?
       who can   guarantee this matter remove   worry cause no fear
       "What do the virtuous and holy seek? To have no worries up to the end. Who
       can guarantee this – to remove all worries and fears?"

(281–316 AC Shengjing, Western Jin)[19]

Later in the period it appears in performative use with explicit first person subject (*chen* "I, your subject"). In the excerpt in (34), the Minister Xichao seeks to allay the fears of the emperor who has been disturbed by an omen.

(34)   Chao yue da   sima   fang jiang wai gu   feng
       Chao say senior war-minister just take out strengthen seal
       jiang   nei zhen sheji.   bi   wu ruo ci   zhi   lü.
       border in   settle society sure no like this POSS worry

---

[17] Many thanks to Shiao-Wei Tham for the data in 5.4.2.

[18] Chaofen Sun and Nina Lin, p. c.

[19] A Buddhist text translated by Fahu; also dated as early fifth century AC.

chen   wei bixia   yi   bai   kou   *bao*   zhi.
I-subject   for   your-highness   use   hundred   mouth   guarantee   this
"Chao said, 'The senior war minister has just strengthened our borders exter-
nally and internally has settled the society. Surely there will be no such dangers.
I guarantee this to your highness with the lives of a hundred [people] [i.e. with
my family].'"

(5th century AC, Shishuoxinyu, Yanyu)

As is typical of developments we have discussed throughout this book, the original
physical meaning "defend" continued to coexist with the speech act meaning, including its declarative performative use, eventually becoming distinguished from
the speech act meaning by compounding: *baowei* "defend (physically)," *baozheng*
"defend (verbally), guarantee."

5.4.3   *Another declarative: Japanese* aisatu

Our third case study is the development of a formal greeting. According
to Searle's classification of illocutionary acts, a greeting is an expressive. Its sincerity condition is to express the speaker's psychological state, and has no direction
of fit:

> in performing an expressive, the speaker is neither trying to get the world to
> match the words, nor the words to match the world, rather the truth of the
> expressed proposition is presupposed. Thus, for example, when I apologize
> for having stepped on your toe, it is not my purpose either to claim that your
> toe was stepped on or to get it stepped on.
>
> (Searle 1976: 12)

However, such an approach depends heavily on the English syntax of expressives
(they do not take *that-* complements). As Verschueren (1999: 132) points out, it
severely threatens Searle's own classification of illocutionary verbs (see 5.1), since
it could encompass all kinds of expression of belief and liking. Furthermore, it
ignores the fact that, like a declarative, a greeting, if successful, ratifies or brings
into being a social relationship between SP/W and AD/R. We therefore broadly
construe GREET as a declarative, in other words a performative act that neither
directs nor represents, but brings a state of affairs into being: in this case, one of
social relationships within the speech situation.

Aisatu "greetings" is used frequently as part of a declarative performative in PDJ.
As a greeting, it appears as a predicate noun in constructions with the pro-verb *suru*
"do," *iu* "say," or one of the corresponding honorific verbs for these meanings, e.g.
go-aisatu moosiagemasu "say (HUMIL) polite greetings" or *go-aisatu itasimasu*
"do (HUMIL) polite greetings." As these examples show, it is typically marked
with the honorific nominal prefix *go-*, which in this construction functions as an

addressee honorific (see 2.3.4). Such constructions make explicit the function in the speech event of what is said, i.e. that the discourse is a welcoming, benediction, or expression of general goodwill toward AD/R. As noted in 5.1, a performative construction containing *aisatu* often appears both at the beginning and end of such a speech event, so that the performative expression additionally functions as a global discourse bracketing device. Spoken *aisatu* discourses are usually pronounced by a distinguished or otherwise honored person and typically involve the use of distinctly higher degrees of formality and honorification than are found in ordinary (polite) conversation. Examples of spoken *aisatu* discourses include quite lengthy opening or closing remarks by an emeritus professor at an academic conference, a convocation by a district superintendent at a school graduation, a speech by a relative of the groom or bride at a wedding reception, etc. In addition, there are written *aisatu* discourses, such as an opening salutation in a book by someone other than the authors (e.g. a distinguished scholar in the field) or personal letters that are not directive or commissive.

In Jp. the noun *aisatu* can be used descriptively as the name for such discourses themselves. It also describes a visit that is made merely to express politeness or keep in touch, rather than to conduct specific business; for example, it is common to visit major business clients to express *aisatu* on the first business day of the year. In the earlier period of MdJ, *aisatu* appears as a descriptive speech act predicate noun meaning "greeting, respects, salutations" in phrases such as *aisatu o kawasu* "exchange greetings" and *aisatu ni iku* "go to pay one's respects." MdJ *aisatu* could even refer to nonlinguistic greetings, as in *te o hutte aisatu o suru* "greet (someone) with a wave of the hand, wave in greeting."

The lexeme *aisatu* entered the Japanese language as a loanword from Ch. Its source meaning appears to have been some type of physical action that involves space and boundary, but analysts differ in regard to the details: Ohno (Ohno, Satake, and Maeda 1990 [1974]: 2) holds that the two Ch. characters that spell *aisatu* mean "push against each other" when used in this combination. Nakamura (1981: 14) says that the meaning of *aisatu* combines "touch lightly" (*ai*) with "touch hard, hit" (*satu*). In his etymological Ch. character dictionary, Ueda (1977 [1918]: 944, 949) holds that *ai* means "push open" or "push aside and move forward," and *satu* means "draw near." Ueda further notes (ibid.) that *aisatu* is found in SAV meanings primarily after its importation into Japan.

While the exact etymology may be a matter of dispute, it is agreed that the original term referred to physical action. Ohno, Ueda, and others, e.g. Yamaguchi (1998: 8), also agree that the word first entered the Japanese language as a religious technical term in Zen Buddhism, which came into Japan in the thirteenth century. *Aisatu* does not appear even once in the massive *Enkyobon* manuscript of the *Heike Monogatari* (1309–10), and so at this point the word may not yet have spread into the community much beyond Zen circles. As a Zen technical term, *aisatu* referred to a locutionary dialectic practice in which a teacher asked a challenging question to a disciple (monk in training), who had to answer back. The goal of the activity was to test the disciple's progress toward enlightenment and possibly help him along the way. This practice was also referred to at that time by the phrase *iti-ai issatu* "one *ai*, one *satu*" (Yamaguchi 1998, Nakamura 1981). Nakamura (ibid.), a dictionary of Buddhist terminology, under *aisatu* first cites the meaning "a teacher exchanges questions-and-answers and tests a student's enlightenment" and then states that the meaning of the word "changes to mean 'answer, give a return gift,'" as in:

(35) [Aite   ga][20] kitune naru koto wo sire-domo
      interlocutor SUBJ fox   COP thing DO know-although
      yoku *aisatu* si-te   kaesu.
      well   answer do-GER return (something)
      "Although [he] knew that his interlocutor was a fox, he answered [its magical questions/challenges] well in return."
                          (LMJ, Kobisyoo [Ohno, Satake, and Maeda 1990 [1974]: 2])

Here *aisatu* appears to be used only as a description of a speech act, and not performatively. The change from "question-and-answer" to "answer" (a meaning still sometimes found in MdJ) is reminiscent of the kinds of changes like those undergone by *let's* discussed in 4.4 in which SP/W has commandeered a word that earlier referred to a dialog between two interlocutors in order to refer to SP/W's part in that dialog; similarly in ME *answer again* "answer back" (a reciprocal two-person exchange) came to be understood as "answer in repeated action" (a single person's act).

From "answer," *aisatu* came to be used to refer to various speaking events, from introducing one person to another to acts expressing congratulations, gratitude, or honor to one's interlocutor in keeping with a particular occasion. In linked verse poetry parties (in which each participant was expected to add a line of verse), which became very popular from the MJ period into the EMdJ period, *aisatu* expressed the adding of a line of verse that was congratulatory or showed honor to one's host (Ohno, Satake, and Maeda 1990 [1974]). In the *Nippo Jisho* (Japanese–Portuguese dictionary of 1603), *aisatu* is cited with the meaning "receive and entertain guests with language"; the entry also cites the idiom *aisatu no yoi hito* (original transcription *aisatno yoifito*) (lit.) "a person good at *aisatu*" with the meaning "a person who entertains well and uses language that makes guests feel good" (Doi, Morita, and Chonan 1980: 18).

It appears that *aisatu* was still not used performatively at the beginning of the seventeenth century. The word is conspicuously absent from Rodriguez' *Arte da*

---

[20] The square brackets indicate an abbreviation provided in Ohno's dictionary.

lingoa de Japam (1604–8). In addition to a thorough description of the grammar of Japanese at that time, Rodriguez' grammar contains major chapters on letter-writing and on other instructions about protocol for the missionaries in communicating with the Imperial Court and other nobles. Despite lengthy lists of types of letters and other communications, there is not even a passing reference to *aisatu*.

By the middle of the seventeenth century, however, *aisatu* comes to be used (with verbs for "say" or "do") to describe the act of greeting, as in (36):

(36) *aisatu*   wo ihu-te toor-azu   ha   naru-mai.
greetings-DO say-GER pass:through-NEG FOC become-NEG:PROB
"Surely [the guard] will let [you] through the gate [lit. probably won't not let you pass] when you say a greeting."
(*c.* 1640 Tora-akira ms., kyogen play [NKD vol. I, 21])

As in PDJ, the word is used to refer to a formal segment of discourse, in the case in (37), the speech act of providing a compliment to the host at the beginning of a linked verse party:

(37) Mukasi   wa   kanarazu   kyaku yori *aisatu*   dai-iti ni
past-times TOP without:fail guest from greetings first LOC
hakku   o   nasu.
make:a:verse DO make:happen
"[Since] times past, a guest would give a verse of greetings first of all."
(1704 Sansatuko [NKD vol. I, 22])

In EMdJ it also comes to be used to describe the giving or answering of a personal letter. NKD cites examples from the records of the Uesugi family and similar documents, all of which are in *kanbun*. These examples, however, still appear to be descriptive rather than performative. In the NKD entry for *aisatu*, the performative meaning of the word is listed, but without any source examples. This is usually an indication that the meaning is relatively recent.

The meaning of *aisatu* "greeting" as in (36) and (37) rather than "answer" focuses more on the image needs and feelings of AD/R in the ongoing speech event than do earlier meanings. The developments that began in EMdJ thus reflect increased intersubjectification: SP/W establishes a mutual link between the world talked about (the content of the discourse) and the world of the speech event by explicitly naming the communicative and social purpose of the particular act of speaking. In MdJ this intersubjectivity is also supported by descriptive constructions such as *go-aisatu dake* "just greetings," a phrase that is commonly used in requesting a meeting with a busy person. The intent of this phrase is to indicate that the meeting will not require preparation on the part of the person visited and will not be a major disruption.

In summary, *aisatu* originated in a non-speech act lexeme, in this case one that is an example of manipulation of an object (meaning source type (vii) in 5.3). It entered Japanese as a Zen term for a particular type of religious training that involved speech events. It first underwent subjectification as its meaning shifted from "question-and-answer" to "answer." The word then came to be used descriptively for the act of providing linguistic communications in keeping with the social expectations associated with a particular type of occasion. It subsequently became associated with the speech act of "greeting," apparently first as an indirect way of describing this act and more recently as a declarative performative to name a particular speech act as one of greetings. This last development reflects increasing intersubjectification.

5.5   On the recruitment of modals for performative uses

The last topic to be addressed in this chapter is the relationship between explicit lexical performative constructions on the one hand and modal expressions on the other in a language like Eng. (and other languages in which modals are members of a distinct grammatical category).

It is reasonable to conclude that when a pre-modal acquires root/deontic modal meaning it can be used (given the right person and tense, and the right conditions) with something akin to illocutionary force. Second person singular present tense permission and obligation of the type *You may X, You must X* would appear to have potential directive performative uses approximately equivalent to *I allow you to X* and *I order you to X*. This force is, however, indirect since, as a modal, the verb does not occur in an *I X you S* construction. Given evidence from the development of full lexical verbs like *promise*, we might suspect that performative uses of modals are relatively late. We show below that this is indeed the case; the recruitment of modals to use with indirect performative meanings is a direct correlate of the degree of subjectification undergone: the more subjective the modal, the more likely that it will be conventionalized as equivalent to a performative expression.

Consider first *must*. As we saw in chapter 3, *mot-* was originally a verb of permission in OE, often used in clauses subordinate to commands and wishes. Many early examples of obligation *mot-* are also embedded in clauses subordinate to explicit locutionary verbs (whether used performatively or not), and indeed we suggested that the conventionalizing of the past tense form may have been enabled precisely by this tendency to be used in such subordinate clauses. Over time, increasingly subjective uses of *mot-/most-* are found. From the perspective of performativity, participant-external deontics must be construed as statements about requirements imposed by others (God, institution, etc.). Thus in the context of regulations for nuns, when we find in *Hali Meidhad* a large number of "thou must X"

constructions, of which (38) below is one, these appear to be statements about behaviors that are necessary conditions for the good life, ordained by God and church,
upheld and implemented by the author(s) of the text, but hardly equivalent to the
subjective form "I command you to X."

(38)   þah   þu riche beo &   nurrice habbe þu *most* as moder
       though you rich   be   and nurse   have you must as mother
       carien for al þet hire limpeð   to donne.
       care   for all that her is:proper to do
       "Although you are rich and have a nurse you must take responsibility like a
       mother for the appropriateness of everything she does."
                                                      (*c.* 1225 Hali Meidhad, p. 156)

When they can be used with participant-internal meanings (SP/W is the source of
authority for requiring something of AD/R), then they acquire indirect performative
force:

(39)   Notwithstanding, by mine advice if ye have this letter ... when
       notwithstanding by my   advice, if you have this letter   when
       ye come ye *must* be suer of a great excuse.
       you come you must be sure of a great excuse
       "All the same, I advise that if you have this letter ... when you come you must
       be sure of having a significant excuse."
                                                     (1461 Paston, Clement, p. 201)

Our data show few clear examples of indirect performative use until the seventeenth century. Among these later examples is the following explicit *I say you must*,
repeated in a list of very personal terms laid out by Tom to Joan:

(40)   I could find in my heart to make thee Mistriss of my household, and Lady of
       my family, all which you know Ione ("Joan") is honour in abundance, but first
       I say you *must* subscribe and consent to my divers causes and
       considerations ... I say once again (and be sure you remember this last
       Article of our agreement) you *must* destroy, kill, and slay them all [the fleas],
       if possible.
                                     (1684–85 Pepys, Penny Merriments, pp. 268–269)

(40) clearly expresses an indirect directive (albeit in a blustering, comic context),
partly because the main verbs are activity verbs (*subscribe, destroy*). Despite the
modal strength of *must*, this expression leaves more options open, and is therefore
more indirect, than the explicit performative *but first I command/order you to sub-*
scribe, or the imperative *first I say subscribe*. Note here the use of *I say*, which,
according to the OED (*say* 12) is a formula to introduce a joke. Such uses presumably derived from sensitivity to the M-heuristic ("prolix expression warns 'marked
situation'") arising from the use of a native word for explicit performative purposes.

220

As mentioned in 5.1, *I say* was associated with religious discourse; it was also used as a declarative in formal speech and writing in the sixteenth century, as in

> (41) I knowe, *I saye* I know it, that all the debt he oweth had bine saved another way if he had bine here.
>
> (1586, Dudley)

In a less formal context such as (40), declarative *I say* was regarded as comical; Nevertheless, it could have performative force, reinforcing insistence, and the sub-jectivity of that insistence. *Must*, occurring as it does in the clause subordinate to *I say*, is understood as obligation deriving from an authority that is highly personal (and one can infer, arbitrary).

The modal *must* has indirect illocutionary force only in the context of activity verbs. In the context of stative verbs of cognition, such as *understand* in (42), there is none (note the explicit performative would be ill-formed since one cannot well command someone to understand something). Here *must* expresses a wish on the part of the speaker, not a command:

> (42) There I saw Mount Benawne, with a furr'd mist vpon his snowie head in stead of a nightcap: (for you *must* vnderstand, that the oldest man aliue neuer saw but the snow was on the top of diuers of those hills).
> "There I saw Mount Benawn, with a furry mist on his head instead of a nightcap (you must understand that the oldest man alive never saw anything but snow on top of any of those hills)."
>
> (1630 Taylor, Penniless Pilgrimage, p. 135)

As is to be expected, the extent to which a modal can be used to indirectly convey performative force depends not only on the type of verb with which it occurs, but also on the person of the subject. Originating in permission and acquiring the meaning of obligation, *must* is not performative in first person (*I must*). However, it can be with second person subjects and (given appropriate authority) third person subjects:

> (43) You/John *must* leave tomorrow.

(This is, of course, ambiguous out of context between on the one hand a statement about obligations imposed by individuals other than SP/W and on the other an indirect performative use in which SP/W establishes an obligation based on his or her own authority.)

Another modal that can be used for indirect performative purposes in MdE is *will*. When the subject is the first person it can be used to express a promise as in *Don't worry, I'll go*, or more frequently, a prediction (the "future," a type of epistemic; see Fleischman 1982). When the subject is the second person, as in *You will go*, it can be used as a directive meaning "I require you to go, whether you like it or not"; in this use it is typically stressed.

Willan originally meant "to desire" and, as a lexical verb followed by a sentential complement, meant "to will." In OE its use in a promissory, i.e. directive and commissive, sense emerges with non-finite complements (when the subject of the infinitive is in identity with the subject of *will-*). It arises naturally out of volition in first person contexts, since promises are self-imposed acts based on one's own volition:

(44) Lazarus ure freond slæpþ ac ic *wylle* gan   &
     Lazarus our friend sleeps but I will go-INF and
     awreccan hyne of   slæpe ...
     a-wake   him from sleep
     Se Hælend hit cwæð be   his deaþe. Hi   wendon soðlice
     the Savior it said about his death. They thought truly
     þæt he hyt sæde be   swefnes   slæpe.
     that he hit said about dream-GEN sleep
     ða   cwæð se Hælend openlice to him, Ladzarus ys dead.
     then said the savior openly to them, Lazarus is dead
     "'Our friend Lazarus is sleeping, but I will go and wake him up from his sleep'... The Savior said it about Lazarus' death. They thought, however, that he said it about the sleep of dreams. Then the Savior said openly to them: 'Lazarus is dead.'"

     (*c*. 1000 West Saxon Gospels, p. 104)

In (44) the disciples take what Christ says to be a statement of his ordinary desires and intentions ("I want to go and wake him"), since they think Lazarus is literally sleeping. But Christ then tells them Lazarus is dead. In this context Christ's words must be reinterpreted as a commitment to act despite improbable circumstances ("I commit myself to go and wake him"), but certainly less direct than *gehat-* would be. When Hroþgar thanks Beowulf for rescuing him and his kingdom from the ravages of Grendel, he is presumably not just expressing his desire to love Beowulf as a son but also his commitment to doing so (with its attendant responsibilities):

(45) Nu ic, Beowulf, þec,
     now I Beowulf you
     secg   betsta, me   for sunu *wylle*
     men:GEN best   1Sg:DAT as son will
     freogan on ferhþe.
     love   in heart
     "Now, Beowulf, best of men, I will love you in my heart as a son."
     (8th century, Beowulf, 946 [Arnovick 1994: 176])

But again, the force seems considerably weaker than that of (*ge*)*hat-*. By MdE the promissory (and ultimately volitional) force is primarily restricted to negative refusals as in *We won't go* (as in the anti-war slogan; contrast negative statements, in which *will* expresses the future), and emphatics such as *I will do it* (with stress on *will*). The predominant meaning in first person contexts is no longer an indirect illocutionary commissive but rather epistemic likelihood (futurity), as in the e-mail message *We'll be seeing you soon.*

Assuming that *will-* in OE is fully performative and the major lexical representation of promising, Arnovick (1994) has suggested that over time greater circumlocution has come to be needed in English to express promises. She attributes this to the grammaticalization of *will* (and *shall*) as tense markers of futurity. However, since from our perspective *will* has never been as explicit a performative verb of promising as *(ge)hat-* (or later *promise*), the correlation Arnovick hypothesizes with grammaticalization appears to be too strong.

The history of *will* illustrates the fact that when we consider the development of modals, especially with reference to their development of indirect performative uses, we must consider a large range of issues. Among them are its relation to lexical performative speech act verbs like *(ge)hat-*, and also to other modals like *shall*.[21] Of special interest in the seventeenth century is the codification by a mathematician, Bishop John Wallis, in *Grammatica Linguae Anglicanae* (1653) of a suppletive paradigm involving *shall* and *will*, depending on person. Epistemic prediction/futurity are expressed by *I shall, you/she will*, deontic promise (also threats and warnings) by *I will, you/she shall* (deontic). Boyd and Boyd (1980) argue that this distinction is by no means arbitrary but well grounded in the history of the modals in question. Arnovick (1989) further argues that the Wallis rules actually sought to reinstate their (indirect) illocutionary force. Wallis' attempted intervention did not, however, prevent the two modals from overlapping semantically, and, in the case of American English, the almost complete loss of *shall*.

The shift from intentional, commissive meanings to epistemic futurity is the kind of shift that we have seen before from non-epistemic to epistemic. Is the fact that there is a decrease in indirect performative force a counterexample to the shift to increasingly discourse-based meanings? While not addressing this issue directly, Aijmer (1985) argues that the development of futurity without promissory overtones can be traced to second and third person contexts. In these contexts the invited inference of futurity from reported intention became a predominant polysemy by ME and then spread to first person. If this is correct, we can think of the development of first person intention to commissive as an example of increasingly discursive use in first person contexts, while the development of the epistemic is an independent development in second and especially third person contexts. In this case, it would

---

[21] Kytö (1991) traces the quantitative development of *will* and *shall* (also other modals) in British English as represented by the Helsinki Corpus and in early American English.

not be a counterexample. Rather, it would support yet again the high degree of context-sensitivity of semantic change.

The modals that in English have been recruited into indirect directive use (especially with second person) are most notably *must, shall*[22] (obligation), *may* (permission), and *will* (obligation with second person, promise with first person). One that has been changing its status during the twentieth century is *can* (permission). Leech (1971: 67, 70) points out that *can* has been limited to permission of only a general sort in formal British English, cf. the contrast between:

(46) a. You *may* smoke in this room. (= You are permitted (by me) to smoke)
b. You *can* smoke in this room. (= You are allowed to smoke)

However, in informal styles *can* is coming to be widely used in a more subjective way (the authority for the permission is preempted by the speaker).[23] One of the characteristics of *ought to*, in contrast to *must*, is that it is only marginally subjective. It expresses general social obligation; only rarely and only recently is the authority for the obligation an individual, specifically the speaker. This accounts for why *ought to* typically does not have indirect performative force. The same is also true of *have to*, which, like *ought to*, tends to be used when obligation is of a general sort. However, given the tendency for modals to be used in increasingly subjective ways, by hypothesis we can expect increased subjectification of these modals as well.

The conclusion that we can draw from these examples is that modals can be used for indirect performative purposes only after the modal in question has undergone sufficient subjectification to allow the invited inference that the speaker has authority for the obligation, permission, promise, etc. As in the case of lexically full verbs, when a modal auxiliary comes to be used with performative force, this force is unstable. This instability is hardly surprising considering the highly contextualized conditions under which performative force comes into being. In the case of the modals, this instability is particularly prominent because the modals have primarily grammatical and therefore multiple functions.

5.6 Conclusion

In conclusion, we have seen that the development of performative uses of lexical verbs or of modals follows the regularities we have seen in earlier chapters.

---

[22] Largely obsolescent.

[23] Leech also discusses ironic uses such as *You can jump in the lake* suggesting that "the speaker sarcastically offers someone the choice of doing something that cannot be avoided, or something no one would choose to do anyway" (Leech 1971: 70). The role of irony in the changes discussed here deserves special attention.

224

Pre-SAV		SAV		Performative		Parenthetical
	>		>		>	
content			>	content/procedural	>	procedural
s-w-proposition	>	s-o-proposition	>	s-o-discourse		
nonsubjective	>			subjective	>	intersubjective

Figure 5.2. Correlated paths in the development of performative uses of nonperformative verbs.

The developments illustrate non-epistemic > epistemic, subjectification, and pre-emption to discursive, metatextual purposes. They are highly dependent on person, tense, and SP/W–AD/R social statuses and interactions (and no doubt the negotiations of these through intonation, though this cannot be addressed here). A schematic representation of the correlated paths in the development of performative uses of nonperformative lexical verbs discussed in this chapter is presented in figure 5.2. Note that in the case of the Jp. *aisaṭu* construction, intersubjectification arises along with the speech act meaning of greeting, in other words somewhat earlier than figure 5.2 suggests; this is in part because of the particular speech act meaning in question, and because of the highly intersubjective nature of Jp. language use. However, the overall order of changes is not different for *aisatu* and *promise*. In claiming that the development of performative speech act verbs involves subjectification and intersubjectification, we intend to highlight the way in which meanings are preempted from the world of description to that of discourse, and attention to the SP/W–AD/R dyad in that discourse. This is a semasiological claim regarding the histories of particular Ls.

Cultural norms differ considerably with respect to the extent to which types of speech acts will be expressed and distinguished lexically. They also differ with respect to the extent to which speech act expressions will be used performatively, or will be expressed indirectly. But by hypothesis, the direction of change will be as outlined in figure 5.2. In Latin and subsequently in much of the history of the later European languages, there has at times been a marked shift toward explicit coding of subjectivity (which can then be subject to intersubjectification).

We have seen that performative verb constructions such as *I promise* can develop highly intersubjective functions. In the next and final set of case studies we turn to the development of markers of politeness, most specifically honorifics. These are linguistic markers the prime function of which is to make intersubjectivity explicit. Among other examples, we will see how the performative expression *I pray you* came to be used as a marker of politeness (*pray*).

6
The development of social deictics

6.1 Introduction

Previous chapters have alluded to the indexical properties of epistemic modals, discourse markers, and performative verbs. In these domains the indexicality is the encoded link between the world of the conceptualized described event (CDE) and the world of the conceptualized speech event (CSE). We now turn to another class of linguistic items that provide such a link: social deictics (SDs). We define SDs as directly encoding within their semantic structures the conceptualized relative social standing (superiority/inferiority, (non)intimacy, in-group versus out-group status, etc.) of a participant either in the CDE or in the CSE by "pointing" to that social standing from the deictic ground (perspective) of SP/W relative to AD/R and other elements of the CSE.[1]

SDs include contrasting second person singular *tu/vous* (T-V) pronouns in European languages like French and German; parentheticals such as *I pray (you)*, sentence adverbials such as *please*; and, in a few languages such as Japanese and Korean, large systems of lexical items, derivational formulae, and affixes that are often termed "referent" and "addressee" honorifics. Referent SDs index the social status of one or more participants in the CDE (here termed "referents") relative to a deictic ground in the CSE. Addressee SDs, by contrast, index the relative social status of the speech event participants conceptualized independently of their possible roles in the CDE. Although most SDs are politeness markers, SDs also include a much smaller subset of linguistic items that directly encode an attitude of denigration.[2] Examples of denigratory SDs in MdJ include the noun suffix *-me* (compare *ano hito* "that person" with *ano hito-me* "that person I belittle") and the

---

[1] SDs thus include the class described by Brown and Levinson (1987 [1978]: 23) as "grammaticalized" politeness markers; however, we prefer the term "encoded" over "grammaticalized," because many SDs are lexemes with independent status and not affixes.

[2] In Japanese linguistics, the term *taiguu hyoogen* "expressions of rank" is used in reference both to honorifics and denigratives, but the analyses do not explicitly distinguish linguistic items whose semantic structures directly encode social deixis from nondeictic euphemisms or other items that convey politeness or denigration via convention.

verb suffix V-*yagaru* "(subject person I belittle) does V." These will not be considered in this chapter.

6.2 Some more detailed distinctions relevant to honorifics

In this section we discuss some distinctions that we will be drawing on in our case studies: first the distinction between referent and addressee honorifics, and second the relationship between politeness and honorific SDs. We also develop diagrammatic models of spatial and social deixis.

6.2.1 Referent and addressee honorifics

As mentioned above, social deictics are usually divided into two main classes:

(i) SDs that point to the social position (relative status or intimacy) of a participant in the CDE, relative to a deictic ground in the CSE,

(ii) SDs that point to social relationships or relative social positions among participants in the CSE, independently of their roles in the CDE.

Following well-known terminology, we use the term "referent SD" for class (i). "Referent" should be understood as a participant in the CDE: it is a cognitive construct without the truth-conditional implications associated with the term in traditional semantics. Despite what might appear to be the case on first thought, second person pronouns that express T-V distinctions are referent rather than addressee SDs. This is because they can only index the social status of AD/R by including AD/R as a participant (i.e. a "referent") in the CDE (Comrie 1976, Brown and Levinson 1987 [1978]). Class (ii) of SDs includes "addressee SDs," which are discussed in more detail in 6.3.[3]

Like most if not all deictic systems, SDs even in a language such as Japanese comprise a relatively simple system in which only a few canonical types of relative social status and (non)intimacy are distinguished. In use, however, SDs are exploited in order to achieve many nuances of expression, including sarcasm through overuse, and insult. A strikingly self-conscious violation of SD norms for purposes of insult (metaphorically indexing the attorney's assessment of the defendant's moral as opposed to social standing) is illustrated in (1). This is from the trial of Sir Walter Raleigh at the beginning of the seventeenth century, a time when *you* was the V term in English, and *thou* the T term:

---

[3] Yet other SDs (not discussed in this book) express additional axes of social indexing that are distinct from the CDE, such as speaker-setting and possibly speaker–bystander status (see Comrie 1976).

(1) *Ral.:* I do not hear yet, that *you* have spoken one word against me; here is no Treason of mine done: If my Lord Cabham be a Traitor, what is that to me?

   Att.: All that he did was by *thy* Instigation, *thou* Viper, for I *thou* thee, *thou* Traitor.

(1603 Raleigh)[4]

In the sections that follow we distinguish referent and addressee honorifics in more detail, and we introduce some of the most important canonical types of relative social status and (non)intimacy. For this discussion, and for several of the case studies in this chapter, we focus on the SD system of Japanese honorifics. Studies of Japanese honorifics comprise a very large body of works in the Japanese language; books by Tsujimura (1967) and Ooishi (1983) have been particularly influential in traditional approaches, and Kikuchi (1996) is a recent major work. Analyses of the Japanese honorific system that have appeared in English have been given by, e.g., Martin (1964, 1975) and Harada (1976). More recent works in English have focused on particular problems in honorific meaning (e.g. Yoshiko Matsumoto 1997) and pragmatic analyses of patterns of use (e.g. Mizutani and Mizutani 1987, Okamoto 1999).

6.2.2   *Politeness and honorific social deictics*

Since most SDs express politeness, a discussion of the nature of soci-olinguistic politeness is an important prerequisite to an understanding of the category "SD." There have been a variety of approaches to politeness. One focuses on conversational maxims (Leech 1983). Another that has been particularly influential is Brown and Levinson's (1987 [1978]) analysis of politeness in terms of universal strategies that diffuse "face threatening acts" (FTAs). Their view of politeness is based on Goffman (1967), and assumes that every individual seeks to claim a self-image for him- or herself that is two-sided: (i) negative face, which is the basic claim to territories and to freedom from imposition, and (ii) positive face, which is the desire that the self-image be appreciated by the interactants (Brown and Levinson 1987 [1978]: 61). However, this view of "face" has been shown to be grounded in a view of the individual that is hardly consistent with the politeness expectations of speakers of Japanese and many other Asian languages (Yoshiko Matsumoto 1988, Okamoto 1999). For speakers of these languages, at least, the role of the individual and defense of individual territory is less important than that of the group: "A person's self-image in Japan is not as an independent individual but as a group member

---

[4] This example was cited by Irma Taavitsainen and Andreas H. Jucker in a workshop presentation on "Pragmatic space in historical linguistics: speech acts and speech act verbs in the history of English," ICHL XIV, Vancouver, 1999.

having certain relations to others" (Yoshiko Matsumoto 1988: 423).[5] In particular, "preservation of face in Japanese culture is intimately bound up with showing recognition of one's relative position in the communicative context and with maintenance of the social ranking order" (ibid. p. 415). Furthermore, "[t]he Japanese concept of deference must include not merely the speaker's humbling him/herself, but the raising of the addressee's level" (ibid. p. 413). Speakers express politeness in the MdJ speech community primarily through distancing strategies. A speaker of MdJ who attempts to create an in-group relationship with AD/R via linguistic means associated with "positive face" (equivalent to *Come here, mate/honey/buddy* cited in Brown and Levinson 1987 [1978]: 108) is likely instead to be evaluated as rude or crass. Because of the differences in the social construction of politeness, we have avoided the term "face" in favor of a concept of politeness that represents SP/W's explicit addressing, in a constructive manner, of the "image" needs of AD/R. Similarly, Held focuses on "image needs" rather than face and on "polite behaviour as a continual sounding out of the reciprocal image needs of ego and alter" (Held 1999: 22). Politeness is thus not only intrinsically subjective, as Brown and Levinson's approach might suggest, but also intrinsically intersubjective.

The conceptualization of image needs and the concomitant modes of expressing politeness are closely intertwined with the ideologies of power in the social system in which a language is used, and are clearly subject to change. Brown and Gilman (1960) discuss the shift in use of the T-V pronoun systems of various European languages from expressing power relationships (superior–inferior) to expressing solidarity (intimate vs. nonintimate). For example, T or V forms now tend to be used reciprocally by both interlocutors in a conversation, whereas in the past they were used nonreciprocally. A similar shift in the usage and social value of honorifics has been noted in comparing pre- and post-World War II speech communities in Japan (Mizutani and Mizutani 1987). Held summarizes shifts in power relations as a social process of redistribution in terms of transfer from, for example, social rank to social value (through the "bourgeoisisation" of society), and from vertical to horizontal distance, in which social hierarchy is replaced by "psychological, affective components of proximity, familiarity" (Held 1999: 24). Such transfers reflect societal transformations. They are represented and indeed constituted in shifts in linguistic practice, but are independent of the types of regularity in semantic change discussed here. Our focus will not be on

---

[5] In this connection it is interesting to note that the expression "lose face" in English and also *perdre la face* in French seem to have been calqued from Chinese *diu lian* in the nineteenth century (the first entry in the OED is from 1876), largely as a technical term in psychology and sociology; however, it has been interpreted in academic circles from the "Indo-European" perspective of individual rights and territory, rather than from an Asian perspective of the group and maintenance of the hierarchic position of that group (Ervin-Tripp, Nakamura, and Guo 1995).

the societal shifts, nor on ways in which individuals may switch from polite to nonpolite to express attitudes such as contempt or displeasure, but rather on (i) the ways in which terms are recruited from content meanings to deictic procedurals that make explicit SP/W's social attitude to participants in the communicative event, and on (ii) the evidence they provide for subjectification and intersubjectification.

SDs constitute only one type out of many linguistic resources that SP/Ws can use strategically to express politeness (Brown and Levinson 1987 [1978]). As semantically coded meanings, they need to be distinguished from conventionally implied meanings (GIINs). For example, T-V pronouns semantically encode social deictic contrasts and so are to be classed as SDs. In contrast, the use in PDE of third person expressions (e.g. *the professor* or *the doctor*) and even first person plural expressions (as in *Have we eaten yet?*) as ways of referring to the second person (see 2.3.4) represents politeness strategies that are used in recognized and systematic ways, but are not semantically encoded in the meanings of those lexical items.

In accordance with the IITSC, some GIINs become semanticized as SDs. MdJ *anata*, a second person pronoun, originates in LOJ *anata*, a spatial deictic noun that signaled a location similar to Eng. "over there." *Anata* came to be used as a third person (pro)noun for "person over there" from EMJ (Yamaguchi 1998: 34). This new meaning represented the semanticization of a GIIN that is common throughout the history of Japanese: the use of an L referring to location in order to metonymically implicate reference to a person in that location. *Anata* subsequently shifted from third person pronoun meaning to second person pronoun meaning in EMdJ around 1750 (ibid.). Compare the shift from third to second person pronominal function noted in Harris (1978) with respect to changes from Classical to Vulgar Latin discussed in 1.3.1. In addition, *anata* came to be used to implicate politeness in a way that is common in Japanese: deictic distance is exploited to express politeness. When the GIIN of politeness became semanticized *anata* became an SD, specifically a member of the class of referent honorifics.

As implied by the fact that honorific SDs are a subset of politeness markers, a further distinction is to be made between SDs and nondeictic sociolinguistically marked Ls (here called "euphemisms") that are used in order to express a social attitude. Thus, while Brown and Levinson (1987 [1978]: 181–182) describe Ls such as *dine* for *eat*, *gentleman* for *man*, or *volume* for *book* as "referent honorifics," we do not include such items in the SD category. The distinction between an SD and a nondeictic euphemism is illustrated by contrasting *yasumu* and *motomeru* in MdJ. The MdJ verb *yasumu* "rest" is a well-established euphemism for "sleep." Its euphemistic meaning represents the output of an "off-record" strategy in which SP/W invites AD/R to infer a meaning indirectly from a closely associated one (Brown and Levinson 1987 [1978]: 211). Although the selection of *yasumu* over *neru* "(go to) sleep" or *nemuru* "(physically) sleep" expresses an attitude of sociolinguistic politeness, *yasumu* is nondeictic because it does not point to the social status of any participant in the CDE or the CSE relative to SP/W's point of view regarding social positioning in the particular speech event. *Yasumu* may be selected to express the concept "sleep," regardless of the intimacy versus nonintimacy of the social relationship between SP/W and AD/R or their relationships to the subject referent of the expression. In contrast, MdJ *motomeru* "demand" (used euphemistically for "buy") specifies in its euphemistic meaning that the subject referent (the buyer) is socially superior to SP/W. In this meaning, the word is typically used only with second and third person subject referents. The euphemistic meaning of *motomeru* incorporates the point of view of SP/W in the CSE as a deictic ground, and so in this meaning the word falls into a class of referent honorific SDs, specifically respectful honorifics.

In sum, we have defined honorifics as semanticized social deictic expressions (SDs), and we have distinguished between SDs and nonsemanticized, implied expressions of politeness, and between SDs and nondeictic euphemisms. It has long been noted with respect to the history of Japanese that new honorifics arise only in the referent honorific category, and all addressee honorifics develop from previously existing referent honorifics (Tsujimura 1968, Lewin 1969). Dasher (1995) analyzed these regular patterns of change among Jp. predicate honorifics as representing a grammaticalization cline of functional shift from (i) indexing participants in the CDE toward (ii) indexing participants and discourse elements of the CSE. The present study builds on that work and examines case studies from the history of Japanese predicate honorifics and also the history of English. The data demonstrate regularities in semantic change that parallel those in the domains previously studied in this book: shifts from conceptual to procedural meaning, subjectification, and intersubjectification.

6.2.3 A model of deixis

Prior to discussion of the meaning structures of Japanese honorifics, it will be useful to examine the deictic spatial pronoun *here* to illustrate deictic semantic structure as we conceptualize it for purposes of this chapter. A model of the relationship between the meaning and use of PDE *here* is given in figure 6.1. The relationship between the utterance use of *here* by SP/W in the actual speech event (the "physical action realm") and its semantically encoded meaning M in the "shared cognitive realm" is shown in figure 6.1 by a simple line to a box including M. (Structural syntactic and phonological components of the L *here* are omitted from this and subsequent figures, as are the IINs and GIINs that arise in the flow of speech.) Like most deictics, *here* has both deictic and nondeictic elements

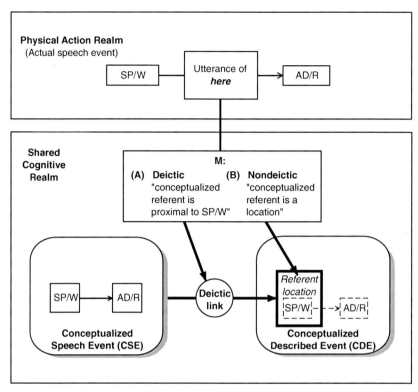

Figure 6.1. Schematic model of the meaning-in-use of PDE *here* (in this and subsequent figures, → = linguistic utterance; ➤ = "informing," i.e. enriching shared cognitive realm).

of meaning (Fillmore 1997 [1971]). The nondeictic M-element of *here* signifies a "location," while its deictic M-element individuates a particular location as "proximal to SP/W."

When a lexeme is selected in the speech stream, its meaning interacts with and adds to the shared cognitive realm (knowledge of cognitive constructs) that interlocutors share, at least in part, as speakers of the language who are building common ground in a communicative situation (see H. Clark 1996). We use the word "inform" for this interaction and enrichment, and we illustrate this informing with arrows from the M box to relevant cognitive constructs. The dynamic nature of the negotiation of meaning in communication is meant to be evoked by the shaded edges of the boxes that represent key cognitive constructs, which include the interlocutors' conceptualization of:

(i)   a world that is spoken about (the conceptualized described event, CDE),
(ii) the world of their speech event (CSE).

The turn-taking effects themselves are, however, not modeled in this or subsequent figures.

Individual Ls need not include a representation of both of these conceptualized worlds. Many Ls inform only the conceptualization of the described event, e.g. *table*, *woman*. Some inform only the conceptualization of the speech event, e.g. *in fact* in its DM meaning. Deictic M-elements, however, typically inform conceptualized links between these two worlds, e.g. deictic or anaphoric references. These links are represented by an arrow from CSE to CDE, because the conceptualized arrangement of participants (and other elements) in the CSE forms the deictic "grounding" in terms of which SP/W points to the arrangement of elements in the CDE (see also discussion below). In figure 6.1, the deictic M-element of *here* informs the link between CSE and CDE by individuating a particular CDE location as "proximal to SP/W," while the nondeictic M-element informs only CDE by signifying that the word stands for a "location."

Although most individual Ls are not deictic, most utterances are. The pervasiveness with which CDEs are "anchored" or "grounded," i.e. oriented relative to the CSE through the use of deictic links, is well known (see e.g. Jakobson 1957, Fillmore 1997 [1971], Silverstein 1976a, Lyons 1977, 1982, Levinson 1983, Hanks 1992). In English, for example, main clauses are tensed, that is, they are located with reference to SP/W's conceptualization of speech-time. What is important for our purposes here is that the conceptualized relationship between SP/W and AD/R in the CSE is "copied" into the representation of the CDE, and serves as its deictic "grounding." For example, in *Kim came here*, neither SP/W nor AD/R are participants in the CDE; however, the *here* cannot be understood unless SP/W and AD/R are projected ("copied") onto the abstract schema *Kim moved to a place*. This copying is represented in figure 6.1 by the dotted line boxes. Although the box that represents *"here* space" is drawn as excluding AD/R (its characteristic use), this L can refer to space that includes AD/R as well as SP/W. For example, in *Kim asked Bella to come here today*, the spatial goal of the motion may include both SP/W and also AD/R (a defeasible GIIN). The thickness of the box around referent location space in the CDE represents the high salience awarded to the figure of the deictic expression (Hanks 1992).

In languages that encode social relationships of the T-V kind, when one of the participants in the CDE is a second person, the social deixis involved can be modeled in similar ways. Figure 6.2 represents the relationship between a SP/W who positions him- or herself at a distance from AD/R, as in Fr. *Je vous souhaite bonnes vacances* "I wish you (second person singular, polite) a good vacation." Note that the meaning of *vous* has two meaning elements: one (A) deictic, the other (B) nondeictic ("human being," or other being appropriate as

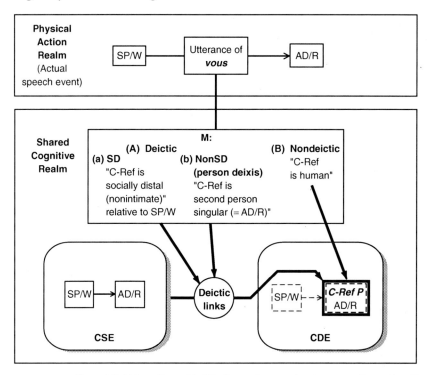

Figure 6.2. Schematic model of the "second person singular pronoun" meaning of French *vous* (C-Ref = conceptualized referent; C-Ref P = conceptualized referent person).

AD). Deictic (A) in turn has separate subcomponents: (i) the SD meaning element "socially distal (nonintimate) relative to SP/W," and (ii) nonSD deictic meaning "second person singular." Both of the deictic meaning elements inform the deictic link between CSE and CDE. The person deixis indicates that the referent person is AD/R, as is shown by the congruence between the referent box and the copy of the AD/R box in the CDE. The choice of the SD pronoun that is used for the linguistic expression of the CDE sets the tone for the subsequent interaction between SP/W and AD/R (including shifts to indicate displeasure, insult, etc.).

We turn now to a discussion of canonical M-structures and paths of functional change among honorific SDs for predicate items in Japanese (verbs, adjectives, and the copula). These comprise a rich system that distinguishes between referent and addressee honorific categories. Like T-V items in other languages, honorific pronouns in Japanese are all referent SDs.

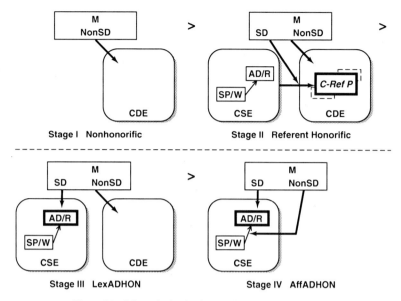

Figure 6.3. Schematic for the CDE > CSE development of Japanese predicate honorifics (C-Ref P = conceptualized referent person).

6.3 Classes of honorifics and patterns of semantic change in Japanese

Japanese predicate honorific SDs can be organized according to four unidirectional stages of development, from informing CDE to informing CSE.[6] These are diagrammed schematically in figure 6.3. The "stages" in the figure illustrate only key categorial features for classes of honorifics. Individual honorific forms have more complex structures, as was seen in figure 6.2.

The top-left (Stage I) diagram of figure 6.3 represents the meaning structures of nonhonorific Ls whose meanings inform only the CDE. Into this category fall Ls such as *table* and *woman*, and Ls with more complex semantic frames, e.g. *command*, *achieve*, *deliver*. The frames of the latter, although relational, are internal to the CDE, not situated according to a deictic grounding in the CSE. As is discussed in more detail in section 6.4, a subset of such nonhonorifics constitutes a source of referent honorifics in Japanese, which are modeled in the top-right diagram (Stage II) of figure 6.3. Sources of referent honorifics in Japanese also include Ls with spatial deictic meanings; their Ms are structured similarly to Stage II, although their deictic M-element is spatial rather than social (see also figure 6.1).

---

[6] Section 6.3 is based on Dasher (1995: chapter 2), where further details can be found.

Referent honorifics for predicate items in Japanese include a sizeable inventory of verbs (e.g. *motomeru* "RESP:buy" (i.e. a respected person buys)), productive formulae for marking referent honorification on nonhonorific verbs, and copula forms.[7] As shown in figure 6.3, the SD meaning element of referent SDs informs a deictic link (the bold arrow) between CSE and CDE. This link points to the social position of a CDE participant ("referent person") or relationships among referent persons who are conceptualized as part of the semantic frame of the L in question. Two classes of referent honorific indexing in Japanese are discussed in more detail below. The deictic pointing is made from a grounding in the CSE, namely SP/W's conceptualization of his or her status vis-à-vis AD/R. The CSE thus enters into the M-structure of this class, but the primary function of referent honorifics is to inform CDE. Referent honorific SDs address AD/R's image needs positively but indirectly by indexing referents.

Referent honorifics in Japanese can be divided into two classes, "respectful" and "humiliative," depending on the conceptualized social standing of the subject referent. These are illustrated in (2) and (3), respectively:

(2) Mikan   o   *mesiagat*-ta.
tangerine DO RESP:eat-PAST
"[Respected subject] ate a tangerine."

(3) Mikan   o   *itadai*-ta.
tangerine DO HUMIL:receive/eat/drink-PAST
"[Humble subject] received a tangerine" or "[Humble subject] ate a tangerine."

Both of these classes of Japanese referent honorifics place primary salience on the CDE participant who (if overtly expressed) is realized as the subject of the expression (the "subject referent"): that is, they highlight the subject referent as the figure of the deictic expression.[8]

As shown by the square brackets in (2) and (3), subject referents in Japanese need not be overtly expressed; referents that are considered by SP/W to be identifiable from context and from the selection of linguistic forms elsewhere in the sentence,

---

[7] Referent honorific formulae, e.g. *HonP-verb ni naru* "RESP:verb" have nonSD meaning elements that are procedural rather than contentful, and so – strictly speaking – their M-structure is somewhat different from that diagrammed in Stage II of figure 6.3. Nevertheless, such formulae are not found to develop into addressee honorific lexemes or addressee honorific affixes in Japanese.

[8] There have been various definitions and analyses of "subject" in Japanese. For the purpose of this chapter, "subject" can be considered to be an abstract syntactic function to which an argument of a predicate is assigned. In MdJ, overtly expressed subject NPs may be marked with the particle *ga*, or (for any of several communicative and cognitive motivations that relate to CSE) with the topic particle *wa*; for details see e.g. Kuno (1973), Shibatani (1990: 262–280). Fujii (1991) provides a historical study of "subject" marking in Japanese.

including any honorific marking on the predicate, are typically left unexpressed (see Martin 1975: 183–185). As these examples illustrate, the argument structure role of the subject referent indexed by the referent honorific may vary depending on the semantic frame of the L: Agent in the case of (2), Recipient in the case of (3). Hence humble subjects can also be Agents, as in *mikan o sasiage-ta* "(Humble subject) gave a tangerine."

The class of honorifics illustrated in (2) points *respectfully* to the social stand-ing of the subject referent, and the class shown in (3) points *humiliatively* to the subject referent. Another approach to classifying Japanese honorifics differenti-ates subject honorifics, which are equivalent to respectful honorifics, from object (or non-subject) honorifics (e.g. Martin 1975, Harada 1976, Yoshiko Matsumoto 1997). In such frameworks, the non-subject honorific category appears to involve the (implied) presence in the CDE of a respectfully indexed non-subject referent, but this is questionable for (3) in the meaning "HUMIL:eat." By contrast, in the respectful–humiliative framework, (2) and (3) represent alternative ways of index-ing the subject referent from the deictic ground of the SP/W–AD/R relationship in the CSE; see figure 6.4.

As shown by the orientation of the SP/W and AD/R boxes in the CSE, the canonical use of referent honorifics in Japanese assumes a deictic ground in which AD/R is superior to SP/W. Conversely, the use of referent honorifics has the expressive effect of elevating AD/R to "higher" social standing in what may be metaphorically conceived as socially "vertical" space (Yoshiko Matsumoto 1988: 413). In MdJ, as in many T-V languages, referent honorifics are now often used reciprocally (see 6.2.2). This reciprocal elevating of AD/R status and lowering of SP/W status may be a means of expressing SP/W's own cultural elegance or refinement in MdJ (Miller 1967, Okamoto 1999). However, in such situations, some asymmetry in the selection of referent honorifics or in other strategies for expressing deference will typically still reveal one interlocutor to have (or be treated as having) higher social standing. In this respect, while they have much in common with T-V SDs, MdJ referent honorifics differ in partially retaining what in Europe were largely older vertical relationships. They also differ in so far as first and third persons may be honorifically marked: respected subject referents are mostly second or third persons, while humble subject referents are typically first person references.

Social deixis in modern Japanese is sensitive to group membership. Thus, in speaking to an outsider, SP/W is likely to use humiliative forms in reference to third persons who fall into SP/W's social group, as well as in reference to him- or herself. In figure 6.4, this characteristic is shown first by the designations SP/W+ and AD/R+ in the copies of those boxes in the CDE; in other words, the deictic ground of the CDE includes the social groups of SP/W and AD/R as well as the interlocutors themselves. In addition, sensitivity to group membership is shown by

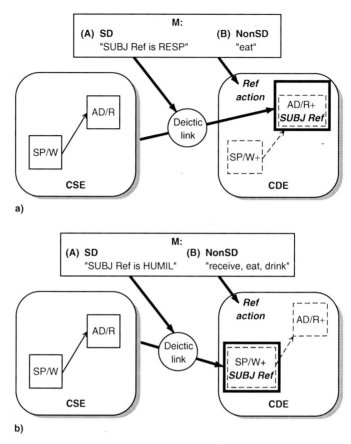

Figure 6.4. Respectful and humiliative referent honorific M-structures in Modern Japanese (Ref action = conceptualized referred-to action; SUBJ Ref = conceptualized subject referent; SP/W+ = speaker and speaker's social group; AD/R+ = addressee and addressee's social group). a) *mesiagaru* "RESP:eat" and b) *itadaku* "HUMIL:receive, eat, drink."

the overlap of the subject referent box (the figure of the deictic reference) with the AD/R+ box (respectful honorifics) and the SP/W+ box (humiliative honorifics). The salience of group membership in Japanese society is situation-sensitive. The same two individuals may be conceptualized as part of the same social group on some occasions (e.g. when speaking to a third person outsider) and as belonging to different groups on other occasions (e.g. when in confrontation with each other; see e.g. Ishida 1984).

Respectful referent predicate honorifics in MdJ have in common a social deictic meaning structure in which they index their subject referent as being:

(i)   socially superior to SP/W (in MdJ restricted to second and third person referents)

(ii) typically socially superior to any non-subject argument referents, and

(iii) typically associated with AD/R or AD/R's social group.

While (i) is a crucial element of the meanings of honorifics in this class, (ii) and (iii) are defeasible. For example, (ii) can be ignored when SP/W uses a respectful honorific to request that AD/R (who is thereby treated as a social superior) perform an action vis-à-vis an even higher ranking third person; in MdJ one says the equivalent of *Please RESP:tell our teacher hello* (not *HUMIL:tell*, even though the teacher has higher status than either interlocutor). Similarly, with regard to (iii), a third person subject referent need not be associated with a member of AD/R's social group, e.g. when SP/W talks about her respected teacher. Figure 6.4a illustrates (i) by means of the difference in relative height of the subject referent box and the dotted-line SP/W+ box. Property (ii) is not shown, as the semantic frame of *mesiagaru* includes no relevant non-subject referent. Property (iii) is shown in that the subject referent box completely encloses the dotted-line AD/R+ box and additionally includes other "space," into which fall respectfully indexed third persons not associated with AD/R or AD/R's social group.

Humiliative referent predicate honorifics in MdJ index that:

(i)   the subject referent is inferior in status relative to a non-subject argument referent or to AD/R,

(ii) the subject referent is associated with SP/W or SP/W's social group, and

(iii) the non-subject argument referent participating in this deixis is typically associated with AD/R or AD/R's group.

While (i) and (ii) are crucial properties of meaning for humiliative honorifics in MdJ, (iii) is defeasible. For example, in (3) SP/W could have received the tangerine from a respected person not associated with AD/R (e.g. "I HUMIL:received a tangerine from my teacher"). Figure 6.4.2 illustrates (i) via the difference in relative height of the subject referent box and the dotted-line AD/R+ box. In (3), the semantic frame of *itadaku* in the meaning "HUMIL:eat" does not include a non-subject referent other than the object consumed; the sole point of reference (grounding) for the humiliative "lowering" of the subject referent is the SP/W–AD/R relationship. Property (ii) is shown by the congruence of the bold-line subject referent box with the dotted-line SP/W+ box. Property (iii) is not shown. However, in the meaning "HUMIL:receive," *itadaku* may include in its semantic frame a non-subject referent who is the source of the object undergoing transfer. The SD positioning of such a non-subject source referent would be drawn as a solid-line box to indicate that this referent is indexed by the deictic expression. In accordance with (i), that box would be located higher than the subject referent box. In accordance with (iii), the source referent box would completely enclose the dotted-line AD/R+ box and also include additional "space" for other third persons not associated with AD/R. Nevertheless, the line around the non-subject referent box would be less bold than that of the subject referent, which is the primary figure of the deictic expression.

From OJ through the EMJ period, the deictic M structures of referent honorifics exhibited less sensitivity to group membership than in subsequent periods of the language. Respectful honorifics were often used in reference to third persons of higher social rank than SP/W, regardless of any social affiliation of the referent with SP/W or AD/R. Similarly, there were many instances of humiliative Ls used in reference to actions of third persons not associated with SP/W, provided that the subject referent had lower social status than did a non-subject argument referent. The gradual increase in concern with group membership is likely to reflect language-external social changes and is in keeping with the power-to-solidarity trend found in European language communities by Brown and Gilman (1960). In the highly stratified, monolithic court society of those early periods of Japan, many instances of honorific use reflected status differences that were generally recognized in society; subjective grounding in the SP/W–AD/R relationship is sometimes not obvious. Nevertheless, even in those eras, a given SP/W might select different forms for the same referent in different situations (Morino 1971: 100–103). For example, the late tenth century writer Sei Shonagon in *Makura no soosi* ("The Pillow Book") wrote that she disliked it when servants used the RESP form in reference to their masters when speaking to outsiders; she thought that HUMIL forms should be used instead (Tsujimura 1971: 15). This early indication of in-group/out-group sensitivity points out that (at least in some language users' opinion) HUMIL forms should be used subjectively according to the point of view of SP/W in the speech event; in other words, these forms reveal the shifting meanings characteristic of deictics among at least some speakers from early on.

Returning to figure 6.3, we see that referent honorifics (Stage II) may develop into addressee honorific lexemes (LexADHONs, Stage III), some of which further develop into addressee honorific affixes (AffADHONs, Stage IV). In fact, referent honorifics are the only source of addressee honorifics in Jp. (Tsujimura 1968, Lewin 1969). While referent honorifics (both respectful and humiliative) point to the social standing of at least one "referent," i.e. participant in the CDE, addressee honorifics directly encode the social deictic positioning of AD/R relative to SP/W independently of their possible roles in the CDE. Example (4) includes both subclasses of addressee honorifics in Japanese.

> (4)　Saikin　zuibun atataka-ku　nat-te　　*mairi-masi*-ta.
> 　　　recently very　warm-ADV become-GER　go/come:POL-POL-PAST
> 　　　"Recently, [the weather] has gradually become very warm."

The LexADHON *mairu* "go/come:POL" functions in (4) as a serialized verb signifying gradual entry into a state. (By "serialized" verb, we mean a verb that is adjoined as V_2 to another verb. Typically this V_2 has undergone a semantic change, whereas V_1 has not.) The AffADHON subclass is represented by the verb suffix *-masu*.

Following terminology familiar in Japanese linguistics, we use the term "polite" (POL) to refer to the type of social standing that these items deictically award to AD/R. In MdJ, the politeness expressed by an addressee honorific involves the indexing of nonintimate social distance between SP/W and AD/R as well as possible elevation of AD/R. At present, the reciprocal use of addressee honorifics by both interlocutors is characteristic of most business and social settings outside of the family home, regardless of the relative social status of the interlocutors. Addressee honorifics are now the primary (but not exclusive) markers of distinct speech registers or styles often called "speech levels" in discussions of Jp. and Korean (Martin 1964). In MdJ, the "polite" register (characterized especially by the addressee honorific verb suffix *masu* and the copula form *desu*) contrasts on the one hand with a "very polite" (VPOL) speech register, which is characterized by the VPOL "be" verb *gozaimasu* (which also appears as an element of the VPOL copula *de-gozaimasu*) and by relatively heavy use of referent honorifics as well as addressee honorific Ls. On the other hand the POL register contrasts with a "plain" speech level, which is characterized by forms that are unmarked for social deixis but whose use is usually considered to indicate a sociolinguistically significant absence of "polite" marking. The "plain" sentence that corresponds to (4) is (5):

(5)   Saikin   zuibun atataka-ku nat-te   *ki*-ta.
      recently very   warm-ADV become-GER come-PAST
      "Recently, [the weather] has gradually become very warm."

Note that the Eng. translations of (4) and (5) are identical. The meaningful distinctions between the two sentences in Jp. appear in the way they inform the conceptualization of SP/W–AD/R relations in the CSE, not of any facet of the CDE.

The distinction between LexADHONs and AffADHONs is based on their nonSD meaning element(s). As shown in figure 6.3, the SD M-element of both subclasses directly informs the AD/R box in the CSE. LexADHONs continue to inform the CDE through their nonSD meaning element(s), which name, describe, or modify the action or state of the CDE. The nonSD M-elements may include spatial or temporal deictic elements as well as nondeictic M-elements; in (4) the directed motion meaning of *mairu* describes a characteristic of the CDE, i.e. "gradual entry into a state." In contrast, the nonSD M-element of AffADHONs such as *-masu* is procedural rather than contentful: it plays a role in the marking of discourse structure by orienting the utterance in which it appears to the ongoing discourse

(Dasher 1995: chapter 3). In figure 6.3, Stage IV, the nonSD M-element accordingly informs the small arrow that represents the linguistic interaction between SP/W and AD/R in the CSE.

This section has provided an overview of classes of honorifics in Japanese and introduced their canonical M-structures and stages of functional development. The Ms of most nonhonorific Ls inform only the CDE. Referent honorifics have Ms that primarily inform the CDE but secondarily inform the CSE, which serves as the grounding for their deictic reference to a CDE participant. In contrast, addressee honorifics attach salience to the AD/R as the figure of the deictic expression, thereby serving primarily to inform the CSE. While the nonSD M-element(s) of LexADHONs continue to inform the CDE, those of AffADHONs inform only the CSE. We now consider the development of referent SD function (section 6.4) and the shift from referent to addressee SD function (section 6.5) in greater detail.

6.4   The development of referent social deictic function

In this section we give a sketch of some case studies from Jp. and Eng., showing how SD meanings may develop from nonSD meanings.[9] Although most texts provide some evidence for politeness forms, particularly rich sources are provided by, on the formal level, petitions, and often on a less formal level, letters. Drama and other representations of conversational interaction provide evidence for not only politeness but also for its inverse – insult, and rudeness – and for cooperativeness versus conflict in general (see Jucker and Taavitsainen 2000 for a proposal about how to study the pragmatic space of insults in historical texts). For the history of English a particularly rich source is the trials recorded from the EMdE period on (see e.g. Hargrave 1730).

The history of the Japanese language provides a wealth of examples of nonSD Ls and constructions acquiring SD function. Although referent honorifics have figured prominently in most styles of Jp. since the earliest recorded texts, there has been an almost complete turnover in the large inventories of Jp. predicate honorifics and SD personal pronouns.

Throughout the recorded history of Jp., source predicate Ls and constructions exhibit one or more of the recurring patterns of semantic change listed below in their development of referent honorific from nonhonorific source meanings.

(i) PREDICATE ITEMS THAT REPRESENT DIRECTED MOTION COME TO ENCODE THE SOCIAL STATUS OF SUBJECT AND OBJECT REFERENT RELATIVE TO SP/W. Examples include EMJ *kudasaru* "be sent

---

[9] Section 6.4 is based on Dasher (1995: chapter 5), which includes additional examples and further details. The case studies that follow, however, represent new investigations.

down" > "RESP:give" (see 6.4.1), OJ *ageru* "move something from low to high position" > LMJ "HUMIL:give (to a superior)," and LMJ *sin-zuru* "HUMIL:give" (Ch. character-based action-noun for "put forward, advance something" + *suru* "do").

(ii) PREDICATES OF MOTION ACROSS A SPATIAL BOUNDARY COME TO ENCODE THE SOCIAL STATUS OF A REFERENT RELATIVE TO SP/W. This pattern includes two different pragmatic associations in Japanese culture. On the one hand, areas that are considered sacred or otherwise accessible only by certain persons, e.g. Shinto shrines and the Imperial court, are conceptualized as bounded areas (Sansom 1952: 55–57). This association is illustrated graphically by an ornamental rope tied around a shrine building, a sacred tree, rock, etc. Entry into such an area is associated with motion directed toward a respected goal or with the power/authority to enter it. Examples include the OJ construction *mawi-iru* (*mau* "HUMIL:go/come" + *iru* "enter") > LOJ *ma(w)iru* "HUMIL:go/come (in)to a respected place" (> MdJ *mairu*); and the LMJ respectful formula *ira-seraru* (*iru* "enter" + *-seraru* "VRESP") > EMdJ *irassyaru* "RESP:go/come/be." On the other hand, onstage arenas such as public or official settings, e.g. the capital city, are conceptualized as unbounded areas that are associated with culture and prestige; thus, in MdJ one says *mati ni deru* "go out (emerge) to (the/a) city." Motion out to an unbounded area is thus associated with motion toward a respected goal or with the power/authority to come out to such a location. Examples include the OJ construction *mawi-idu* (*mau* "HUMIL:go/come" + *idu* "go out, emerge") > LOJ *maudu* "HUMIL:go/come (out) to a respected place," which survives in the MdJ idiom *hatu moode* "first visit of the year to a Shinto shrine" (a New Year's custom involving large crowds); and also *idu* in various constructions built from honorific formulae, e.g. LMJ *odyaru* (< HonP-*ide*, the nominalized form of *idu*, + *aru* "be"), EMdJ *oide nasaru*, and MdJ *oide ni naru*, all of which express general existence or motion but mark respectful referent honorification on the subject: "RESP:go/come/be."

(iii) PREDICATES DENOTING THE SUCCESSFUL ATTAINMENT OF A GOAL OR ACCOMPLISHMENT OF AN ACTION COME TO ENCODE THE ACTION OF A SOCIAL SUPERIOR. Examples include the EMJ formula *nas-aru* (*nasu* "achieve, create, make, cause to become" + *-(r)aru* "RESP") > LMJ pro-verb *nasaru* "RESP:do"; OJ *wataru* "transit (across, from one end to another)" > EMJ "RESP:go/come/be"; OJ *kosu* "go over, overtake" > EMdJ formula *okosi nasaru* "RESP:go/come"; OJ *hakobu* "carry" > EMdJ formula *ohakobi nasaru* "RESP:go/come"; and OJ *hirou* "pick up, obtain (unintentionally), walk with care" > EMdJ formula *ohiroi nasaru* "RESP:go/come (especially on foot)."[10]

---

[10] *Hakobu* and *hirou* are both found in constructions with the meaning "walk" that pre-date their honorific use, e.g. LOJ *ayumi wo hakobu* lit. "carry [one's] footsteps" = "walk" (Ohno, Satake, and Maeda 1990: 1055), LMJ *asi wo hirou* lit. "pick up [one's] feet" (ibid. p. 1144).

(iv) PREDICATES FOR STATIVE CONCEPTS AND LACK OF ACTION COME TO ENCODE HUMILIATIVE MEAN-INGS. Examples include OJ *samoraFu* "attend a superior, wait for an order" > LOJ *saburahu* "HUMIL:be"; OJ stative verb form *wi-ari* "be sitting, crouching, motionless" > LMJ *oru* "HUMIL:be"; and OJ *ukagau* "peer, watch/wait (for an opportunity)" > LMJ "HUMIL:ask, inquire" (later "HUMIL:hear, visit").

(v) PREDICATES FOR MEANINGS THAT IMPLY SOCIAL STATUS COME TO ENCODE BOTH A METONYMI-CALLY RELATED NONDEICTIC M AND SOCIAL DEIXIS. Examples include OJ *oFosu* "command (speech act verb)" > LOJ "RESP:say" (and its related EMJ construction *o(h)ose-raru* "RESP:say" > MdJ *ossyaru* "RESP:say"); OJ *makaru* "receive permission to withdraw, leave a superior" > LOJ "HUMIL:go/come (from a respected place)"; and OJ *itasu* "cause to reach, deliver, devote (one's entire strength) to" > LMJ "HUMIL:do" (i.e. a pro-verb).

(vi) PREDICATE ITEMS THAT REFLECT THE OUTPUT OF SOCIOLINGUISTIC DEPERSONALIZATION STRATEGIES, E.G. PASSIVE, CAUSATIVE, OR NOMINALIZED CONSTRUCTIONS, COME TO ENCODE SD. Various referent honorific formulae reflect this pattern, e.g. the LOJ passive/potential/spontaneous suffix V-*(r)aru* "V is done, (subject) is able to do V, V occurs spontaneously" > early EMJ "RESP:V"; and honorific prefix + nominalized verb + *ni naru* "it becomes an honorable V-ing" > MdJ "RESP:V"; similarly, collocations such as *o-me ni kakaru* (RESP-"eye" + DAT + *kakaru* "be attached to") > LMJ "HUMIL:meet (respected person)"; and Ls such as the OJ passive verb form *kikoyu* "be heard, is heard (spontaneously)" > early LOJ "HUMIL:say" > LOJ pro-verb "HUMIL:do." Honorific constructions built of nominalized verbs or Ch.-character-based action nouns + a pro-verb "do" likewise exhibit this pattern.

Only a subset of the Ls and constructions with meanings in each of the above categories are ever exploited as honorifics. Many of these patterns of semantic change may appear to represent metaphoric shifts across conceptual domains, e.g. spatial deixis > social deixis. However, on closer examination, it is consistently the case that new predicate honorifics in Japanese develop from those Ls and constructions that index social status marking as a GIIN; other semantically similar items do not acquire honorific function. For example, OJ *itadaku* "elevate, hold up (something) to the top of one's head" signified a gesture that is still used in Japanese culture in order to show appreciation or reverence for a gift received from a social superior; the L may derive from *ita* "summit, (upper) limit" + *daku* "embrace, hold in one's arms" (Ohno, Satake, and Maeda 1990 [1974]: 100). In LMJ *itadaku* comes to encode the referent honorific meaning "HUMIL:receive, eat/drink." *Itadaku* thus exemplifies pattern (i) (see the motion of the gesture) and possibly pattern (v) (see the social significance of the gesture). In contrast, semantically similar LMJ *motiageru* "lift up" (*motu* "hold" + *ageru* "raise") lacks any such GIIN and fails to develop into an honorific; instead, this L develops the meanings "increase one's possessions or status" and "lift up with praise" by EMdJ. Similar evidence of the relevance of prior pragmatic associations with social status marking will be discussed in the history of *kudasaru* (6.4.1). The consideration of which Ls and constructions develop semantically encoded referent honorific meanings in the history of Japanese supports a view that privileges invited inferencing as the mechanism of change.

The development of SD meaning from nonSD meaning intrinsically involves the development of procedural meaning. It also intrinsically involves subjectification: an SD meaning depends on SP/W's point of view as the deictic ground for the individuation of the subject referent. Thus, while prehonorific OJ *oFosu* "command (speech act verb)" was typically used in reference to actions by individuals of high social standing (such as allowed them to give commands), LOJ *o(h)osu* in its referent honorific meaning "RESP:say" was additionally applied to other acts of speaking and to the actions of other persons whom SP/W recognized through the selection of this L as having superior social status relative to SP/W. In other words, the subject of LOJ *o(h)osu* need not be a commander, merely a social superior of SP/W.

Furthermore, the development of SD meaning intrinsically involves intersubjectification, because SDs serve to express SP/W's attention to AD/R's image needs. However, in the patterns of semantic development among SDs, as in other domains examined in this book, subjectification dominates in the early stages, and then some items undergo increasing intersubjectification (nonhonorifics first develop referent honorific function, and some referent honorifics subsequently shift to addressee honorific function in Japanese). Referent honorifics do not directly index the social status of AD/R; instead, they address the image needs of AD/R indirectly via their indexing of the social status of a referent in the CDE. Therefore, subjectification dominates in the development of referent honorific function. Increasing intersubjectification is found in the shift from referent to addressee honorific function.

6.4.1   Japanese **kudasaru** *"RESP:give to SP/W (group)"*

As a RESP referent honorific, MdJ *kudasaru* is characteristically used with second and third person subject referents, and not with first person subject referents. MdJ *kudasaru* is further restricted to actions directed toward SP/W+, i.e. SP/W or a member of the SP/W social group, but there is no contrasting RESP verb for "give out from SP/W+." The set of contrasting SD verbs for "give" in MdJ is shown in figure 6.5. In addition to use as a full verb, *kudasaru* may appear as V$_2$ in a serialized verb construction to indicate that V$_1$ is done as a favor. In MdJ, *kudasaru* appears with high frequency in the imperative form in this serialized verb construction (*V-te kudasai*) in order to express a directive built on V$_1$. The sociolinguistic function of this construction is similar to that of *please* in MdE directives, e.g. *kaite kudasai* "RESP:give SP/W (the favor of) writing" = "(please) RESP:write."

	Referent honorific		Nonhonorific
	Respectful	Humiliative	
"give to SP/W+"	kudasaru	0	kureru
"give out from SP/W+"	0	sasiageru	ageru (yaru)

Figure 6.5. Deictic donatory verbs in Modern Japanese.

Stage I: kudasaru₁*: "send down"*

Kudasaru first appears in EMJ as a derivational form of OJ *kudasu* "send down" + the verb suffix -(*r*)*aru*. The development of referent honorific meaning by *kudasu* in EMJ reflects pattern (i) above, namely the use of an item that represents directed motion to encode relative social status. The suffix -(*r*)*aru* (older form -(*r*)*ayu*) preexisted its suffixation to *kudasu*. It is found from OJ on with the meanings "passive, potential, spontaneous" (i.e. "V is done," "(subject) can do V," "V occurs naturally, spontaneously"). Around the time of the transition between LOJ and EMJ (early twelfth century), -(*r*)*aru* additionally came to be used as a respectful referent honorific formula (for details, see Tsujimura 1971, Karashima 1993). Verbs with this suffix attached reflect a sociolinguistic depersonalization strategy; see meaning change type (vi) in section 6.4.

Both *kudasu* and its intransitive counterpart *kudaru* have GIINs with socially marked change of location from OJ on, e.g. uses such as "send from the capital city to the provinces" (NKD v. 2:499, 506). From LOJ, both verbs are found to refer to the sending down or promulgation of an order or judgment, a CDE that is associated with authority or high status of the subject. However, not all verbs that have such GIINs with socially marked change of location develop semanticized honorific status. For example, *noboru* "climb up" appears frequently in LMJ texts for the action "go up to the capital city," but this L does not go on to develop the SD function of deictically encoding social status. Furthermore, there are a number of semantically similar verbs in Japanese that do not have such GIINs of social status and do not develop honorific meanings, e.g. *sageru* "lower (one's head, etc.), hang (a sign from a pole, etc.)"; *orosu* "lower (a sail), let down (a ladder), bring/take down (from a high shelf), drop off (a passenger), etc."; *furu* "(rain, snow) falls."

Stage II: kudasaru₂*: "RESP:give"*

The use of *kudasaru* as a referent honorific with the meaning "RESP:give" (*kudasaru₂*) is marginal in the Enkyobon text of the *Heike Monogatari* (*Tale of the Heike*, 1309–10 AC). In this text *kudasaru* occurs sixty-five times as a full verb and an additional sixty-five times as a serialized verb. Of the full verb examples, fifty-five involve the sending down or handing down of various sorts of imperial edicts and orders (including twenty-four examples with *senzi* "imperial edict" and sixteen with *inzen* "order by the retired emperor"), e.g. (6):

(6) Tenka   ryooan   no   senzi   wo
     entire:country mourning ASSOC imperial:edict DO
     kudas-aru.
     send:down-PASS/RESP:send:down
     "An imperial edict of mourning over the entire country was sent down."
                    (1309–10, Enkyobon Heike Monogatari [Kitahara and Ogawa 1996:
                                                              vol. I, 92.7])

Kudasaru in (6) presumably carries a GIIN of relative social status between the subject and indirect object referents, but it is not honorific since there appears to be no SD grounding in the point of view of SP/W. Example (6) illustrates well the difficulties of determining how to interpret the use of *kudasaru*. The Chinese character with which -(*r*)*aru* is written in (6), and in many other examples in this text, stands for passive. However, the fact that *senzi* "imperial edict" is case-marked with the direct object particle *wo* appears to support the analysis of -(*r*)*aru* as a respectful formula without passive meaning, specifically as a respectful subject marker, at least as an implicature. Note, however, that the subject itself is unspecified. *In* "retired emperor who has taken the tonsure as a monk" is the subject of the previous sentence, and from the story line it is likely that the promulgation of this edict is to be associated with him. *Senzi* were written documents with the seal of the emperor, who may either have promulgated them himself, in which case he would be the implied subject of the sentence, or through someone else, in which case the subject would be an indefinite pronoun. Despite the possibility that -(*r*)*aru* is being used here to mark the subject respectfully, the meaning of *kudasaru* in this example appears to be "send down" rather than "give" because it involves no change of ownership; (6) is therefore at best a potential transitional example of the shift to *kudasaru₂*. The remaining ten examples of full verb *kudasaru* involve the sending down of imperial servants or messengers from the capital to perform some task in another location, i.e. *kudasaru₁*.

In forty-five of the serialized verb examples in this text, *kudasaru* is adjoined to the verb *o(h)osu*. In many of these instances, *o(h)osu* appears to have its earlier nonhonorific meaning "(issue a) command." In some instances, however, it seems to have a newer SD referent honorific meaning "RESP:say/command" (a metonymic derivative of "send down a (written) edict"). In such contexts, *kudasaru* can be interpreted as having a harmonically honorific meaning, at least as a GIIN. Consider (7):

(7) Midoo no   gosyo   he   mesi,
     (place) ASSOC Imperial:palace GOAL   RESP:summon
     kenzyoo   no   koto ha   ika-ni to
     award:for:service ASSOC thing TOP   how   QUOT

o(h)ose   *kudasaru*.
RESP:say RESP:give/RESP:send:down
"[The retired emperor] summoned [Chikanori, who was in charge of the award ceremony] to the Mido Palace and RESP:asked [him] the favor of [telling] how the matter of the award [of rank for service] [was coming along]"/"... and RESP:sent:down the command that he should [tell] how the matter of the award [was coming along]."

> (1309–10, Enkyobon Heike Monogatari [Kitahara and Ogawa 1996: vol. I, 46.16])

Although *o(h)ose-kudasaru* in (7) can be interpreted, as in the first gloss, to mean "RESP:give (me the favor of) saying" (*kudasaru₂*), it can also be interpreted as "RESP:send:down the commanding" (*kudasaru₁*), as in the second gloss. The communication could have been transmitted in the palace to Chikanori in written form or indirectly through an intermediary. In an additional eight of the serialized verb examples, V₁ is a verb that expresses the preparation or transfer of written commands or similar documents, a context that favors a *kudasaru₁* interpretation.

A further eleven serialized verb examples of *kudasaru* in the Enkyobon Heike text involve actions in which the direct object that undergoes transfer is a person, e.g. *mesi-kudasaru* "RESP:summon and RESP:send:down from the capital" (seven examples) and *ohi-kudasaru* "RESP:chase out and RESP:send:down from the capital." In the one remaining serialized verb example, *kudasaru* appears in a predicate that seems to involve transfer of ownership:

(8)   Tada   tabi   *kudasare*-soora(h)e   to
       just/only RESP:give RESP:send:down-POL:IMP   QUOT
       moos-are-kere-ba.
       HUMIL:say-RESP-PAST-and:so
       "[Yoshitsune] said 'Just give it to me.'"

> (1309–10, Enkyobon Heike Monogatari [Kitahara and Ogawa 1996: vol. II, 476.15])

In (8), *kudasaru* is adjoined to *tabi*, a form of the verb *tabu*, itself a contraction of the referent honorific verb *tama(h)u* "RESP:give" (instantiated since OJ); *kudasaru* appears to reinforce the social superior-to-inferior relationship that is indexed by *tabu*. This example also includes the addressee honorific *sooroo*, whose presence supports the interpretation of the preceding clause as a direct quotation (see 6.5). The attachment of *-(r)aru* (here most likely a RESP suffix) to *moosu* "HUMIL:say" indicates that the subject (Yoshitsune) is higher in social standing than SP/W (the narrator), while *moosu* itself indexes Yoshitsune as lower than his addressee. *Moosu* thus reinforces the relative status of the subject and indirect object of *kudasaru*.

Kudasaru is only rarely instantiated in other texts until the end of the LMJ period. This is most likely due to the establishment around this time of a classical literary model based on the earlier language forms of LOJ literature, in which "RESP:give" continues to be expressed by *tama(h)u* and its various derivatives (especially *tamawaru*, which is formed with the RESP suffix -*(r)aru*). An examination of five Noh plays attributed to Kan'ami (d. 1384) revealed no examples of *kudasaru* but numerous examples of *tama(h)u* and its derivatives. Sato (1974) notes only sporadic examples of *kudasaru* in *Otogi Zoosi* (a fourteenth century collection of didactic stories) and Buddhist literature through the fifteenth century. In a word frequency study, Hisatake (1974) likewise finds only infrequent examples of *kudasaru* until the so-called "Christian materials" (late sixteenth century roman-letter translations into Japanese of Aesop's fables, a modernized vernacular version of the *Heike Monogatari*, etc.). In these texts, *kudasaru* is one of the most frequent lexical items.

By the end of LMJ (late sixteenth to early seventeenth century), *kudasaru* has become the dominant verb for "RESP:give" in colloquial passages, while *tamau* and its derivatives, such as *tamawaru*, continue to be found in styles that follow the classical literary model. Thus, *kudasaru* is the most frequent verb for "RESP:give" in comic Kyogen plays (recorded in the seventeenth century based on orally transmitted dialog from LMJ). In *Daikoku Renga* ("Daikoku's Linked Verse," Kitagawa and Yasuda 1972: 81–86), however, two worshippers use *tamawaru* in regard to the action of the god Daikoku in a poem that serves as an act of worship to praise the god. When Daikoku subsequently appears in person in response to their poem, they use *kudasaru₂* in a directive that requests the god to come closer or continue the dialog with them:

> (9) Haa, arigato-o   gozaru.   Madu   kooko-o
>   Haa auspicious-ADV be:POL   first/by:all:means here-ADV
>   go-rairin   nasare-te *kudasare*-i.
>   RESP-attendance RESP:do-GER RESP:give-IMPER
>   (Both worshippers in unison): "Oh, how auspicious! By all means, give (us the favor of) your attendance."
>   (before 17th century, Kyogen, Daikoku Renga [Kitagawa and Yasuda 1972: 84.11])

In a subsequent passage cited as a special recitative, Daikoku uses *tamau* and other archaic RESP forms with self-reference in recounting his origin to the worshippers.[11] Near the end of the play, the worshippers likewise use another

---

[11] Examples of RESP honorifics for self-reference are also found in the recorded speech of the emperor and the highest rank of nobility from OJ through LMJ. Various explanations have been proposed (see Dasher 1995: 149–150 for details). In this particular text, it is also possible that the actor playing the god has been assigned the point of view of a more neutral narrator in recounting the god's origin and exploits.

archaic form, *tabi-tama-e* "RESP:give-RESP-IMPER" in a directive seeking bless-ings from Daikoku, who is still on-stage. The use of *kudasaru* (as opposed to *tamau*) in reference to the god's action in (9) may express the speakers' sur-prise at the sudden entrance and self-introduction by the god, but the details of stylistic nuance await further sociolinguistic analysis of similar texts and LMJ in general.

The association of *tamau* and its derivatives with accepted classical liter-ary models may explain the puzzling absence of *kudasaru* from the lists of RESP honorifics in the 1604–8 grammar by Rodriguez (Doi, tr. 1955), although Rodriguez uses *kudasaru* as a respectful form in quite a few example sentences throughout that massive work. The contemporary 1603 *Nippo Jisho* (Japanese–Portuguese Dictionary) cites the meaning "give from a superior to an inferior" for *kudasaru* (Doi, Morita, and Chonan 1980: 162). However, in addition to this mean-ing, which assigns RESP to the subject, *Nippo Jisho* additionally cites the meaning "HUMIL:eat/drink" for *kudasaru*. This secondary meaning, which assigns HUMIL to the subject, derives from the ambiguity in the meaning of the -(*r*)*aru* suffix dur-ing MJ discussed with reference to (6) above. If the suffix has passive meaning, the construction *kudas-aru* means "be sent down by, or receive from a superior," and the meaning is "receive," not "give." The semantic field of HUMIL verbs for "re-ceive" throughout the history of Japanese includes the actions "eat/drink," probably through a metonymic extension with "receive food/drink." During MJ, *tamawaru* (*tamau* "RESP:give" + -(*r*)*aru*) exhibits the same polysemy: "RESP:give" and also "HUMIL:receive/eat/drink." In EMdJ, the conjugational pattern of *kudasaru* di-verged from that of -(*r*)*aru*, so that the composition of the L became opaque, and association with the passive was lost. Accordingly, *kudasaru* ceased to be found in the HUMIL meaning that had been based on the passive meaning of the suffix.

The development of SD function by *kudasaru* involves the development of a procedural meaning: the honoring of the subject as respectful (or the humbling of the subject in the secondary meaning discussed above). It also involves subjectifi-cation. While a nonhonorific meaning does not necessarily involve SP/W's point of view, SD meaning by definition incorporates the SP/W point-of-view as the ground for the SD reference. As shown by the examples in the Enkyobon Heike, the pre-honorific M of *kudasaru* ("send down") is associated with a GIIN of gener-ally recognized social superior–inferior relationships; any dependence on SP/W's subjective assessment of the participants in the CDE is minimal. By the time of the Kyogen plays, the deictic ground of *kudasaru₂* has become established as being defined from SP/W's point of view: LMJ speakers use *kudasaru* to award social superiority not only to obviously high ranking members of society, but also to sec-ond and third person subject referents to whom they think a deferential attitude may be appropriate in a particular situation. Example (10) illustrates reciprocal use:

(10)   *Taro:* Nanitozo   sono suehirogari akinoo-te *kudasare*-i
                by:all:means that suehirogari sell-GER RESP:give-IMPER
        Huckster: Ika-nimoima dai-te   o-maso-o.
                certainly now bring:out-GER HONP[12]-HUMIL:give-INTENT
        "*Taro:* By all means, please sell me that 'suehirogari.'
        Huckster: I shall certainly bring it out right now."
                (before 17th century, Kyogen, Suehirogari [Kitagawa and Yasuda 1972:
                                                              71.16–72.1])

In this dialog, the main character Taro, a servant sent by his master to the capital city to buy a *suehirogari* "auspiciously shaped fan," has encountered a huckster in the guise of a merchant. The huckster takes advantage of Taro's ignorance of the word *suehirogari* by selling him an old umbrella instead. In Japanese society of the time, merchants held relatively low social rank, even when they had considerable economic power. The relative social status of the servant Taro and the huckster is somewhat ambiguous: honorific use between Taro and the huckster is largely reciprocal, although Taro appears to use somewhat more deferential language than does the huckster throughout the play. Accordingly, in (10) Taro uses RESP *kudasaru* in reference to the action of the huckster; in reply the huckster uses mildly HUMIL *omasu* (< EMJ *mairasu* "HUMIL:give") in reference to that same act from the huckster's first person point of view. The selection of honorifics is subjective and determined by each SP/W's assessment of the participants' social standings and other aspects of the situation.

The meaning of *kudasaru₂* underwent further subjectification when its meaning was narrowed to its modern meaning "RESP:give:to:SP/W+" (see figure 6.5). This development appears to have occurred after *kudasaru* became a referent honorific, most likely in EMdJ. The paucity of examples until late LMJ, however, may have obscured the early stages of this narrowing, and the range of uses of *kudasaru₂* during EMdJ awaits future study. Nevertheless, the contrasting nonhonorific verb *kureru* may provide indirect evidence that the meaning of *kudasaru₂* was not restricted to actions directed toward SP/W or SP/W's group until EMdJ. Like *kudasaru₂*, *kureru* is used in standard MdJ only for "give:to:SP/W (SP/W group)." This restriction did not apply to *kureru* in earlier stages of the language (Ohno, Satake, and Maeda 1990 [1974]: 436). Examples cited by Ohno, Satake, and Maeda (1990 [1974]) and by NKD (vol. VII, 10) suggest that the restriction of the meaning of *kureru* to "give

---

[12] The generalized honorific prefix (HONP) *o-* originated in the narrower RESP meaning. In this example it has addressee honorific meaning. In other contemporary examples, RESP meaning can still be found.

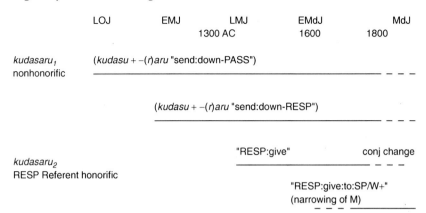

Figure 6.6. Time-line for the development of the Japanese RESP referent honorific *kudasaru* (conj. change = change in conjugational class, which obscured the relationship to the suffix *-(r)aru* "PASS, RESP").

to SP/W+" did not occur until late in EMdJ, or possibly around the beginning of MdJ (latter half of the nineteenth century). Like other marked items in contrasting marked–unmarked pairs, the meaning of an honorific typically neutralizes semantic distinctions found in the meaning of its nonhonorific counterpart. Consequently, it is unlikely that the meaning of *kudasaru₂* as a donatory verb was ever more narrowly restricted than that of *kureru*.

A summary of the development of *kudasaru* is in figure 6.6.

This case study illustrates that subjectification rather than intersubjectification predominates at the stage of the development of referent honorific function, although the development of honorific status intrinsically involves some attention to the image needs of AD/R. Referent honorifics show politeness only indirectly to AD/R through their SD marking of referents (participants in the CDE). The range of subjects of *kudasaru₂* in MdJ includes respected third persons (e.g. teachers) not connected with AD/R, as well as those who fall into the AD/R social group. As we will eventually see, intersubjectification is a major process in the development of addressee honorific meaning by referent honorifics. But first we look at a couple of expressions that developed referent honorific meaning in English.

6.4.2   English pray *(ADV)*

In this section we outline the development of *pray* as a pragmatic marker with SD function from a parenthetical expression, and ultimately from a main clause performative expression.

As was pointed out in 5.2, first person directive performative uses of the verb *prec-* "ask" came to be used in addition to, and often in preference to, second person petitions in prayer formulae in Latin of the first century BC. The verb *preie-* "pray" was borrowed from French into English in the thirteenth century, and it eventually replaced OE *bidd-* "pray" (which had both performative and epistetmic uses like those that *preie-* developed). The main use of *preie-* was as a lexical verb introducing a subordinate clause. Performative uses typically involved the construction: first person subject + Verb-present + second person indirect object (T or V form) followed by a subordinate clause (a complement *that*-clause as in (11a), an imperative as in (11b), or an interrogative):

(11) a. *I preie you* þat ye wende with me.
          I ask   you that you go   with me
          "I ask that you go with me."
                          (*c.* 1300 Havelok 1440 [MED *preien* 1.b.(b)])

      b. *I pray yow* telle me what was wreton vnder the mares fote.
          "I pray you tell me what was written under the mare's foot."
                          (1481 Caxton, p. 59)

The Helsinki Corpus does not provide any examples of performative uses of *preie-* in the early period (1250–1350), nor of the parenthetical to be discussed immediately below, but according to the MED both were attested before 1350.

Whereas the performative main clause construction is sentence-initial, the paren-thetical (which may be of the form *I pray you,* or *I pray thee,* or just *I pray*), occurs in a variety of positions. Its parenthetical status is unambiguous when it occurs clause-internally or clause-finally:

(12) Myldeliche   myne,   *y preie,* al þat þou se.
      Compassionately think-about I pray   all that you see
      "Think about all you see compassionately, I pray."
                          (*c.* 1325 Iesu swete is 40 [MED *preien* 5])

However, in instances where the *I pray you* construction is clause-initial and precedes an imperative, it is ambiguous with the main clause construction. Thus (11b) might be parenthetical. In other words, it might be used not primarily with the force of an explicit performative, but rather as a formula introducing an imperative, more saliently expressing deference to AD/R, i.e. intersubjective attitude.

With respect to the development of parenthetical *I pray thee* to *prithee* and *I pray you* to *pray*, it is important to note that several of the examples that can be construed as clause-initial parentheticals introduce a directive, either an imperative, as in (11b) and (13):

(13) Comly kyng of mankyn, *I pray the* here my stevyn.
      "Noble king of mankind, I pray you hear my voice."
                          (after 1460 Wakefield Plays, p. 16)

or an interrogative, as in (14).

> (14) *I pray you*, are they then no diphthongs?
>
> > (1596 Coote, 14 [Fries 1998: 94])

In such contexts they can be understood to invite the inference that SP/W is paying attention to the image-needs of AD/R and is being deferential. This seems especially likely when the addressee is God and is named, and in particular when something of direct benefit to SP/W is being asked for, as in (13).

By the sixteenth century two new forms without the subject pronoun appear: *prithee* and, without any pronoun, *pray*.[13] These forms are adverbial in function and their development has been discussed by Akimoto (2000) in terms of grammaticalization. Their role as pragmatic particles in EMdE court trials is discussed in Kryk-Kastovsky (1998) and in EMdE instructional texts by Fries (1998). In the case of *prithee* the SD function of the T form of the pronoun is maintained, as can be seen in the denigratory switch in (15) from *you* to *prithee* (rather than using *pray*):

> (15) *Lord Chief Justice:* But just now, you swore he staid out all Night?
> > *Mrs. Duddle:* No, my Lord.
> > *Lord Chief Justice:* Yes, but you did though; *prithee* mind what thou art about.
> > > (1685 Lisle, p. 74)

In the case of *pray*, absent the referent social deictic *you*, it came to function as an SD. It contrasts with absence of any politeness formula, and deictically with *prithee*, being the more polite of the two forms. Examples of SD *pray* are restricted to imperative or interrogative environments ((16a) and (16b, c) respectively). Thus AD/R is always at least implied as a participant in the directive speech event (*I ask you do X/I ask you answer Y*). Frequently a direct address form is present, as in (16b):

> (16) a. *Pray* let my love be remembered to Mrs. Parr.
> > > (1613 Cornwallis)
>
> > b. *Att. Gen.:* ... we first call Sir Thomas Whitegrave, who is a Justice of the Peace, and a worthy Gentleman; a Member of the Church of England in that County...
> > > *Sol. Gen.:* *Pray*, Sir Thomas, will you be pleas'd to give the Court an account, whether you saw Mr. Ireland in Staffordshire 1678, and what time it was?
> > > > (1685 Oates, p. 85)

---

[13] This dating is on the evidence of the OED (*pray* 8.d.). The first examples in the Helsinki Corpus appear in the period 1640 on.

    c. Since both *shall*, and *will* do certainly shew the Verb they precede to be future:
        Pray when must I use *shall*, and when *will*?

                                             (1700 Brown, 20 [Fries 1998: 94])

At first *pray* is largely used with more deference than *prithee*, frequently with honorific titles, such as *Sir X, Your honour*, as in (16b), i.e. to signal greater social distance than *prithee*, presumably because of its origin in the form *I pray you*. However, with the loss of the T-V distinction in English during the eighteenth and nineteenth centuries, and with the consequent loss of *prithee*, it came to index simple social distance from AD/R, who is implicit as a referent in the CDE of the imperative clause.

6.4.3 *English* please *(ADV)*

      Pray continued to be used as a politeness marker in the nineteenth century, but was recessive to *please*, another form originally borrowed from French. As in the case of *pray*, the history of this form has been studied primarily in the context of changes in its grammatical structure (e.g. Allen 1995). From a lexicosyntactic perspective the main interest in *please* is that it occurs in the two[14] constructions illustrated in PDE by (17):

(17) a. The plan *pleased the children.*
       b. Women have the constitutional right to attend whichever public school *they*
          please.

                                      (1991 Apr. 11, United Press Intl.)

In the type illustrated by (17a) there are typically two arguments: one an Experiencer expressed as an oblique (dative) in postverbal position, the other a Cause or Causer expressed as a preverbal subject (nominative). This type was borrowed from French in the fourteenth century, and is known as the "impersonal type" because the Experiencer is in the dative. A ME example is:

(18)   and they may nat *plese hym.*
       and they may not please him
       "and they cannot please him."
            (?late 1390s Chaucer, CT, Parson, p. 293, l. 224 [Allen 1995: 278])

By contrast, the second type which is illustrated by (17b), and is presumably the source of the politeness marker, has only one overt argument, the Experiencer, which is expressed in the nominative, and is in subject position. It is very rarely

---

[14] Other constructions occurred, with an Experiencer and an overt proposition, such as *It pleases me to be able to respond*, and *I am pleased to be able to respond*. They do not appear to be directly related to the SD development of *please*, though they did, no doubt, have some influence on it.

attested unambiguously in texts until the sixteenth century (Allen 1995: 280–281), and appears to be an innovation in English. The earliest example Allen claims to have found is:

(19) Ye may excuse yow   by me, if *ye please*, tyl the next terme.
      you may excuse yourself by me if you wish   until the next term
      "You may excuse yourself on my account, if you wish, until the next term."
                                       (1462 Paston Letters, 662.15 [Allen 1995: 281])

Allen's prime interest in the construction is the use of subject or oblique case (this is unambiguous if a pronoun is used – *I/thou/ he/she/we/ye/they* are subject forms, *me/thee/him/her/us/you/them* are oblique forms until the sixteenth century when the *ye/you* distinction was lost – or if the Experiencer is postverbal), especially in *if*-clauses. She points out that among the factors controlling the choice in Shakespeare's plays there are four of special importance.

(i) One is that Experiencer is typically subject if it is coreferential with the main clause, as in (19),

(ii) The second is that the more agentive and in control the Experiencer is represented to be, the more likely it is to be in subject position with nominative morphology. In particular, in *if*-clauses the original postverbal oblique form is used to refer to a hypothetical situation which will occur when the speaker positions Experiencer as thinking that the situation is "suitable or acceptable," as in (20a), even if it is not desirable, whereas the newer subject/nominative form is used when the speaker invokes the "polite fiction" that the Experiencer thinks he or she "wishes it to happen" (20b) (Allen 1995: 288):

(20) a. And ("if") *please* your majesty, let his neck answer for it.
                          (1599 Shakespeare, Henry V, IV.viii.43 [Allen 1995: 290])

      b. This young maid might do her a shrewd turn, if *she pleas'd*.
                          (1602–3 Shakespeare, All's Well, III.v.67 [Allen 1995: 291])

(iii) The third factor is that if the *if*-clause introduces new information rather than setting up a logical conditional, the Experiencer is always oblique (Allen 1995: 288); she relates this to criterion (ii), since the Experiencer addressee has no control over the information. We may note that in the period under consideration, the "information-*please*" with postverbal Experiencer, had become a formula often used in letters, with or without *if*, as in (21), which is addressed to King James I:

(21) *Please* your Majesty,
      I am glad to have heard of your Majesties recovery, before I understood of
      your distemper by the heat of the weather.
                                                (1608 Henry Prince of Wales)

(iv) A fourth criterion that Allen notes in connection with Shakespeare's choice of *please* constructions is politeness, which interacts with (ii) and (iii) above.

Support for Allen's hypothesis that word order was used primarily to project social distance is provided by the fact that during the nineteenth century the postverbal oblique construction was largely recessive. This may be correlatable with the loss of the T-V distinction. The subject/nominative construction *if you please* became the default polite formula, as in:

(22) We will, *if you please*, say no more on this subject.

(1871–72 Eliot, p. 317 [Allen 1995: 299])

Meanwhile, *please* without overt expression of either the *if* or the Experiencer came to be used as a pragmatic marker of politeness. According to the OED this use of *please* "may have been unknown to Shakespeare" (*please* II.6.c.). By the beginning of the twentieth century it had almost completely taken over from *pray*. Playful attempts to differentiate between Experiencer's perceived reluctance versus willingness led in the mid-twentieth century to such highly elaborate (and often humorous) devices as the wheedling formula captured in:

(23) She was saying, *Please. Pretty please.*

(1959 Sinclair, Breaking of Bumbo, v. 74 [OED *pretty* D])

The history of *please* is on one level very different from that of *pray*; for example, it did not originate in an explicit performative, and it is not limited to directive speech acts. *Please* with its second person pronoun (*if you please*) focuses on AD/R, first as expressed, then as implied subject. By contrast, *pray* with its first person pronoun (*I pray you/thee*) focuses on SP/W, first as expressed, then as implied subject. Indeed, the replacement of *pray* by *please* has been seen as a shift to paying attention to "negative face" (Busse 1998).[15] Busse suggests that the replacement may be connected with a shift in pragmatic strategies noted by Kopytko (1993) from positive to negative politeness more generally in Modern British. If so, this is a change in social values, independent of the semasiological development of the constructions themselves, as are other shifts in usage such as the one Myhill notes among the modals from group-oriented uses of the modals like *must, ought to*, and intentional *will*, to more individualized uses of modals like *got to, should*, and *gonna* (see 3.2.5). Despite these differences between *please* and *pray*, there are significant similarities. Beyond the obvious routinization of a construction with meaning at the propositional level to a pragmatic marker with functions at the sociodiscourse level, both *I pray you/prithee* and *if it please you/if you please* illustrate the development of referent honorific meaning. Note AD/R is always a participant, either explicitly

---

[15] Thanks to Jonathan Culpeper for this reference.

or implicitly, in the CDE (including CDEs that are wished-for outcomes of directives). Neither *prithee/pray* nor *please* serves addressee honorific functions, since they cannot be used independently of their possible roles in the CDE, thus *(You) Give her the book, please/pray* but not **I gave her the book please/pray*. Both also show subjectification: preemption by SP/W to the negotiation of discourse. Finally, with the loss of the pronouns, *pray* and *please* underwent intersubjectification: conceptualized image-needs of AD/R that were formerly expressed by T or V came to be encoded in the bare adverb; both acquired referent SD politeness function.

6.5   The development of predicate addressee honorifics in Japanese

As discussed in 6.2.1, referent honorifics show politeness to AD/R indirectly by SD indexing of a CDE participant (a "referent"). The referent may be the same person as one of the interlocutors, but is not necessarily so. Thus, speakers of Jp. employ the same class of referent predicate honorifics (RESP honorifics) with respected third person subjects as with respected second person subjects; conversely, they use HUMIL honorifics with third person subjects associated with SP/W as well as with first person subjects. In contrast, addressee honorifics directly mark SP/W's conceptualization of AD/R's social standing relative to SP/W, independently of their possible roles in the CDE. Consequently, in Jp. addressee honorifics for verbs and other predicate forms can be used with any subject allowed by their semantic frame: first, second, or third person, animate or inanimate, generic or specific, definite or indefinite.

Noting that languages with addressee honorifics are rare in comparison to languages with referent honorifics, and citing some instances of overlap between referent and addressee honorific categories, Brown and Levinson (1987 [1978]: 276–280) suggest that referent honorifics are basic and that addressee honorifics are derived, at least in part, from referent honorifics. In Japanese addressee honorifics have been claimed to develop exclusively from referent honorifics (Tsujimura 1968, Lewin 1969). Figure 6.7 provides a relatively comprehensive list of the predicate items that develop regular use as addressee honorifics during the history of Japanese as it is available to us from texts. As shown in the figure, in the recorded history of Jp., only a small number of referent honorific verbs have developed regularly recurring uses as addressee honorifics. It is noteworthy that certain semantic categories that are regularly populated with referent honorific lexemes are not found to yield addressee honorifics in Jp., e.g. mental/sensory activities and states ("think," "know," "hear," "see," etc.) and certain inherently relational activities ("meet," "visit"). Those lexemes that do become addressee honorifics probably comprise less than ten percent of the total number of referent honorific verbs at any one period, not counting many derivatives and compound forms. All addressee honorifics in Jp. arise from items whose nondeictic meanings participate in relatively high frequency constructions,

Item	Earlier (Referent Hon.) Meaning	Referent Honorific Dates	Dates as Addressee Honorific
haberi	HUMIL:be	OJ–MJ	LOJ (early 11th C)–EMdJ Restricted to classical literary registers from LMJ
saburahu > sooroo	HUMIL:be	LOJ–MJ	end LOJ (c. 12th C)–EMJ >*sooroo*, EMJ–EMdJ
oru	HUMIL:be	LMJ–MdJ	EMdJ (c. 18th C)–MdJ
mairu	HUMIL:go/come	OJ–MdJ	LMJ (c. 15th C)–MdJ
mairasu(ru) > -masu	HUMIL:give	EMJ–LMJ	LMJ (from c. 15th C) >-*masu*, end LMJ–MdJ
[ageru]	HUMIL:give	LMJ (14th C)–MdJ	EMdJ (c. 17th C)–MdJ
tamau (u-e conj)	HUMIL:receive/eat/drink	OJ–EMJ	LOJ (c. 11th C)–EMJ
tabu (u-e conj)	HUMIL:receive/eat/drink	OJ–EMdJ	LOJ (c. 11th C)–MdJ
[itadaku]	HUMIL:receive/eat/drink	LMJ (14th C)–MdJ	EMdJ (late 19th C)–MdJ
moosu	HUMIL:say	OJ–MdJ	LOJ (c. 11th C)–MdJ
[itasu]	HUMIL:do	LMJ–MdJ	end LMJ (c. 16th C)–MdJ
goza-aru > gozaru	RESP:be/go/come	LMJ–EMdJ	end LMJ (c. 16th C)–MdJ
o(n) iri aru > oryaru	RESP:be/go/come	LMJ–EMdJ	end LMJ (c. 16th C)–EMdJ
o(n) ide aru > odyaru desu	RESP:be/go/come	LMJ–EMdJ	end LMJ (c. 16th C)–EMdJ contraction of existing ADR honorific COPULA EMdJ (19th C)–MdJ

Figure 6.7. Japanese predicated items that developed addressee honorific meaning (expanded from Dasher 1995: chapter 5.4) (items enclosed in [ ] are not accepted as addressee honorifics by all speakers).

typically as V_2 in a serialized verb construction. For example, in Jp. "be" verbs appear as V_2 in a serialized verb construction that signifies stative (or iterative) aspect and as an identifiable element of many copula and adjectival predicate forms; verbs for "go/come" likewise occurring as V_2 in serialized verb constructions signify gradual change of state; verbs for "give" and "receive" appearing as V_2 indicate deictically that the action benefits someone. Since the items in the figure appear to develop addressee honorific meaning in their full verb uses as early as they do in their serialized verb uses, it is not clear what if any role the serialized verb constructions had in the development of addressee honorific meaning. However, they had a significant impact on frequency of use.

In figure 6.7 we cite predicate addressee honorific function from the approximate date when that function appears to have become semanticized. In other words, from that date on there are regularly occurring instances in which the item in question directly indexes SP/W's polite attitude toward AD/R independently of SP/W's and AD/R's possible roles as participants in the CDE. As shown in the figure, the earlier referent honorific meaning typically persists alongside the newer meaning, sometimes until much later. Some MdJ items in figure 6.7 with well-established addressee honorific uses are still treated by many sources as referent honorifics. For example, in popular-press books for native speakers of Japanese, Atooda (1980) and Yoshizawa (1985) classify *mairu*, *moosu*, and *oru* as HUMIL referent honorifics and describe their addressee honorific uses as mistakes, despite the long history of addressee honorific uses of these items (since the eleventh century in the case of *moosu*), and their occurrence in PDJ as addressee honorifics in registers such as railway station announcements and TV news broadcasts. In MdJ, *ageru*, *itadaku*, and *itasu* are likewise used as addressee honorifics by some speakers. However, their use as addressee honorifics appears not yet to have become as widely accepted as has that of *mairu*, *moosu*, and *oru* (for details, see Dasher 1995: 47–49).

Figure 6.7 is arranged according to the referent honorific source meanings of the linguistic items. As shown, most addressee honorifics for predicate items in Jp. develop from HUMIL referent honorifics. Only one set of addressee honorifics develops from RESP referent honorifics. This set contains three items, all of which are built on the RESP referent honorific formula "RESP:prefix-nominalized verb + *aru* 'be'" and have the earlier referent honorific meaning "RESP:be/go/come." (*Goza* of *goza-aru* appears to have been an LMJ innovative repronunciation of the Chinese characters used to spell an earlier verb for "RESP:be/go/come," namely *owasu*.) All three items develop addressee honorific function at about the same time (near the end of the LMJ period); Rodriguez (1604–8) includes them in his list of RESP verbs but cites their addressee honorific function in a special note (Doi 1955: 591–593). Thus, except for this exceptional set of three items, the dominant path of change in Jp. is

HUMIL > POL (addressee honorific). Instances of this change are found at various historical periods and among items with several different nondeictic meanings.

As noted in 6.4, the development of referent honorific meaning by a nonhonorific predicate item in Jp. typically involves a change in its nondeictic meaning in addition to its development of an SD component of meaning. In contrast, the initial development of addressee honorific meaning by a referent honorific in Jp. does not involve a change in non SD meaning. For example, *moosu* ("HUMIL:say" > "say:POL") has a similar range of uses in its addressee honorific function as in its earlier humiliative referent honorific function: it continues to serve as the matrix predicate for indirect or direct quotations of speech, including name-giving and other speech acts, and for the recounting of the participants, time, manner or other characteristics of a CDE. The development of addressee honorific function in Jp. thus primarily involves a change in the SD meaning component of the item, which comes to have no connection to the CDE (and instead directly marks the SP/W–AD/R relationship). The non SD meaning component of a new addressee predicate honorific in Jp. continues to inform the conceptualization of the described event by naming or describing the referent action or state.

Three of the addressee honorific lexemes in figure 6.7, however, subsequently go on to develop a more highly grammaticalized function in which their non SD meaning component likewise ceases to inform the conceptualization of the described event. These items are *haberi*, *saburahu* (>*sooroo*), and *mairasu* (>-*masu*) (for details see Dasher 1995: chapter 6). Another highly grammaticalized addressee honorific in MdJ is *desu*. The precise etymology of *desu* is disputed by Japanese scholars (see Martin 1975: 1032 for details), but *desu* almost certainly developed from a contraction of an earlier copula form that incorporated an addressee honorific such as *sooroo* or -*masu*. Tsujimura (1968) differentiates addressee honorific lexemes (*bikago* "beautifying words" in his terminology) from these highly grammaticalized forms (*taisya keigo* "interpersonal honorifics") as different categories of (addressee) honorifics. In their newer function, the highly grammaticalized items serve primarily to mark a "polite" speech register or style; they secondarily contribute to the demarcation of units of discourse (Maynard 1993, Dasher 1995: chapter 3). Analyses of pragmatic factors in the patterns of use of MdJ -*masu* and *desu* continue to be refined (e.g. Cooke 1998 and Okamoto 1999). Since the present study focuses on the development of addressee honorific function, rather than on their subsequent grammaticalization, we will not discuss these developments further.

In their cross-linguistic discussion of honorifics, Brown and Levinson propose to account for the development from referent to addressee honorific status as follows. Referent honorifics, which are often used in order to show SP/W's deference indirectly to AD/R (via the SD marking of a referent associated with AD/R), may "stabilize . . . so that they may only be used in reference to the addressee's associates or belongings" (1987 [1978]: 282). Brown and Levinson posit that "via the recurrent use of referent honorifics in situations where the referent–addressee relation is a close one . . . they may evolve into direct addressee honorifics" (ibid.). However, as they note elsewhere (ibid. p. 185), honorifics with the closest association to AD/R, namely T-V second person pronouns, are to be classified as referent honorifics. Although such pronouns always refer to AD/R, they can do so only by including AD/R as a participant in the CDE. Consequently, stabilization of reference to AD/R is insufficient to account for the development of addressee honorific function. In our framework, this development involves (i) loss of the referent honorific's SD link to the CDE, and (ii) shift from the mere grounding of deictic point of view in the SP/W–AD/R dyad to the salient indexing of AD/R in the CSE as the figure of the deictic expression. This shift to direct indexing of AD/R and the concomitant increase in the salience of AD/R as the figure of the deictic expression exemplifies intersubjectification.

As shown in figure 6.7, the earliest addressee honorifics appear in LOJ. Scholars of Japanese agree that the addressee honorific category itself was lacking in OJ. Therefore, the initial appearances of addressee honorifics in LOJ represent a major systemic development in the history of the Jp. honorifics. This and also the development of a distinction between two distinct levels of RESP honorification (VRESP in reference to the emperor and highest ranking nobility, RESP for most other participants of court society) may be related to language-external changes (Lewin 1969). From the time of the establishment of the permanent capital in Kyoto (794 AC), the historical event that is usually taken to mark the transition from OJ to LOJ, Jp. court society became larger and noticeably more complex. While the development of the category of addressee honorifics appears to be directly correlated with this societal change, the development of addressee honorific meaning by individual linguistic items appears not to have any identifiable correlation with language-external events; nor does the subsequent development of the highly grammaticalized subcategory of addressee honorifics. Although major turnovers in honorific vocabulary have occurred since LOJ, the honorific system itself has remained relatively stable.

The one area in which the honorific system has changed since LOJ is in the range of the deictic meaning structure. As noted in 6.3, MdJ HUMIL honorifics crucially index (i) that their subject referent is lower in status than a non-subject referent or AD/R, and (ii) that this subject referent is associated with SP/W or SP/W's social group. In earlier stages of the language, the restriction of subject referent to SP/W or SP/W's social group appears not to have applied. Thus, in LOJ, one finds frequent examples of predicates marked with a HUMIL form that indexes the subject referent as lower in standing than a non-subject referent, and additionally a RESP form that indexes the subject referent as higher in standing than SP/W. The gradual rise in salience of the association between subject referent and SP/W social group may reflect an external societal change similar to that which is reflected in the trend from indexing power relationships to indexing solidarity relationships as noted by Brown and Gilman (1960). As Japanese society underwent a shift from a unitary social hierarchy centered on the Heian imperial court (LOJ) to more complex systems of competing social groups in the feudal era and subsequent periods of modernization and democratization, the nature of the social relationships that were indexed by referent honorifics underwent change. Similarly, nonreciprocal uses of addressee honorifics in Jp. appear to be found more frequently in premodern periods than at the present time, in which reciprocal use appears to predominate in many situations. Accordingly, the meaning structure of the category itself may have shifted from indexing AD/R as socially superior to indexing AD/R as nonintimate.

We now turn to a case study of the development of addressee honorific function in Japanese.

6.5.1   *Japanese* saburahu *"HUMIL:be"* > *"be:POL"*

In this section, we examine the historical development of the Jp. verb *saburahu*. Among the semantic polysemies it involves is the well-known triad LOCATIVE–POSSESSIVE–EXISTENTIAL (see Lyons 1968, E. Clark 1978). In keeping with the topic of the present chapter, we focus not on this triad, but on *saburahu*'s development of referent honorific meaning ("HUMIL:be") early in LOJ (tenth century) and its subsequent development into an addressee honorific ("be:POL(ite)") near the end of LOJ (twelfth century). By early EMJ, *saburahu* was being used as a verb suffix with primarily procedural meaning as marker of POLITE register; in its subsequent history it became highly grammaticalized as a style marker. In this it had similarities to *-masu* in MdJ. However, unlike *-masu*, it was used both as a full verb and as an addressee honorific element in constructions that are characteristic of "be" verbs in Jp., i.e. copula, adjective predicates, and stative/iterative aspect verb forms. During MJ, the pronunciation of *saburahu* came to be *sooroo*.[16] Near the end of LMJ, *sooroo* was replaced in colloquial registers by newer addressee honorifics: by *-masu* in its highly grammaticalized verb suffix function and by *gozaru*, *odyaru*, and *oryaru* in its "be" verb uses. *Sooroo*

---

[16] The overall path of phonetic change is clear, but it is frequently not possible to determine the precise pronunciation of *saburahu* in a given text, because orthographic conventions diverged from the spoken language from LOJ into MJ, and because from LOJ on the verb stem was typically written with a Chinese character used as an ideogram, not as a phonetic symbol. Consequently, we have generalized the representation of the word to three forms that are relatively clearly attested: *samoraFu* for OJ (see also *saFuraFi* in (25b)), *saburahu* for LOJ, and *sooroo* for EMJ and subsequent stages of the language; NKD (vol. XII, 330) provides more details about likely intermediate pronunciations.

nonetheless persisted in some text types throughout EMdJ, e.g. serving as the characteristic style marker of personal letters into the first half of the twentieth century (Martin 1975: 1039). Although obsolete in standard PDJ, *sooroo* is familiar to educated native speakers through their study of classical literature, historical television dramas, and occasionally songs and poems; forms related to *sooroo* may still be found in some outlying island dialects (ibid.). These post-thirteenth century developments will not concern us further here.

Stage I: saburahu₁*: "wait on"*

It is generally agreed among Japanese linguists that LOJ *saburahu* developed from the OJ verb form *samoraFu*, which had the nonhonorific meaning "wait on/for."

In some OJ uses, e.g. when it expresses the waiting for an opportunity, occasion, condition, or event, *samoraFu* has no apparent pragmatic association with social status:

> (24) Kase *samoraFu* to   iFu ni   kakotuke-te,
>   wind wait:for/on QUOT say DAT   make:excuse-PERF/GER
>   Fisasi-ku   totomaru koto tuki wo kazoFe-nu.
>   long:time-ADV stop/stay thing month DO count-PERF
>   "Having made the excuse, saying that (he/they) will wait for/on the wind,
>   months pass (lit., one counts the months) as (the ship) remain(s) (there) for a
>   long time ..."
>   (720 Nihon Shoki, "7th Year of Yuuryaku" [NKD vol. IX, 141])

In other OJ examples, *samoraFu* expresses waiting for an order or summons in a specific location. (The noun *samurai* originates from a nominalized form of *saburahu* in this meaning.) This use of *saburahu* likewise involves no shifting deictic orientation relative to the CSE, and so there is no honorific meaning. However, there is a GIIN that the subject referent has a subservient relationship. In (25a) this subservient relationship is to the anticipated giver of the order, in (25b) to the emperor (implicated by the word *mi-kaki* "[Imperial] partition"):

> (25) a. Fimukasi no   tagi   no   mi-kado ni
>   east   ASSOC waterfall ASSOC RESP-gate LOC
>   *samoraFe*-do kinoFu   mo keFu mo
>   wait-although yesterday FOC today FOC
>   mesu   koto mo nasi.
>   RESP:summon thing FOC not:be
>   "Although [I] *wait* at the [Imperial] Gate of the Eastern Waterfall
>   [= a location in the Imperial Palace], there is no summons yesterday or today."
>   (before 760 Man'yooshuu 2:184, [Takagi, Gomi, and Ohno 1957: vol I, 101])

b. Mi-kaki   no   moto ni   *saFuraFi*,
  RESP-partition ASSOC base LOC be:in:attendance
  omoFi no   Foka   ni   sonaFu
  thought ASSOC other:than MANNER make:preparations
  "*Being in attendance* in the immediate vicinity of the [imperial] partition [i.e.
  within the imperial chambers], [1/3rd person] made extraordinary
  preparations."

             (720 Nihon Shoki, "51st Year of Keiko" [NKD vol. IX, 122])

The meaning "be in attendance in order to serve" (or possibly "serve in a location") continues to be found in many instances of *saburahu* throughout LOJ. A well-known example is in the opening line of the *Tale of Genji* (26):

(26) Idure no   o(ho)n-toki   ni   ka,
      which ASSOC RESP-time/era LOC Q
      nyoogo kooi   amata *saburahi*-tamahi-ker-u   naka ni . . .
      consort court:lady many   serve-RESP-PAST-one(s) among LOC
      "In the time of some emperor, among the many consorts and ladies who served
      [were in attendance] [at court] . . ."

           (*c.* 1006 Genji Monogatari [Abe, Akiyama, and Imai 1970: 93.1])

In (26), the productive RESP referent honorific suffix -*tamahu* deictically marks the subjects (consorts and ladies at court) as having superior social status relative to SP/W (the narrator). In contrast, *saburahu* "serve (at court), be in attendance (to serve at court)" does not index a social deictic relationship between the court ladies and SP/W/narrator; rather, it shows a fixed (nondeictic) status relationship between the ladies and the emperor.

Stage II: saburahu$_2$: *referent honorific*
    In examples (25) and (26) there is a GIIN arising out of the conceptual frame associated with the relationship between the subject and another participant in the described event of "wait on," namely that the subject is socially inferior to the other participant. By early in the tenth century there are sporadic examples in which *saburahu* appears to be used in the meaning "be in the vicinity of a high ranking person," not "waiting for service." Consider (27):

(27) . . . nige-te   iru   sode wo torahe-tamahe-ba
          flee-PERF enter sleeve DO seize-RESP-and:then
      omote wo hutagi-te *saburahe*-do,
      face   DO hide-PERF HUMIL:be-although
      hazime yo-ku   goranzi-ture-ba, . . .
      first:time good-ADV VRESP:see-PERF-and:then

"[The emperor] seized the sleeve [of Princess Kaguya as she] fled into [an adjoining room], and then, although she *was* [waiting] there with her face concealed, he saw her well for the first time, and then . . ."

(early 10th century Taketori Monogatari [Matsuo 1961: 172.10])

Although it is possible that *saburahu* in (27) may be construed to imply that the emperor thought that Princess Kaguya was waiting to serve him, from the narrator's perspective all that is involved appears to be presence in the location. In the next lines of the story, Princess Kaguya reveals herself not to be from earth and vanishes when the emperor tries to take her with him. Since the conceptual frame here does not intrinsically involve a servant–master relationship, the choice of *saburahu* over another verb for "be" (or "wait") appears to reflect the indexing of the relative social status between the subject, Princess Kaguya, and the Emperor from the point of view of SP/W/narrator. On this interpretation, *saburahu* in (27) involves HUMIL referent honorific function (*saburahu₂*).

Saburahu became established as a "HUMIL:be" verb during the tenth century only very gradually, as can be seen by comparison with *haberi*, which had earlier developed "HUMIL:be" meaning and at the time was already in transition from referent honorific to addressee honorific ("be:POL") function. In *Taketori Monogatari*, at the beginning of the century, there are four examples of *saburahu*, including (27), versus twenty-eight of *haberi*. Moreover, in two of the other three examples, *saburahu* clearly has the nonhonorific meanings "wait for an opportunity" and "serve [be in attendance] at court." Later in the tenth century, *saburahu* is still not often found as V_2 in serialized verb or other predicate constructions that are characteristic of "be" verbs throughout the recorded history of Jp. In *Kageroo Nikki* (before 974), *saburahu* appears twenty-three times, all as a morphosyntactically full verb. In contrast, *haberi* appears over forty times as a full verb and an additional forty-five times as a serialized verb or other predicate construction element.[17]

Given the layering of older and newer meanings, it is not surprising that many examples of *saburahu* in *Kageroo Nikki* and subsequent LOJ texts are ambiguous between nonhonorific "be in attendance (to serve)" and referent honorific "HUMIL:be." However, *Kageroo Nikki*, from the later tenth century, contains examples, all in represented conversation, in which the meaning "HUMIL:be" is unambiguous, e.g. (28):

(28) Mune-hasiru-made oboe-haberu   wo
      heart-run-extent   feel-(be:)HUMIL/POL but
      kono mi-su   no   uti   ni   dani
      this RESP-screen ASSOC inside LOC even: FOC

---

[17] Recall that V2 in serialized constructions differs from the polysemous full verb form in both nondeictic and in SD meaning (see 6.3).

saburahu   to   omohi-tamahe-te,[18]   maka-de-n.
HUMIL:be QUOT think-HUMIL-PERF HUMIL:take:leave-go:out-INTENT
"(I) am feeling as though my heart is pounding, but I intend to *be* inside this
screen (to talk directly with you), and then I will leave (go out)."
(before 974 Kageroo Nikki [Saeki and Imuta 1981: 228.11])

In (28), the meaning "HUMIL:be in the vicinity of a RESP person" is evidenced by
the use of *mi-* "RESP" + *su* "screen." This example is from a represented conversation in which SP is a nobleman who desires the hand in marriage of the diarist's
adopted daughter. AD is the diarist herself. Frustrated by the diarist's refusals to
consider his suit for some time, the nobleman has come calling to her home in the
evening. Among Japanese nobility at this period, women remained separated from
men callers on most occasions by a screen or blind, except in intimate situations.
SP's agitated emotional state and also the purpose of the linguistic interaction, may
explain his extensive use of HUMIL forms, including *saburahu*, even though his
social status is not obviously lower than that of the diarist (the nobleman is probably the younger brother of the diarist's husband).[19] The shifting nature of the social
deictic reference expressed by *saburahu* is thus clear. The lexeme *haberi* also occurs
in (28). While *saburahu* appears to be closely associated with locative "HUMIL:be
in a RESP location," *haberi* lacks any locative meaning and instead functions as an
adjoined "be" verb denoting stative/iterative aspect with addressee honorific meaning. In this example, *haberi* may have HUMIL referent honorific or POL addressee
honorific meaning.

Examination of *saburahu* in the first two volumes of *The Tale of Genji* (*c.* 1006) in
the edition by Abe, Akiyama, and Imai (1970) likewise revealed many examples, e.g.
(26) above, in which *saburahu* continued to be used in its older nonhonorific meaning
saburahu₁ "serve, be in attendance (to serve)" and a number of examples, mostly
in represented conversation, in which the word functions as a HUMIL referent
honorific for "be" (*saburahu₂*).[20] Uses in *The Tale of Genji* reveal several apparent
innovations over uses in the *Kageroo Nikki*: *saburahu* is found to mean existential
as well as locative "be," and it appears in the full range of predicate constructions
that are characteristic of "be" verbs in Jp., including copula, predicate adjective, and
serialized verb constructions. In (29), *saburahu* means "HUMIL:be" and functions
as a serialized verb signifying stative aspect:

---

[18] In (29), the suffix *-tamahe* is a HUMIL form conjugated according to the "u-e" (*simonidan*)
class, not RESP *-tamahu* (which is conjugated according to the *yodan* "four vowels" class).
[19] See Seidensticker (1964:147–148 and n. 108) for details.
[20] In 126 examples, the ratio of HUMIL to nonhonorific instances appears to be about 1:4, although
a precise quantitative analysis is impossible due to many ambiguous instances. Frequent collocations such as *saburahu hitobito* "the serving people in attendance" (nineteen examples) also
increase the relative number of nonhonorific examples.

(29) Kaku-nomi   komori-*saburahi*-tamah-u   mo
this:way-EXCL:FOC be:shut:up-HUMIL:be-RESP-thing also
ohotono   no   o(ho)n-kokoro itohosi-kere-ba
father:in:law ASSOC RESP-feelings unpleasant-PAST-and:so
maka-de-tamah-eri.
HUMIL:take:leave-go:out-RESP-PERF
"[Genji] being shut up all the time [in the Imperial palace] would likewise be
upsetting to [Genji's] father-in-law, and so [Genji] set out [from the palace for
his father-in-law's mansion]."

(*c*. 1006 Genji Monogatari [Abe, Akiyama, and Imai 1970: 167.6])

The RESP suffix -*tamahu* marks Genji as higher in status than the narrator. The
HUMIL marking *saburahu* is relative to some non-subject entity that is higher in
status than Genji. At this stage of the novel, Genji is a captain of the Imperial Palace
guards, and so HUMIL *saburahu* may mark Genji's inferior status relative to the
palace (and, by association, the emperor), or it may mark his status relative to his
father-in-law. Since the location involved is the palace, Genji's "being" there may
be equivalent to "serving" or "being in attendance to serve," an interpretation that
would favor the older, nonhonorific meaning of *saburahu*. However, it is unlikely
that the father-in-law would be upset at Genji fulfilling his duty of service. Instead,
it is more likely that Genji's father-in-law would be upset at Genji's presence in the
palace (and therefore away from his wife) at a time when service to the emperor
is not necessary. Thus, the meaning "HUMIL:be" is more likely than the meaning
"serve." Nevertheless, it is not clear in this example whether *saburahu* should be
interpreted as signifying locative "be" (in the palace) or whether it can be interpreted
as a general "be" verb that here expresses stative aspect.

By the time of the *Konjaku Monogatari-shuu* (1130–40), *saburahu* had become
well established as a HUMIL referent honorific:

(30) Yahara akumi-yori-te   kokuoo ni   moosi-te
slowly on:knees-approach-GER king   DAT HUMIL:say-GER
ihaku, onore koso sono tama ha   nusumi-te
saying, myself FOC that   jewel EMPH steal-GER
moti-te *saburahe*.
hold-GER HUMIL:be
"Slowly approaching on his knees, [a state minister] said to the king, 'it is I
who have stolen the jewel, and I *have* it.'"

(1130–40 Konjaku Monogatari-shuu [Yamada et al. 1959: vol. I, 347.11])

In (30), *saburahu* occurs in a construction that consists of *motu* "hold" plus a
(serialized) "be" verb, a collocation that expresses "have, possess" throughout the
history of Jp. The selection of *saburahu* indexes the first person subject referent as
lower in social status than the king, who is the AD of the direct quotation and also

the rightful owner of the jewel under discussion. In this example, *saburahu* indexes the subject referent (a participant in the CDE), and therefore it functions as HUMIL *saburahu₂*. However, the context and careful description of the setting immediately before the represented speech suggest that use of *saburahu* focuses on the king as AD, rather than on his implicit role in the CDE as the owner/source of the object stolen. As we will see in greater detail below, such use represents a step on the way to addressee honorific function.

> *Stage III:* saburahu₃ *"addressee honorific"*
>
> As was found with *kudasaru* (6.4.1), the development of *saburahu₂* involves the acquisition of a (deictic) procedural meaning element alongside a change in its contentful meaning "be in existence." In addition, this development involves subjectification: deictic meaning indexes social status from the point of view of SP/W. As a referent honorific, *saburahu₂* serves as a means for SP/W to address the image needs of AD/R, both through socially appropriate indexing of participants in the CDE and through contributing to an elegant tone of language use. Consequently, the development of referent honorific function by definition involves intersubjectification as well, but AD/R's status is only part of the deictic ground, not its figure. The subsequent development of *saburahu* into an addressee honorific, *saburahu₃*, however, reflects increasing intersubjectification beyond that of its referent honorific use. As an addressee honorific, the item highlights AD/R status or the SP/W–AD/R social relationship as the figure of deictic reference, thereby making it salient (Hanks 1992).

Although some possible tenth century examples of the development of *saburahu* into an addressee honorific have been cited, it does not occur with any frequency until after the mid-eleventh century (Morino 1971: 158–159).[21] A major indication that a referent honorific has developed addressee honorific function is the dropping of selectional restrictions on its range of subject referents. As noted in 6.3, the restrictions on the subjects of referent honorifics in earlier stages of Japanese society coincided more with the power relationships of contemporary feudal and court societies than with the solidarity relationships of modern-day Japan (Dasher 1995: chapter 4). Consequently, HUMIL honorifics from OJ through EMJ are often used with third person subjects who are not aligned with the SP/W social group, but who are lower in status than a non-subject referent (from the point of view of SP/W). Therefore evidence of the development of addressee honorific function by a HUMIL referent honorific can be found during those periods in the broadening

---

[21] NKD (vol. IX, 122) cites two examples of the addressee honorific use of *saburahu* in the early and mid-tenth century. The context of the earliest example, from *Taketori Monogatari* [Matsuo 1961: 76.1–2], before 909) strongly suggests a referent not an addressee honorific function.

of honorific's range of subject referents to include inanimate subjects not associated with any CDE participant, generic reference statements, and second person subjects.

Morino (1971: 158–161) finds scattered examples of *saburahu* with inanimate subjects in tenth and early eleventh century texts. Our examination of two volumes of Genji Monogatari found out of over 125 instances of *saburahu* only one likely addressee honorific example with an inanimate subject that is not associated with the social group of any human referred to or implicitly alluded to in the CDE : *koto* "(intangible) thing" in (31):

> (31) Kore yori   medurasiki koto ha
>   this more:than unusual   thing TOP
>   *saburahi*-nan   ya to   te wori.
>   be:POL-EMPH Q QUOT say be:seated
>   "[Shikibu] said, 'Is there a more unusual thing [than the story I just told]?' and
>   sat down."
>   (*c*. 1006 Genji Monogatari [Abe, Akiyama, and Imai 1970: 164.12])

In (31) *saburahu* appears not to index any participant in the CDE. The quoted speech in (31) is a response to a challenge by Genji and another listener that a story Shikibu just told could not be true. Since use of *saburahu₂* was relatively innovative at the time, *saburahu* may have been felt to be more expressive than *haberi*, the productive addressee honorific for "be" in the early eleventh century, and therefore more suitable than *haberi* for Shikibu's emotionally charged retort.

A similar distinction in expressiveness between *saburahu* and *haberi* is found in *Konjaku Monogatari-shuu*, in which *saburahu* exhibits characteristics of transition toward addressee honorific function. In the Fifth Book (scroll), a myth from India, which is set in a state that exiled seniors at seventy years of age, a wise minister (who has hidden his mother away rather than exile her) consistently uses *haberi* in his speech to the king until the end of the story. At that point the minister reveals the secret behind his wise guidance and argues for a change in the country's laws. In this final page of the story, the minister uses *saburahu* extensively; an excerpt is in (32):

> (32) Sore-ni tosi ohi-taru   mono   ha   kiki
>   however year grow:old-PERF HUMIL:person TOP knowledge
>   hiro-ku   *saburahe*-ba,   mosi
>   broad-ADV HUMIL:be(possess)-and:so perhaps
>   kiki-oki-taru   koto ya   *saburahu*
>   ask-for:future:use-PERF thing INDEF:SUBJ HUMIL:be
>   to-mo, makari-ide-tu,   tohi-*saburahi*-te   sono
>   if-FOC HUMIL-go:out-PERF inquire-be:HUMIL-GER those

koto wo motite   mina   moosi-*saburahi*-si   nari.
words DO by:means:of everything HUMIL:say-HUMIL:be-PAST COP
"However, an old person *has* broad knowledge, and when[ever] there *was* something [I] should find out, [I] left [the royal court] and, *having* asked [my mother], with her words I *have* told you everything [and that is why I appear to be a wise minister]."

             (1130–40, Konjaku Monogatari-shuu [Yamada et al. 1959:
             vol. I, 402.8–9])

In (32) *saburahu* appears twice as a full verb for existential "be" and twice as a serialized verb or auxiliary. The first clause has generic reference, suggesting that the first example could be interpreted as *saburahu₃*; however, the appearance of HUMIL *mono* "person" as the subject also supports the interpretation of it as *saburahu₂*, i.e. as a HUMIL referent honorific, under some sort of pragmatic agreement phenomenon, and this is how we have glossed it. The next instance of *saburahu* in this example is with the inanimate subject *koto* "(intangible) thing," which here refers to "occasions" or "times." However, *koto* is modified by the verb *kiku* "ask," which here has a first person subject; in context *kiki-okitaru-koto* means "occasions when I have something to ask." The referent "time/occasion" of *koto* is thus associated with the first person, a CDE role that supports an interpretation of *saburahu* in this instance as a HUMIL referent honorific. The following two instances of *saburahu* in (32) are as a serialized form. Both instances have first person subjects and signify aspectual Ms that derive from the full verb M "be."

The four instances of *saburahu* in (32) thus all appear to mark the social status of the subject referent, but at least the first three instances also mark that status relative to AD, who has no role as a participant in the CDE. Only the final clause includes the king in the semantic frame of the CDE (as the recipient of the action "say"). Since they mark the social status of a CDE participant, these examples are to be classified as HUMIL referent honorifics. Nevertheless, because the SD indexing is also relative to AD/R independently of the CDE these examples are transitional. A fully semanticized instance of addressee honorification would require that SP/W's attitude to AD/R is independent of the status of any CDE participant, which is not the case here. In the first two (full verb) instances, the association between the subject and the SP + group is only indirect or is otherwise tenuous. Moreover, speech event considerations appear to be a prominent motivation behind the choice of more deferential *saburahu* over *haberi*: the example occurs inside the minister's confession that he has been violating the law and his petition that the law be changed. Attention to AD appears to have been more salient than the SD marking of the subject.

Examination of *saburahu* in the first five scrolls of the early–mid-twelfth century *Konjaku Monogatari-shuu* (Mabuchi and Ariga 1982, Yamada et al. 1959: vol. I) revealed several instances of transitional uses, such as those in (32), but no instances with a second person subject were found. In a detailed comparison of *saburahu* and *haberi* in the entire *Konjaku Monogatari-shuu*, Sakurai (1966) classifies a number of instances of *saburahu* as an addressee honorific, but his classification appears to rest on the presence versus absence of a RESP non-subject referent in the semantic frame. Even by this definition, Sakurai notes that addressee honorific uses of *saburahu* are found only in represented speech, not in narrative passages. By comparing the relative status of the interlocutors involved in each instance of use, he holds that *saburahu* as an addressee honorific expresses a higher degree of deference than does *haberi* in this work, and that *haberi* shows signs of a weakening of its honorific force.

In considering the use of *saburahu* with second person subjects, it is important to note an asymmetry in honorific use during LOJ and EMJ. Very high ranking persons sometimes used HUMIL forms for second person reference in speaking to lower ranking individuals. Such uses did not positively address the image needs of AD, but rather reinforced the lower status of the second person referent relative to the higher ranking SP. Such examples are thus not addressee honorifics. Thus, in the later twelfth century *Imakagami, saburahu* appears in several quoted directives, most of which do not appear to express politeness to AD. Nevertheless, this text includes examples such as (33), in which *saburahu* is used in reference to the action of a third person who is marked by a RESP form as being socially superior to SP/W:

> (33) ika yoo ni ka go-sata *saburahu*-ramu
> how manner ADV Q RESP-procedure be:POL-PROB
> nado omohikake-zu . . . to moosi-kere-ba
> et:cetera think:of-NEG QUOT HUMIL:say-PAST-and:then
> "[The workman] said, '[The priest] didn't even think about, "how will the procedure *be* [done]?" ' "
>
> (1174–75 Imakagami [Sakakibara et al. 1984: 262.1])

In (33), a messenger from a priest is reporting back to the priest about the status of a project that the latter had ordered to be carried out. It is difficult to ascertain whether the messenger is providing a word-for-word direct quotation of the workman's speech, or has imposed his own point of view on the report. In either case, *saburahu* appears in this example with a subject (*sata* "procedure") that is marked with the honorific prefix *go-*, which has RESP meaning.[22] Context, along with the

---

[22] The honorific prefix *go-* is an allomorph of *o(n)-*. *Go-* is used with words that originated from (written) Chinese or words invented in Japan according to Chinese word-building patterns, and *o(n)-* is used with words that appear to native speakers to be of native Jp. origin. The prefix *o(n)-* has generalized in meaning, so that in some instances in MdJ the prefix indicates RESP referent honorific function and in others it has addressee honorific function. However, the allomorph *go-* appears to have remained more associated with RESP marking, as can be illustrated by a few items that can take either prefix. In MdJ, *go-benkyoo* can only mean "(your) RESP study," while *obenkyoo* can mean "(anyone's) study (POLITE to AD/R)."

RESP marking on *sata*, indicates that the subject referent "procedure" is associated with the highest ranking participant in the ongoing series of CDEs, namely the priest. Therefore, one cannot interpret *saburahu* as indexing the priest as having lower social status than some other CDE participant. This example thus reveals a clear dissociation of the deictic M of *saburahu* from the CDE. The selection of *saburahu* over other possible "be" verbs in this example instead deictically indexes AD as being socially superior to SP. Example (33) thus reflects addressee honorific function (*saburahu₃*).

In general, our examination of the range of uses of *saburahu* in the *Konjaku Monogatari-shuu* and the *Imakagami* supports the view that SP/Ws were sometimes using the lexeme with addressee honorific function in the mid-twelfth century but that this new function was not yet well established. *Haberi* still appeared to be more productive as an addressee honorific for "be." Many examples of *saburahu* were ambiguous between HUMIL and addressee honorific function. The use of *saburahu* with respected subjects, which, as in (33), is a clear indicator of dissociation from the earlier HUMIL meaning, still appeared to be rare. Therefore, we conclude that the transition of *saburahu* from referent honorific to addressee honorific function was probably completed sometime near the end of the twelfth or early thirteenth century.

About one hundred years later, the Enkyobon text of the *Heike Monogatari* (1309–10) reveals *saburahu* to be quite productive as an addressee honorific in the colloquial language. The pronunciation of the lexeme in men's speech by this time had probably become *soorau* (NKD vol. XII, 330). However, it continued to be pronounced as *sabura(h)u* in women's speech throughout MJ. In represented speech, *soorau/sabura(h)u* occurs as a full verb for existential and locative "be," as a serialized verb with aspectual meaning, and as an element of predicate adjective and copula constructions. It appears with a variety of inanimate, intangible, and nonspecific subject referents, e.g. (34):

(34) Soo   hitori ...   hoo-oo   no   on-mae   ni
        monk one:person cloistered:emperor ASSOC RESP-presence LOC
        mairi-te,   makoto nite-*soorau*-yaran ...
        HUMIL:come/go-GER truth   COP-POL-HEARSAY
        "A monk ... came into the presence of the cloistered emperor [and said], 'They
        say that this is the truth ...' "
                (1309–10 Enkyobon Heike Monogatari [Kitahara and Ogawa 1996: 20.1])

In (34) *soorau* appears in a phrase that functions as the discourse opener for a relatively long statement of a petition by a monk who is unknown to the very high ranking AD[23] and other nobles present. *Soorau* does not index the social status of any

---

[23] The "cloistered emperor" had abdicated the throne and taken the tonsure as a monk, but he still exercised great power.

participant in the CDE; instead, it marks the attitude of SP toward AD, i.e. it is clearly *saburahu₃*. The copula construction refers to the truth of what is about to be said; the HEARSAY suffix (*ya* "Question" + (a) r (u) "be" + *amu* "future, probability") depersonalizes the source of the information. In the Enkyobon *Heike Monogatari*, *soorau* occurs in directives with socially superior second person subjects, as in (35):

> (35) Naisi si-go-nin ai-tomonaw-ase-owasimasi-te
> female:attendant four-five-person together-accompany-CAUS-VRESP:be-GER
> kyoo e on-nobori-*soora*-e.
> capital:city GOAL RESP-go:up-POL-IMPER
> "Taking four or five women shrine attendants along [with you], go up to the capital."
>
> (1309–10 Enkyobon Heike Monogatari [Kitahara and Ogawa 1996: 67.1])

The VRESP (very respectful) marking of the preceding predicate, and the honorific prefix attached to the nominalized form of *noboru* "go up," make it clear that the subject has socially superior status. The selection of *soorau* rather than a suffixed donatory verb (the most common pattern for expressing a directive in Jp.) probably indicates that SP conceptualizes the directive as a recommendation that will lead to success for the person going up to the capital, not as a personal favor to SP. A RESP referent honorific verb for "be" would have been possible in place of *soorau* in this example; there were several in the EMJ vocabulary in addition to *owasimasu*. The appearance of *soorau* in the final predicate position of the sentence however, maintains a POLITE register that is found throughout this instance of represented speech. Example (35) is from a represented speech that extends for thirteen sentences, nine of which end with a form of *soorau*.

A few instances of *soorau* in represented speech in the Enkyobon *Heike Monogatari* may be analyzed as preserving the older HUMIL meaning, but addressee honorific function is the dominant use of *soorau/saburau* in this text. The use of *soorau* in narrative passages of the Enkyobon *Heike Monogatari* is more conservative than in passages of represented speech. In narrative passages, the M "locative be" predominates, and examples that appear to indicate the old non-honorific meaning "be in attendance to serve" can still be found. Nevertheless, *soorau/saburau* appears much more frequently in represented speech: over sixty instances in the first hundred pages of the edition by Kitahara and Ogawa (1996), compared with nine instances in narrative passages. The association of *soorau* with represented speech reflects an emerging MJ stylistic distinction, in which *sooroo* was more characteristic of colloquial registers, while *haberi* was more characteristic of written registers. As noted at the beginning of this case study, *sooroo* in MJ subsequently developed highly grammaticalized function as a suffix whose nondeictic meaning was primarily procedural (and relevant to the bracketing of discourse).

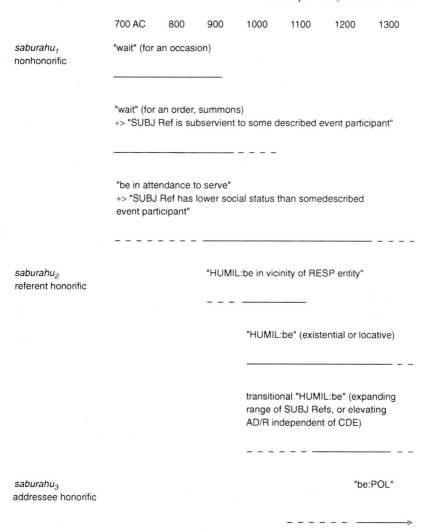

Figure 6.8. Time-line for the development of Japanese *saburahu* ($\longrightarrow$ = continued to be attested beyond the end of time-line).

The present study, however, has focused on the development of *saburahu* as far as the point at which it became an addressee honorific lexeme.

The stages in the development of *saburahu* are shown on a time line in figure 6.8. As shown, the nonhonorific (although pragmatically marked) meaning "be in attendance to serve, serve at a place" (*saburahu₁*) persists until the early fourteenth century (although examples of this meaning are infrequent in comparison to other

Pre-honorific	>	Referent honorific	>	LexADHON	>	AffADHON
informs CDE	>	CDE/$_{CSE}$	>	CSE/$_{CDE}$	>	CSE
content	>	content/procedural	>			procedural
nonsubjective	>	coded subjectivity	>	coded intersubjectivity		

Figure 6.9. Correlated paths in the development of Japanese honorifics.

uses of the lexeme by then). Moreover, there is a relatively short time between the development of HUMIL honorific function (*saburahu₂*) and the development of addressee honorific function (*saburahu₃*). Nevertheless, the relative timing between the development of the two functions is clear.

The development of *saburahu₃* involves several stages. First, the highly restricted meaning "HUMIL:be in the vicinity of a RESP entity" (*saburahu₂*) is generalized to include existential as well as locative "be" (including grammatical constructions characteristic of existential "be" verbs; see (29), (30), (31)). In this latter function, the RESP non-subject entity in the frame of the event becomes less salient. Then, as the range of subject referents increases to include inanimates, intangibles, and generic references (see (31)), the "space" of possible indexed subject referents expands beyond the SP/W+ space. Then, the item is found in examples in which the HUMIL social status is indexed relative to AD (see (32)), and concern about AD's image needs in the CSE appears to be more prominent than is the marking of the subject referent. This represents a major shift of salient indexing from the CDE to the CSE. This shift amounts to intersubjectification. Finally, the range of subject referents further expands to include RESP subjects as well as subjects that are lower ranking relative to some entity in the CDE or AD (see (33)). This stage indicates that there is no longer an indexing of the subject referent and that its SD meaning has become completely dissociated from the CDE.

6.6   Conclusion

In this chapter we have outlined the development of two kinds of politeness markers. First we discussed referent honorifics that signal the social status of a participant in the CDE from the point of view of SP/W's conceptualized relationship to AD/R in the CSE (figure 6.3, Stage II). Secondly, we discussed some examples of addressee honorifics; in Japanese these arise out of referent honorifics, and signal SP/W's conceptualized relationship to AD/R, independent of SP/W's and AD/R's possible roles in the CDE (figure 6.3, Stage III). In this function, addressee honorifics become generalized style markers, and can even come to serve DM-bracketing functions (figure 6.3, Stage IV).

The patterns in the history of Jp. predicate honorifics discussed in this chapter illustrate correlated paths of development that are represented in figure 6.9. The shift from nonhonorific to honorific status involves the general domain shift that has been a theme throughout this book: the shift from informing the CDE to informing the CSE (a shift akin to that from "socio-physical" to "speech act" meaning identified in Sweetser 1990; in the present case, however, the intermediary domain is one of social deixis rather than of reasoning and epistemic deixis). While non-honorifics inform the CDE, referent honorifics not only perform this function but also incorporate the CSE (as the deictic ground) in their SD meaning. In figure 6.9, this function of referent honorifics is indicated by CDE/$_{CSE}$ (conceptualized described event and secondarily conceptualized speech event). In contrast, addressee honorifics primarily inform the CSE but retain some non-SD meaning. This reversal of salience is indicated by CSE/$_{CDE}$. AffADHONs have ceased to inform the CDE, and inform only the CSE. With respect to changes in semantic function, non-honorifics that develop SD status as referent honorifics come to include a procedural meaning element (i.e. their SD meaning) alongside a contentful meaning. Although LexADHONs likewise incorporate both contentful and procedural meaning elements, those that develop into AffADHONs lose their contentful meaning. Referent honorifics encode subjectivity in that they point to one or more "referent" entities in the CDE from the standpoint of SP/W in the speech event. Referent honorifics additionally implicate intersubjectivity as a GIIN; their use typically represents a strategy to address positively the image needs of AD/R. In contrast, addressee honorifics directly encode intersubjectivity; they point to the social status of AD/R independently of the content of what is said.

One question that naturally arises from this sort of study is what the later history of a particular item under discussion may be. Most turnovers of honorific vocabulary (both referent and addressee classes) involve the ultimate replacement of an earlier honorific by a newer (and while new, more expressive) honorific for a similar M (e.g. *pray* by *please*, *haberi* by *sooroo* (< *saburahu*), *sooroo* by *-masu*). Once a newer honorific has appeared, its older counterpart in many instances eventually falls completely from use, although it may survive in particular registers or settings. Relatively recent Jp. translations of the Bible and Christian hymns employ a number of old honorific forms no longer heard outside religious contexts, e.g. *masimasu* "VRESP:be" (used in reference to God). Although the referent honorific *tamahu* "RESP:give" was supplanted in most registers by *kudasaru* during LMJ, its imperative form (*tamae*) survives in MdJ in speech styles associated with rough businessmen or gangsters, typically with denigratory nuances. Because older and newer meanings of Ls coexist at any one period of time, when the honorific meaning is replaced, the original meaning may still be attested (often in a rather different construction or morphosyntactic use). Thus we still use the main verb *pray*, but not its honorific parenthetical (*I pray you*) or its adverbial form (*pray*). Although the persistence of an earlier nonhonorific meaning appears to be the norm, sometimes we find gradual loss of honorific value, i.e. extension of the honorific meaning, instead. For example, Jp. *ageru* developed the referent honorific M "HUMIL:give" in LMJ from the nonhonorific M "move something from a low to a high position" (attested through MdJ). In the last fifty years, however, *ageru* has undergone considerable weakening of its honorific force, so that it has all but supplanted its nonhonorific counterpart *yaru* (the latter survives in uses in which SP/W wishes to highlight the inferior status of the recipient relative to the subject). Given its meaning, the nonhonorific PDJ use of *ageru* for "give" appears to be derived from its honorific use, and not to be a case of persistence of the earlier spatial meaning.

As is hardly surprising, honorific meanings have been shown to arise in conversation. Several times it has been pointed out that changes first appear in quoted conversations (e.g. discussion of the development of *saburahu* in this chapter; see also discussion of *well* in chapter 4). This suggests that they were regarded as conversational, i.e. colloquial, when they were first introduced. However, this is a topic that deserves further study.

7
Conclusion

7.1 Introduction

In this conclusion we briefly summarize the major hypotheses that we have presented, and in doing so essentially reprise the main points of chapter 1. We end with a few suggestions for future research.

7.2 Summary of major findings

Our primary goal has been to show that there are general tendencies in semantic change that are widely attested across a range of semantic fields and languages, and that they result from the interaction of language use with linguistic structure. We have hypothesized that semantic change starts with SP/Ws instantiating a code that they have acquired. Drawing on and exploiting, sometimes consciously, sometimes unconsciously, pragmatic meanings, most especially those kinds of implicatures that we have called "invited inferences," SP/Ws may innovate new uses of extant lexemes. If these new uses spread to AD/Rs and are replicated by them in their role as SP/Ws, then semanticization will take place. We have argued that the main mechanism of semantic change is subjectification (including intersubjectification). This follows from the hypothesis that the seeds of semantic change are to be found in SP/Ws, drawing on and exploiting pragmatic meanings that arise in negotiated interaction. SP/Ws do so for their own ends – to inform, to express beliefs and emotions, and to make explicit what they are (or claim to be) doing with language. Some aspects of what SP/Ws do, most especially projecting innovative metaphorical relations, are primarily self-directed, manifestations of analogical conceptualizing, solving problems of expression, and language play. However, most of what they do with language is metonymic to the SP/W–AD/R dyad (in the sense of associative conceptual metonymy developed in this book). This dyad, though interactive, is not symmetric. SP/Ws exploit their own competence and trust that AD/Rs will understand them; those who do and who adopt the innovations of their interlocutor do so as SP/Ws. One of the outcomes of subjectification is preemption of meaning to the act of speaking itself, hence ultimately to discourse meanings. These are largely procedural in the sense that they point to beliefs, attitudes to the act of speaking that is being engaged in.

Since the interlocutor dyad is the locus of change, and is constrained by the R-, and M-heuristics, innovations are:

(i) constrained by context-dependent pragmatic enrichment
(ii) only minimally different from earlier meanings.

In their early stages they are pragmatic polysemies, extensions on the semasiological dimension. If over time speakers come to use the new pragmatic meanings as part of the linguistic code (i.e. as meanings that function at least in part independent of context), then semantic polysemies will arise. In no case have we found evidence of an older meaning disappearing exactly at the point in time that a new one is semanticized: old and new meanings typically coexist in the same text, e.g. deontic and epistemic meanings of *must* coexist. Only occasionally do old meanings disappear altogether, e.g. the original permission meaning of *must*; more frequently, older meanings survive in highly restricted contexts, e.g. the volitional meaning of *will* remains primarily in negative contexts serving the function of refusal. Semantic change is therefore characterizable as:

(1) $M_1 > M_1 \sim M_2 \, (>M_2)$

This is a variant of the more general claim about language change made in 1.2.2 that:

(2) $A > A \sim B \, (>B)$

Given the tendency for language-users to categorize, new polysemies tend to be attracted to already extant conceptual structures, i.e. they are additions to a given meaningful category on the onomasiological level. However, original meanings tend to persist so that no pure synonyms develop; hence although *indeed, in fact, actually* all underwent similar developments from clause-internal manner or "in respect to which" adverbials to epistemic adversative (sentential) adverbials to DMs, each behaves in a slightly different, unique way.

Innovation of onomasiological categories is rare, but can occur, as we have seen in chapter 6 in connection with the development of addressee honorifics. While deference is probably a universal behavioral strategy, it is only rarely found as a structured linguistic category. We have shown that the development of members of this category in Japanese follows the criteria outlined above: it is constrained by context-dependent pragmatic enrichment, and is only minimally different from earlier meanings.

The process by which new meanings arise has been represented by the IITSC model of semantic change given in 1.3.2 and the typical semantic–pragmatic

Pragmatic–semantic tendencies

a. non-subjective	>	subjective	>	intersubjective
b. content	>	content/procedural	>	procedural
c. s-w-proposition	>	s-o-proposition	>	s-o-discourse
d. truth-conditional		>		non-truth-conditional

Shift from one semantic domain to another

A. CDE	>	CDE/CSE	>	CSE/CDE	>	CSE
B. premodal	>		deontic		>	epistemic
C. ADV$_{manner}$	>	ADV$_{adversative}$	>	ADV$_{elaboration}$	>	ADV$_{hedge}$
D. pre-SAV	>	SAV	>	performative	>	parenthetical
E. pre-honorific	>	referent honorific	>	LexADHON	>	AffADHON

Figure 7.1. Summary of the cross-linguistic regularities in semantic change discussed in this book.

tendencies in semasiological change with respect to function have been summarized in figure 1.4. Instantiations and correlations of semasiological changes in particular domains have been summarized in figure 3.8 for epistemic modals, 4.4 for DMs, 5.2 for performative verbs, and 6.9 for honorifics. The various regular tendencies and their instantiations in semantic domains that we have discussed are summarized in figure 7.1.

It is important to note several things in connection with figure 7.1:

(i) No lexeme is required to undergo the type of change schematized here; each line represents a possible type of change. The hypothesis is that if a lexeme with the appropriate semantics undergoes change, it is probable that the change will be of the type specified. Most importantly, a reverse order of development is hypothesized to be ruled out except under special circumstances such as language engineering or new word formation (e.g. compounding, calquing).

(ii) In actual fact, the trajectories are far more complex than those given here. Because of the principle $M_1 > M_1 \sim M_2$ ($>M_2$) in (1) above, there are polysemous layers at each innovated stage, and in many cases multiple polysemies can coexist over many centuries.

(iii) Figure 7.1 is a summary of the regularities in change we have identified. No lexeme has to undergo the changes, and once a change has started no lexeme will necessarily undergo all possible changes identified. Not every change will necessarily show evidence of the operation of any tendency to the extreme right of the trajectory. The crucial point is that if SP/Ws begin to exploit a lexeme in new ways, and the new meanings are adopted by others, the reverse order of change is not expected.

(iv) It is especially important to note that figure 7.1. is not a hypothesis about correlations among the various regularities. It should not be read vertically, only horizontally (for example, ADV$_{adversative}$ is often epistemic, never deontic, although a vertical reading of lines A and B might suggest a correlation with deontics; likewise AffADHONs are not obviously epistemic).

With respect to the standard taxonomies of historical semantics that date back to Bréal (see 2.2.1), our hypothesis is that they are the outcomes of some very general mechanisms of change. (Conceptual) metonymy is in our view intimately bound up with the mechanism of invited inferencing, and changes identified in the literature as involving metonymic change are typically the outcomes of invited inferencing; changes not identified in the literature as involving metaphorical change are either the direct outcomes of metaphorization or the indirect outcomes of conceptual metonymy. Amelioration and pejoration are the direct outcomes of subjectification at the content level. Generalization and narrowing of meaning are the outcomes of the emergence of differential saliencies in language use.

Bréal considered metaphor, pejoration, and narrowing as the dominant mechanisms of semantic change (Bréal 1964 [1900]). Our position in this book has been that if metaphor appears to predominate, that is an artifact of several practices. It may be a function of the type of lexical domains under investigation; diminutives, when related to eye or seed are more likely to be derived by metaphorization than DMs, SAVs, or markers of honorification. Or it may be a function of focusing on comparison of synchronic stages, and therefore on sources and targets (beginnings and endings) rather than on fine-grained intermediate stages of development. It may also be in part a function of whether we think primarily in terms of decontextualized lexemes and dictionary entries, rather than in terms of actual textual use. Above all, it is a function of thinking of metonymy in a very simplistic, nonconceptual way. If, as we believe, it is true that metonymy in general is "probably even more basic to language and cognition" (Barcelona 2000b: 4), and if conceptual metonymy is intimately bound up with invited inferencing, it should be no surprise that invited inferencing rather than metaphorizing is the principal mechanism that drives semantic change. If pejoration appears to predominate, this is because of social power and prejudice, as Hock and Joseph (1996), among others, have pointed out. As far as narrowing is concerned, it is doubtful that this does predominate; whether narrowing or generalization predominates is largely a function of the domain investigated. For example, wherever semantic change intersects with grammaticalization, generalization tends to predominate.

The regularities we have investigated are major tendencies that are hypothesized to be available for any kind of change that involves semantic development of at least those lexemes that are recruited to the target domains we have discussed here:

modality, DMs, SAVs, and SDs. This means that they can and must be expected to intersect with changes of the types known as grammaticalization and lexicalization. However, they are not coextensive with either. Grammaticalization is in essence a morphosyntactic phenomenon, most crucially the development of functional categories (auxiliary, case, preposition, subordinator, etc.) out of constructions including lexical categories (main verb, nominal in adposition, etc.); it also involves intra-constructional fusion. Even though it is primarily a morphosyntactic phenomenon, by hypothesis grammaticalization is actuated by semantic changes (Fleischman 1982, Hopper and Traugott 1993, Bybee, Perkins, and Pagliuca 1994). It typically involves a subset of the kinds of meaning-change discussed here, most especially invited inferencing in syntagmatic context, subjectification, and, in some cases, intersubjectification. Equally broadly speaking, lexicalization is in essence either (i) a change in the syntactic category status of a lexeme given certain argument structure constraints, e.g. use of the nouns *calendar* or *window* as verbs, or the preemption of a grammatical item under conditions of quotation or "mention" to lexical status, e.g. of *thou* as a verb (see 6.2), or (ii) the formation of a new member of a major category by the combination of more than one meaningful element, e.g. by derivational morphology or compounding. In either case, the process of lexicalization may disrupt the semasiological processes outlined here. By hypothesis any new semasiological change arising after lexicalization has taken place is constrained by both the syntactic or lexical frame realignment involved and by the principle that there are no true synonyms. Many semantic changes involve neither grammaticalization nor lexicalization (e.g. use of *find* or *recognize* as a speech act verb). Whether or not the form (syntactic, derivational, or phonological) of a lexeme changes, the semasiological semantic changes undergone, if any, are predicted to be of the types characterized in figure 7.1.

7.3 Directions for future work

The hypotheses pursued here have necessarily been tested within a limited range of semantic domains. Further research is needed to develop a fuller understanding of several issues, both language-external and language-internal.

With respect to language-external issues, at different periods different onomasiological or conceptual structures may be more active "targets" of change than others; such differences will be very closely tied to the kinds of styles and texts favored at the time, but the individual paths of innovation are hypothesized to be similar, however few or many members are recruited to the semantic class in question. To have a full understanding of the changes discussed here and their impact on language-users, it will be important to know, among other things, in which text-types particular changes are favored, and among which groups of people. For example, it has been suggested (Macaulay 1995) that English speakers in authoritative position, or those who position themselves as having authority, may favor stronger epistemic adverbials (e.g. *in fact, surely*) than others in less authoritative positions. Likewise, as the development of speech act verbs and of honorification shows, speakers of different languages may well find different types of expression salient, and may therefore recruit fewer or more lexemes into particular conceptual categories – whereas explicit encoding of subjectivity may be highly valued in one society or group, explicit encoding of intersubjectivity may be more highly valued in another. Or at one period of time objectivity may be favored over subjectivity. Study of the social and political aspects of the changes highlighted here will give added insight into the relationship between language and culture. We believe that the processes leading to semasiological change will be the same, whether or not these changes spread, and however restricted or rich their onomasiological consequences may be.

With respect to language-internal issues, one important question is the extent to which the separate tendencies identified in figure 7.1 as (b)–(d) are independent of (inter)subjectification and of each other, and under precisely what circumstances they may be correlated. Procedural meanings of the type we have discussed here, such as subjective epistemics, DMs, performatives, and addressee honorifics clearly have scope over the proposition with which they are associated; it is less clear, however, that subjective procedurals such as focus particles (e.g. *mere* < "pure," and *even* < "smooth, flat") have such wide scope; therefore we have considered them separate tendencies. Another issue is whether the kind of reversal of saliency that we identified in (A) with respect to shifts from conceptualized described event to conceptualized speech event will always be identifiable in semasiological changes, although by hypothesis sufficiently fine-grained analyses based on sufficiently extensive textual data are likely to reveal such shifts at intermediary points of development. A third issue is what happens to those polysemies that have developed on the far right hand side of the trajectory of change, in other words, to those lexemes that have developed non-truth-conditional, procedural, scope-over-discourse, and intersubjective meanings. Our hypothesis is that most Ls with such meanings are replaced by newly recruited polysemies from other Ls, i.e. do not continue further semasiologically, but are replaced onomasiologically; their failure to continue along a semasiological trajectory would follow from their being least referential and therefore least tied to non-linguistic categories. However, some Ls that we have not discussed, such as topic markers, are well known to become subject markers, i.e. to be grammaticalized as obligatory markers (e.g. Givón 1979, Shibatani 1991); under what conditions such changes occur and how they are semantically and pragmatically constrained needs to be studied. Further research will also show to what extent the same or other regularities may be found in other semantic areas, e.g. terms for emotion, degree adverbials, markers of indirect speech. This study has been designed to build the foundations for further work along lines such as these.

As work continues, a fuller integration with the formalisms of semantics and pragmatics will continue to give insights into the exact nature of the changes involved, and into the nature of semantic and pragmatic learnability. At the same time, research on evidence for change should allow for a richer understanding of variation in meaning than is often apparent in current formal approaches.

PRIMARY REFERENCES

References in this section are to works cited in examples, where known (not all sources, including the OED, provide full or even any references for data). Citations in square brackets ([ ]) in examples give the source of the example citation, which can be found in the Secondary references. Works that have been used as both primary data and secondary references (e.g. dictionaries like OED, NKD) are cited in Secondary references as well as here.

References from dictionaries and secondary sources are given in the form cited in those sources. Where data has been cited from the OED and another source, e.g. John Gower, *Confessio Amantis*, the more recent source (typically the Helsinki Corpus) only is given. Wherever examples are derived from electronic data bases these data bases are referenced at the end of the entry.

ÆCHom I, 17(App). Second Sunday after Easter. *Ælfric's "Catholic Homilies" First Series*, ed. P. A. M. Clemoes. Cambridge University dissertation, 614–627, 1955–56. (DOE)

ÆCHom II, 42. Martyrs. *Ælfric's "Catholic Homilies" Second Series, Text*, ed. M. Godden. Early English Text Society S.S. 5, 310–317. London: Oxford University Press, 1979 [1922]. (DOE)

Ælfric, Grammar. *c*. 1000. *Aelfrics Grammatik und Glossar; Text und Varianten*, ed. Julius Zupitza. Berlin: Max Niehans, 1966 [1880].

ÆLS I: *Ælfric's Lives of the Saints*, vol. I., ed. W. W. Skeat. Early English Text Society 76, 1966 [1881–1900]. (DOE)

Alfred, Boethius. *King Alfred's Version of Boethius' De Consolatione Philosophiae*, ed. W. J. Sedgefield. Darmstadt 1968 [1899]. (DOE)

Alfred, Preface to Cura Pastoralis. *King Alfred's West-Saxon Version Of Gregory's Pastoral Care*, Part I, ed. H. Sweet. Early English Text Society O. S. 45. London: Oxford University Press, 1958 [1871]. (HCET)

Ancrene Wisse, ed. J. R. R. Tolkien. Early English Text Society 249. London: Oxford University Press, 1962. (HCET)

Appeal London: *A Book Of London English 1384–1425*, ed. R. W. Chambers and M. Daunt. Oxford: Clarendon, 1967 [1931]. (HCET)

Austen, Jane. 1816. Emma, ed. R. W. Chapman, *The Novels of Jane Austen*. Oxford: Clarendon, 5 vols., 1926.

Austen, Jane. 1818. Northanger Abbey, ed. R. W. Chapman, *The Novels of Jane Austen.* Oxford: Clarendon, 5 vols., 1926.

Austen, Jane. 1818. Persuasion, ed. R. W. Chapman, *The Novels of Jane Austen.* Oxford: Clarendon, 5 vols., 1926.

Bede. ?900. *Ecclesiastical History.* Schipper (OED) p. 276 (Jucker 1997)

Beowulf. eighth century. *Beowulf with the Finnesburgh Fragment*, ed. C. L. Wrenn and W. F. Bolton. Exeter; University of Exeter Press, 1988 [1953].

Berkeley, George. 1732. *Alciphron*, ed. A. A. Luce and T. E. Jessop, *The Works of George Berkeley, Bishop of Gloyne.* London: Nelson, 1948; repr. Nendeln: Kraus, 1979.

Boxer, Diana. 1993. *Complaining and Commiserating: a Speech Act View of Solidarity in Spoken American English.* New York: Peter Lang.

Boyle, Electricity: Robert Boyle. 1675–76. *Electricity and Magnetism. Old Ashmolean Reprints* 7. Series ed., R. W. T. Gunther. Oxford: University of Oxford, 1927. (HCET)

Brown, Richard. *The English School Reformed*, 1969 (see Fries, 1998, in Secondary references).

Brown Corpus. 1961. W. N. Francis and H. Kucera. *A Standard Corpus of Present-Day Edited American English.* Providence, RI: Brown University. (Included in ICAME.)

Brut. *The Brut or The Chronicles of England*, Part I, ed. F. W. D. Brie. Early English Text Society, O.S. 131. London: Oxford University Press, 1960 [1906].

Buchan, John. 1924. *The Three Hostages.*

Carroll, Lewis. 1865. *Alice in Wonderland: Authoritative Texts of Alice's Adventures in Wonderland, Through the Looking-Glass, The Hunting of the Snark: Backgrounds; Essays in criticism*, ed. Donald J. Gray. New York: Norton, 1971.

Cato. *Marcius Porcius Cato, On Agriculture; Marcus Terentius Varro, On Agriculture*, trans. William Davis Hooper, rev. Harrison Boyd Ash, Loeb Classical Library. Cambridge, MA: Harvard University Press.

Caxton, William. *The History of Reynard the Fox, trans. from the Original by William Caxton*, ed. N. Blake. Early English Text Society 263. London: Oxford University Press, 1970.

CEEC. *The Corpus of Early English Correspondence*, compiled by Terttu Nevalainen, Helena Raumolin-Brunberg, et al. University of Helsinki, 1998. (ICAME)

Charter (Harm). Writ of King Edward, Bury St. Edmunds. P. H. Sawyer, *Anglo-Saxon Charters: An Annotated List and Bibliography.* London, 1968. (DOE)

Chaucer, Geoffrey. *The Riverside Chaucer*, ed. Larry D. Benson. Boston: Houghton Mifflin, 1987, 3rd ed.

Chauliac (1). ?1425. Anonymous Translation of Guy de Chauliac's Grande Chirurgie: Microfilm print of New York Academy of Medicine ms.

Chauliac (2). *c.* 1420. Microfilm print of Paris Angl. 25 ms.

Chikamatsu. Early 18th century. *Chikamatsu Monzaemon-shuu* [Collected Plays of Chikamatsu Monzaemon], vol. I, ed. Shuu Mori, Bunzoo Torigoe, and Ciyoji Nagatomo. Nihon Koten Bungaku Zenshuu (NKBZ) series 43, Tokyo: Shogakukan, 1972.

Primary references

ChronA. *Two of the Saxon Chronicles Parallel*, 2 vols., ed. C. Plummer. Oxford: Oxford University Press, 1952 [1892–99].

ChronE. *Two of the Saxon Chronicles Parallel*, 2 vols., ed. C. Plummer. Oxford: Oxford University Press, 1952 [1892–99]. (DOE)

Chronicle Capgrave. 1452. *John Capgrave's Abbreuiacioun of Cronicles*, ed. P. J. Lucas. Early English Text Society, O.S. 285. Oxford: Oxford University Press, 1983. (HCET)

Clowes, William. 1602. *Treatise for the Artificial Cure of Struma, 1602*. The English Experience 238. Amsterdam: Theatrvm Orbis Terrarvm and New York: Da Capo Press, 1970. (HCET)

Congreve: William Congreve. *The Comedies of William Congreve*, ed. Eric S. Rump, New York: Viking Penguin, 1985.

Coote: Edmund Coote. 1596. *The English Schoole-Master*, 1968 (see Fries, 1998, in Secondary references).

Cornwallis, Jane. 1613. Letter to Elnathan Parr. (CEEC)

Daikoku Renga ["Linked Verse for Daikoku"]. Before 17th century. *Kyoogenshuu* [Collected Kyogen plays], eds. Tadahiko Kitagawa and Akira Yasuda. Nihon Koten Bungaku Zenshuu (NKBZ) series 35, 81–86. Tokyo: Shogakukan.

Defoe, Daniel. 1722. *A Journal of the Plague Year 1722*, 1754.

Deloney, Thomas. 1619. *Jack of Newbury (1619). The Novels of Thomas Deloney*, ed., M. E. Lawlis. Bloomington: Indiana University Press. (HCET)

Dickens, Charles. 1837/38. *Oliver Twist*, ed. P. Fairclough. London: Penguin, 1985.

Digby Plays. *c.* 1500. *The Late Medieval Religious Plays of Bodleian MSS Digby 133 and E Museo 160*, ed. D. C. Baker, J. L. Murphy, and L. B. Hall, Jr. Early English Text Society 283. Oxford: Oxford University Press, 1982. (HCET)

Digges. 1571. Digges, Leonard and Thomas Digges. *A Geometrical Practice Named Pantometria*, 1591.

Documents Chancery. 15th century. *An Anthology of Chancery English*, ed. J. H. Fischer, M. Richardson, and J. L. Fisher. Knoxville: University of Tennessee Press, 1984. (HCET)

Documents Harmer. 9th–10th century. *Select English Historical Documents of the Ninth and Tenth Centuries*, ed. F. E. Harmer. Cambridge: Cambridge University Press, 1914. (HCET)

DOE: *Dictionary of Old English Corpus in Electronic Form*. Compiled by Angus Cameron, Ashley Crandell Amos, Sharon Butler, Antonette diPaolo Healey. University of Toronto: Dictionary of Old English Project. <http://www.doe.utoronto.ca/webcorpus. html>

Doyle, Arthur Conan. 1894. *The Annotated Sherlock Holmes*, vol. I, ed. William S. Baring-Gould. New York: Clarkson N. Potter, 1967.

Dudley: Robert Dudley. 1586. Letter XCI. The Earl of Leycester to Mr. Secretary Walsyngham. (CEEC)

Dunhuang Bianwen Ji. ?900. *Renmin Wenxue Chubanshe*, eds. Yiliang Zhou, Gong Qi, Yigong Zeng, Zhongmin Wang, Qinshu Wang, and Da Xiang. Beijing, 1984.

Eguchi. 14th century. Noh play by Kan'ami (1333–84). *Yookyoku-shuu [Selected Noh Plays]*, eds. and annot. Mario Yokomichi and Akira Omote. Nihon Koten Bungaku Taikei (NKBT) series 40. Tokyo: Iwanami Shoten, 1960.

Eliot, George. 1860. *Mill on the Floss*. London: Cavendish, 1986.

Eliot, George. 1871–72. *Middlemarch*. Penguin Classics. Harmondsworth: Penguin, 1986.

Elyot, Thomas. 1531. *The Boke Named the Governour (1531)*, ed. E. Rhys, intro. by F. Watson. Everyman's Library. London and New York: J. M. Dent. (HCET)

English Wycliffite Sermons. *c*. 1400. *English Wycliffite Sermons*, vol. I, ed. A. Hudson. Oxford: Clarendon. (HCET)

Enkyobon Heike Monogatari [Enkyobon Text, Tale of the Heike]. 1309–10, eds. Yasuo Kitahara and Eiichi Ogawa. Tokyo: Benseisha, 1996, 4 vols.

Equatorie of the Planets. *c*. 1392. *The Equatorie of the Planets*, ed. D. J. Price. Cambridge: Cambridge University Press. (HCET)

Exodus. ?eighth century. *The Old English Version of The Heptateuch*, ed. S. J. Crawford. Early English Text Society 160. Oxford: Oxford University Press, 1969.

Farquhar, George. 1707. *The Beaux' Stratagem*, ed. Charles N. Fifer. Lincoln: University of Nebraska Press, 1977.

Fates of the Apostles. *c*. 1000. *The Exeter Book. The Anglo-Saxon Poetic Records* vol. III, ed. George Philip Krapp and Elliott van Kirk Dobbie. New York: Columbia University Press, 1932. (HCET)

Fitzherbert. 1534. *The Book of Husbandry (1534)*, ed. W. W. Skeat. English Dialect Society 37. Vaduz: Kraus Reprint Ltd., 1965 [1882]. (HCET)

Floris. *c*. 1300 (?1250). *King Horn, Floriz and Blauncheflur, the Assumption of our Lady*, 1st ed. J. R. Lumby, 1866; re-ed., G. H. McKnight, Early English Text Society, 14, London: Oxford University Press, 1901.

Fox and Wolf. *c*. 1300. *The Fox and the Wolf in the Well: Middle English Humorous Tales in Verse*, ed. G. H. McKnight. NY: Gordian, 1971 [1913]. (HCET)

Fraser, B and M. Malamud-Makowski. 1996. English and Spanish contrastive discourse markers. *Language Sciences* 18: 863–881.

Gawain. after 1345. *Sir Gawain and the Green Knight*, ed. J. R. R. Tolkien and E. V. Gordon. Oxford: Clarendon, 1930.

Genesis. 8th century. *The Junius Manuscript: The Anglo-Saxon Poetic Records*, vol. I, ed. G. P. Krapp. London: Routledge and NY: Columbia University Press, 1931. (HCET)

Genji Monogatari [Tale of Genji]. *c*. 1006. Monash University, Australia: The Monash Nihongo FTP Archive. *<ftp://ftp.cc.monash.edu.au/pub/nihongo/genji.euc.gz>* electronic file of complete text, with page number references to hard-copy published editions.

Genji Monogatari [Tale of Genji]. *c*. 1006. *Genji Monogatari*, vols. I, II, eds. Akio Abe, Ken Akiyama, and Gen'e Imai. Tokyo: Shogakukan. Nihon Koten Bungaku Zensoo (NKBZ) series 12, 13, 1970.

GD. *c*.1000. *Bischof Wœrferths von Worcester Übersetzung der Dialoge Gregors des Grossen*, 2 vols., ed. H. Hecht. Leipzig: Wigand.

Primary references

Gower, John. after 1393. *Confessio Amantis: The English Works of John Gower*, vol. I, ed. G. C. Macaulay. London, 1957 [1900]. (HCET)

Grafton, Rochard. 1543. *A Continuation of the Chronicles of England, Begynning where J. Hardyng Left (1470–1543)*, 1812.

Gregory, William. 1475. *Gregory's Chronicle. The Historical Collections of a Citizen of London in the Fifteenth Century*, ed., J. Camden. Camden Society, N.S. XVII. Westminster, 1876. (HCET)

Hali Meidhad. *c.* 1225. *The Katherine Group. Edited from MS. Bodley 34*, ed. S. T. R. O. d'Ardenne. Bibliothèque de la Faculté de Philosophie et Lettres de l'Université de Liège, CCXV. Paris: Société d'Édition "Les Belles Lettres," 1977. (HCET)

Hargrave, F. ed. 1730. *A Complete Collection of State-trials and Proceedings for High-treason, and other Crimes and Misdemeanours, from the Reign of King Richard II to the End of the Reign of King George I*. London: J. Walthoe.

Havelok. *c.* 1300. *Havelok*, ed. G. V. Smithers. Oxford: Clarendon, 1987. (HCET)

Havelok. *c.* 1300. *The Lay of Havelok the Dane*, ed. W. W. Skeat. Early English Text Society E.S. 4. Oxford: Oxford University Press, 1868. (MED)

HCET. *Helsinki Corpus of English Texts, Diachronic Part*. See Rissanen, Kytö, and Palander-Collin, eds., 1993 and Kytö 1993 [1991]. (Included in ICAME.)

Helsinki Corpus: see HCET.

Henry Prince of Wales. 1608. Letter 254 to King James I. (CEEC).

Hilton, Walter. *c.* 1450. *Walter Hilton's Eight Chapters on Perfection*, ed. F. Kuriyagawa. Tokyo: Keio Institute of Cultural and Linguistic Studies, 1967. (HCET)

HomU. Homilies for Unspecified Occasions. *Wulfstan, Sammlung englischer Denkmäler* 4. Berlin, 1883, repr. by K. Ostheeren, 1967.

Hooker, Richard. 1614. *Two Sermons upon Part of S. Jude's Epistle, 1514*. The English Experience 195. Amsterdam: Theatrvm Orbis Terrarvm and NY: Da Capo, 1969. (HCET)

Horn, Laurence R. 1991. Given as new: when redundant affirmation isn't. *Journal of Pragmatics* 15: 313–336.

Hume, David. 1748. Enquiry Concerning Human Understanding, ed. Eugene F. Miller, *Essays, Moral, Political, and Literary: David Hume*. Indianapolis: Liberty Classics, 1987.

Hume, David. 1779. Dialogues Concerning Natural Religion, ed. Eugene F. Miller, *Essays, Moral, Political, and Literary: David Hume*. Indianapolis: Liberty Classics, 1987.

ICAME. *International Computer Archives of Modern English*. Bergen: Norwegian Computing Centre for the Humanities. CD-ROM.

Imakagami ["The New Mirror"]. 1174–75. *Imakagami honbun oyobi soosakuin* [Text and comprehensive index to the Imakagami], ed. Kunihiko Sakakibara, Kazuyoshi Fujikake, and Kiyoshi Tsukahara. Tokyo: Kasama Shoin, 1984.

Kageroo Nikki ["The Gossamer Diary"]. Early 10th century. *Kageroo nikki soo-sakuin* [Comprehensive index of the *Kageroo Nikki* with annotated text], ed. Umetomo Saeki and Tsunehisa Imuta. Tokyo: Kazama Shobo, 1981.

Kempe, Margery. after 1438. *The Book of Margery Kempe*, vol. I, ed. S. B. Meech and H. E. Allen. Early English Text Society, London: Oxford University Press, 1940. (HCET)

Konjaku Monogatari-shuu ["Tales of Times Now Past"]. 1130–40. Eds. Yoshio Yamada, Tadao Yamada, Hideo Yamada, and Toshio Yamada. Nihon Koten Bungaku Taikei (NKBT) series 22–23. Tokyo: Iwanami Shoten, 1959.

Kyoogen [short comic plays]. Before 17th century. *Kyoogen-shuu* ["Anthology of kyogen plays"], eds. Tadahiko Kitagawa and Akira Yasuda. Nihon koten bungaku zenshuu (NKBZ) series 35. Tokyo: Shogakukan, 1972.

Lacnunga. *Anglo-Saxon Magic and Medicine, Illustrated Specially from the Semi-Pagan Text "Lacnunga,"* ed. J. H. G. Grattan and C. Singer. Publications of the Wellcome Historical Medical Museum, N.S. 3., 1972 [1952]. (HCET)

Lampeter Corpus of Early Modern English Tracts, compiled by Josef Schmied and Eva Hertel, 1991–. (Included in ICAME)

Langacker, Ronald W. 1995. Raising and transparency. *Language* 71: 1–62.

Latimer: Hugh Latimer, *Sermon on the Ploughers, 18 January 1549; Seven Sermons Before Edward VI, on Each Friday in Lent, 1549*, ed. E. Arber. English Reprints. London: Alex Murray, 1968. (HCET)

LawGer. *Gerefa*, in Liebermann, vol. I: 453–455, 1903–16.

Lay Brut: *c*. 1225 (?1200). *Laȝamon's Brut, or Chronicle of Britain*, ed. F. Madden. London: Society of Antiquaries of London, 1847.

Lee, Sophia and Harriet. 1798. *Canterbury Tales*, 1797–1801.

Lewis, Eleanor. 1996. "We're going to look at your life insurance today": an analysis of pronouns in life insurance sales. Senior honors thesis, Department of Linguistics, Stanford University.

Life of St. Edmund. *c*. 1450. The Life of St. Edmund, ed. N. F. Blake. *Middle English Religious Prose*. York Medieval Texts. London: Arnold, 1972. (HCET)

Lindisfarne Gospels. *The Four Gospels in Anglo-Saxon, Northumbrian, and Old Mercian Versions*, ed. W. W. Skeat. Darmstadt 1970 [1871–87]. (DOE)

Lisle, Lady Alice. 1685. The Trial of Lady Alice Lisle. Hargrave, 1730, vol. IV. (HCET)

Locke, John. 1693. *Directions Concerning Education*, ed. F. G. Kenyon. Oxford: Roxburghe Club, 1933. (HCET)

MacWard, Robert. 1671. *The True Non-Conformist (anon.)*.

Malory, Thomas. *c*. 1470. *The Works of Sir Thomas Malory*, ed. E. Vinaver. London: Oxford University Press, 1954.

Man'yooshuu. [Man'yoshu, The Ten-Thousand Leaves]. Before 760. Eds. and annot. Ichinosuke Tagaki, Tomohide Gomi, and Susumu Ohno. Nihon Koten Bungaku Taikei (NKBT) series 4–7. Tokyo: Iwanami Shoten, 1957–60.

MED: *The Middle English Dictionary*. 1956–. Ann Arbor: University of Michigan Press. (See also <http://www.hti.umich.edu/dict/med/>)

Mengzi. 300BC. *Mengzi yinde [A Concordance to Meng Tzu]*, Harvard-Yenching Institute Sinological Index Series, Supplement No. 16. Peiping: Yenching University Press, 1940.

Monk of Evesham. 1482. *The Revelation to the Monk of Evesham*, ed. E. Aber. London, 1869.

Mulford, Clarence Edward. 1913. *The Coming of Cassidy – and Others*.

Mursili II's prayer. *Das hethitische Gebet der Gassulijawija*, ed. Johann Tischler. Innsbrucker Beiträge zur Sprachwissenschaft 37. Innsbruck: Institut für Sprachwissenschaft der Universität.

Nesbit, E. 1909. *Harding's Luck*. London: T. Fisher Unwin, 1923.

Nihon Shoki [Chronicles of Japan]. 720. Eds. Taroo Sakamoto, Saburoo Ienaga, Mitsusada Inoue, Susumu Ohno. Nihon Koten Bungaku Taikei (NKBT) series 67–68. Tokyo: Iwanami Shoten, 1967.

Nippo Jisho [Vocabulario da Lingoa de Iapam; Japanese–Portuguese Dictionary]. 1603. *Hooyaku Nippo Jisho* [Japanese translation of Nippo Jisho], eds. Tadao Doi, Takeshi Morita, and Minoru Choonan. Tokyo: Iwanami Shoten, 1980.

NKD: *Nihon Kokugo Daijiten* [*Unabridged Dictionary of the Japanese Language*]. 1972–76. Tokyo: Shogakukan, 20 vols.

Nrf. Gild. Ret. *Norfolk Gild Returns: English Gilds*, ed. T. Smith and L. T. Smith, Early English Text Society 40. London: Oxford University Press, 1870, rev. 1892.

Oates, Titus. 1685. *The Trial of Titus Oates*. Hargrave 1730, vol. IV. (HCET)

OED: *The Oxford English Dictionary*. 1989. Oxford: Clarendon, 2nd ed. (also OED2/e CD-ROM V 2.0, 1999); *Oxford English Dictionary Online*. 2000. Oxford: Oxford University Press, 3rd. ed. <http://dictionary.oed.com/>

Orosius. *c*. 880. *King Alfred's Orosius*, ed. H. Sweet. Early English Text Society, O.S. 79. London: Oxford University Press, 1959 [1883].

Paston, Clement. *Paston Letters and Papers of the Fifteenth Century*, Part I, ed. N. Davis. Oxford: Clarendon. (HCET)

Paston. *The Paston Letters, A.D. 1422–1509*, ed. J. Gairdner, 1904.

Paston Letters: *Paston Letters and Papers of the Fifteenth Century*, ed. N. Davis. Oxford: Clarendon, 1971. (HCET)

Pepys, Diary. 1666. *Samuel Pepys. Memoirs, Comprising his Diary from 1659 to 1669, and a Selection from his Private Correspondence 16...*

Pepys, Penny Merriments. 1684–85. *Samuel Pepys' Penny Merriments*, ed. R. Thompson. London: Constable, 1976. (HCET)

Purvey, Wycliffe. *The Prologue to the Bible, the Holy Bible, Containing the Old and New Testaments, with the Apocryphal Books, in the Earliest English Versions Made from the Latin Vulgate by John Wycliffe and his Followers*, vol. I, ed. J. Forshall and F. Madden. Oxford: Oxford University Press, 1850. (HCET)

Queen Elizabeth. 1593. *Queen Elizabeth's Englishings of Boethius, De Consolatione Philosophiae, A. D. 1593, Plutarch De Curiositate, Horace, De Arte Poetica, A. D. 1598*, ed. C. Pemberton. Early English Text Society, O.S. 113. London: Oxford University Press, 1899. (HCET)

Radcliffe, Ann, Mrs. 1797. *The Italian, or the Confession of the Black Penitents, a Romance.*

Raleigh, Walter. *c*. 1603. The Trial of Sir Walter Raleigh. Hargrave 1730, vol. I. (HCET)

Rodriguez, P. João. 1604–8. *Arte da lingoa de Japam. Nihon daibunten* [Japanese translation of *Arte da lingoa de Japam*], ed. and trans. Tadao Doi. Tokyo: Sanseido, 1967.

Sansatsuko [Haikai comic verse] by Hattori Doboo. 1704. *Koohon Bashoo Zenshuu* [Comparative Texts of the Collected Works of Bashoo].

Sawles Warde. *The Katherine Group. Edited from MS Bodley 34*, ed. S. T. R. O. d'Ardenne. Bibliothèque de la Faculté de Philosophie et Lettres de l'Université de Liège, CCXV, Paris: Société d'Édition "Les Belles Lettres," 1977. (HCET)

Scott, Walter. 1822. *Peveril of the Peak.*

Shakespeare, William. *The Riverside Shakespeare*, ed. G. Blakemore Evans. Boston: Houghton Mifflin, 1974.

Shengjing. 228–316. Academica Sinica, Online Corpus of Chinese.

Shiji. 104–91 BC. Zhonghua Shuju. Beijing, 1992.

Shishuoxinyu. 5th century. Liu, Yiqing. Academica Sinica, Online Corpus of Chinese.

Shizen koji. 14th century. Noh play by Kan'ami (1333–84), probably revised by Zeami (1363–1443). *Yookyoku-shuu* [Selected Noh Plays], eds. and annot. Mario Yokomichi and Akira Omote. Nihon Koten Bungaku Taikei (NBKT) series 40. Tokyo: Iwanami Shoten, 1960.

Sidgwick, Henry. 1886. *Outlines of the History of Ethics for English Readers*. Boston: Beacon, 1960.

Smith, Adam. 1776. *An Inquiry into the Nature and Causes of the Wealth of Nations*, vol. II, ed. R. H. Campbell and A. S. Skinner. Indianapolis: Liberty Fund, 1981.

Suehirogari ["The Auspicious Fan"]. Before 17th century. *Kyoogenshuu* [Collected Kyogen Plays], eds. Tadahiko Kitagawa and Akira Yasuda. Nihon Koten Bungaku Zenshuu (NKBZ) series 35, pp. 66–86. Tokyo: Shogakugakan.

Sunzi. 5th century BC. Sun, Wu. Academica Sinica, Online Corpus of Chinese.

Taketori Monogatari [Bamboo Cutter's Tale]. early 10th century. *Taketori monogatari zenshaku.* [Complete annotated edition of the *Taketori Monogatari*], ed. Hajime Matsuo. Tokyo: Musashino Shoin, 1961.

Taylor, John. 1630. *All The Workes of John Taylor the Water Poet, 1630. With An Introductory Note By V. E. Neuburg*. London: Scolar, 1977.

Tillotson, John. 1671. *Sermons on "The Folly of Scoffing at Religion" and "Of the Tryall of the Spirits." Three Restoration Divines: Barrow, South, Tillotson: Selected Sermons*, vol. II.ii, ed. S. T. R. O. d'Ardenne. Bibliothèque de la Faculté de Philosophie et Lettres de l'Université de Liège, CCXV. Paris: Société d'Édition "Les Belles Lettres," 1976. (HCET)

Tora-akira ms., Kyoogen. *c.* 1640. *Kohon Noh-kyoogenshuu* [Old ms. of Noh and Kyoogen Plays], ed. Ken Sasano. Tokyo: Iwanami Shoten, 1943–44.

Tsurezure-gusa. [Essays in Idleness]. *c.* 1330. *Tsurezure-gusa soosakuin* [Comprehensive Index of the Tsurezure-gusa, with annotated text], ed. Motoki Tokieda. Tokyo: Shibundo, 1967.

UA Hem. Mag. *United Airlines Hemisphere Magazine.*

United Press Intl.: United Press International. Top stories syndicated by UPI for the years 1991 and 1992.

Primary references

Vanbrugh. John. 1697. *The Relapse*, ed. Bernard Harris. New York: Norton, 1986.

Vices and Virtues. *c.* 1200. *The Book of Vices and Virtues*, ed. E. Holthausen. Early English Text Society, O.S. 89. London: Oxford University Press, 1888. (HCET)

Wakefield Plays. *The Wakefield Pageants in the Towneley Cycle*, ed. A. C. Cawley. Old and Middle English Texts. Manchester: Manchester University Press, 1958. (HCET)

Weller, M. 1970. Moonchildren. In T. Hoffman, ed., *Famous American Plays of the 1970's*. New York: Dell, 1981.

West Saxon Gospels. *The Holy Gospels in Anglo-Saxon, Northumbrian, and Old Mercian Versions*, ed. W. W. Skeat. Cambridge: Cambridge University Press, 1871–1887.

Witches. *George Gifford. A Handbook on Witches and Witchcraftes, 1593*. Shakespeare Association Facsimiles 1, with an introduction by B. White. London: Humphrey Milford and Oxford University Press, 1931.

Wycherley, William. 1674/75. *The Country Wife*, ed. John Dixon Hunt. New York: Norton, 1988.

York Plays: *The York Plays*, ed. Richard Beadle. York Medieval Texts. London: Arnold, 1982. (HCET)

Zhuzi Yulei Scrolls. 1200. Academica Sinica, Online Corpus of Chinese.

SECONDARY REFERENCES

Abe, Akio, Ken Akiyama, and Gen'e Imai, eds. and annot. 1970. *Genji Monogatari* [The Tale of Genji], vols. I & II. Nihon Koten Bungaku Zenshuu series, 12 vols. Tokyo: Shogakukan.

Abraham, Werner. 1991. The grammaticalization of the German modal particles. In Traugott and Heine, vol. II, 331–380.

Adamson, Sylvia. 1995. From empathetic deixis to empathetic narrative: stylisation and (de-)subjectivisation as processes of language change. In Stein and Wright, 195–224.

Ahlqvist, Anders, ed. 1982. *Papers from the 5th International Conference on Historical Linguistics*. Amsterdam: Benjamins.

Aijmer, Karin. 1985. The semantic development of *will*. In Fisiak, 11–21.

1986. Why is *actually* so popular in spoken English? In Gunnel Tottie and Ingegard Bäcklund, eds., *English in Speech and Writing: a Symposium*, 119–129. Uppsala: Almqvist and Wiksell.

1996. *I think* – an English modal particle. In Swan and Westvik, 1–47.

Aissen, Judith. 1992. Topic and focus in Mayan. *Language* 68: 43–80.

Akatsuka, Noriko. 1992. Japanese modals are conditionals. In Diane Brentari, Gary N. Larson, and Lynn A. MacLeod, eds., *The Joy of Grammar*, 1–10. Amsterdam: Benjamins.

1997. Negative conditionality, subjectification, and conditional reasoning. In Athenasiadou and Dirven, 323–354.

Akatsuka, Noriko and Sung-Ock S. Sohn. 1994. Negative conditionality: the case of Japanese -*tewa* and Korean -*taka*. In Noriko Akatsuka, ed., *Japanese/Korean Linguistics* 4: 203–219. Stanford University: Center for the Study of Language and Information.

Akimoto, Minoji. 2000. The grammaticalization of the verb "pray." In Olga Fischer, Annette Rosenbach, and Dieter Stein, eds., *Pathways of Change: Grammaticalization in English*, 67–84, Amsterdam: Benjamins.

Allen, Cynthia, L. 1995. On doing as you please. In Jucker, 275–308.

Allerton D. and A. Cruttenden. 1974. English sentence adverbials: their syntax and their intonation in British English. *Lingua* 34: 1–30.

American Heritage Dictionary of the English Language, The. 2000. Boston: Houghton Mifflin. 4th ed.

Amino, Yoshihiko. 1991. *Nihon no rekisi o yomi-naosu* [Rereading the History of Japan]. Tokyo: Tsukuma Shobo.

Andersen, Henning. 1973. Abductive and deductive change. *Language* 49: 765–793.

Anderson, Lloyd B. 1982. Universals of aspect and parts of speech: parallels between signed and spoken languages. In Paul J. Hopper, ed., *Tense–Aspect: between Semantics and Pragmatics*, 91–114. Amsterdam: Benjamins.

Andrews, Edna. 1995. Seeing is believing: visual categories in the Russian lexicon. In Ellen Contini-Morava and Barbara Sussman Goldberg, with Robert S. Kirsner, eds., *Meaning as Explanation: Advances in Linguistic Sign Theory*, 363–377. Berlin: Mouton de Gruyter.

Anscombre, Jean-Claude and Oswald Ducrot. 1989. Argumentativity and informativity. In Michael Meyer, ed., *From Metaphysics to Rhetoric*, 71–87. Dordrecht: Kluwer.

Anttila, Raimo. 1989 [1972]. *Historical and Comparative Linguistics*. Amsterdam: Benjamins, 2nd ed.

  1992. Historical explanation and historical linguistics. In Garry W. Davis and Gregory K. Iverson, eds., *Explanation in Historical Linguistics*, 17–39. Amsterdam: Benjamins.

Archangeli, Diana. 1997. Optimality Theory: an introduction to linguistics in the 1990s. In Diana Archangeli and D. Terence Langendoen, eds., *Optimality Theory: an Overview*, 1–32. Oxford: Blackwell.

Ariel, M. 1994. Pragmatic operators. In Asher and Simpson, vol. VI: 3250–3253.

Arnovick, Leslie Katherine. 1989. The Wallis rules as speech act prescription: an illocutionary re-evaluation. *General Linguistics* 29: 150–158.

  1994. The expanding discourse of promises in Present-Day English: a case study in historical pragmatics. *Folia Linguistica Historica* 15: 175–191.

Asher, R. E. and J. M. Y. Simpson, eds. 1994. *The Encyclopedia of Language and Linguistics*. Oxford: Pergamon, 6 vols.

Athanasiadou, Angeliki and René Dirven, eds. 1997. *On Conditionals Again*. Amsterdam: Benjamins.

Atlas, Jay D. and Stephen C. Levinson. 1981. *It*-clefts, informativeness, and logical form. In Peter Cole, 1–61.

Atooda, Toshiko. 1980. *Nihongo Zyoosiki Tesuto* [Tests of Common Sense about Japanese (Usage)]. Tokyo: Ikeda Shoten.

Austin, J. L. 1962. *How to Do Things with Words*. Oxford: Oxford University Press.

Axmaker, Shelley, Annie Jaisser, and Helen Singmaster, eds. 1988. *Proceedings of the Fourteenth Annual Meeting of the Berkeley Linguistics Society*. Berkeley: Berkeley Linguistics Society.

Bach, Ulrich. 1995. Wills and will making in 16th and 17th century England: some pragmatic aspects. In Jucker, 125–144.

Baker, Philip and Anand Syea, eds. 1996. *Changing Meanings, Changing Functions*. Westminster Creolistics Series. London: University of Westminster Press.

Banfield, Ann. 1973. Narrative style and the grammar of direct and indirect speech. *Foundations of Language* 10: 1–39.

1982. *Unspeakable Sentences: Narration and Representation in the Language of Fiction.* Boston: Routledge and Kegan Paul.

Barcelona, Antonio, ed. 2000a. *Metaphor and Metonymy at the Crossroads: a Cognitive Perspective.* Berlin: Mouton de Gruyter.

2000b. Introduction: the cognitive theory of metaphor and metonymy. In Barcelona 2000a: 1–28.

Baron, Naomi. 1977. *Language Acquisition and Historical Change.* Amsterdam: North-Holland.

Bartsch, Renate. 1984. Norms, tolerance, lexical change, and context-dependent meaning. *Journal of Pragmatics* 8: 367–393.

Benveniste, Emile. 1968. Mutations of linguistic categories. In Lehmann and Malkiel, 85–94.

1971a [1958]. Subjectivity in language. In *Problems in General Linguistics*, 223–230. Trans. by Mary Elizabeth Meek. Coral Gables, FL: University of Miami Press. (Publ. as De la subjectivité dans le langage, *Problèmes de Linguistique Générale*, 258–266. Paris: Gallimard, 1966); Orig. publ. in *Journal de psychologie* 55: 267f. 1958).)

1971b [1958]. Delocutive verbs. In *Problems in General Linguistics*, 239–246. Trans. by Mary Elizabeth Meek. Coral Gables, FL: University of Miami Press. (Publ. as Les verbes délocutifs, *Problèmes de Linguistique Générale*, 277–285. Paris: Gallimard, 1966 [1958]; Orig. publ. in A. G. Hatcher and K. L. Selig, eds., *Studia Philologica et Litteraria in Honorem L. Spitzer*, 57–63, Bern, 1958.)

1973. *Indo-European Language and Society.* Trans. by E. Palmer. Coral Gables, FL: University of Miami Press.

Bergner, Heinz. 1998. Dialogue in the Medieval drama. In Borgmeier, Grabes, and Jucker, 75–83.

Berlin, Brent and Paul Kay. 1969. *Basic Color Terms: their Universality and Evolution.* Berkeley: University of California Press.

Biber, Douglas. 1988. *Variation across Speech and Writing.* Cambridge: Cambridge University Press.

Biber, Douglas and Edward Finegan. 1988. Adverbial stance types in English. *Discourse Processes* 11: 1–34.

1989. Styles of stance in English: lexical and grammatical marking of evidentiality and affect. *Text* 9: 93–124.

Bickerton, Derek. 1984. The language bioprogram hypothesis. *Behavioral and Brain Sciences* 7: 173–221.

Bjork, Robert E. and Anita Obermeier. 1997. Date, provenance, author, audiences. In Robert E. Bjork and John D. Niles, eds., *A Beowulf Handbook*, 13–34. Lincoln: University of Nebraska Press.

Blake, Norman F. 1992–93. Shakespeare and discourse. *Stylistica* 2/3: 81–90.

Blakemore, Diane. 1987. *Semantic Constraints on Relevance.* Oxford: Blackwell.

1988. *So* as a constraint on relevance. In Ruth Kempson, ed., *Mental Representation: the Interface between Language and Reality*, 183–195. Cambridge: Cambridge University Press.

1990. Constraints on interpretation. In Kira Hall, Jean-Pierre Koenig, Michael Meacham, Sondra Reinman, and Laurel A. Sutton, eds., *Proceedings of the Sixteenth Annual Meeting of the Berkeley Linguistics Society*, 363–370. Berkeley: Berkeley Linguistics Society.

1996. Are apposition markers discourse markers? *Journal of Linguistics* 32: 325–348.

Blank, Andreas. 1997. *Prinzipien des lexikalischen Bedeutungswandels am Beispiel der romanischen Sprachen*. Tübingen: Niemeyer.

1999. Why do new meanings occur? A cognitive typology of the motivations for lexical semantic change. In Blank and Koch, 61–89.

Blank, Andreas and Peter Koch, eds. 1999. *Historical Semantics and Cognition*. Berlin: Mouton de Gruyter.

Blass, Regina. 1996. *Relevance Relations in Discourse*. Cambridge: Cambridge University Press.

Bloch, Oscar and Walter von Wartburg. 1960. *Dictionnaire étymologique de la langue française*. Paris: Presses Universitaires de France, 3rd ed.

Bloomfield, Leonard. 1984 [1933]. *Language*. New York: Holt, Rinehart, and Winston.

Blum-Kulka, Shoshana, Juliane House, Gabriele Kasper, eds. 1989. *Cross-cultural Pragmatics: Requests and Apologies*. Norwood, NJ: Ablex.

Bolinger, Dwight. 1971. Semantic overloading: a restudy of the verb *remind*. *Language* 47: 522–547.

1979. To catch a metaphor: *you* as norm. *American Speech* 54: 194–209.

Borgmeier, Raimund, Herbert Grabes, and Andreas H. Jucker, eds. 1998. *Historical Pragmatics: Anglistentag 1997 Giessen Proceedings*. Giessen: WVT Wissenschaftlicher Verlag.

Bourdieu, Pierre. 1991. *Language and Symbolic Power*. Ed. and introduced by John B. Thompson; trans. by Gino Raymond and Matthew Adamson. Cambridge, MA: Harvard University Press.

Bowler, P. J. 1975. The changing meaning of "evolution." *Journal of the History of Ideas* 36: 95–114.

Boyd, Julian and Zelda Boyd. 1980. "Shall" and "will." In Leonard Michaels and Christopher Ricks, eds., *The State of the Language*, 43–53. Berkeley: University of California Press.

Boyd, Julian and J. P. Thorne. 1969. The semantics of modal verbs. *Journal of Linguistics* 5: 57–74.

Bréal, Michel. 1964 [1900]. *Semantics: Studies in the Science of Meaning*. Trans. by Mrs. Henry Cust. New York: Dover.

1991 [1882]. *The Beginnings of Semantics: Essays, Lectures and Reviews*. Ed. and trans. by George Wolf. Stanford: Stanford University Press.

Brinton, Laurel J. 1988. *The Development of English Aspectual Systems*. Cambridge: Cambridge University Press.

1996. *Pragmatic Markers in English: Grammaticalization and Discourse Function*. Berlin: Mouton de Gruyter.

Brown, Cecil H. and Stanley R. Witkowski. 1983. Polysemy, lexical change and cultural importance. *Man* (N.S.) 18(7): 2–89.

Brown, Keith. 1992. Double modals in Hawick Scots. In Peter Trudgill and J. K. Chambers, eds., *Dialects of English: Studies in Grammatical Variation*, 74–103. London: Longman.

Brown, Penelope and Stephen C. Levinson. 1987 [1978]. *Politeness: some Universals in Language Usage*. Cambridge: Cambridge University Press.

Brown, Roger and Albert Gilman. 1960. The pronouns of power and solidarity. In Thomas A. Sebeok, ed., *Style in Language*, 253–276. Cambridge, MA: MIT Press.

Brugman, Claudia. 1984. The *very* idea: a case study in polysemy and cross-lexical generalization. *Papers from the Twentieth Meeting of The Chicago Linguistic Society, Parasession on lexical semantics*, 21–38. Chicago: Chicago Linguistic Society.

    1988. *The Story of Over: Polysemy, Semantics, and the Structure of the Lexicon*. New York: Garland.

Bryson, Bill. 1991. *Mother Tongue: the English Language*. London: Penguin.

Buck, Carl Darling. 1949. *A Dictionary of Selected Synonyms in the Principal Indo-European Languages*. Chicago: University of Chicago Press.

Bühler, Karl. 1990 [1934]. *Theory of Language: the Representational Function of Language*. Trans. by Donald Fraser Goodwin. Amsterdam: Benjamins. (Orig. publ. as *Sprachtheorie*, Jena: Fischer, 1934.)

Busse, Ulrich. 1998. *Prithee now, say you will, and go about it: prithee* vs. *pray you* as discourse markers in the Shakespeare corpus. In Fritz-Wilhelm Neumann and Sabine Schilling, eds., *Anglistentag 1998, Erfurt: Proceedings*. Trier: Wissenschaftlicher Verlag.

Bybee, Joan L. 1985. *Morphology: a Study of the Relation between Meaning and Form*. Amsterdam: Benjamins.

    1988. Semantic substance vs. contrast in the development of grammatical meaning. In Axmaker, Jaisser, and Singmaster, 247–264.

    1995. The semantic development of past tense modals in English. In Bybee and Fleischman, 503–517.

Bybee, Joan and Suzanne Fleischman, eds. 1995. *Modality in Grammar and Discourse*. Amsterdam: Benjamins.

Bybee, Joan L. and William Pagliuca. 1985. Cross-linguistic comparison and the development of grammatical meaning. In Fisiak, 59–83.

    1987. The evolution of future meaning. In Giacalone Ramat, Carruba, and Bernini, 108–122.

Bybee, Joan L., William Pagliuca, and Revere D. Perkins. 1991. Back to the future. In Traugott and Heine, vol. II: 17–58.

Bybee, Joan L., Revere Perkins, and William Pagliuca. 1994. *The Evolution of Grammar: Tense, Aspect, and Modality in the Languages of the World*. Chicago: University of Chicago Press.

Secondary references

Cameron, Angus, Ashley Crandell Amos, Sharon Butler, and Antonette diPaolo Healey. 1980. *The Dictionary of Old English Corpus in Electronic Form*. University of Toronto: Dictionary of Old English Project.

Campbell, Lyle. 1999 [1998]. *Historical Linguistics: an Introduction*. Cambridge, MA: MIT Press.

Carston, Robyn. 1995. Quantity maxims and generalized implicature. *Lingua* 96: 213–244.

Casad, Eugene H., ed. 1996. *Cognitive Linguistics in the Redwoods: the Expansion of a New Paradigm in Linguistics*. Berlin: Mouton de Gruyter.

Chafe, Wallace. 1994. *Discourse, Consciousness, and Time: the Flow and Displacement of Conscious Experience in Speaking and Writing*. Chicago: Univerisity of Chicago Press.

Chafe, Wallace and Johanna Nichols, eds. 1986. *Evidentiality: the Linguistic Coding of Epistemology*. Norwood: Ablex.

Chao, Yuenren. 1968. *A Grammar of Spoken Chinese*. Berkeley: University of California Press.

Chomsky, Noam. 1986. *Knowledge of Language: its Nature, Origin, and Use*. New York: Praeger.

Chou, Fa-kao. 1953. Notes on Chinese Grammar. *Bulletin of the Institute of History and Philology* 24: 224–247.

Chung, Sandra and Alan Timberlake. 1985. Tense, aspect, and mood. In Shopen, vol. III: 202–258.

Cinque, Guglielmo. 1999. *Adverbs and Functional Heads: a Cross-linguistic Perspective*. Oxford: Oxford University Press.

Clark, Eve V. 1978. Locationals: existential, locative, and possessive constructions. In Greenberg, Ferguson, and Moravcsik, vol. IV: 85–126.

Clark, Eve V. and Herbert H. Clark. 1979. When nouns surface as verbs. *Language* 55: 767–811.

Clark, Herbert H. 1992. *Arenas of Language Use*. Chicago: University of Chicago Press. 1996. *Using Language*. Cambridge: Cambridge University Press.

Clark, Herbert H. and Thomas B. Carlson. 1982. Hearers and speech acts. *Language* 58: 332–373.

Coates, Jennifer. 1983. *The Semantics of the Modal Auxiliaries*. London: Croom Helm. 1995. The expression of root and epistemic possibility in English. In Bybee and Fleischman, 55–66.

Cole, Peter. 1975. The synchronic and diachronic status of conversational implicature. In Cole and Morgan, 257–288. 1981. *Radical Pragmatics*. New York: Academic Press.

Cole, Peter and Jerry Morgan, eds. 1975. *Syntax and Semantics*, vol. III: *Speech Acts*. New York: Academic Press.

Coleman, Linda and Paul Kay. 1981. Prototype semantics: the English word *lie*. *Language* 57: 26–44.

Comrie, Bernard. 1976. Linguistic politeness axes: speaker-addressee, speaker-referent, speaker-bystander. *Pragmatics Microfiche* 1(7): A3. Cambridge University: Department of Linguistics.

Cook, Haruko Minegishi. 1998. Situational meanings of Japanese social deixis: the
mixed use of the *masu* and plain forms. *Journal of Linguistic Anthropology* 8(1):
87–110.

Croft, William. 1990. *Typology and Universals*. Cambridge: Cambridge University Press.
1993. The role of domains in the interpretation of metaphors and metonymies. *Cognitive Linguistics* 4: 335–370.
1995. Autonomy and functionalist linguistics. *Language* 71: 490–532.

Crowley, Tony. 1996. *Language in History: Theories and Texts*. London: Routledge.

Cruse, D. Alan. 1986. *Lexical Semantics*. Cambridge: Cambridge University Press.
2000. *Meaning in Language: an Introduction to Semantics and Pragmatics*. Oxford:
Oxford University Press.

Culpeper, Jonathan and Elena Semino. 2000. Constructing witches and spells: speech acts
and activity types in Early Modern England. *Journal of Historical Pragmatics*
1: 97–116.

Dahlgren, Kathleen. 1978. The nature of linguistic stereotypes. In D. Farkas, W. M.
Jacobsen, and K. W. Todrys, eds., 58–70.
1985. Social terms and social reality. In Suzanne Romaine and Elizabeth Closs Traugott,
eds., *Folia Linguistica Historica* 6: 107–125.

Dancygier, Barbara. 1992. Two metatextual operators: negation and conditionality in
English and Polish. In Laura A. Buszard-Welcher, Lionel Wee, and William Weigel,
eds., *Proceedings of the Eighteenth Annual Meeting of the Berkeley Linguistics
Society*, 61–75. Berkeley: Berkeley Linguistics Society.

Danet, Brenda. 1997. Speech, writing and performativity: an evolutionary view of the
history of constitutive ritual. In Britt-Louise Gunnarsson, Per Linell, and Bengt
Nordberg, eds., *The Construction of Professional Discourse*, 1–41. London: Longman.

Danet, Brenda and Bryna Bogoch. 1994. Orality, literacy, and performativity in Anglo-
Saxon wills. In John Gibbon, ed., *Language and the Law*, 100–135. Harlow: Longman.

Dasher, Richard B. 1983. The semantic development of honorific expressions in Japanese.
Papers in Linguistics 2: 217–228.
1995. Grammaticalization in the System of Japanese Predicate Honorifics. PhD
dissertation, Stanford University.

Dekeyser, Xavier. 1998. Loss of prototypical meanings in the history of English semantics
or semantic redeployment. In Hogg and van Bergen, 63–71.

Denison, David. 1990. Auxiliary + impersonal in Old English. *Folia Linguistica Historica*
9: 139–166.
1992. *Counterfactual may have*. In Gerritsen and Stein, 229–256.
1993. *English Historical Syntax*. Oxford: Oxford University Press.
1998. Syntax. In Suzanne Romaine, ed., *The Cambridge History of the English
Language*, vol. IV: *1776–1997*, 92–328. Cambridge: Cambridge University Press.

Derrig, Sandra. 1978. Metaphor in the color lexicon. In Farkas, Jacobsen, and Todrys,
85–96.

Diewald, Gabriele. 1993. Zur Grammatikalisierung der Modalverben im Deutschen.
Zeitschrift für Sprachwissenschaft 12: 218–234.

1999. *Die Modalverben im Deutschen: Grammatikalisierung und Polyfunktionalität.* Tübingen: Niemeyer.

Dixon, R. M. W. 1972. *The Dyirbal Language of North Queensland.* Cambridge: Cambridge University Press.

1979. Ergativity. *Language* 55: 59–138.

DOE: *Dictionary of Old English Corpus in Electronic Form.* Compiled by Angus Cameron, Ashley Crandell Amos, Sharon Butler, and Antonette diPaolo Healey. University of Toronto: Dictionary of Old English Project. (http://www.doe.utoronto.ca/ webcorpus.html)

Doi, Tadao, tr. 1955. *Nihon daibunten* [Translation of *Arte da lingoa de Japam*, by P. João Rodriguez (1604–8)]. Tokyo: Sanseido.

Doi, Tadao, Takesi Morita, and Minoru Chonan, eds. 1980. *Nippo Jisho* [Modern Japanese translation of the *Vocabulario da Lingoa de Iapam* (Japanese–Portuguese dictionary, 1603)]. Tokyo: Iwanami Shoten.

Dowty, David R. 1985. On recent analyses of the semantics of control. *Linguistics and Philosophy* 8: 291–331.

Du Bois, John W. 1985. Competing motivations. In Haiman, 343–365.

Ducrot, Oswald. 1983. Operateurs argumentatifs et visée argumentative. *Cahiers de Linguistique Française* 5: 7–36.

Duranti, Alessandro and Charles Goodwin, eds. 1992. *Rethinking Context: Language as an Interactive Phenomenon.* Cambridge: Cambridge University Press.

Eckert, Penelope. 1989. *Jocks and Burnouts.* New York: Teachers College, Columbia University.

Enkvist, Nils E. and Brita Wårvik. 1987. Old English *þa*, temporal chains, and narrative structure. In Giacalone Ramat, Carruba, and Bernini, 221–237.

Erman, Britt and Ulla-Britt Kotsinas. 1993. Pragmaticalization: the case of *ba'* and *you know. Studier i modern språkvetenskap* 10: 76–93. Stockhom: Almqvist Wiksell.

Ernst, Thomas Byden. 1984. *Towards an Integrated Theory of Adverb Position in English.* Indiana University Linguistics Club.

Ervin-Tripp, Susan, Kei Nakamura, and Jiansheng Guo. 1995. Shifting face from Asia to Europe. In Shibatani and Thompson, 43–71.

Evans, Nicholas. 1994. Kayardild. In Goddard and Wierzbicka, 203–228.

Faarlund, Jan Terje. 1990. *Syntactic Change.* Berlin: Mouton de Gruyter.

Faingold, Eduardo D. 1991. Evidence of seventeenth century uses of *shall* and *will* compatible with markedness-reversal. *Papiere zur Linguistik* 44–45/1–2: 57–63.

Faltz, Leonard M. 1989. A role for inference in meaning change. *Studies in Language* 13: 317–331.

Farkas, Donka, Wesley M. Jacobsen, and Karol W. Todrys, eds. 1978. *Papers from the Parasession on the Lexicon.* Chicago: Chicago Linguistic Society.

Fauconnier, Gilles. 1975. Polarity and the scale principle. In Robin E. Grossman, L. James San, and Timothy Vance, eds., *Papers from the Eleventh Regional Meeting of the Chicago Linguistic Society*, 188–199. Chicago: Chicago Linguistic Society.

Ferrara, Kathleen. 1997. Form and function of the discourse marker *anyway*: implications for discourse analysis. *Linguistics* 35: 343–378.

Fillmore, Charles J. 1978. On the organization of semantic information in the lexicon. In Farkas, Jacobsen, and Todrys, 148–173.

1982. Frame semantics. *Linguistics in the Morning Calm*, 111–137. Seoul: Hanshin.

1985. Frames and the semantics of understanding. *Quadierni di Semantica* 6: 222–255.

1997 [1971]. *Lectures on Deixis*. Stanford, CA: CSLI.

Fillmore, Charles J., Paul Kay, and Mary Catherine O'Connor. 1988. Regularity and idiomaticity in grammatical constructions: the case of *let alone*. *Language* 64: 501–538.

Finegan, Edward. 1995. Subjectivity and subjectivisation: an introduction. In Stein and Wright, 1–15.

Fischer, Olga. 1994. The development of quasi-auxiliaries in English and changes in word order. *Neophilologus* 78: 137–164.

Fisiak, Jacek, ed. 1985. *Historical Semantics: Historical Word-formation*. Berlin: Mouton de Gruyter.

Fleischman, Suzanne. 1982. *The Future in Thought and Language*. Cambridge: Cambridge University Press.

1983. From pragmatics to grammar: diachronic reflections on complex pasts and futures in Romance. *Lingua* 60: 183–214.

1989. Temporal distance: a basic linguistic metaphor. *Studies in Language*. 13: 1–50.

1990. *Tense and Narrativity: from Medieval Performance to Modern Fiction*. Austin: University of Texas Press.

1991. Discourse as space/discourse as time: reflections on the metalanguage of spoken and written discourse. *Journal of Pragmatics* 16: 291–306.

1992. Discourse and diachrony: the rise and fall of Old French SI. In Gerritsen and Stein, 433–473.

Fleischman, Suzanne and Marina Yaguello. Forthcoming. Discourse markers across languages? Evidence from English and French. In C. L. Moder and A. Martinovic-Zic, eds., *Discourse across Languages and Cultures*. Amsterdam: Benjamins.

Fludernik, Monika. 1993. *The Fictions of Language and the Language of Fiction*. London: Routledge.

Fong, Vivienne. 1997. The Order of Things: what Directional Locatives Denote. PhD dissertation, Stanford University.

Foolen, Ad. 1996. Pragmatic particles. In Jef Verschueren, Jan-Ola Östman, Jan Blommaert, and Chris Bulcaen, eds., *Handbook of Pragmatics 1996*, 1–24. Amsterdam: Benjamins.

Frajzyngier, Zygmunt. 1991. The *de dicto* domain in language. In Traugott and Heine, vol. 1: 218–251.

Fraser, Bruce. 1975. Hedged performatives. In Cole and Morgan, 187–210.

1988. Types of English discourse markers. *Acta Linguistica Hungarica* 38: 19–33.

1990. An approach to discourse markers. *Journal of Pragmatics* 14: 383–395.

1996. Pragmatic markers. *Pragmatics* 6: 167–190.

Secondary references

Fraser, B. and M. Malamud-Makowski. 1996. English and Spanish contrastive discourse markers. *Language Sciences* 18: 863–881.

Frawley, William. 1992. *Linguistic Semantics*. Hillsdale, NJ: Lawrence Erlbaum.

Fries, Udo. 1998. Dialogue in instructional texts. In Borgmeier, Grabes, and Jucker, 85–96.

Fritz, Gerd. 1998. *Historische Semantik*. Stuttgart: Metzler.

Fujii, Noriko. 1991. *Historical Discourse Analysis: Grammatical Subject in Japanese*. Berlin: Mouton de Gruyter.

Gamon, David. 1994. On the development of epistemicity in the German modal verbs *mögen* and *müssen*. *Folia Linguistica Historica* 14: 125–176.

Geeraerts, Dirk. 1983. Reclassifying semantic change. *Quaderni di Semantica* 4: 217–240.
    1992. Prototypicality effects in diachronic semantics: a round-up. In Kellermann and Morrissey, 183–203.
    1995. Specialization and reinterpretation in idioms. In Martin Everaert, Erik-Jan van der Linden, André Schenk, and Rob Schreuder, eds., *Idioms: Structural and Psychological Perspectives*, 57–73. Hillsdale, NJ: Erlbaum.
    1997. *Diachronic Prototype Semantics: a Contribution to Historical Lexicology*. Oxford: Clarendon.

Geis, Michael L. and Arnold M. Zwicky. 1971. On invited inferences. *Linguistic Inquiry* 2: 561–566.

Geluykens, Ronald. 1992. *From Discourse Process to Grammatical Construction: on Left-dislocation in English*. Amsterdam: Benjamins.

Gerritsen, Marinell and Dieter Stein, eds. 1992. *Internal and External Factors in Syntactic Change*. Berlin: Mouton de Gruyter.

Giacalone Ramat, Anna. 2000. On some grammaticalization patterns for auxiliaries. In Smith and Bentley, 125–154.

Giacalone Ramat, Anna, Onofrio Carruba, and Giuliano Bernini, eds. 1987. *Papers from the 7th International Conference on Historical Linguistics*. Amsterdam: Benjamins.

Gibbs, Raymond W. 1993. Process and products in making sense of tropes. In 1993 edition of Ortony 1993 [1979] 252–276.

Givón, Talmy. 1979. *On Understanding Grammar*. New York: Academic Press.

Goddard, Cliff and Anna Wierzbicka, eds. 1994. *Semantic and Lexical Universals: Theory and Empirical Findings*. Amsterdam: Benjamins.

Goffman, Erving. 1967. *Interaction Ritual: Essays on Face to Face Behavior*. Garden City, NY: Anchor.

Goldberg, Adele E. 1995. *Constructions: a Construction Grammar Approach to Argument Structure*. Chicago: University of Chicago Press.

Goossens, Louis. 1982. The development of the modals and of the epistemic function in English. In Ahlqvist, 74–84.
    1985. Framing the linguistic action scene in Old and Present-Day English: OE *cweþan, secgan, sp(r)ecan* and present-day English *speak, talk, say,* and *tell* compared. In Jacek Fisiak, ed., *Papers from the 6th International Conference on Historical Linguistics*, 149–170. Amsterdam: Benjamins.

1987a. Modal tracks: the case of *magan* and *motan*. In A. M. Simon-Vandenbergen, ed., *Studies in Honor of René Derolez*, 216–236. Genl. Seminarie voor Engelse en Oud-Germaanse Taalkunds.

1987b. Modal shifts and predication types. In Johan van der Auwera and Louis Goossens, eds., *Ins and Outs of the Predication*, 21–37. Dordrecht: Foris.

1992. *Cunnan, conne(n), can*: the development of a radial category. In Kellermann and Morrissey, 377–394.

1995a. Metaphtonymy: the interaction of metaphor and metonymy in figurative expressions for linguistic action. In Goossens et al., 159–174.

1995b. From three respectable horses' mouths: metonymy and conventionalization in a diachronically differentiated data base. In Goossens et al., 175–204.

1996. *English Modals and Functional Models: a Confrontation*. Antwerp Papers in Linguistics 86. University of Antwerp.

1999. Metonymic bridges as modal shifts. In Klaus-Uwe Panther and Günter Radden, ed., *Metonymy on Language and thought*, 193–210. Amsterdam: Benjamins.

2000. Patterns of meaning extension, "parallel chaining", subjectification, and modal shifts. In Barcelona 2000a, 149–169.

Goossens, Louis, Paul Pauwels, Brygida Rudzka-Ostyn, Anne-Marie Simon-Vandenbergen, and Johan Vanparys, eds. 1995. *By Word of Mouth: Metaphor, Metonymy and Linguistic Action in a Cognitive Perspective*. Amsterdam: Benjamins.

Gould, Stephen Jay. 1977. *Ontogeny and Phylogeny*. Cambridge, MA: Belknap Press of Harvard University.

Greenbaum, Sidney. 1969. *Studies in English Adverbial Usage*. London: Longman.

Greenberg, Joseph H. 1966 [1963]. Some universals of language with particular reference to word order of meaningful elements. In Joseph H. Greenberg, ed., *Language Universals, with Special Reference to Feature Hierarchies*, 178–194. The Hague: Mouton, 2nd ed.

1978. How does a language acquire gender markers? In Joseph H. Greenberg, Charles A. Ferguson, and Edith Moravcsik, eds., *Universals of Human Language*, vol. III: 249–295. Stanford: Stanford University Press.

1985. Some iconic relationships among place, time, and discourse deixis. In Haiman, 271–287.

1993. The second person is rightly so called. In Mushira Eid and Gregory Iverson, eds., *Principles and Predictions: the Analysis of Natural Languages: Papers in Honor of Gerald Sanders*, 9–14. Amsterdam: Benjamins.

Greenberg, Joseph H., Charles A. Ferguson, Edith Moravcsik, eds. 1978. *Universals of Human Language*. Stanford: Stanford University Press, 4 vols.

Grice, Paul. 1989 [1975]. Logic and conversation. In his *Studies in the Way of Words*, 22–40. Cambridge, MA: Harvard University Press. (Orig. publ. in Cole and Morgan 1975, 41–58.)

Groefsema, Marjolein. 1995. *Can, may, must* and *should*: a Relevance theoretic account. *Journal of Linguistics* 31: 53–79.

Guiraud, Pierre. 1955. *La sémantique*. Que sais-je? 655. Paris: Presses Universitaires de France.

Secondary references

Gussenhoven, Carlos. 1984. *On the Grammar and Semantics of Sentence Accents*. Dordrecht: Foris.

Györi, Gábor. 1996. Historical aspects of categorization. In Casad, 175–206.

Haiman, John. 1980. The iconicity of grammar. *Language* 56: 515–540.

ed. 1985. *Iconicity in Syntax*. Amsterdam: Benjamins.

Haiman, John and Sandra A. Thompson, eds. 1988. *Clause Combining in Grammar and Discourse*. Amsterdam: Benjamins.

Halle, Morris. 1964. Phonology in generative grammar. In Jerry A. Fodor and Jerrold J. Katz, eds., *The Structure of Language: Readings in the Philosophy of Language*, 334–352. Englewood Cliffs, NJ: Prentice-Hall.

Halliday, M. A. K. 1970. Functional diversity in language as seen from a consideration of modality and mood in English. *Foundations of Language* 6: 322–365.

1977. *Functional Linguistics*. London: Arnold.

1990. Linguistic perspectives on literacy: a systemic–functional approach. In F. Christie and E. Jenkins, eds., *Literacy in Social Processes*. Sidney: Literacy Technologies.

1994 [1985]. *An Introduction to Functional Grammar*. London: Edward Arnold, 2nd ed.

Halliday, M. A. K. and Ruqaia Hasan. 1976. *Cohesion in English*. London: Longman.

Hanks, William F. 1992. The indexical ground of deictic reference. In Alessandro Duranti and Charles Goodwin, eds., *Rethinking Context: Language as an Interactive Phenomenon*, 46–76. Cambridge: Cambridge University Press.

Hansen, Maj-Britt Mosegaard. 1998. *The Function of Discourse Particles*. Amsterdam: Benjamins.

Hanson, Kristin. 1987. On subjectivity and the history of epistemic expressions in English. *Papers from the Twenty-third Regional Meeting of the Chicago Linguistic Society*, 133–147. Chicago: Chicago Linguistic Society.

Harada, Shin-ichi. 1976. Honorifics. In Masayoshi Shibatani, ed., *Syntax and Semantics*, vol. V: *Japanese Generative Grammar*, 499–561. New York: Academic Press.

Harkins, Jean. 1994. *Bridging Two Worlds: Aboriginal English and Crosscultural Understanding*. St. Lucia: University of Queensland Press.

1995. Desire in Language and Thought: a Study in Crosscultural Semantics. PhD dissertation, Australian National University.

Harris, Alice C. and Lyle Campbell. 1995. *Historical Syntax in Cross-Linguistic Perspective*. Cambridge: Cambridge University Press.

Harris, Martin. 1978. *The Evolution of French Syntax: a Comparative Approach*. New York: Longman.

Haspelmath, Martin. 1997. *From Space to Time: Temporal Adverbials in the World's Languages*. LINCOM Studies in Theoretical Linguistics 3. Munich: LINCOM EUROPA.

1998. Does grammaticalization need reanalysis? *Studies in Language* 22: 315–351.

Hattori, Shiro. 1967. Descriptive linguistics in Japan. In Thomas A. Sebeok, ed., *Current Trends in Linguistics*, vol. II: 530–584. The Hague: Mouton.

Hayashi, Shiroo, and Fujio Minami, eds. 1973–74. *Keigo Kooza* [Monographs Series on Honorifics]. Tokyo: Meiji Shoin, 10 vols.

Healey, Antonette di Paolo, et al. 1994. *Dictionary of Old English, fascicle A*. Microfiche, Dictionary of Old English Project, Center for Medieval Studies, University of Toronto.

Heeschen, Volker. 1983. The metalinguistic vocabulary of a speech community in the Highlands of Irian Jaya (West New Guinea). *Deutsche Forschungsgemeinschaft*, Publ. 15: *Man, Culture, and Environment in the Highlands of Irian Jaya*.

Heine, Bernd. 1993. *Auxiliaries: Cognitive Forces and Grammaticalization*. Oxford: Oxford University Press.

1995. Agent-oriented vs. epistemic modality: some observations on German modals. In Bybee and Fleischman, 17–53.

1997. *Cognitive Foundations of Grammar*. Oxford: Oxford University Press.

Heine, Bernd, Ulrike Claudi, and Friederike Hünnemeyer. 1991. *Grammaticalization: a Conceptual Framework*. Chicago: University of Chicago Press.

Heine, Bernd, Tom Güldemann, Christa Kilian-Katz, Donald A. Lessau, Heinz Roberg, Mathias Schladt, and Thomas Stolz. 1993. *Conceptual Shift: a Lexicon of Grammaticalization Processes in African Languages*. Afrikanistische Arbeitspapiere 34/35. University of Cologne.

Heine, Bernd and Mechthild Reh. 1984. *Grammaticalization and Reanalysis in African Languages*. Hamburg: Buske.

Held, Gudrun. 1999. Submission strategies as an expression of the ideology of politeness: reflections on the verbalisation of social power relations. *Pragmatics* 9: 21–36.

Herring, Susan C., Pieter van Reenen, and Lise Schøsler, eds. 2000. *Textual Parameters in Older Languages*. Amsterdam: Benjamins.

Higgins, Roger. 1990. By mishap and out of control: on the meaningful descent of raising in English. Ms., University of Massachusetts, Amherst.

Hinds, John. 1976. *Aspects of Japanese Discourse Structure*. Tokyo: Kaitakusha.

Hinds, John, Senko Maynard, and Shoichi Iwasaki, eds. 1987. *Perspectives on Topicalization: the Case of Japanese wa*. Amsterdam: Benjamins.

Hisatake, Akiko. 1974. Syoomotu, kirisitan siryoo no keigo [Honorifics in the *Syoomotu* (collections of LMJ lecture notes and commentaries about literary or religious works) and Christian materials]. In Hayashi and Minami 1973–74, vol. III: 223–258.

Hobbes, Thomas. 1969 [1650]. *The Elements of Law, Natural and Politic*. Ed. Ferdinand Tönnies. New York: Barnes and Noble, 2nd ed.

Hock, Hans Henrich. 1991 [1986]. *Principles of Historical Linguistics*. Berlin: Mouton de Gruyter, 2nd ed.

Hock, Hans Henrich and Brian D. Joseph. 1996. *Language History, Language Change, and Language Relationship: an Introduction to Historical and Comparative Linguistics*. Berlin: Mouton de Gruyter.

Hoenigswald, Henry H. 1992. Semantic change and "regularity": a legacy of the past. In Kellermann and Morrissey, 85–105.

Hogg, Richard M. and Linda van Bergen, eds. 1998. *Historical Linguistics 1995*, vol. II: *Germanic Linguistics*. Amsterdam: Benjamins.

Secondary references

Hopper, Paul J. 1979. Aspect and foregrounding in discourse. In Talmy Givón, ed., *Syntax and Semantics*, vol. XII: *Discourse and Syntax*, 213–241. New York: Academic Press.

1991. On some principles of grammaticization. In Traugott and Heine, vol. I: 17–35.

Hopper, Paul J. and Sandra Annear Thompson. 1980. Transitivity in grammar and discourse. *Language* 56: 251–299.

Hopper, Paul J. and Elizabeth Closs Traugott. 1993. *Grammaticalization*. Cambridge: Cambridge University Press.

Horn, Laurence R. 1972. On the Semantic Properties of Logical Operators in English. PhD dissertation, University of California, Los Angeles.

1984. Toward a new taxonomy for pragmatic inference: Q-based and R-based implicature. In Deborah Schiffrin, ed., *Meaning, Form, and Use in Context: Linguistic Applications; Georgetown University Round Table '84*, 11–42. Washington DC: Georgetown University Press.

1985. Metalinguistic negation and pragmatic ambiguity. *Language* 61: 121–174.

1989. *A Natural History of Negation*. Chicago: University of Chicago Press.

1991. Given as new: when redundant affirmation isn't. *Journal of Pragmatics* 15: 313–336.

1998. Conditionals 'R' us: from IF to IFF via R-based implicature. Paper presented at Stanford University, May.

Hoye, Leo. 1997. *Adverbs and Modality in English*. London: Longman.

Hughes, Geoffrey. 1992. Social factors in the formulation of a typology of semantic change. In Kellermann and Morrissey, 107–124.

Iizumi, Rokuroo. 1963. *Kido-airaku-go Ziten* [Dictionary of Words for Emotions]. Tokyo: Tokyodo Shuppan.

Ipsen, G. 1924. Der alte Orient und die Indogermanen. In J. Friedrich et al., eds., *Stand und Aufgaben der Sprachwissenschaft. Festschrift für Streitberg*, 200–237. Heidelberg: Winter.

Ishida, Takeshi. 1984. Conflict and its accommodation: *omote-ura* and *uchi-soto* relations. In Ellis Krauss, Thomas Rohlen, and Patricia Steinhoff, eds., *Conflict in Japan*, 16–38. Honolulu: University of Hawaii Press.

Iwasaki, Shoichi. 1993. *Subjectivity in Grammar and Discourse: Theoretical Considerations and a Case Study of Japanese Spoken Discourse*. Amsterdam: Benjamins.

Jackendoff, Ray S. 1972. *Semantic Interpretation in Generative Grammar*. Cambridge, MA: MIT Press.

1983. *Semantics and Cognition*. Cambridge, MA: MIT Press.

1990. *Semantic Structures*. Cambridge, MA: MIT Press.

1997. *The Architecture of the Language Faculty*. Linguistic Inquiry Monograph 28. Cambridge, MA: MIT Press.

Jacobs, Andreas and Andreas H. Jucker. 1995. The historical perspective in pragmatics. In Jucker, 3–33.

Jakobson, Roman. 1957. *Shifters, Verbal Categories, and the Russian Verb*. Cambridge, MA: Harvard University Russian Language Project.

Jakobson, Roman and Morris Halle. 1971. *Fundamentals of Language*. The Hague: Mouton.

Janda, Richard D. 1995. From agreement affix to subject "clitic" – and bound root: *-mos* > *-nos* vs. *(-)nos(-)* and *nos-otros* in New Mexican and other regional Spanish dialects. In Audra Dainora, Rachel Hemphill, Barbara Luka, Barbara Need, and Sheri Pargman, eds., *Papers from the Thirty-first Regional Meeting of the Chicago Linguistic Society*, vol. II: *The Parasession on Clitics*, 118–139. Chicago: Chicago Linguistic Society.

2001. Beyond "pathways" and "unidirectionality": on the discontinuity of language transmission and the counterability of grammaticalization. *Language Sciences* 23: 265–340.

Jespersen, Otto. 1924. *The Philosophy of Grammar*. London: Allen and Unwin.

Jucker, Andreas H., ed. 1995. *Historical Pragmatics*. Amsterdam: Benjamins.

1997. The discourse marker *well* in the history of English. *English Language and Linguistics* 1: 91–110.

Jucker, Andreas H. and Irma Taavitsainen. 2000. Diachronic speech act analysis: insults from flyting to flaming. *Journal of Historical Pragmatics* 1: 67–95.

Jucker, Andreas H. and Yael Ziv, eds., 1998. *Discourse Markers: Descriptions and Theory*. Amsterdam: Benjamins.

Jurafsky, Daniel. 1996. Universal tendencies in the semantics of the diminutive. *Language* 72: 533–578.

Justus, Carol F. 1993. Mood correspondences in older Indo-European prayer petitions. *General Linguistics* 33: 129–161.

Kahr, Joan Casper. 1975. Adposition and locationals: typology and diachronic development. *Working Papers on Language Universals* 19: 21–54. Department of Linguistics, Stanford University.

Kakehi, Iori. 1980. Ueda Kazutosi [Biography of K. Ueda]. *Kokugogaku Daijiten*, 58–59.

Kakouriotis, Athanasios and Eliza Kitis. 1997. The case of "vob/lai" and other psychological verbs. In Amalia Mozer, ed., *Proceedings of the 3rd International Conference on Greek Linguistics*, 131–140. Athens: Ellinika Grammata.

Karashima, Mie. 1993. *Ru, raru* no sonkei-yoohoo no hassei to tenkai: komonzyota no yoorei kara [Derivation and development of the honorific uses of *-ru* and *-raru*: based on examples taken from Komonjo [official documents] and other ancient texts]. *Kokugogaku* 172: 1–14.

Katz, Jerrold J. and Jerry A. Fodor. 1963. The structure of a semantic theory. *Language* 39: 170–210.

Kay, Paul. 1975. Synchronic variability and diachronic change in basic color terms. *Language in Society* 4: 257–270.

1990. Even. *Linguistics and Philosophy* 13: 59–111. (Repr. in Kay, 1997: 49–98.)

1997. *Words and the Grammar of Context*. Stanford University: CSLI.

Keenan, Edward L. and Bernard Comrie. 1977. Noun phrase accessibility and universal grammar. *Linguistic Inquiry* 8: 63–99.

Keller, Rudi. 1994. *On Language Change: the Invisible Hand in Language*. Trans. by Brigitte Nerlich. (Orig. publ. as *Sprachwandel: Von der unsichtbaren Hand in der Sprache*, Tübingen: Francke, 1990.)

1995. The epistemic *weil*. In Stein and Wright, 16–30.

Kellermann, Günter and Michael D. Morrissey, eds. 1992. *Diachrony within Synchrony: Language History and Cognition. Papers from the International Symposium at the University of Duisburg, 26–28 March 1990*. Frankfurt-am-Main: Peter Lang.

Kemenade, Ans van. 1999. Functional categories, morphosyntactic change, grammaticalization. *Linguistics* 37: 997–1010.

Kemmer, Suzanne. 1993. *The Middle Voice*. Amsterdam: Benjamins.

Kempson, Ruth. 1980. Ambiguity and word meaning. In Sidney Greenbaum, Geoffrey Leech, and Jan Svartvik, eds., *Studies in English linguistics*, 7–16. London: Longman.

Kiefer, Ferenc. 1994. Modality. In Asher and Simpson, vol. V: 2515–2520.

Kiefer, Ferenc. 1997. Modality and pragmatics. *Folia Linguistica. Acta Societatis Linguisticae Europeae* 31: 241–253.

Kikuchi, Yasuto. 1996. *Keigo Sainyuumon* [Re-introduction to (Japanese) Honorifics]. Tokyo: Maruzen.

Kiparsky, Paul. 1982 [1968]. Linguistic universals and linguistic change. *Explanation in Phonology*, 13–43. Dordrecht: Foris. (Orig. publ. in Emmon Bach and Robert T. Harms, eds., *Universals in Linguistic Theory*, 171–202. Holt, Rinehart and Winston, 1968.)

1992. Analogy. In William Bright, ed., *International Encyclopedia of Linguistics*, vol. I: 56–60. New York: Oxford University Press.

1995. Indo-European origins of Germanic syntax. In Adrian Battye and Ian Roberts, eds., *Clause Structure and Language Change*, 140–169. Oxford: Oxford University Press.

Kleparski, Grzegorz. 1986. *Semantic Change and Componential Analysis: an Inquiry into Pejorative Developments in English*. Regensburg: Pustet.

1990. *Semantic Change in English: a Study of Evaluative Developments in the Domain of Humans*. Lublin: Redakcja Wydawnictw Kul.

Kluge, F. and E. Seebold. 1995. *Etymologisches Wörterbuch der deutschen Sprache*. Berlin: de Gruyter, 3rd ed.

Kokugogaku Daijiten. [Dictionary of Japanese Linguistics]. 1980. Tokyo: Tokyodo Shuppan.

Komatsu, Hideo. 1980. Zisyo [Dictionaries]. *Kokugogaku Daijiten*, 460–464.

König, Ekkehard. 1986. Conditionals, concessive conditionals and concessives: areas of contrast, overlap and neutralization. In Elizabeth Closs Traugott, Alice ter Meulen, Judy Snitzer Reilly, and Charles A. Ferguson, eds., *On Conditionals*, 229–246. Cambridge: Cambridge University Press.

1991. *The Meaning of Focus Particles: a Comparative Perspective*. London: Routledge.

König, Ekkehard and Peter Siemund. 1999. Intensifiers as targets and sources of semantic change. In Blank and Koch, 237–257.

König, Ekkehard and Elizabeth Closs Traugott. 1982. Divergence and apparent convergence in the development of "yet" and "still." In Monica Macaulay, Orin Gensler, Claudia Brugman, Inese Civkulis, Amy Dahlstrom, Katherine Krile, and Rob Sturm, eds., *Proceedings of the Eighth Annual Meeting of the Berkeley Linguistics Society*, 170–179. Berkeley: Berkeley Linguistics Society.

Kopytko, Roman. 1993. *Polite Discourse in Shakespeare's English*. Poznan: Adam Miskiewicz University Press.

1995. Linguistic politeness strategies in Shakespeare's plays. In Jucker, 515–540.

Kortmann, Bernd. 1992. Reanalysis completed and in progress: participles as sources of prepositions and conjunctions. In Kellermann and Morrissey, 429–453.

1997. *Adverbial Subordination: a Typology and History of Adverbial Subordinators Based on European Languages*. Berlin: Mouton de Gruyter.

Kövecses, Zoltán. 2000. The scope of metaphor. In Barcelona 2000a, 79–92.

Kövecses, Zoltán and Günter Radden. 1998. Metonymy: developing a cognitive linguistic view. *Cognitive Linguistics* 9: 37–77.

Koyama, Hiroshi, ed. and annot. 1960. *Kyoogen-syuu* [Anthology of Kyogen Plays]. Nihon Koten Bungaku Taikei (NKBT) series 42. Tokyo: Iwanami Shoten.

Kratzer, Angelika. 1977. What "must" and "can" must and can mean. *Linguistics and Philosophy* 1: 337–355.

Kroch, Anthony S. 1989. Reflexes of grammar in patterns of language change. *Language Variation and Change* 1: 199–244.

Kronasser, Heinz. 1952. *Handbuch der Semasiologie: Kurze Einführung in die Geschichte, Problematik und Terminologie der Bedeutungslehre*. Heidelberg: Winter.

Kroon, Caroline H. C. 1995. *Discourse Particles in Latin: a Study of Nam, Enim, Autem, Vero and At*. Amsterdam Studies in Classical Philology 4. Amsterdam: J. C. Gieben.

Krug, Manfred G. 1998. *Gotta* – the tenth central modal in English? Social, stylistic and regional variation in the British National Corpus as evidence of ongoing grammaticalization. In Hans Lindquist, Staffen Klintborg, Magnus Levin, and Maria Estling, eds., *The Major Varieties of English: Papers from MAVEN 97*, 177–191. Växjö: Acta Wexioninsia.

Krug, Manfred G. 2000. *Emerging English Modals: a Corpus-Based Study of Grammaticalization*. Berlin: Mouton de Gruyter.

Kryk-Kastovsky, Barbara. 1998. Pragmatic markers in Early Modern English court trials. In Borgmeier, Grabes, and Jucker, 47–56.

Kuhn, Thomas S. 1996 [1962]. *The Structure of Scientific Revolutions*. Chicago: University of Chicago Press, 3rd ed.

Kuno, Susumo. 1973. *The Structure of the Japanese Language*. Cambridge, MA: MIT Press.

Kuno, Susumo and Etsuko Kaburaki. 1977. Empathy and syntax. *Linguistic Inquiry* 8: 627–672.

Kuroda. S.-Y. 1973. Where epistemology, style, and grammar meet: a case study from Japanese. In Stephen R. Anderson and Paul Kiparsky, eds., *A Festschrift for Morris Halle*, 377–391. New York: Holt, Rinehart and Winston.

Kurylowicz, Jerzy. 1975. Metaphor and metonymy. *Esquisses Linguistiques*, vol. II: 88–92. Munich: Wilhelm Fink.

Kurzon, Dennis. 1986. *It is Hereby Performed: Legal Speech Acts*. Amsterdam: Benjamins.

Kytö, Merja. 1991. *Variation and Diachrony, with Early American English in Focus*. Frankfurt-am-Main: Peter Lang.

1993 [1991]. *Manual to the Diachronic Part of the Helsinki Corpus of English Texts*. Helsinki: Helsinki University Press.

Labov, William. 1974. On the use of the present to explain the past. In Luigi Heilman, ed., *Proceedings of the 11th International Congress of Linguists*, 825–852. Bologna: Mulino.

1994. *Principles of Linguistic Change: Internal Factors*. Cambridge: Cambridge University Press.

Lakoff, George. 1972. Hedges: a study in meaning criteria and the logic of fuzzy concepts. In Paul M. Peranteau, Judith N. Levi, and Gloria G. Phares, eds., *Papers from the Eighth Regional Meeting of the Chicago Linguistic Society*, 183–225. Chicago: Chicago Linguistic Society.

1987. *Women, Fire, and Dangerous Things: what Categories Reveal about the Mind*. Chicago: Chicago University Press.

1993. The contemporary theory of metaphor. In 1993 edition of Ortony 1993 [1974], 202–251.

Lakoff, George, and Mark Johnson. 1980. *Metaphors we Live by*. Chicago: University of Chicago Press.

Lakoff, Robin. 1972. Language in context. *Language* 48: 907–927.

Lambrecht, Knud. 1994. *Information Structure and Sentence Form: Topic, Focus and the Mental Representations of Discourse Referents*. Cambridge: Cambridge University Press.

Langacker, Ronald W. 1977. Syntactic reanalysis. In Charles Li, ed., *Mechanisms of Syntactic Change*, 57–139. Austin: University of Texas Press.

1985. Observations and speculations on subjectivity. In Haiman, 109–150.

1987/91. *Foundations of Cognitive Linguistics*. Stanford: Stanford University Press, 2 vols.

1990. Subjectification. *Cognitive Linguistics* 1: 5–38.

1993. Universals of construal. In Joshua S. Guenter, Barbara A. Kaiser, and Cheryl C. Zoll, eds., *Proceedings of the Nineteenth Annual Meeting of the Berkeley Linguistics Society*, 447–463. Berkeley: Berkeley Linguistics Society.

1995. Raising and transparency. *Language* 71: 1–62.

1999. Losing control: grammaticalization, subjectification, and transparency. In Blank and Koch, 147–175.

Lass, Roger. 1980. *On Explaining Language Change*. Cambridge: Cambridge University Press.

1997. *Historical Linguistics and Language Change*. Cambridge: Cambridge University Press.

2000. Remarks on (Uni)directionality. In Olga Fischer, Anette Rosenbach, and Dieter Stein, eds., *Pathways of Change: Grammaticalization in English*, 207–227. Amsterdam: Benjamins.

Lau, D. C. 1970. *Mencius*. London: Penguin.

Leech, Geoffrey N. 1970. *Towards a Semantic Description of English*. Bloomington: Indiana University Press.

1971. *Meaning and the English Verb*. London: Longman.

1983. *Principles of Pragmatics*. London: Longman.

Legge, James. 1984. *The Chinese Classics* II: *The Works of Mencius*. Oxford: Oxford Press.

Lehmann, Christian. 1985. Grammaticalization: synchronic variation and diachronic change. *Lingua e Stile* 20: 303–318.

1988. Towards *a typology* of clause linkage. In Haiman and Thompson, 181–225.

1995 [1982]. *Thoughts on Grammaticalization*. Munich: LINCOM EUROPA. (Orig. publ. as *Thoughts on Grammaticalization: a Programmatic Sketch*, vol. I. Arbeiten Des Kölner Universalien-Projekts 48. Cologne: University of Cologne, Institut für Sprachwissenschaft, 1982.)

Lehmann, Winfred P. and Yakov Malkiel, eds. 1968. *Directions for Historical Linguistics: a Symposium*. Austin: University of Texas Press.

Lehrer, Adrienne. 1974. *Semantic Fields And Lexical Structure*. Amsterdam: North-Holland.

1985. The influence of semantic fields on semantic change. In Fisiak, 283–295.

Lehrer, Adrienne and Eva Feder Kittay, eds. 1992. *Frames, Fields, and Contrasts: New Essays in Semantic and Lexical Organization*. Hillsdale, NJ: Erlbaum.

Lehti-Eklund, Hanna. 1990. *Från Adverb till Markör i Text. Studier i Semantisk-syntaktisk Utveckling i Äldre Svenska*. Helsingfors: Humanistika Avhandlingar.

Lepschy, Giulio. 1981. Enantiosemy and irony in Italian lexis. *The Italianist* 1: 82–88.

Levin, Beth. 1993. *English verb classes and alternations: a preliminary investigation*. Chicago: University of Chicago Press.

Levin, Beth and Malka Rappaport Hovav. 1995. *Unaccusativity: at the Syntax–Lexical Semantics Interface*. Linguistic Inquiry Monograph 25. Cambridge, MA: MIT Press.

Levinson, Stephen C. 1979. Pragmatics and social deixis: reclaiming the notion of conventional implicature. In John Kingston, Eve E. Sweetser, James Collins, Huruko Kawasaki, John Manley-Baser, Dorothy W. Marschak, Catherine O'Connor, David Shaul, Marta Tobey, Henry Thompson, and Katherine Turner, eds., *Proceedings of the Fifth Annual Meeting of the Berkeley Linguistics Society*, 206–223. Berkeley: Berkeley Linguistics Society.

1983. *Pragmatics*. Cambridge: Cambridge University Press.

1995. Three levels of meaning. In F. R. Palmer, ed., *Grammar and Meaning: Essays in Honor of Sir John Lyons*, 90–115. Cambridge: Cambridge University Press.

2000. *Presumptive Meanings: the Theory of Generalized Conversational Implicature*. Cambridge, MA: MIT Press, Bradford.

Lewandowska-Tomaszczyk, Barbara. 1985. On semantic change in a dynamic model of language. In Fisiak, 297–323.

Lewin, Bruno, ed. 1969. *Beiträge zum Interpersonalen Bezug im Japanischen*. Wiesbaden: Otto Harrassowitz.

Li, Dong-yi. 1992. *Hanzi Yanbian Wubaili* [The Evolution of Five Hundred Chinese Characters]. Beijing: Beijing Language Institute Press, 3rd ed., revised.

Lichtenberk, Frantisek. 1991. Semantic change and heterosemy in grammaticalization. *Language* 67: 474–509.

Secondary references

Lightfoot, David. 1979. *Principles of Diachronic Syntax*. Cambridge: Cambridge University Press.

1991. *How to Set Parameters: Arguments from Language Change*. Cambridge, MA: MIT Press.

1999. *The Development of Language: Acquisition, Change, and Evolution*. Malden, MA: Blackwell.

Lipka, Leonhard. 1990. *An Outline of English Lexicology: Lexical Structure, Word Semantics, and Word-Formation*. Tübingen: Niemeyer.

Longacre, Robert E. 1976. Mystery particles and affixes. In Salikoko Mufwene, Carol A. Walker, and Sanford B. Steever, eds., *Papers from the Twelfth Regional Meeting of the Chicago Linguistic Society*, 468–475. Chicago: Chicago Linguistic Society.

Lord, Carol. 1993. *Historical Change in Serial Verb Constructions*. Amsterdam: Benjamins.

Lyons, John. 1968. *Introduction to Theoretical Linguistics*. Cambridge: Cambridge University Press.

1977. *Semantics*. Cambridge: Cambridge University Press, 2 vols.

1982. Deixis and subjectivity: *Loquor, ergo sum*? In Robert J. Jarvella and Wolfgang Klein, eds., *Speech, Place, and Action: Studies in Deixis and Related Topics*, 101–124. New York: Wiley.

1994. Subjecthood and subjectivity. In Marina Yaguello, ed., *Subjecthood and Subjectivity: the Status of the Subject in Linguistic Theory*, 9–17. Paris: Ophrys; London: Institut Français du Royaume-Uni.

1995. *Linguistic Semantics: an Introduction*. Cambridge: Cambridge University Press.

Mabuchi, Kazuo and Kazuko Ariga. 1982. *Konzyaku Monogatari-syuu Ziritu-go Sakuin* [Index of Independent Words in the *Konjaku Monogatari-shuu* (1130–40 "Tales of Times Now Past")]. Tokyo: Kasama Shoin.

Macaulay, Ronald K. S. 1995. The adverbs of authority. *English World-Wide* 16: 37–60.

McCawley, James D. 1968. Lexical insertion in a transformational grammar without deep structure. In Bill J. Darden, Charles-James N. Bailey, and Alice Davidson, eds., *Papers from the Fourth Regional Meeting of the Chicago Linguistic Society*, 71–80. Chicago: Chicago Linguistic Society.

1988. *The Syntactic Phenomena of English*, vol. II. Chicago: University of Chicago Press.

McConnell-Ginet, Sally. 1982. Adverbs and logical form: a linguistically realistic theory. *Language* 58: 144–187.

MacMahon, April M. S. 1994. *Understanding Language Change*. Cambridge: Cambridge University Press.

McWhorter, John. 1997. *Towards a New Model of Creole Genesis*. New York: Peter Lang.

Manoliu, Maria M. 2000. From *deixis ad oculos* to discourse markers via *deixis ad phantasma*. In Smith and Bentley, 243–260.

Marchello-Nizia, Christiane. Forthcoming. Language Evolution and Semantic Representations: from "Subjective" to "Objective" in French.

Martin, Samuel. 1964. Speech levels in Japan and Korea. In Dell Hymes, ed., *Language in Culture and Society*, 407–415. New York: Harper and Row.

1975. *A Reference Grammar of Japanese*. New Haven: Yale University Press.

314

Masuda, Koh, ed. 1974. *Kenkyusha's New Japanese–English Dictionary*. Tokyo: Kenkyusha, 4th ed.

Matisoff, James A. 1973. *The Grammar of Lahu*. Berkeley: University of California Press.

Matoré, Georges. 1953. *La méthode en lexicologie: Domaine français*. Paris: Didier.

Matsumoto, Yo. 1988. From bound grammatical markers to free discourse markers: history of some Japanese connectives. In Axmaker, Jaisser, and Singmaster, 340–351.

Matsumoto, Yoshiko. 1985. A sort of speech act qualification in Japanese: *Chotto*. *Journal of Asian Culture* 11: 143–159.

1988. Reexamination of the universality of face: politeness phenomena in Japanese. *Journal of Pragmatics* 12: 403–426.

1997. The rise and fall of Japanese nonsubject honorifics: the case of "*o*-Verb-*suru*." *Journal of Pragmatics* 28: 719–740.

Matsuo, Hajime, ed. and annot. 1961. *Taketori Monogatari zenshaku* [Complete annotated edition of the Bamboo Cutter's Tale]. Tokyo: Musashino Shoin.

Matthiessen, Christian and Sandra A. Thompson. 1988. The structure of discourse and "subordination". In Haiman and Thompson, 275–329.

Maynard, Senko K. 1993. *Discourse Modality: Subjectivity, Emotion, and Voice in the Japanese Language*. Amsterdam: Benjamins.

MED: *The Middle English Dictionary*. 1956 –. Ann Arbor: University of Michigan Press. (see also http://www.hti.umich.edu/dict/med/)

Meillet, Antoine. 1958 [1905–6]. Comment les mots changent de sens. In his *Linguistique historique et linguistique générale*, 230–280. Paris: Champion (Repr. from *Année sociologique* 1905–06.)

1958 [1912]. L'évolution des formes grammaticales. In his *Linguistique historique et linguistique générale*, 130–148. Paris: Champion. (Repr. from *Scientia (Rivista di scienza)* XII, 1912.)

1958 [1915–16]. Le renouvellement des conjonctions. In his *Linguistique historique et linguistique générale*, 159–174. Paris: Champion. (Repr. from *Annuaire de l'École Pratique des Hautes Études*, 1915–16.)

Mey, Jacob L. 1993. *Pragmatics: an Introduction*. Oxford: Blackwell.

Michaelis, Laura A. 1993. "Continuity" within three scalar models: the polysemy of adverbial *still*. *Journal of Semantics* 10: 193–237.

Miller, Roy Andrew. 1967. *The Japanese Language*. Chicago: University of Chicago Press.

Milroy, James. 1992. *Linguistic Variation and Change: on the Historical Sociolinguistics of English*. Oxford: Blackwell.

1993. On the social origins of language change. In Charles Jones, ed., *Historical Linguistics: Problems and Perspectives*, 215–236. London: Longman.

Milroy, James and Lesley Milroy. 1985. Linguistic change, social network and speaker innovation. *Journal of Linguistics* 21: 339–384.

Milroy, Lesley. 1980. *Language and Social Networks*. Baltimore: University Park Press.

Mitchell, Bruce. 1986. *A Guide to Old English*. Oxford: Blackwell, 2 vols.

Mizutani, Osamu and Nobuko Mizutani. 1987. *How to Be Polite in Japanese*. Tokyo: Japan Times.

Secondary references

Montgomery, Michael B. and Stephen J. Nagle. 1993. Double modals in Scotland and the southern United States: trans-atlantic inheritance or independent development? *Folia Linguistica Historica* 14: 91–107.

Morgan, Jerry L. 1993 [1979]. Observations on the pragmatics of metaphor. In Ortony, 124–134.

Mori, Shu, Bunzo Torigoe, and Chiyoji Nagatomo, eds. 1972. *Tikamatu Monzaemon Syuu* [Collected works of Chikamatsu Monzaemon], vol. I. Nihon Koten Bungaku Zenshuu series 43. Tokyo: Shogakukan.

Morino, Muneaki. 1971. Kodai no keigo II [Honorifics of Late Old Japanese]. In Tsujimura, 97–182.

Mossé, Fernand. 1952. *A Handbook of Middle English*. Trans. by James A. Walker. Baltimore: Johns Hopkins.

Mushin, Ilana. 1998. Evidentiality and epistemological stance in Macedonian, English and Japanese narrative. PhD dissertation, SUNY, Buffalo.

Myhill, John. 1995. Change and continuity in the functions of the American English modals. *Linguistics* 33: 157–211.

1996. The development of the strong obligation system in American English. *American Speech* 71: 339–388.

1997. *Should* and *ought:* the rise of individually oriented modality in American English. *Journal of English Linguistics* 1: 3–23.

Myhill, John and Laura A. Smith. 1995. The discourse and interactive functions of obligation expressions. In Bybee and Fleischman, 239–292.

Nakamura, Hajime. 1981. *Bukkyoogo Daijiten* [Dictionary of Buddhist terms]. Tokyo: Tokyo Shoseki Kabushiki Gaisha.

Nakamura, Michio, ed. and annot. 1957. *Ukiyo-buro* [Public Bath of the Floating World (1808)]. Nihon Koten Bungaku Taikei series 63. Tokyo: Iwanami Shoten.

Nakata, Iwao and Yutaka Tsukijima. 1980. Kokugo-si [History of the Japanese language]. *Kokugogaku Daijiten*, 399–404.

Nelson, Andrew N. 1962. *The Modern Reader's Japanese–English Character Dictionary*. Tokyo: Tuttle.

Nerlich, Brigitte and David D. Clarke. 1992. Outline of a model for semantic change. In Kellermann and Morrissey, 125–141.

1999. Synecdoche as a cognitive and communicative strategy. In Blank and Koch, 197–213.

Nevalainen, Terttu and Helena Raumolin-Brunberg. 1995. Constraints on politeness: the pragmatics of address formulae in Early English correspondence. In Jucker, 541–601.

Nevis, Joal A. 1986. Decliticization and deaffixation in Saame: abessive *taga*. *Ohio State University Working Papers in Linguistics* 34: 1–19.

Newmeyer, Frederick J., ed. 1988. *Linguistics: the Cambridge Survey*. Cambridge: Cambridge University Press, 4 vols.

1998. *Language Form and Language Function*. Cambridge, MA: MIT Press, Bradford.

Nicolle, Steve. 1997. A relevance-theoretic account of *be going to*. *Journal of Linguistics* 33: 355–377.

1998. A relevance theory perspective on grammaticalization. *Cognitive Linguistics* 9: 1–35.

Nikiforidou, Kiki. 1996. Modern Greek *as*: a case study in grammaticalization and grammatical polysemy. *Studies in Language* 20: 599–632.

Nippo Jisho. See Doi, Morita, and Chonan, 1980.

NKD: *Nihon Kokugo Daijiten* [Unabridged Dictionary of the Japanese Language]. 1972–76. Tokyo: Shogakukan, 20 vols.

Nølke, Henning. 1992. Semantic constraints on argumentation: from polyphonic micro-structure to argumentative macro-structure. In Frans H. van Eemeren, ed., *Argumentation Illuminated*, 189–200. Amsterdam: SICSAT.

Nordlinger, Rachel and Elizabeth Closs Traugott. 1997. Scope and the development of epistemic modality: evidence from *ought to*. *English Language and Linguistics* 1: 295–317.

Nunberg, Geoffrey. 1978. *The Pragmatics of Reference*. Bloomington, IN: Indiana University Linguistics Club.

1979. The non-uniqueness of semantic solutions: polysemy. *Linguistics and Philosophy* 3: 143–184.

Nuyts, Jan. 1998. Subjectivity as an evidential dimension in epistemic modal expressions. Paper presented at the 6th International Conference on Pragmatics, Reims, July.

O'Connor, Patricia. 1994. "You could feel it through the skin": agency and positioning in the prisoners' stabbing stories. *Text* 14: 45–75.

OED: *The Oxford English Dictionary*. 1989. New York: Oxford University Press, 2nd ed. (also OED2/e CD-ROM V 2.0, 1999); *Oxford English Dictionary Online*. 2000. Oxford: Oxford University Press, 3rd. ed. (http://dictionary.oed.com/)

Ohno (also Ono, Oono), Susumu. 1980. Imi henka [Meaning change]. *Kokugogaku Daijiten*, 35–37.

Ohno, Susumu, and Toshiko Karashima, eds. 1972. *Ise Monogatari Soosakuin* [Comprehensive Index to the *Ise Monogatari* (Tales of Ise)]. Tokyo: Meiji Shoin.

Ohno, Susumu, Akihiro Satake, and Kingoro Maeda, eds. 1990 [1974]. *Iwanami Kogo Jiten* [The Iwanami Dictionary of Old Japanese Words]. Tokyo: Iwanami Shoten, revised ed.

Ohori, T., ed. 1998. *Studies in Japanese Grammaticalization: Cognitive and Discourse Perspectives*. Tokyo: Kurosio.

Okamoto, Shigeko. 1999. Situated politeness: manipulating honorific and non-honorific expressions in Japanese conversations. *Pragmatics* 9(1): 51–74.

Olson, David R. 1994. *The World on Paper: the Conceptual and Cognitive Implications of Writing and Reading*. Cambridge: Cambridge University Press.

Ong, Walter J. 1982. *Orality and Literacy: the Technologizing of the Word*. London: Methuen.

Onodera, Noriko Okada. 1993. Pragmatic change in Japanese: conjunctions and interjections as discourse markers. PhD dissertation, Georgetown University.

1995. Diachronic analysis of Japanese discourse markers. In Jucker, 393–437.

Secondary references

Ooishi, Hatsutaroo. 1983. *Gendai Keigo Kenkyuu* [Research into Honorifics of Modern Japanese]. Tokyo: Chikuma Shoboo.

Ormelius-Sandblom, Elisabet. 1997. *Die Modalpartikel ja, doch und schon*. Stockholm: Almqvist and Wiksell.

Ortony, Anthony, ed. 1993 [1979]. *Metaphor and Thought*. Cambridge: Cambridge University Press, 2nd ed.

Östman, Jan-Ola. 1981. *You Know: a Discourse-functional Approach*. Amsterdam: Benjamins.

Pagliuca, William, ed. 1994. *Perspectives on Grammaticalization*. Amsterdam: Benjamins.

Palmer, F. R. 1986. *Mood and Modality*. Cambridge: Cambridge University Press.

1990 [1979]. *Modality and the English Modals*. New York: Longman, 2nd ed.

Papi, Marcella Bertuccelli. 2000. Is a diachronic speech act theory possible? *Journal of Historical Pragmatics* 1: 57–66.

Paul, Hermann. 1920 [1880]. *Prinzipien der Sprachgeschichte*. Tübingen: Niemeyer, 5th ed.

Pauwels, Paul, and Anne-Marie Simon-Vandenbergen. 1995. Body parts in linguistic action: underlying schemas and value judgments. In Goossens et al., 35–69.

Pederson, Eric, Eve Danciger, David Wilkins, Stephen Levinson, Sotara Kita, and Gunter Senft. 1998. Semantic typology and spatial conceptualization. *Language* 74: 557–589.

Peirce, Charles Sanders. 1955 [1898]. *Philosophical Writings of Peirce*. Ed. by Justus Bucher. New York: Dover.

Pérez, Aveline. 1990. Time in motion: grammaticalisation of the *be going to* construction in English. *La Trobe University Working Papers in Linguistics* 3: 49–64.

Perkins, Michael R. 1983. *Modal Expressions in English*. Norwood, NJ: Ablex.

Perret, Michèle. 1982. De l'espace romanesque à la matérialité du livre. L'espace énonciatif des premiers romans en prose. *Poétique* 50: 173–182.

Peyraube, Alain. 1999. On the modal auxiliaries of possibility in Classical Chinese. In H.S. Wang, F. Tsao and C. Lien, eds., *Selected Papers from the 5th International Conference on Chinese Linguistics*, 27–52. Taipei: Crane.

Pinkster, Harm. 1987. The strategy and chronology of the development of future and perfect tense auxiliaries in Latin. In Martin B. Harris and Paolo Ramat, eds., *The Historical Development of Auxiliaries*, 193–223. Berlin: Mouton de Gruyter.

Plank, Frans. 1984. The modals story retold. *Studies in Language* 8: 305–364.

Pokorny, Julius. 1959/69. *Indogermanisches Etymologisches Wörterbuch*. Bern: Francke, 2 vols.

Pons Bordería, Salvador. 1998. *Conexión y Conectores: Estudio de su Relación en el Registro Informal de la Lengua*. Cuadernos de Filología 27. University of Valencia: Departamento de Filología Española.

Powell, Mava Jo. 1992a. The systematic development of correlated interpersonal and metalinguistic uses in stance adverbs. *Cognitive Linguistics* 3: 75–110.

1992b. Folk theories of meaning and principles of conventionality: encoding literal attitude via stance adverb. In Lehrer and Kittay 1992, 333–353.

Prince, Ellen. 1988. Discourse analysis: a part of the study of linguistic competence. In Newmeyer, vol. II: 164–182.

Prokosch, E. 1938. *A Comparative Germanic Grammar*. Baltimore: Linguistic Society of America.

Pustejovsky, James. 1995. *The Generative Lexicon*. Cambridge, MA: MIT Press.

Quirk, Randolph, Sidney Greenbaum, Geoffrey Leech, and Jan Svartvik. 1985. *A Comprehensive Grammar of the English Language*. New York: Longman.

Radden, Günter. 2000. How metonymic are metaphors? In Barcelona 2000a, 93–108.

Ramat, Paolo and Davide Ricca. 1998. Sentence adverbs in the languages of Europe. In Van der Auwera with Baoill, 187–275.

Reddy, Michael J. 1993 [1979]. The conduit metaphor: a case of frame conflict in our language about language. In Ortony, 164–201.

Rescher, N. 1968. *Topics in Philosophical Logic*. Dordrecht: Reidel.

Rissanen, Matti. 1986. Variation and the study of English historical syntax. In David Sankoff, ed., *Diversity and Diachrony*, 97–109. Amsterdam: Benjamins.

Rissanen, Matti, Merja Kytö, and Minna Palander-Collin, eds. 1993. *Early English in the Computer Age: Explorations through the Helsinki Corpus*. Berlin: Mouton de Gruyter.

Robert. 1992. *Dictionnaire historique de la langue française*. Paris: Dictionnaires Le Robert.

Roberts, Ian G. 1993. A formal account of grammaticalisation in the history of Romance futures. *Folia Linguistica Historica* 13: 219–258.

Roberts, Sarah Julianne. 1998. The role of diffusion in the genesis of Hawaiian Creole. *Language* 74: 1–39.

Rodriguez, João. See Doi 1955.

Romaine, Suzanne. 1982. *Socio-historical Linguistics: its Status and Methodology*. Cambridge: Cambridge University Press.

Rosaldo, Michelle Z. 1982. The things we do with words: Ilongot speech acts and speech act theory in philosophy. *Language in Society* 11: 203–237.

Rosch, Eleanor. 1975. Cognitive representations of semantic categories. *Journal of Experimental Psychology* 104: 192–233.

1994. Expressive sentence types – a contradiction in terms: the case of exclamation. *Sprache und Pragmatik* 33: 38–68. Lund.

Rosengren, Inger. 1992. Zur Grammatik und Pragmatik der Exklamation. In Inger Rosengren, ed., *Satz und Illokution*, vol. I: 263–306. Linguistische Arbeiten 278. Tübingen: Germanistisches Institut der Universität Lund.

Rossari, C. 1994. *Les opérations de reformulation: Analyse du processus et des marques dans une perspective contrastive français-italien*. Bern: Peter Lang.

Rouchota, Villy. 1996. Discourse connectives: what do they link? In J. Harris and R. Backley, eds., *1996 University College London Working Papers in Linguistics*, 199–212.

Roulet, E. 1987. Complétude interactive et connecteurs reformulatifs. *Cahiers de Linguistique Française* 8: 111–140.

Rudolph, Elisabeth. 1988. Connective relations – connective expressions – connective structures. In János S. Petöfi, ed., *Text and Discourse Constitution: Empirical Aspects, Theoretical Approaches*, 97–133. Berlin: de Gruyter.

1996. *Contrast: Adversative and Concessive Relations and their Expressions in English, German, Spanish, Portuguese on Sentence and Text Level.* Berlin: Walter de Gruyter.

Rudzka-Ostyn, Brygida. 1995. Metaphor, schema, invariance: the case of verbs of answering. In Goossens et al., 205–243.

Saeki, Umetomo and Tsunehisa Imuta, eds. 1981. *Kageroo Nikki Soosakuin* [Comprehensive Index and Text of the *Kageroo Nikki* ("Gossamer Years Diary," mid-10th century)]. Tokyo: Kazama Shobo.

Sakurai, Mitsuaki. 1966. *Konzyaku Monogatari-syuu no Gohoo no Kenkyuu.* [Studies of word use in the Konjaku Monogatari-shuu ("Tales of Times Now Past," mid-12th century)]. Tokyo: Meiji Shoin.

Sanders, José and Wilbert Spooren. 1996. Subjectivity and certainty in epistemic modality: a study of Dutch epistemic modifiers. *Cognitive Linguistics* 7: 241–264.

Sankoff, Gilian. 1980. *The Social Life of Language.* Philadelphia: University of Pennsylvania Press.

Sansom, George B. 1952. *Japan: a Short Cultural History.* Stanford: Stanford University Press.

Sato, Shigeru. 1974. Otogi-Zoosi, Bukkyoo bungaku no keigo [Honorifics in *Otogi-Zooshi* (LMJ collections of short stories) and Buddhist literature]. In Hayashi and Minami 1973–74, vol. III: 177–222.

Saussure, Ferdinand de. 1967 [1879]. Mémoire sur le système primitif des voyelles dans les languages indo-européennes, Paris: Vieweg. (Trans. by Winfred P. Lehmann as "On the primitive system of vowels in the Indo-European languages," in Winfred P. Lehmann, ed., *A Reader in Nineteenth Century Historical Indo-European Linguistics*, 217–224. Bloomington: Indiana University Press, 1967.)

1996 [1916]. *Course in General Linguistics.* Trans. by Roy Harris. Chicago: Open Court.

Schiffrin, Deborah. 1987. *Discourse Markers.* Cambridge: Cambridge University Press.

1988. Conversation analysis. In Newmeyer, vol. IV: 251–276.

1990a. The principle of intersubjectivity in communication and conversation. *Semiotica* 80: 121–151.

1990b. Between text and context: deixis, anaphora, and the meaning of *then. Text* 10: 245–270.

1992. Anaphoric *then*: aspectual, textual, and epistemic meaning. *Linguistics* 30: 753–792.

1994. *Approaches to Discourse.* Oxford: Blackwell.

Schlieben-Lange, Brigitte. 1983. *Traditionen des Sprechens: Elemente einer pragmatischen Sprachgeschichtsschreibung.* Stuttgart: Kohlhammer.

1992. The history of subordinating conjunctions in some Romance languages. In Gerritsen and Stein, 341–354.

Schourop, Lawrence C. 1985. *Common Discourse Particles in English Conversation: Like, Well, Y'Know.* New York: Garland.

Schwenter, Scott A. 1999. *Pragmatics of Conditional Marking: Implicature, Scalarity and Exclusivity.* New York: Garland.

Schwenter, Scott A. and Elizabeth Closs Traugott. 1995. The semantic and pragmatic development of substitutive complex prepositions in English. In Jucker, 243–273.

2000. Invoking scalarity: the development of *in fact*. *Journal of Historical Pragmatics* 1: 7–25.

Searle, John R. 1965. What is a speech act? In Max Black, ed., *Philosophy in America*, 221–239. Ithaca: Cornell University Press.

1969. *Speech Acts: an Essay in the Philosophy of Language*. Cambridge: Cambridge University Press.

1976. A classification of illocutionary acts. *Language in Society* 5: 1–23.

1979. *Expression and Meaning: Studies in the Theory of Speech Acts*. Cambridge: Cambridge University Press.

Seeley, Christopher. 1991. *A History of Writing in Japanese*. Leiden: Brill.

Seidensticker, Edward G., trans. 1964. *The Gossamer Years (Kageroo Nikki): a Diary by a Noblewoman of Heian Japan*. Tokyo and Rutland, VT: Charles E. Tuttle.

trans. 1980. *The Tale of Genji*. New York: Knopf.

Seiler, Hansjakob. 1983. *Possession as an Operational Dimension of Language*. Tübingen: Narr.

Shepherd, Susan C. 1981. Modals in Antiguan Creole, language acquisition, and history. PhD dissertation, Stanford University.

1982. From deontic to epistemic: an analysis of modals in the history of English, creoles, and language acquisition. In Ahlqvist, 316–323.

Shibatani, Masayoshi. 1990. *The Languages of Japan*. Cambridge: Cambridge University Press.

1991. Grammaticalization of topic into subject. In Traugott and Heine, vol. II: 93–133.

Shibatani, Masayoshi and Sandra Thompson, eds. 1995. *Essays in Semantics and Pragmatics in Honor of Charles J. Fillmore*. Amsterdam: Benjamins.

Shopen, Timothy, ed. 1985. *Language Typology and Syntactic Description*. Cambridge: Cambridge University Press, 3 vols.

Silverstein, Michael. 1976a. Shifters, linguistic categories, and cultural description. In Keith H. Basso and Henry A. Selby, eds., *Meaning in Anthropology*, 11–55. Albuquerque: University of New Mexico Press.

1976b. Hierarchy of features and ergativity. In R. M. W. Dixon, ed., *Grammatical Categories in Australian Languages*, 112–171. Canberra: Australian Institute of Aboriginal Languages.

Slobin, Dan I. 1977. Language change in childhood and in history. In John MacNamara, ed., *Language Learning and Thought*, 185–214. New York: Academic Press.

1994. Talking perfectly: discourse origins of the present perfect. In Pagliuca, 119–133.

Smith, John Charles and Delia Bentley, eds. 2000. *Historical Linguistics 1995*, vol. I: *General Issues and Non-Germanic Languages*. Amsterdam: Benjamins.

Solomon, Julie. 1995. Local and global functions of a borrowed/native pair of discourse markers in a Yucatec Maya narrative. In Jocelyn Ahlers, Leela Bilmes, Joshua S. Guenter, Barbara A. Kaiser, and Ju Namkung, eds., *Papers from the Twenty-first*

Secondary references

Meeting of the Berkeley Linguistics Society, 287–298. Berkeley: Berkeley Linguistics Society.

Sperber, Dan and Deirdre Wilson. 1995 [1986]. *Relevance: Communication and Cognition*. Oxford: Blackwell, 2nd ed.

Steele, Susan. 1975. Is it possible? *Stanford Working Papers in Language Universals* 18: 35–58.

Stein, Dieter and Susan Wright, eds. 1995. *Subjectivity and Subjectivisation in Language*. Cambridge: Cambridge University Press.

Stenström, Anna-Brita. 1998. From sentence to discourse: *Cos (because)* in teenage talk. In Jucker and Ziv, 127–165.

Stern, Gustaf. 1968 [1931]. *Meaning and Change of Meaning*. Bloomington: Indiana University Press. (Orig. publ. Göteborg, Elanders boktryckeri aktiebolag, 1931.)

Stubbs, Michael. 1986. "A matter of prolonged field work": notes toward a modal grammar of English. *Applied Linguistics* 7: 1–25.

Sun, Chaofen. 1996. *Word Order Changes and Grammaticalization in the History of Chinese*. Stanford: Stanford University Press.

  1998. Aspectual categories that overlap: a historical and dialectal perspective of the Chinese ZHE. *Journal of East Asian Linguistics* 7: 153–174.

Suzuki, Ryoko. 1998. From a lexical noun to an utterance-final pragmatic particle: *wake*. In Toshio Ohori, ed., *Studies in Japanese Grammaticalization*, 67–92. Tokyo: Kurosio.

  1999. Grammaticization in Japanese: a study of pragmatic particle-ization. PhD dissertation, University of California, Santa Barbara.

Svorou, Soteria. 1993. *The Grammar of Space*. Amsterdam: Benjamins.

Swan, Toril. 1988. *Sentence Adverbials in English: a Synchronic and Diachronic Investigation*. Oslo: Novus.

  1991. Adverbial shifts: evidence from Norwegian and English. In Dieter Kastovsky, ed., *Historical English Syntax*, 409–438. Berlin: Mouton de Gruyter.

  1997. From manner to subject modification: adverbialization in English. *Nordic Journal of Linguistics* 20: 179–195.

Swan, Toril and Olaf Jansen Westvik, eds. 1996. *Modality in Germanic Languages*. Berlin: Mouton de Gruyter.

Sweetser, Eve E. 1988. Grammaticalization and semantic bleaching. In Axmaker, Jaisser, and Singmaster, 389–405.

  1990. *From Etymology to Pragmatics: Metaphorical and Cultural Aspects of Semantic Structure*. Cambridge: Cambridge University Press.

Sweetser, Eve E. and Gilles Fauconnier. 1996. Cognitive links and domains: basic aspects of mental space theory. In Gilles Fauconnier and Eve E. Sweetser, eds., *Spaces, World, and Grammars*, 1–28. Chicago: University of Chicago Press.

Taavitsainen, Irma and Andreas H. Jucker. 1999. Pragmatic space in historical linguistics: speech acts and speech act verbs in the history of English. Paper presented at the Workshop on Historical Pragmatics, 14th International Conference on Historical Linguistics. Vancouver, August 1999.

Tabor, Whitney. 1994a. Syntactic innovation: a connectionist model. PhD dissertation, Stanford University.

1994b. The gradual development of degree modifier *sort of* and *kind of*: a corpus proximity model. In Katharine Beals, Gina Cooke, David Kathman, Sotaro Kita, Karl-Erik McCullough, and David Testen, eds., *Papers from the Twenty-ninth Regional Meeting of the Chicago Linguistic Society*, 451–465. Chicago: Chicago Linguistics Society.

Takagi, Ichinosuke, Tomohide Gomi, and Susumu Ohno, eds. and annot. 1957–60. *Man' yooshuu* [The Ten Thousand Leaves]. Tokyo: Iwanami Shoten. Nihon Koten Bungaku Taikei (NKBT) series: 4–7.

Takemitsu, Makoto. 1998. *Nitizyoogo no Yurai Ziten* [Etymological Dictionary of Everyday Words in Japanese]. Tokyo: Tokyodo Shuppan.

Talmy, Leonard. 1985. Lexicalization patterns: semantic structure in lexical forms. In Shopen, vol. III: 57–149.

1988. Force dynamics in language and cognition. *Cognitive Science* 2: 49–100.

Tamba, Irene. 1986. Approche du "signe" et du "sens" linguistiques à travers les systèmes d'écriture japonais. In Jean-Claude Chevalier, Michel Launay, and Maurice Molho, eds., *Langages: Le signifiant* 82: 83–100.

Taylor, John R. 1996. On running and jogging. *Cognitive Linguistics* 7: 21–34.

1997 [1989]. *Linguistic Categorization: Prototypes in Linguistic Theory*. Oxford: Clarendon, 2nd ed.

Thomas, Francis-Noël and Mark Turner. 1994. *Clear and Simple as the Truth: Writing Classic Prose*. Princeton: Princeton University Press.

Thompson, Sandra A. and Anthony Mulac. 1991. A quantitative perspective on the grammaticization of epistemic parentheticals in English. In Traugott and Heine, vol. II: 313–329.

Tiersma, Peter. 1986. The language of offer and acceptance: speech acts and the question of intent. *California Law Review* 74: 189–232.

1999. *Legal Language*. Chicago: University of Chicago Press.

Tobler, Adolf 1921 [1882]. Il ne faut pas que tu meures "du darfst nicht sterben". Repr. in *Vermischte Beiträge zur französischen Grammatik*, vol. I: 201–205. Leipzig: Hirzel, 3rd ed.

Tokieda, Motoki. 1941. *Kokugogaku-si Genron* [Fundamental Principles of Japanese Linguistics]. Tokyo: Iwanami Shoten.

Traugott, Elizabeth Closs. 1978. On the expression of spatio-temporal relations in language. In Joseph H. Greenberg, Charles A. Ferguson, and Edith A. Moravcsik, eds., *Universals of Human Language*, vol. III, 369–400. Stanford: Stanford University Press.

1980. Meaning-change in the development of grammatical markers. *Language Sciences* 2: 44–61.

1982. From propositional to textual and expressive meanings; some semantic–pragmatic aspects of grammaticalization. In Winfred P. Lehmann and Yakov Malkiel, eds., *Perspectives on Historical Linguistics*, 245–271. Amsterdam: Benjamins.

Secondary references

1985a. On conditionals. In Haiman 1985, 289–307.

1985b. On regularity in semantic change. *Journal of Literary Semantics* 14: 155–173.

1986. Is internal semantic–pragmatic reconstruction possible? In Caroline Duncan-Rose and Theo Vennemann, eds., *On Language: Rhetorica, Phonologica, Syntactica: a Festschrift for Robert P. Stockwell from his Friends and Colleagues*, 128–144. London: Routledge.

1987. Literacy and language change: the special case of speech act verbs. In Judith Langer, ed., *Language, Literacy, and Culture: Issues of Society and Schooling*, 11–27. Norwood, NJ: Ablex.

1988. Pragmatic strengthening and grammaticalization. In Axmaker, Jaisser, and Singmaster, 406–416.

1989. On the rise of epistemic meanings in English: an example of subjectification in semantic change. *Language* 57: 33–65.

1994. Grammaticalization and lexicalization. In Asher and Simpson, vol. III: 1481–1486.

1991. English speech act verbs: a historical perspective. In Linda R. Waugh and Stephen Rudy, eds., *New Vistas in Grammar: Invariance and Variation*, 387–406. Amsterdam: Benjamins.

1995a. Subjectification in grammaticalization. In Stein and Wright 1995, 31–54.

1995b. The role of discourse markers in a theory of grammaticalization. Paper presented at the 12th International Conference on Historical Linguistics, Manchester, August 1995. (http://www.stanford.edu/~traugott/traugott.html)

1996. Subjectification and the development of epistemic meaning: the case of *promise* and *threaten*. In Swan and Westvik, 185–210.

1996/97. Semantic change: an overview. *Glot International* 2 (9/10): 3–6.

1999a. The role of pragmatics in semantic change. In Jef Verschueren, ed., *Pragmatics in 1998: Selected Papers from the 6th International Pragmatics Conference*, vol. II, 93–102. Antwerp: International Pragmatics Association.

1999b. The rhetoric of counter-expectation in semantic change: a study in subjectification. In Blank and Koch 1999, 177–196.

Forthcoming. Constructions in grammaticalization. In Richard Janda and Brian Joseph, eds., *A Handbook of Historical Linguistics*. Oxford: Blackwell.

Traugott, Elizabeth Closs and Richard Dasher. 1987. On the historical relation between mental and speech act verbs in English and Japanese. In Giacalone Ramat, Carruba, and Bernini, 561–573.

Traugott, Elizabeth Closs and Bernd Heine, eds. 1991. *Approaches to Grammaticalization*. Amsterdam: Benjamins, 2 vols.

Traugott, Elizabeth Closs and Ekkehard König. 1991. The semantics–pragmatics of grammaticalization revisited. In Traugott and Heine, vol. I: 189–218.

Trier, Jost. 1931. *Der deutsche Wortschatz im Sinnbezirk des Verstandes*. Heidelberg: Winter.

Tsujimura, Toshiki. 1967. *Gendai no Keigo* [Honorific Language of Modern Japanese]. Tokyo: Kyoobunsha.

1968. *Keigo no Si-Teki Kenkyuu* [Historical Studies of Japanese Honorifics]. Tokyo: Tokyodo.

ed. 1971. *Keigo-Si* [The History of Japanese Honorifics]. Kooza Kokugosi, 5 [Monograph Series on the History of the Japanese Language 5]. Tokyo: Taishuukan Shoten.

Ueda, Kazutoshi ("Bannen"), et al. 1977 [1918]. *Daiziten* [Chinese-Character Dictionary]. Tokyo: Kodansha.

Ullmann, Stephen. 1957. *The Principles of Semantics*. Oxford: Blackwell, 2nd ed.

 1964. *Semantics: an Introduction to the Science of Meaning*. Oxford: Basil Blackwell.

Vallduví, Enric. 1992. *The Informational Component*. New York: Garland.

Van der Auwera, Johan. 1997. Conditional perfection. In Athanasiadou and Dirven, 169–190.

 1999. On the semantic and pragmatic polyfunctionality of modal verbs. In Ken Turner, ed., *The Semantics–Pragmatics Interface from Different Points of View*, 49–64. Amsterdam: Elsevier.

 Forthcoming. On the typology of negative modals. In Jack Hoeksema, ed., *Perspectives on Negation and Polarity Items*. Amsterdam: Benjamins.

Van der Auwera, Johan with Dónall P. Ó Baoill, eds. 1998. *Adverbial Constructions in the Languages of Europe*. Berlin: Mouton de Gruyter.

Van der Auwera, Johan and Vladimir A. Plungian. 1998. Modality's semantic map. *Linguistic Typology* 2: 79–124.

Vanparys, Johan. 1995. A survey of metalinguistic metaphors. In Goossens et al., 1–34.

Verhagen, Arie. 1995. Subjectification, syntax, and communication. In Stein and Wright, 103–128.

 1996. Sequential conceptualization and linear order. In Casad, 793–817.

 2000. "The girl that promised to become something": an exploration into diachronic subjectification in Dutch. In Thomas F. Shannon and Johan P. Snapper, eds., *The Berkeley Conference on Dutch Linguistics 1997: the Dutch Language at the Millennium*, 197–208. Lanham, MD: University Press of America.

Verschueren, Jef. 1995. The conceptual basis of performativity. In Masayoshi Shibatani and Sandra Thompson, eds., *Essays in Semantics and Pragmatics in Honor of Charles J. Fillmore*, 299–321. Amsterdam: Benjamins.

 1999. *Understanding Pragmatics*. London: Arnold.

Viberg, Åke. 1983. The verbs of perception: a typological study. *Linguistics* 21: 123–162.

Victorri, Bernard. 1997. La polysémie: un artefact de la linguistique? *Revue de Sémantique et Pragmatique* 2: 41–62.

Vincent, Nigel. 1982. The development of the auxiliaries HABERE and ESSE in Romance. In Nigel Vincent and Martin Harris, eds., *Studies in the Romance Verb*, 71–96. London: Croom Helm.

 1994. Lectures on historical syntax. Australian Linguistics Institute, La Trobe, July.

Visser, F. Th. 1969. *An Historical Syntax of the English Language*, vol. III, part 1. Leiden: Brill.

Voyles, Joseph B. 1973. Accounting for semantic change. *Lingua* 31: 95–124.

Warner, Anthony R. 1990. Reworking the history of the English auxiliaries. In Sylvia Adamson, Vivien Law, Nigel Vincent, and Susan Wright, eds., *Papers from the 5th*

Secondary references

International Conference on English Historical Linguistics, 537–558. Amsterdam: Benjamins.

1993. *English Auxiliaries: Structure and History*. Cambridge: Cambridge University Press.

Warren, Beatrice. 1992. *Sense-developments: a Contrastive Study of the Development of Slang Sense and Novel Standard Senses in English*. Stockholm: Almqvist and Wiksell.

1998. What *is* metonymy? In Hogg and van Bergen, 301–310.

Wartburg, Walther von. 1928–66. *Französisches etymologisches Wörterbuch*. Basel: Zbinden.

Watkins, Calvert. 1985. *The American Heritage Dictionary of Indo-European Roots*. Boston: Houghton Mifflin.

Watts, Richard J. 1995. Justifying grammars: a socio-pragmatic foray into the discourse community of Early English grammarians. In Jucker, 145–185.

Wegener, Heide. 1998. Zur Grammatikalisierung von Modalpartikeln. In Irmhild Barz and Günther Öhlschläger, eds., *Zwischen Grammatik und Lexicon*, 37–55. Tübingen: Niemeyer.

Weinreich, Uriel. 1964. *Webster's Third*: a critique of its semantics. *International Journal of American Linguistics* 30: 405–409.

Weinreich, Uriel, William Labov, and Marvin I. Herzog. 1968. Empirical foundations for a theory of language change. In Lehmann and Malkiel, 97–195.

Wierzbicka, Anna. 1985a. *Lexicography and Conceptual Analysis*. Ann Arbor: Karoma.

1985b. A semantic metalanguage for a crosscultural comparison of speech acts and speech genres. *Language in Society* 14: 491–514.

1985c. *English Speech Act Verbs: a Semantic Dictionary*. Orlando: FL: Academic Press.

1992. *Semantics, Primes, and Universals*. Oxford: Oxford University Press.

1994. Semantic primitives across languages: a critical review. In Goddard and Wierzbicka, 445–500.

1995. *Cross-Cultural Pragmatics*. Berlin: Mouton de Gruyter.

1997. *Understanding Cultures through their Key Words*. New York: Oxford University Press.

Wilkins, David. 1996. Natural tendencies in semantic change and the search for cognates. In Mark Durie and Malcolm Ross, eds., *The Comparative Method Reviewed: Regularity and Irregularity in Language Change*, 264–304. New York: Oxford University Press.

Williams, Joseph M. 1976. Synaesthetic adjectives: a possible law of semantic change. *Language* 52: 461–478.

Williams, Raymond. 1985 [1976]. *Keywords: a Vocabulary of Culture and Society*. New York: Oxford University Press, 2nd ed.

Wilson, Deirdre and Dan Sperber. 1993. Linguistic form and relevance. *Lingua* 90: 1–25.

Wolf, George. 1991. Translator's introduction: the emergence of the concept of semantics. In Michel Bréal, *The Beginnings of Semantics: Essays, Lectures and Reviews* (ed. and trans by George Wolf), 3–17. Stanford: Stanford University Press.

Yamada, Tadao, ed. 1958. *Taketori Monogatari Soosakuin* [Comprehensive Index of the Taketori Monogatari ("Bamboo Cutter's Tale," early 10th century)]. Tokyo: Musashino Shoin.

Yamada, Yoshio, Tadao Yamada, Hideo Yamada, and Toshio Yamada, eds. 1959. *Konjaku Monogatari-shuu* [1130–40 "Tales of Times Now Past"]. Nihon Koten Bungaku Taikei series 22–23. Tokyo: Iwanami Shoten.

Yamaguchi, Yoshinori. 1998. *Kurashi no Kotoba: Gogen Jiten* [Etymological Dictionary of Everyday Words]. Tokyo: Kodansha.

Yang, Ping. 1989. The development and structure of V *de* O. *Zhongguo Yuwen* [Chinese Grammar] 2: 126–136.

Yoshizawa, Norio. 1985. *Doko-ka Okasii Keigo* [Honorific (Usage in Japanese) that is Somehow Odd]. Tokyo: Goma Shobo.

Zipf, George Kingsley. 1965 [1949]. *Human Behavior and the Principle of Least Effort.* New York: Hafner.

INDEX OF LANGUAGES

INDEX OF NAMES

Names in this index are authors of secondary references

Index of names

GENERAL INDEX

This index includes lexemes that are discussed in some detail. They are typically cited in their historically most recent spellings; verbs appear in their stem form; languages other than Modern English are specified.

In the case of topics that are discussed throughout the book, e.g. "regularity," entries are typically limited to the first two chapters, where they are introduced.

Lightning Source UK Ltd.
Milton Keynes UK
UKOW041820311012

201492UK00001B/40/A